California Family Law Judicial Council Forms for Paralegals
2019 Edition

A compilation of Family Law Judicial Council forms. Printed with permission.

ISBN: 9781796922134

The forms
are presented in
chronological order

0001

PARTY WITHOUT ATTORNEY OR ATTORNEY	STATE BAR NUMBER:	FOR COURT USE ONLY
NAME:		
FIRM NAME:		
STREET ADDRESS:		
CITY: STATE: ZIP CODE:		
TELEPHONE NO.: FAX NO.:		
E-MAIL ADDRESS:		
ATTORNEY FOR (name):		

SUPERIOR COURT OF CALIFORNIA, COUNTY OF
STREET ADDRESS:
MAILING ADDRESS:
CITY AND ZIP CODE:
BRANCH NAME:

PETITIONER:

RESPONDENT:

PETITION FOR	☐ **AMENDED**	CASE NUMBER:
☐ **Dissolution (Divorce) of:** ☐ Marriage ☐ Domestic Partnership		
☐ **Legal Separation of:** ☐ Marriage ☐ Domestic Partnership		
☐ **Nullity of:** ☐ Marriage ☐ Domestic Partnership		

1. **LEGAL RELATIONSHIP** *(check all that apply)*:
   a. ☐ We are married.
   b. ☐ We are domestic partners and our domestic partnership was established in California.
   c. ☐ We are domestic partners and our domestic partnership was NOT established in California.

2. **RESIDENCE REQUIREMENTS** *(check all that apply)*:
   a. ☐ Petitioner ☐ Respondent has been a resident of this state for at least six months and of this county for at least three months immediately preceding the filing of this *Petition. (For a divorce, at least one person in the legal relationship described in items 1a and 1c must comply with this requirement.)*
   b. ☐ Our domestic partnership was established in California. Neither of us has to be a resident or have a domicile in California to dissolve our partnership here.
   c. ☐ We are the same sex, were married in California, but currently live in a jurisdiction that does not recognize, and will not dissolve, our marriage. This *Petition* is filed in the county where we married.
   Petitioner lives in *(specify)*: Respondent lives in *(specify)*:

3. **STATISTICAL FACTS**
   a. ☐ (1) Date of marriage *(specify)*: (2) Date of separation *(specify)*:
      (3) Time from date of marriage to date of separation *(specify)*: Years Months
   b. ☐ (1) Registration date of domestic partnership with the California Secretary of State or other state equivalent *(specify below)*:
      (2) Date of separation *(specify)*:
      (3) Time from date of registration of domestic partnership to date of separation *(specify)*: Years Months

4. **MINOR CHILDREN**
   a. ☐ There are no minor children.
   b. ☐ The minor children are:

Child's name	Birthdate	Age	Sex

   (1) ☐ continued on Attachment 4b. (2) ☐ a child who is not yet born.
   c. If any children listed above were born before the marriage or domestic partnership, the court has the authority to determine those children to be children of the marriage or domestic partnership.
   d. If there are minor children of Petitioner and Respondent, a completed *Declaration Under Uniform Child Custody Jurisdiction and Enforcement Act (UCCJEA)* (form FL-105) must be attached.
   e. ☐ Petitioner and Respondent signed a voluntary declaration of paternity. A copy ☐ is ☐ is not attached.

Form Adopted for Mandatory Use
Judicial Council of California
FL-100 [Rev. July 1, 2016]

PETITION—MARRIAGE/DOMESTIC PARTNERSHIP
(Family Law)

Family Code, §§ 297, 299, 2320, 2330, 3409;
www.courts.ca.gov

PETITIONER:	CASE NUMBER:
RESPONDENT:	

Petitioner requests that the court make the following orders:

5. **LEGAL GROUNDS** (Family Code sections 2200–2210, 2310–2312)

    a. ☐ Divorce   or   ☐ Legal separation   of the marriage or domestic partnership based on *(check one):*
        (1) ☐ irreconcilable differences.   (2) ☐ permanent legal incapacity to make decisions.

    b. ☐ Nullity of void marriage or domestic partnership based on
        (1) ☐ incest.   (2) ☐ bigamy.

    c. ☐ Nullity of voidable marriage or domestic partnership based on
        (1) ☐ petitioner's age at time of registration of domestic   (4) ☐ fraud.
            partnership or marriage.
        (2) ☐ prior existing marriage or domestic partnership.   (5) ☐ force.
        (3) ☐ unsound mind.   (6) ☐ physical incapacity.

6. **CHILD CUSTODY AND VISITATION (PARENTING TIME)**

	Petitioner	Respondent	Joint	Other
a. Legal custody of children to	☐	☐	☐	☐
b. Physical custody of children to	☐	☐	☐	☐
c. Child visitation (parenting time) be granted to	☐	☐		☐

    As requested in   ☐ form FL-311   ☐ form FL-312   ☐ form FL-341(C)
                   ☐ form FL-341(D)   ☐ form FL-341(E)   ☐ Attachment 6c(1)

7. **CHILD SUPPORT**

    a. If there are minor children born to or adopted by Petitioner and Respondent before or during this marriage or domestic partnership, the court will make orders for the support of the children upon request and submission of financial forms by the requesting party.

    b. An earnings assignment may be issued without further notice.

    c. Any party required to pay support must pay interest on overdue amounts at the "legal" rate, which is currently 10 percent.

    d. ☐ Other *(specify):*

8. **SPOUSAL OR DOMESTIC PARTNER SUPPORT**

    a. ☐ Spousal or domestic partner support payable to   ☐ Petitioner   ☐ Respondent

    b. ☐ Terminate (end) the court's ability to award support to   ☐ Petitioner   ☐ Respondent

    c. ☐ Reserve for future determination the issue of support payable to   ☐ Petitioner   ☐ Respondent

    d. ☐ Other *(specify):*

9. **SEPARATE PROPERTY**

    a. ☐ There are no such assets or debts that I know of to be confirmed by the court.

    b. ☐ Confirm as separate property the assets and debts in   ☐ *Property Declaration* (form FL-160).   ☐ Attachment 9b.
        ☐ the following list.   Item   Confirm to

PETITION—MARRIAGE/DOMESTIC PARTNERSHIP
(Family Law)

0003

PETITIONER:	CASE NUMBER:
RESPONDENT:	

10. COMMUNITY AND QUASI-COMMUNITY PROPERTY

a. ☐ There are no such assets or debts that I know of to be divided by the court.

b. ☐ Determine rights to community and quasi-community assets and debts. All such assets and debts are listed
☐ in *Property Declaration* (form FL-160)   ☐ in Attachment 10b.
☐ as follows *(specify):*

11. OTHER REQUESTS

a. ☐ Attorney's fees and costs payable by   ☐ Petitioner   ☐ Respondent

b ☐ Petitioner's former name be restored to *(specify):*

c. ☐ Other *(specify):*

☐ Continued on Attachment 11c.

12. I HAVE READ THE RESTRAINING ORDERS ON THE BACK OF THE SUMMONS, AND I UNDERSTAND THAT THEY APPLY TO ME WHEN THIS PETITION IS FILED.

I declare under penalty of perjury under the laws of the State of California that the foregoing is true and correct.

Date:

_____
(TYPE OR PRINT NAME)

▶ _____
(SIGNATURE OF PETITIONER)

Date:

_____
(TYPE OR PRINT NAME)

▶ _____
(SIGNATURE OF ATTORNEY FOR PETITIONER)

FOR MORE INFORMATION: Read *Legal Steps for a Divorce or Legal Separation* (**form FL-107-INFO**) and visit "Families Change" at **www.familieschange.ca.gov** — an online guide for parents and children going through divorce or separation.

NOTICE: You may redact (black out) social security numbers from any written material filed with the court in this case other than a form used to collect child, spousal or partner support.

NOTICE—CANCELLATION OF RIGHTS: Dissolution or legal separation may automatically cancel the rights of a domestic partner or spouse under the other domestic partner's or spouse's will, trust, retirement plan, power of attorney, pay-on-death bank account, survivorship rights to any property owned in joint tenancy, and any other similar thing. It does not automatically cancel the right of a domestic partner or spouse as beneficiary of the other partner's or spouse's life insurance policy. You should review these matters, as well as any credit cards, other credit accounts, insurance polices, retirement plans, and credit reports, to determine whether they should be changed or whether you should take any other actions. Some changes may require the agreement of your partner or spouse or a court order.

ATTORNEY OR PARTY WITHOUT ATTORNEY *(Name, State Bar number, and address)*:	FOR COURT USE ONLY
TELEPHONE NO.: FAX NO. *(Optional)*: E-MAIL ADDRESS *(Optional)*: ATTORNEY FOR *(Name)*:	

SUPERIOR COURT OF CALIFORNIA, COUNTY OF

STREET ADDRESS:

MAILING ADDRESS:

CITY AND ZIP CODE:

BRANCH NAME:

PETITIONER:	*(This section applies only to family law cases.)*
RESPONDENT:	
OTHER PARTY:	

(This section apples only to guardianship cases.)	CASE NUMBER:
GUARDIANSHIP OF *(Name)*: Minor	

DECLARATION UNDER UNIFORM CHILD CUSTODY JURISDICTION AND ENFORCEMENT ACT (UCCJEA)

1. **I am a party** to this proceeding to determine custody of a child.

2. ☐ My present address and the present address of each child residing with me is confidential under Family Code section 3429 as I have indicated in item 3.

3. There are *(specify number):*   minor children who are subject to this proceeding, as follows:
   (Insert the information requested below. The residence information must be given for the last FIVE years.)

a. Child's name	Place of birth	Date of birth	Sex
Period of residence	**Address**	**Person child lived with** *(name and complete current address)*	**Relationship**
to present	☐ Confidential	☐ Confidential	
to	Child's residence *(City, State)*	Person child lived with *(name and complete current address)*	
to	Child's residence *(City, State)*	Person child lived with *(name and complete current address)*	
to	Child's residence *(City, State)*	Person child lived with *(name and complete current address)*	

b. Child's name ☐ Residence information is the same as given above for child a. *(If NOT the same, provide the information below.)*	Place of birth	Date of birth	Sex
Period of residence	**Address**	**Person child lived with** *(name and complete current address)*	**Relationship**
to present	☐ Confidential	☐ Confidential	
to	Child's residence *(City, State)*	Person child lived with *(name and complete current address)*	
to	Child's residence *(City, State)*	Person child lived with *(name and complete current address)*	
to	Child's residence *(City, State)*	Person child lived with *(name and complete current address)*	

c. ☐ Additional residence information for a child listed in item a or b is continued on attachment 3c.

d. ☐ Additional children are listed on form *FL-105(A)/GC-120(A)*. *(Provide all requested information for additional children.)*

Page 1 of 2

DECLARATION UNDER UNIFORM CHILD CUSTODY JURISDICTION AND ENFORCEMENT ACT (UCCJEA)

0005

SHORT TITLE:	CASE NUMBER:

4. Do you have information about, or have you participated as a party or as a witness or in some other capacity in, another court case or custody or visitation proceeding, in California or elsewhere, concerning a child subject to this proceeding?

☐ Yes ☐ No *(If yes, attach a copy of the orders (if you have one) and provide the following information):*

Proceeding	Case number	Court *(name, state, location)*	Court order or judgment *(date)*	Name of each child	Your connection to the case	Case status
a. ☐ Family						
b. ☐ Guardianship						
c. ☐ Other						

Proceeding	Case Number	Court *(name, state, location)*
d. ☐ Juvenile Delinquency/ Juvenile Dependency		
e. ☐ Adoption		

5. ☐ One or more domestic violence restraining/protective orders are now in effect. *(Attach a copy of the orders if you have one and provide the following information):*

Court	County	State	Case number *(if known)*	Orders expire *(date)*
a. ☐ Criminal				
b. ☐ Family				
c. ☐ Juvenile Delinquency/ Juvenile Dependency				
d. ☐ Other				

6. Do you know of any person who is not a party to this proceeding who has physical custody or claims to have custody of or visitation rights with any child in this case? ☐ Yes ☐ No *(If yes, provide the following information):*

a. Name and address of person	b. Name and address of person	c. Name and address of person
☐ Has physical custody ☐ Claims custody rights ☐ Claims visitation rights	☐ Has physical custody ☐ Claims custody rights ☐ Claims visitation rights	☐ Has physical custody ☐ Claims custody rights ☐ Claims visitation rights
Name of each child	Name of each child	Name of each child

I declare under penalty of perjury under the laws of the State of California that the foregoing is true and correct.

Date:

▶

_____
(TYPE OR PRINT NAME)

_____
(SIGNATURE OF DECLARANT)

7. ☐ Number of pages attached:_____

NOTICE TO DECLARANT: You have a continuing duty to inform this court if you obtain any information about a custody proceeding in a California court or any other court concerning a child subject to this proceeding.

0006

CASE NAME:	CASE NUMBER:

ATTACHMENT TO
DECLARATION UNDER UNIFORM CHILD CUSTODY JURISDICTION AND ENFORCEMENT ACT (UCCJEA)

_____ Child's name	Place of birth	Date of birth	Sex
[ ] Residence information is the same as given on form FL-105/GC-120 for child a. *(If NOT the same, provide the information below.)*			

Period of residence	Present address	Person child lived with *(name and complete current address)*	Relationship
to present	[ ] Confidential	[ ] Confidential	
to	Child's residence *(City, State)*	Person child lived with *(name and complete current address)*	
to	Child's residence *(City, State)*	Person child lived with *(name and complete current address)*	
to	Child's residence *(City, State)*	Person child lived with *(name and complete current address)*	

_____ Child's name	Place of birth	Date of birth	Sex
[ ] Residence information is the same as given on form FL-105/GC-120 for child a. *(If NOT the same, provide the information below.)*			

Period of residence	Address	Person child lived with *(name and complete current address)*	Relationship
to present	[ ] Confidential	[ ] Confidential	
to	Child's residence *(City, State)*	Person child lived with *(name and complete current address)*	
to	Child's residence *(City, State)*	Person child lived with *(name and complete current address)*	
to	Child's residence *(City, State)*	Person child lived with *(name and complete current address)*	

_____ Child's name	Place of birth	Date of birth	Sex
[ ] Residence information is the same as given on form FL-105/GC-120 for child a. *(If NOT the same, provide the information below.)*			

Period of residence	Address	Person child lived with *(name and complete current address)*	Relationship
to present	[ ] Confidential	[ ] Confidential	
to	Child's residence *(City, State)*	Person child lived with *(name and complete current address)*	
to	Child's residence *(City, State)*	Person child lived with *(name and complete current address)*	
to	Child's residence *(City, State)*	Person child lived with *(name and complete current address)*	

Page____ of ____

Form Adopted for Mandatory Use
Judicial Council of California
FL-105(A)/GC-120(A)
[New January 1, 2009]

ATTACHMENT TO
DECLARATION UNDER UNIFORM CHILD CUSTODY JURISDICTION
AND ENFORCEMENT ACT (UCCJEA)

Family Code, § 3400 et seq.;
Probate Code, §§ 1510(f), 1512
www.courtinfo.ca.gov

FL-107-INFO | Legal Steps for a Divorce or Legal Separation

STEP 1. Start Your Case

- The **petitioner** (the person who files the first divorce or legal separation forms with the court) fills out and files with the court clerk at least a *Petition—Marriage/Domestic Partnership* (form FL-100) and a *Summons* (form FL-110) and, if there are children of the relationship, a *Declaration Under Uniform Child Custody Jurisdiction and Enforcement Act* (form FL-105).
- The forms needed to start your case and information about filing fees and fee waivers are available at "Filing Your Case," at *courts.ca.gov/filing*.
- The court clerk will stamp and return copies of the filed forms to the **petitioner**.

STEP 2. Serve the Forms

- **Someone 18 or older**–not the **petitioner**–serves the spouse or domestic partner (called the **respondent**) with all the forms from Step 1 plus a blank *Response—Marriage/Domestic Partnership* (form FL-120) and files with the court a proof-of-service form, such as *Proof of Service of Summons* (form FL-115), telling when and how the respondent was served. (To *serve* means "to give in the proper legal way.") For more information, see "Serving Your First Set of Court Forms" at *courts.ca.gov/filing*.
- The **respondent** has 30 days to file and serve a *Response*. So, the **petitioner** must wait 30 days before starting Step 4.

STEP 3. Disclose Financial Information

- At the same time as Step 1 or within 60 days of filing the *Petition*, the **petitioner** must fill out and have these documents served on the **respondent**: *Declaration of Disclosure* (form FL-140), *Income and Expense Declaration* (form FL-150), *Schedule of Assets and Debts* (form FL-142) or *Property Declaration* (form FL-160), and all tax returns filed by the party in the two years before serving the disclosure documents. These disclosure documents are not filed with the court.
- If the **respondent** files a *Response*, he or she must also complete and serve the same disclosure documents on the **petitioner** within 60 days of filing the *Response*.
- The 60-day time frame for serving the disclosures may be changed by written agreement between the parties or by court order.
- The **petitioner** and **respondent** each file a *Declaration Regarding Service* (form FL-141) with the court saying disclosures were served. If the **respondent** does not serve disclosures, the **petitioner** can still finish the case without them. For more information, see "Fill Out and Serve Your Financial Declaration of Disclosure Forms" at *courts.ca.gov/filing* (click on Step 4).

STEP 4. Finish the Divorce or Legal Separation Case in One of Four Ways

Respondent does not file a *Response* (called "default")		Respondent files a *Response*	
No *Response* and NO written agreement: Petitioner waits 30 days after Step 2 is complete and prepares a proposed *Judgment* (form FL-180), together with all other needed forms. See "True Default Case" at *courts. ca.gov/truedefault*.	**No *Response* BUT written agreement:** Petitioner attaches the signed and notarized agreement to the proposed *Judgment* (form FL-180), together with all other needed forms. See "Default Case with Written Agreement" at *courts. ca.gov/defaultagree*.	***Response* AND written agreement:** Either party files *Appearance, Stipulations, and Waivers* (form FL-130) and the proposed *Judgment* with written agreement attached and other needed forms. See "Uncontested Case" at *courts. ca.gov/uncontested*.	***Response* and NO agreement:** Parties must go to trial to have a judge resolve the issues. See "Contested Case" at *courts.ca.gov/contested*.

IMPORTANT NOTICES

- The earliest you can be divorced is six months and one day from one of these three dates (whichever occurs first): (1) the date Respondent was served with the *Summons* (form FL-110) and *Petition* (form FL-100), (2) the date the *Response* (form FL-120) was filed, or (3) the date *Appearance, Stipulations, and Waivers* (form FL-130) was filed. Legal separation has no waiting period. You are NOT divorced or legally separated until the court enters a *Judgment* in your case.
- If you need court orders for child support, custody, parenting time (visitation), spousal or partner support, restraining orders, or other issues, file a *Request for Order* (form FL-300) asking for temporary orders. See "Request for Order Information" at *courts.ca.gov/divorcerequests* for more information.
- Annulments: See *courts.ca.gov/annulment* for information about annulments.
- You must keep the court and the other party informed of any change in your mailing address or other contact information. File and serve a *Notice of Change of Address or Other Contact Information* (form MC-040) on the other party or his or her attorney to let them know about the change in your contact information.

Judicial Council of California, *www.courts.ca.gov*
Revise January 1, 2015, Optional Form
Cal. Rules of Court, rule 5.83

Legal Steps for a Divorce or Legal Separation

FL-107-INFO, Page 1 of 2

→

FL-107-INFO Legal Steps for a Divorce or Legal Separation

Do you have a registered domestic partnership? The process for a divorce or legal separation of a domestic partnership is the same as on page 1. For information about ending your domestic partnership in the superior court, see *courts.ca. gov/filing*. To find out if you are eligible to end your domestic partnership through the Secretary of State, see *courts.ca. gov/summdissodp*. Note: There may be differences in federal taxes and other issues for domestic partnerships. Seek advice from an attorney experienced in domestic partner law.

What if you want a legal separation? The process on page 1 is the same, except you will **NOT** get a *Judgment* for legal separation unless both parties agree to a legal separation OR if **respondent** has not filed a *Response*. If both parties agree to be legally separated but do not agree on other issues, the parties must go to trial to have a judge resolve those issues. You are **NOT** legally separated until you receive a *Judgment* signed by the court. For more information, see "Legal Separation" at *courts.ca.gov/legalseparation*. AFTER the court enters a judgment for legal separation, if you decide you want a divorce, you must start a new case to request a divorce and pay another filing fee.

Getting help to resolve divorce or legal separation cases

You may prefer to resolve some or all of the issues in your divorce or legal separation case without having the court decide for you. You and your spouse or domestic partner can put your agreement in writing and file it in your case. But your agreement must follow all legal requirements.

Court Services

- **Family Law Facilitators and Self-Help Centers** help with court forms and instructions. They can provide samples of agreements and other information and, in some cases, help with mediation.

- **Family Court Services**. If you and the other parent already have a family law case and have filed a *Request for Order* (form FL-300) seeking orders about child custody and visitation (parenting time), the court will refer you to Family Court Services. They provide child custody mediation or child custody recommending counseling to try to help you both make a parenting plan that is in the best interest of your child. Note: They cannot help with financial issues.

- **Settlement Conferences**. An informal process in which a judge or an experienced lawyer meets with the parties and their lawyers to discuss the case and their positions and suggests a resolution. The parties can either agree to the suggestions or use the suggestions to help in further settlement discussions.

Private services (which you can hire to help you resolve your case):

- **Lawyers.** Also called attorneys, lawyers can help work out agreements between the parties and represent you at court hearings and trials.

- **Collaborative Lawyers**. Lawyers who represent each party but do not go to court. They try to reach an agreement. If court is necessary, the parties must hire new lawyers.

- **Mediators**. A lawyer or counselor who helps the parties communicate to explore options and reach a mutually acceptable resolution.

Where can I get help?

This information sheet gives you only basic information on the divorce or legal separation and is not legal advice. If you want legal advice, ask a lawyer for help. You may also:

- Contact the family law facilitator or self-help center in your court for information, court forms, and referrals to local legal resources. For more information, see *courts.ca.gov/courtresources.*

- Find a lawyer through a certified lawyer referral service on the State Bar of California's website: *calbar.ca.gov/LRS* or by calling 866-442-2529 (toll-free).

- Hire a private mediator. For more information about court and private services, see *courts.ca.gov/selfhelp-adr. htm.*

- Find information on the California Courts Online Self-Help Center website: *courts.ca.gov/selfhelp*.

- *Find free and low-cost legal help (if you qualify) at lawhelpcalifornia.org.*

- Find information at your local law library or public library.

What if there is domestic violence?

If there is domestic violence or a protective or restraining order, talk to a lawyer, counselor, or mediator before making agreements.

For domestic violence help, call the National Domestic Violence Hotline: 800-799-7233; TDD: 800-787-3224; or 211 (if available in your area).

0009

SUMMONS (Family Law)

FL-110

CITACIÓN (Derecho familiar)

NOTICE TO RESPONDENT *(Name):*
AVISO AL DEMANDADO (Nombre):

You have been sued. Read the information below and on the next page.

Lo han demandado. Lea la información a continuación y en la página siguiente.

Petitioner's name is:
Nombre del demandante:

CASE NUMBER *(NÚMERO DE CASO):*

You have **30 calendar days** after this *Summons* and *Petition* are served on you to file a *Response* (form FL-120) at the court and have a copy served on the petitioner. A letter, phone call, or court appearance will not protect you.

If you do not file your *Response* on time, the court may make orders affecting your marriage or domestic partnership, your property, and custody of your children. You may be ordered to pay support and attorney fees and costs.

For legal advice, contact a lawyer immediately. Get help finding a lawyer at the California Courts Online Self-Help Center *(www.courts.ca.gov/selfhelp)*, at the California Legal Services website *(www.lawhelpca.org)*, or by contacting your local county bar association.

*Tiene **30 días de calendario** después de haber recibido la entrega legal de esta Citación y Petición para presentar una Respuesta (formulario FL-120) ante la corte y efectuar la entrega legal de una copia al demandante. Una carta o llamada telefónica o una audiencia de la corte no basta para protegerlo.*

Si no presenta su Respuesta a tiempo, la corte puede dar órdenes que afecten su matrimonio o pareja de hecho, sus bienes y la custodia de sus hijos. La corte también le puede ordenar que pague manutención, y honorarios y costos legales.

Para asesoramiento legal, póngase en contacto de inmediato con un abogado. Puede obtener información para encontrar un abogado en el Centro de Ayuda de las Cortes de California (www.sucorte.ca.gov), en el sitio web de los Servicios Legales de California (www.lawhelpca.org) o poniéndose en contacto con el colegio de abogados de su condado.

NOTICE—RESTRAINING ORDERS ARE ON PAGE 2:
These restraining orders are effective against both spouses or domestic partners until the petition is dismissed, a judgment is entered, or the court makes further orders. They are enforceable anywhere in California by any law enforcement officer who has received or seen a copy of them.

AVISO—LAS ÓRDENES DE RESTRICCIÓN SE ENCUENTRAN EN LA PÁGINA 2: Las órdenes de restricción están en vigencia en cuanto a ambos cónyuges o miembros de la pareja de hecho hasta que se despida la petición, se emita un fallo o la corte dé otras órdenes. Cualquier agencia del orden público que haya recibido o visto una copia de estas órdenes puede hacerlas acatar en cualquier lugar de California.

FEE WAIVER: If you cannot pay the filing fee, ask the clerk for a fee waiver form. The court may order you to pay back all or part of the fees and costs that the court waived for you or the other party.

EXENCIÓN DE CUOTAS: Si no puede pagar la cuota de presentación, pida al secretario un formulario de exención de cuotas. La corte puede ordenar que usted pague, ya sea en parte o por completo, las cuotas y costos de la corte previamente exentos a petición de usted o de la otra parte.

[SEAL]

1. The name and address of the court are *(El nombre y dirección de la corte son):*

2. The name, address, and telephone number of the petitioner's attorney, or the petitioner without an attorney, are: *(El nombre, dirección y número de teléfono del abogado del demandante, o del demandante si no tiene abogado, son):*

Date *(Fecha):* _____ Clerk , by *(Secretario, por)* _____ , Deputy *(Asistente)*

Page 1 of 2

Form Adopted for Mandatory Use
Judicial Council of California
FL-110 [Rev. January 1, 2015]

SUMMONS
(Family Law)

Family Code, §§ 232, 233, 2024.7, 2040, 7700;
Code of Civil Procedure, §§ 412.20, 416.60–416.90
www.courts.ca.gov

STANDARD FAMILY LAW RESTRAINING ORDERS	ÓRDENES DE RESTRICCIÓN ESTÁNDAR DE DERECHO FAMILIAR

Starting immediately, you and your spouse or domestic partner are restrained from:

1. removing the minor children of the parties from the state or applying for a new or replacement passport for those minor children without the prior written consent of the other party or an order of the court;

2. cashing, borrowing against, canceling, transferring, disposing of, or changing the beneficiaries of any insurance or other coverage, including life, health, automobile, and disability, held for the benefit of the parties and their minor children;

3. transferring, encumbering, hypothecating, concealing, or in any way disposing of any property, real or personal, whether community, quasi-community, or separate, without the written consent of the other party or an order of the court, except in the usual course of business or for the necessities of life; and

4. creating a nonprobate transfer or modifying a nonprobate transfer in a manner that affects the disposition of property subject to the transfer, without the written consent of the other party or an order of the court. Before revocation of a nonprobate transfer can take effect or a right of survivorship to property can be eliminated, notice of the change must be filed and served on the other party.

You must notify each other of any proposed extraordinary expenditures at least five business days prior to incurring these extraordinary expenditures and account to the court for all extraordinary expenditures made after these restraining orders are effective. However, you may use community property, quasi-community property, or your own separate property to pay an attorney to help you or to pay court costs.

En forma inmediata, usted y su cónyuge o pareja de hecho tienen prohibido:

1. *llevarse del estado de California a los hijos menores de las partes, o solicitar un pasaporte nuevo o de repuesto para los hijos menores, sin el consentimiento previo por escrito de la otra parte o sin una orden de la corte;*

2. *cobrar, pedir prestado, cancelar, transferir, deshacerse o cambiar el nombre de los beneficiarios de cualquier seguro u otro tipo de cobertura, como de vida, salud, vehículo y discapacidad, que tenga como beneficiario(s) a las partes y su(s) hijo(s) menor(es);*

3. *transferir, gravar, hipotecar, ocultar o deshacerse de cualquier manera de cualquier propiedad, inmueble o personal, ya sea comunitaria, cuasicomunitaria o separada, sin el consentimiento escrito de la otra parte o una orden de la corte, excepto en el curso habitual de actividades personales y comerciales o para satisfacer las necesidades de la vida; y*

4. *crear o modificar una transferencia no testamentaria de manera que afecte la asignación de una propiedad sujeta a transferencia, sin el consentimiento por escrito de la otra parte o una orden de la corte. Antes de que se pueda eliminar la revocación de una transferencia no testamentaria, se debe presentar ante la corte un aviso del cambio y hacer una entrega legal de dicho aviso a la otra parte.*

Cada parte tiene que notificar a la otra sobre cualquier gasto extraordinario propuesto por lo menos cinco días hábiles antes de realizarlo, y rendir cuenta a la corte de todos los gastos extraordinarios realizados después de que estas órdenes de restricción hayan entrado en vigencia. No obstante, puede usar propiedad comunitaria, cuasicomunitaria o suya separada para pagar a un abogado que lo ayude o para pagar los costos de la corte.

NOTICE—ACCESS TO AFFORDABLE HEALTH INSURANCE: Do you or someone in your household need affordable health insurance? If so, you should apply for Covered California. Covered California can help reduce the cost you pay towards high quality affordable health care. For more information, visit *www.coveredca.com*. Or call Covered California at 1-800-300-1506.

AVISO—ACCESO A SEGURO DE SALUD MÁS ECONÓMICO: ¿Necesita seguro de salud a un costo asequible, ya sea para usted o alguien en su hogar? Si es así, puede presentar una solicitud con Covered California. Covered California lo puede ayudar a reducir el costo que paga por seguro de salud asequible y de alta calidad. Para obtener más información, visite *www.coveredca.com*. O llame a Covered California al 1-800-300-0213.

WARNING—IMPORTANT INFORMATION

California law provides that, for purposes of division of property upon dissolution of a marriage or domestic partnership or upon legal separation, property acquired by the parties during marriage or domestic partnership in joint form is presumed to be community property. If either party to this action should die before the jointly held community property is divided, the language in the deed that characterizes how title is held (i.e., joint tenancy, tenants in common, or community property) will be controlling, and not the community property presumption. You should consult your attorney if you want the community property presumption to be written into the recorded title to the property.

ADVERTENCIA—IMFORMACIÓN IMPORTANTE

De acuerdo a la ley de California, las propiedades adquiridas por las partes durante su matrimonio o pareja de hecho en forma conjunta se consideran propiedad comunitaria para fines de la división de bienes que ocurre cuando se produce una disolución o separación legal del matrimonio o pareja de hecho. Si cualquiera de las partes de este caso llega a fallecer antes de que se divida la propiedad comunitaria de tenencia conjunta, el destino de la misma quedará determinado por las cláusulas de la escritura correspondiente que describen su tenencia (por ej., tenencia conjunta, tenencia en común o propiedad comunitaria) y no por la presunción de propiedad comunitaria. Si quiere que la presunción comunitaria quede registrada en la escritura de la propiedad, debería consultar con un abogado.

0011

ATTORNEY OR PARTY WITHOUT ATTORNEY *(Name, State Bar number, and address)*:	*FOR COURT USE ONLY*
TELEPHONE NO.: FAX NO.: E-MAIL ADDRESS: ATTORNEY FOR *(Name)*:	

SUPERIOR COURT OF CALIFORNIA, COUNTY OF
STREET ADDRESS:
MAILING ADDRESS:
CITY AND ZIP CODE:
BRANCH NAME:

PETITIONER:

RESPONDENT:

PROOF OF SERVICE OF SUMMONS	CASE NUMBER:

1. At the time of service I was at least 18 years of age and not a party to this action. **I served the respondent with copies of:**

   a. ☐ Family Law—Marriage/Domestic Partnership: *Petition—Marriage/Domestic Partnership* (form FL-100), *Summons* (form FL-110), and blank *Response—Marriage/Domestic Partnership* (form FL-120)

   –or–

   b. ☐ Uniform Parentage: *Petition to Establish Parental Relationship* (form FL-200), *Summons* (form FL-210), and blank *Response to Petition to Establish Parental Relationship* (form FL-220)

   –or–

   c. ☐ Custody and Support: *Petition for Custody and Support of Minor Children* (form FL-260), *Summons* (form FL-210), and blank *Response to Petition for Custody and Support of Minor Children* (form FL-270)

   and

   d. ☐
   (1) ☐ Completed and blank *Declaration Under Uniform Child Custody Jurisdiction and Enforcement Act* (form FL-105)

   (2) ☐ Completed and blank *Declaration of Disclosure* (form FL-140)

   (3) ☐ Completed and blank *Schedule of Assets and Debts* (form FL-142)

   (4) ☐ Completed and blank *Income and Expense Declaration* (form FL-150)

   (5) ☐ Completed and blank *Financial Statement (Simplified)* (form FL-155)

   (6) ☐ Completed and blank *Property Declaration* (form FL-160)

   (7) ☐ *Request for Order* (form FL-300), and blank *Responsive Declaration to Request for Order* (form FL-320)

   (8) ☐ Other *(specify)*:

2. Address where respondent was served:

3. I served the respondent by the following means *(check proper boxes)*:

   a. ☐ **Personal service.** I personally delivered the copies to the respondent (Code Civ. Proc., § 415.10)
   on *(date)*:   at *(time)*:

   b. ☐ **Substituted service.** I left the copies with or in the presence of *(name)*:

   who is *(specify title or relationship to respondent)*:

   (1) ☐ **(Business)** a person at least 18 years of age who was apparently in charge at the office or usual place of business of the respondent. I informed him or her of the general nature of the papers.

   (2) ☐ **(Home)** a competent member of the household (at least 18 years of age) at the home of the respondent. I informed him or her of the general nature of the papers.

   on *(date)*:   at *(time)*:

   I thereafter mailed additional copies (by first class, postage prepaid) to the respondent at the place where the copies were left (Code Civ. Proc., § 415.20b) on *(date)*:

   A **declaration of diligence** is attached, stating the actions taken to first attempt personal service.

Page 1 of 2

| **PROOF OF SERVICE OF SUMMONS**
 (Family Law—Uniform Parentage—Custody and Support) | Code of Civil Procedure, § 417.10
 www.courts.ca.gov

PETITIONER:	CASE NUMBER:
RESPONDENT:	

3. c. ☐ **Mail and acknowledgment service.** I mailed the copies to the respondent, addressed as shown in item 2, by first-class mail, postage prepaid, on *(date):*   from *(city):*

    (1) ☐ with two copies of the *Notice and Acknowledgment of Receipt* (form FL-117) and a postage-paid return envelope addressed to me. **(Attach completed *Notice and Acknowledgment of Receipt* (form FL-117).)** (Code Civ. Proc., § 415.30.)

    (2) ☐ to an address outside California (by registered or certified mail with return receipt requested). **(Attach signed return receipt or other evidence of actual delivery to the respondent.)** (Code Civ. Proc., §§ 415.40, 417.20.)

  d. ☐ **Other** *(specify code section):*

    ☐ Continued on Attachment 3d.

4. **Person who served papers**

  Name:

  Address:

  Telephone number:

  This person is

  a. ☐ exempt from registration under Business and Professions Code section 22350(b).

  b. ☐ not a registered California process server.

  c. ☐ a registered California process server: ☐ an employee or ☐ an independent contractor

    (1) Registration no.:

    (2) County:

  d. **The fee** for service was *(specify):* $

5. ☐ **I declare** under penalty of perjury under the laws of the State of California that the foregoing is true and correct.

–or–

6. ☐ **I am a California sheriff, marshal, or constable,** and I certify that the foregoing is true and correct.

Date:

_____
(NAME OF PERSON WHO SERVED PAPERS)

▶

_____
(SIGNATURE OF PERSON WHO SERVED PAPERS)

PROOF OF SERVICE OF SUMMONS
(Family Law—Uniform Parentage—Custody and Support)

0013

ATTORNEY OR PARTY WITHOUT ATTORNEY *(Name, State Bar number, and address):*	*FOR COURT USE ONLY*
TELEPHONE NO.: FAX NO.: E-MAIL ADDRESS: ATTORNEY FOR *(Name)*:	

SUPERIOR COURT OF CALIFORNIA, COUNTY OF
   STREET ADDRESS:
   MAILING ADDRESS:
   CITY AND ZIP CODE:
   BRANCH NAME:

PETITIONER:

RESPONDENT:

NOTICE AND ACKNOWLEDGMENT OF RECEIPT	CASE NUMBER:

(Sender completes items 1 through 4 and signs before mailing. Recipient completes items 5 and 6, signs, then returns)

1. To *(name of individual being served):* _____

NOTICE

The documents identified below are being served on you by mail with this acknowledgment form. You must personally sign, or a person authorized by you must sign, this form to acknowledge receipt of the documents.

If the documents described below include a summons and you fail to complete and return this acknowledgment form to the sender within 20 days of the date of mailing, you will be liable for the reasonable expenses incurred after that date in serving you or attempting to serve you with these documents by any other methods permitted by law. If you return this form to the sender, service of a summons is deemed complete on the date you sign the acknowledgment of receipt below. This is **not** an answer to the action. If you do not agree with what is being requested, you must submit a completed *Response* form to the court within 30 calendar days.

2. Date of mailing *(specify):* _____

3. _____   ▶   _____
      (TYPE OR PRINT SENDER'S NAME)   (SIGNATURE OF SENDER—MUST NOT BE A PARTY IN THIS CASE
                                                  AND MUST BE 18 YEARS OR OLDER)

ACKNOWLEDGMENT OF RECEIPT

4. I agree I received the following:

  a. ☐ Family Law: *Petition—Marriage/Domestic Partnership* (form FL-100), *Summons* (form FL-110), and blank *Response—Marriage/Domestic Partnership* (form FL-120)

  b. ☐ Uniform Parentage: *Petition to Establish Parental Relationship* (form FL-200), *Summons* (form FL-210), and blank *Response to Petition to Establish Parental Relationship* (form FL-220)

  c. ☐ Custody and Support: *Petition for Custody and Support of Minor Children* (form FL-260), *Summons* (form FL-210), and blank *Response to Petition for Custody and Support of Minor Children* (form FL-270)

  d. ☐
    (1) ☐ Completed and blank *Declaration Under Uniform Child Custody Jurisdiction and Enforcement Act* (form FL-105)
    (2) ☐ Completed and blank *Declaration of Disclosure* (form FL-140)
    (3) ☐ Completed and blank *Schedule of Assets and Debts* (form FL-142)
    (4) ☐ Completed and blank *Property Declaration* (form FL-160)

    (5) ☐ Completed and blank *Income and Expense Declaration* (form FL-150)
    (6) ☐ Completed and blank *Financial Statement (Simplified)* (form FL-155)
    (7) ☐ *Request for Order* (form FL-300), and blank *Responsive Declaration to Request for Order* (form FL-320)
    (8) ☐ Other *(specify):*

5. Recipient signed this acknowledgment on *(specify date):* _____

6. _____   ▶   _____
    (TYPE OR PRINT NAME OF PERSON ACKNOWLEDGING RECEIPT)   (SIGNATURE OF PERSON ACKNOWLEDGING RECEIPT)

Page 1 of 1

Form Approved for Optional Use
Judicial Council of California
FL-117 [Rev. January 1, 2015]

NOTICE AND ACKNOWLEDGMENT OF RECEIPT
(Family Law)

Code of Civil Procedure, § 415.30, 417.10
www.courts.ca.gov

0014

PARTY WITHOUT ATTORNEY OR ATTORNEY	STATE BAR NUMBER:	FOR COURT USE ONLY
NAME:		
FIRM NAME:		
STREET ADDRESS:		
CITY:	STATE: ZIP CODE:	
TELEPHONE NO.:	FAX NO.:	
E-MAIL ADDRESS:		
ATTORNEY FOR (name):		

SUPERIOR COURT OF CALIFORNIA, COUNTY OF
    STREET ADDRESS:
    MAILING ADDRESS:
    CITY AND ZIP CODE:
    BRANCH NAME:

PETITIONER:
RESPONDENT:

RESPONSE ☐ **AND REQUEST FOR** ☐ **AMENDED**	CASE NUMBER:
☐ **Dissolution (Divorce) of:** ☐ Marriage ☐ Domestic Partnership	
☐ **Legal Separation of:** ☐ Marriage ☐ Domestic Partnership	
☐ **Nullity of:** ☐ Marriage ☐ Domestic Partnership	

1. **LEGAL RELATIONSHIP** (check all that apply):

  a. ☐ We are married.

  b. ☐ We are domestic partners and our domestic partnership was established in California.

  c. ☐ We are domestic partners and our domestic partnership was NOT established in California.

2. **RESIDENCE REQUIREMENTS** (check all that apply):

  a. ☐ Petitioner ☐ Respondent has been a resident of this state for at least six months and of this county for at least three months immediately preceding the filing of this *Petition*. (For a divorce, at least one person in the legal relationship described in items 1a and 1c must comply with this requirement.)

  b. ☐ Our domestic partnership was established in California. Neither of us has to be a resident or have a domicile in California to dissolve our partnership here.

  c. ☐ We are the same sex, were married in California, but currently live in a jurisdiction that does not recognize, and will not dissolve, our marriage. This *Petition* is filed in the county where we married.
    Petitioner lives in (specify):   Respondent lives in (specify):

3. **STATISTICAL FACTS**

  a. ☐ (1) Date of marriage (specify):   (2) Date of separation (specify):
    (3) Time from date of marriage to date of separation (specify):   Years   Months

  b. ☐ (1) Registration date of domestic partnership with the California Secretary of State or other state equivalent (specify below):
    (2) Date of separation (specify):
    (3) Time from date of registration of domestic partnership to date of separation (specify):   Years   Months

4. **MINOR CHILDREN**

  a. ☐ There are no minor children.

  b. ☐ The minor children are:

Child's name	Birthdate	Age	Sex

    (1) ☐ continued on Attachment 4b.   (2) ☐ a child who is not yet born.

  c. If any children were born before the marriage or domestic partnership, the court has the authority to determine those children to be children of the marriage or domestic partnership.

  d. If there are minor children of Petitioner and Respondent, a completed *Declaration Under Uniform Child Custody Jurisdiction and Enforcement Act (UCCJEA)* (form FL-105) must be attached.

  e. ☐ Petitioner and Respondent signed a voluntary declaration of paternity. A copy ☐ is ☐ is not attached.

Page 1 of 3

RESPONSE—MARRIAGE/DOMESTIC PARTNERSHIP
(Family Law)

FL-120

PETITIONER:	CASE NUMBER:
RESPONDENT:	

Respondent requests that the court make the following orders:

5. **LEGAL GROUNDS** (Family Code sections 2200–2210; 2310–2312)

   a. ☐ **Respondent contends** that the parties never legally married or registered a domestic partnership.

   b. ☐ **Respondent denies** the grounds set forth in item 5 of the petition.

   c. ☐ **Respondent requests**

      (1) ☐ divorce   ☐ Legal separation   of the marriage or domestic partnership based on

         (a) ☐ irreconcilable differences.   (b) ☐ permanent legal incapacity to make decisions.

      (2) ☐ Nullity of void marriage or domestic partnership based on

         (a) ☐ incest.   (b) ☐ bigamy.

      (3) ☐ Nullity of voidable marriage or domestic partnership based on

         (a) ☐ respondent's age at time of registration of domestic partnership or marriage.   (d) ☐ fraud.

         (b) ☐ prior existing marriage or domestic partnership.   (e) ☐ force.

         (c) ☐ unsound mind.   (f) ☐ physical incapacity.

6. **CHILD CUSTODY AND VISITATION (PARENTING TIME)**

	Petitioner	Respondent	Joint	Other
a. Legal custody of children to	☐	☐	☐	☐
b. Physical custody of children to	☐	☐	☐	☐
c. Child visitation (parenting time) be granted to	☐	☐		☐

   As requested in   ☐ form FL-311   ☐ form FL-312   ☐ form FL-341(C)

                      ☐ form FL-341(D)   ☐ form FL-341(E)   ☐ Attachment 6c(1)

7. **CHILD SUPPORT**

   a. If there are minor children born to or adopted by Petitioner and Respondent before or during this marriage or domestic partnership, the court will make orders for the support of the children upon request and submission of financial forms by the requesting party.

   b. An earnings assignment may be issued without further notice.

   c. Any party required to pay support must pay interest on overdue amounts at the "legal" rate, which is currently 10 percent.

   d. ☐ Other (specify):

8. **SPOUSAL OR DOMESTIC PARTNER SUPPORT**

   a. ☐ Spousal or domestic partner support payable to   ☐ Petitioner   ☐ Respondent

   b. ☐ Terminate (end) the court's ability to award support to   ☐ Petitioner   ☐ Respondent

   c. ☐ Reserve for future determination the issue of support payable to   ☐ Petitioner   ☐ Respondent

   d. ☐ Other (specify):

9. **SEPARATE PROPERTY**

   a. ☐ There are no such assets or debts that I know of to be confirmed by the court.

   b. ☐ Confirm as separate property the assets and debts in   ☐ *Property Declaration* (form FL-160).   ☐ Attachment 9b.

      ☐ the following list.   Item   Confirm to

FL-120

PETITIONER:	CASE NUMBER:
RESPONDENT:	

10. **COMMUNITY AND QUASI-COMMUNITY PROPERTY**

   a. ☐ There are no such assets or debts that I know of to be divided by the court.

   b. ☐ Determine rights to community and quasi-community assets and debts. All such assets and debts are listed

       ☐ in *Property Declaration* (form FL-160).   ☐ in Attachment 10b.

       ☐ as follows *(specify):*

11. **OTHER REQUESTS**

   a. ☐ Attorney's fees and costs payable by   ☐ Petitioner   ☐ Respondent

   b ☐ Respondent's former name be restored to *(specify):*

   c. ☐ Other *(specify):*

      ☐ Continued on Attachment 11c.

I declare under penalty of perjury under the laws of the State of California that the foregoing is true and correct.

Date:

_____
(TYPE OR PRINT NAME)

▶ _____
(SIGNATURE OF RESPONDENT)

Date:

_____
(TYPE OR PRINT NAME)

▶ _____
(SIGNATURE OF ATTORNEY FOR RESPONDENT)

FOR MORE INFORMATION: Read *Legal Steps for a Divorce or Legal Separation* (form FL-107-INFO) and visit "Families Change" at www.familieschange.ca.gov — an online guide for parents and children going through divorce or separation.

NOTICE: You may redact (black out) social security numbers from any written material filed with the court in this case other than a form used to collect child, spousal or partner support.

NOTICE—CANCELLATION OF RIGHTS: Dissolution or legal separation may automatically cancel the rights of a domestic partner or spouse under the other domestic partner's or spouse's will, trust, retirement plan, power of attorney, pay-on-death bank account, survivorship rights to any property owned in joint tenancy, and any other similar thing. It does not automatically cancel the right of a domestic partner or spouse as beneficiary of the other partner's or spouse's life insurance policy. You should review these matters, as well as any credit cards, other credit accounts, insurance polices, retirement plans, and credit reports, to determine whether they should be changed or whether you should take any other actions. Some changes may require the agreement of your partner or spouse or a court order.

The original response must be filed in the court with proof of service of a copy on Petitioner.

FL-120 [Rev. July 1, 2016]

RESPONSE—MARRIAGE/DOMESTIC PARTNERSHIP
(Family Law)

Page 3 of 3

0017

ATTORNEY OR PARTY WITHOUT ATTORNEY (Name, State Bar number, and address):	FOR COURT USE ONLY
TELEPHONE NO.: FAX NO. (Optional): E-MAIL ADDRESS (Optional): ATTORNEY FOR (Name):	

SUPERIOR COURT OF CALIFORNIA, COUNTY OF
STREET ADDRESS:
MAILING ADDRESS:
CITY AND ZIP CODE:
BRANCH NAME:

PETITIONER:

RESPONDENT:

APPEARANCE, STIPULATIONS, AND WAIVERS	CASE NUMBER:

1. **Appearance by respondent** *(you must choose one):*

   a. ☐ By filing this form, I make a general appearance.

   b. ☒ I have previously made a general appearance.

   c. ☐ I am a member of the military services of the United States of America. I have completed and attached to this form *Declaration and Conditional Waiver of Rights Under the Servicemembers Civil Relief Act of 2003* (form FL-130(A)).

2. **Agreements, stipulations, and waivers** *(choose all that apply):*

   a. ☐ The parties agree that this cause may be decided as an uncontested matter.

   b. ☐ The parties waive their rights to notice of trial, a statement of decision, a motion for new trial, and the right to appeal.

   c. ☐ This matter may be decided by a commissioner sitting as a temporary judge.

   d. ☐ The parties have a written agreement that will be submitted to the court, or a stipulation for judgment will be submitted to the court and attached to *Judgment (Family Law)* (form FL-180).

   e. ☐ None of these agreements or waivers will apply unless the court approves the stipulation for judgment or incorporates the written settlement agreement into the judgment.

   f. ☐ This is a parentage case, and both parties have signed an *Advisement and Waiver of Rights Re: Establishment of Parental Relationship* (form FL-235) or its equivalent.

3. **Other** *(specify):*

Date: _____

_____
(TYPE OR PRINT NAME)

▶ _____
(SIGNATURE OF PETITIONER)

Date: _____

_____
(TYPE OR PRINT NAME)

▶ _____
(SIGNATURE OF RESPONDENT)

Date: _____

_____
(TYPE OR PRINT NAME)

▶ _____
(SIGNATURE OF ATTORNEY FOR PETITIONER)

Date: _____

_____
(TYPE OR PRINT NAME)

▶ _____
(SIGNATURE OF ATTORNEY FOR RESPONDENT)

Page 1 of 1

Form Approved for Optional Use Judicial Council of California FL-130 [Rev. January 1, 2011]	**APPEARANCE, STIPULATIONS, AND WAIVERS** (Family Law—Uniform Parentage—Custody and Support)	Government Code, § 70673 www.courtinfo.ca.gov

0018

PETITIONER/PLAINTIFF:	CASE NUMBER:
RESPONDENT/DEFENDANT:	
OTHER PARENT:	

DECLARATION AND CONDITIONAL WAIVER OF RIGHTS
UNDER THE SERVICEMEMBERS CIVIL RELIEF ACT OF 2003
Attachment to *Appearance, Stipulations, and Waivers* (form FL-130)

Notice to Servicemember

The Servicemembers Civil Relief Act of 2003 (50 U.S.C. App. §§ 501–596), formerly known as the Soldiers' and Sailors' Civil Relief Act of 1940, is a federal law that provides protections for military members when they enter active duty. You may obtain a copy of the act from the public law library or from the website of the United States Department of Justice at *www.justice.gov.*

By signing this conditional waiver and attaching it to *Appearance, Stipulations, and Waivers* (form FL-130), I declare that I am entitled to the benefits of the Servicemembers Civil Relief Act, title 50 United States Code Appendix, sections 501–596 (SCRA), and:

1. To permit the court to decide this cause as an uncontested matter and enter a judgment that incorporates the terms of the written agreement made between the petitioner and me (a copy of which is attached to this form), I make a knowing, intelligent, and voluntary conditional waiver of the right to seek to set aside a default judgment entered against me in this matter, as provided by section 521 of the SCRA.

2. This waiver is conditioned as follows:

   a. The waiver applies only to a default judgment that incorporates the terms and conditions of the written agreement between the petitioner and me that is titled *(specify):*

      (1) ☐ Stipulation for Judgment

      (2) ☐ Marital Settlement Agreement

      (3) ☐ Other *(specify):*

   b. The court must enter a judgment in this case that incorporates only the terms and conditions of the above written agreement without any change; and

   c. Should the court enter a judgment that changes the above written agreement in any way, then I do not waive any of my rights under the SCRA, including my right to seek to set aside the judgment at any time.

3. This conditional waiver was executed during or after a period of military service.

I declare under penalty of perjury under the laws of the State of California that the foregoing is true and correct.

Date:

_____   _____
(TYPE OR PRINT NAME)   (SIGNATURE OF RESPONDENT)

Attention: Clerk of the Court

By law, a servicemember must not be charged a fee to file *Appearance, Stipulations, and Waivers* (form FL-130).

Page 1 of 1

Form Approved for Optional Use
Judicial Council of California
FL-130(A) [New January 1, 2011]

DECLARATION AND CONDITIONAL WAIVER OF RIGHTS
UNDER THE SERVICEMEMBERS CIVIL RELIEF ACT OF 2003

50 U.S.C. Appen. § 501 et seq.
Government Code, § 70673
www.courts.ca.gov

0019

ATTORNEY OR PARTY WITHOUT ATTORNEY *(Name, State Bar number, and address):*

TELEPHONE NO.:   FAX NO. :

E-MAIL ADDRESS:

ATTORNEY FOR *(Name)*:

SUPERIOR COURT OF CALIFORNIA, COUNTY OF

STREET ADDRESS:

MAILING ADDRESS:

CITY AND ZIP CODE:

BRANCH NAME:

PETITIONER:

RESPONDENT:

OTHER PARENT/PARTY:

DECLARATION OF DISCLOSURE	CASE NUMBER:
☐ Petitioner's ☐ Preliminary	
☐ Respondent's ☐ Final	

DO NOT FILE DECLARATIONS OF DISCLOSURE OR FINANCIAL ATTACHMENTS WITH THE COURT

In a dissolution, legal separation, or nullity action, both a preliminary and a final declaration of disclosure must be served on the other party with certain exceptions. Neither disclosure is filed with the court. Instead, a declaration stating that service of disclosure documents was completed or waived must be filed with the court (see form FL-141).

- *In summary dissolution cases, each spouse or domestic partner must exchange preliminary disclosures as described in* Summary Dissolution Information *(form FL-810). Final disclosures are not required (see Family Code section 2109).*

- *In a default judgment case that is not a stipulated judgment or a judgment based on a marital settlement agreement, only the petitioner is required to complete and serve a preliminary declaration of disclosure. A final disclosure is not required of either party (see Family Code section 2110).*

- *Service of preliminary declarations of disclosure may not be waived by an agreement between the parties.*

- *Parties who agree to waive final declarations of disclosure must file their written agreement with the court (see form FL-144).*

The petitioner must serve a preliminary declaration of disclosure at the same time as the Petition or within 60 days of filing the Petition. The respondent must serve a preliminary declaration of disclosure at the same time as the Response or within 60 days of filing the Response. The time periods may be extended by written agreement of the parties or by court order (see Family Code section 2104(f)).

Attached are the following:

1. ☐ A completed *Schedule of Assets and Debts* (form FL-142) or ☐ A *Property Declaration* (form FL-160) for *(specify):* ☐ Community and Quasi-Community Property ☐ Separate Property.

2. ☐ A completed *Income and Expense Declaration* (form FL-150).

3. ☐ All tax returns filed by the party in the two years before the date that the party served the disclosure documents.

4. ☐ A statement of all material facts and information regarding valuation of all assets that are community property or in which the community has an interest *(not a form)*.

5. ☐ A statement of all material facts and information regarding obligations for which the community is liable *(not a form)*.

6. ☐ An accurate and complete written disclosure of any investment opportunity, business opportunity, or other income-producing opportunity presented since the date of separation that results from any investment, significant business, or other income-producing opportunity from the date of marriage to the date of separation *(not a form)*.

I declare under penalty of perjury under the laws of the State of California that the foregoing is true and correct.

Date:

_____   _____
(TYPE OR PRINT NAME)   SIGNATURE

Page 1 of 1

Form Adopted for Mandatory Use
Judicial Council of California
FL-140 [Rev. July 1, 2013]

DECLARATION OF DISCLOSURE
(Family Law)

Family Code, §§ 2102, 2104,
2105, 2106, 2112
www.courts.ca.gov

0020

ATTORNEY OR PARTY WITHOUT ATTORNEY (Name, State Bar number, and address):

TELEPHONE NO.:   FAX NO. :
E-MAIL ADDRESS:
ATTORNEY FOR (Name):

SUPERIOR COURT OF CALIFORNIA, COUNTY OF
STREET ADDRESS:
MAILING ADDRESS:
CITY AND ZIP CODE:
BRANCH NAME:

PETITIONER:
RESPONDENT:
OTHER PARENT/PARTY:

DECLARATION REGARDING SERVICE OF DECLARATION OF DISCLOSURE AND INCOME AND EXPENSE DECLARATION
☐ Petitioner's   ☐ Preliminary
☐ Respondent's   ☐ Final

CASE NUMBER:

1. I am the ☐ attorney for ☐ petitioner ☐ respondent in this matter.

2. ☐ Petitioner's ☐ Respondent's *Preliminary Declaration of Disclosure* (form FL-140), current* *Income and Expense Declaration* (form FL-150), completed *Schedule of Assets and Debts* (form FL-142) or *Community and Separate Property Declarations* (form FL-160) with appropriate attachments, all tax returns filed by the party in the two years before service of the preliminary disclosures, and all other required information under Family Code section 2104 were served on:

   ☐ the other party ☐ the other party's attorney by ☐ personal service ☐ mail
   ☐ Other (specify):
   on (date):

3. ☐ Petitioner's ☐ Respondent's *Final Declaration of Disclosure* (form FL-140), current* *Income and Expense Declaration* (form FL-150), completed *Schedule of Assets and Debts* (form FL-142) or *Community or Separate Property Declarations* (form FL-160) with attachments, and the material facts and information required by Family Code section 2105 were served on:

   ☐ the other party ☐ other party's attorney by ☐ personal service ☐ mail
   ☐ Other (specify):
   on (date):

4. ☐ Service of ☐ Petitioner's ☐ Respondent's ☐ preliminary ☐ final declaration of disclosure
   ☐ current income and expense declaration has been waived as follows:

   a. ☐ The parties agreed to waive final declaration of disclosure requirements under Family Code section 2105(d.)
      (Form FL-144 may be used for this purpose.) The waiver ☐ was filed on (date):
      ☐ is being filed at the same time as this form.

   b. ☐ The party has failed to comply with disclosure requirements, and the court has granted the request for voluntary waiver of receipt under Family Code section 2107 on (date):

   c. ☐ This is a default proceeding that does not include a stipulated judgment or settlement agreement. Petitioner waives final disclosure requirements under Family Code section 2110.

*Current is defined as completed within the past three months providing no facts have changed. (Cal. Rules of Court, rule 5.260.)

I declare under penalty of perjury under the laws of the State of California that the foregoing is true and correct.

Date:

_____   ▶ _____
(TYPE OR PRINT NAME)   SIGNATURE

NOTE: File this document with the court.
Do not file a copy of the Preliminary or Final Declaration of Disclosure or any attachments to either declaration of disclosure with this document.

Page 1 of 1

Form Adopted for Mandatory Use
Judicial Council of California
FL-141 [Rev. July 1, 2013]

DECLARATION REGARDING SERVICE OF DECLARATION OF DISCLOSURE AND INCOME AND EXPENSE DECLARATION
(Family Law)

Family Code, §§ 2102, 2104,
2105, 2106, 2112
www.courts.ca.gov

THIS FORM SHOULD NOT BE FILED WITH THE COURT

ATTORNEY OR PARTY WITHOUT ATTORNEY *(Name and Address)*:	TELEPHONE NO.:

ATTORNEY FOR *(Name)*:

SUPERIOR COURT OF CALIFORNIA, COUNTY OF

PETITIONER:

RESPONDENT:

SCHEDULE OF ASSETS AND DEBTS ☐ **Petitioner's** ☐ **Respondent's**	CASE NUMBER:

— **INSTRUCTIONS** —

List all your known community and separate assets or debts. Include assets even if they are in the possession of another person, including your spouse. If you contend an asset or debt is separate, put P (for Petitioner) or R (for Respondent) in the first column (separate property) to indicate to whom you contend it belongs.

All values should be as of the date of signing the declaration unless you specify a different valuation date with the description. For additional space, use a continuation sheet numbered to show which item is being continued.

ITEM NO.	ASSETS DESCRIPTION	SEP. PROP	DATE ACQUIRED	CURRENT GROSS FAIR MARKET VALUE	AMOUNT OF MONEY OWED OR ENCUMBRANCE
1.	REAL ESTATE *(Give street addresses and attach copies of deeds with legal descriptions and latest lender's statement.)*			$	$
2.	HOUSEHOLD FURNITURE, FURNISHINGS, APPLIANCES *(Identify.)*				
3.	JEWELRY, ANTIQUES, ART, COIN COLLECTIONS, etc. *(Identify.)*				

Form Approved for Optional Use
Judicial Council of California
FL-142 [Rev. January 1, 2005]

SCHEDULE OF ASSETS AND DEBTS
(Family Law)

Code of Civil Procedure, §§ 2030(c), 2033.5
www.courtinfo.ca.gov

ITEM NO.	ASSETS DESCRIPTION	SEP. PROP	DATE ACQUIRED	CURRENT GROSS FAIR MARKET VALUE	AMOUNT OF MONEY OWED OR ENCUMBRANCE
				$	$
4.	VEHICLES, BOATS, TRAILERS *(Describe and attach copy of title document.)*				
5.	SAVINGS ACCOUNTS *(Account name, account number, bank, and branch. Attach copy of latest statement.)*				
6.	CHECKING ACCOUNTS *(Account name and number, bank, and branch. Attach copy of latest statement.)*				
7.	CREDIT UNION, OTHER DEPOSIT ACCOUNTS *(Account name and number, bank, and branch. Attach copy of latest statement.)*				
8.	CASH *(Give location.)*				
9.	TAX REFUND				
10.	LIFE INSURANCE WITH CASH SURRENDER OR LOAN VALUE *(Attach copy of declaration page for each policy.)*				

ITEM NO.	ASSETS DESCRIPTION	SEP. PROP	DATE ACQUIRED	CURRENT GROSS FAIR MARKET VALUE	AMOUNT OF MONEY OWED OR ENCUMBRANCE
11.	STOCKS, BONDS, SECURED NOTES, MUTUAL FUNDS *(Give certificate number and attach copy of the certificate or copy of latest statement.)*			$	$
12.	RETIREMENT AND PENSIONS *(Attach copy of latest summary plan documents and latest benefit statement.)*				
13.	PROFIT - SHARING, ANNUITIES, IRAS, DEFERRED COMPENSATION *(Attach copy of latest statement.)*				
14.	ACCOUNTS RECEIVABLE AND UNSECURED NOTES *(Attach copy of each.)*				
15.	PARTNERSHIPS AND OTHER BUSINESS INTERESTS *(Attach copy of most current K-1 form and Schedule C.)*				
16.	OTHER ASSETS				
17.	TOTAL ASSETS FROM CONTINUATION SHEET				
18.	TOTAL ASSETS			$	$

ITEM NO.	DEBTS—SHOW TO WHOM OWED	SEP. PROP.	TOTAL OWING	DATE INCURRED
19. STUDENT LOANS *(Give details.)*			$	
20. TAXES *(Give details.)*				
21. SUPPORT ARREARAGES *(Attach copies of orders and statements.)*				
22. LOANS—UNSECURED *(Give bank name and loan number and attach copy of latest statement.)*				
23. CREDIT CARDS *(Give creditor's name and address and the account number. Attach copy of latest statement.)*				
24. OTHER DEBTS *(Specify.):*				
25. TOTAL DEBTS FROM CONTINUATION SHEET				
26. TOTAL DEBTS			$	

27. ☐ *(Specify number):* _____ pages are attached as continuation sheets.

I declare under penalty of perjury under the laws of the State of California that the foregoing is true and correct.

Date:

▶

_____
(TYPE OR PRINT NAME)

_____
(SIGNATURE OF DECLARANT)

0025

FL-144

ATTORNEY OR PARTY WITHOUT ATTORNEY *(Name, State Bar number, and address):*	FOR COURT USE ONLY
TELEPHONE NO.: FAX NO. *(Optional):* E–MAIL ADDRESS *(Optional):* ATTORNEY FOR *(Name):*	

SUPERIOR COURT OF CALIFORNIA, COUNTY OF

STREET ADDRESS:

MAILING ADDRESS:

CITY AND ZIP CODE:

BRANCH NAME:

PLAINTIFF/ PETITIONER:

DEFENDANT/ RESPONDENT:

OTHER:

STIPULATION AND WAIVER OF FINAL DECLARATION OF DISCLOSURE	CASE NUMBER:

1. Under Family Code section 2105(d), the parties agree to waive the requirements of Family Code section 2105(a) concerning the final declaration of disclosure.

2. The parties agree as follows:

   a. We have complied with Family Code section 2104, and the preliminary declarations of disclosure have been completed and exchanged.

   b. We have completed and exchanged a current *Income and Expense Declaration* (form FL-150) that includes all material facts and information on each party's earnings, accumulations, and expenses.

   c. We have fully complied with Family Law section 2102 and have fully augmented the preliminary declarations of disclosure, including disclosure of all material facts and information on

      (1) the characterization of all assets and liabilities,

      (2) the valuation of all assets that are community property or in which the community has an interest, and

      (3) the amounts of all community debts and obligations.

   d. Each of the parties enters into this waiver knowingly, intelligently, and voluntarily.

   e. Each party understands that this waiver does not limit the legal disclosure obligations of the parties but rather is a statement under penalty of perjury that those obligations have been fulfilled.

   f. The parties also understand that if they do not comply with these obligations, the court will set aside the judgment.

The petitioner and respondent declare under penalty of perjury under the laws of the State of California that the foregoing is true and correct.

Date:

_____
(TYPE OR PRINT NAME)

_____
(SIGNATURE OF PETITIONER)

_____
(TYPE OR PRINT NAME)

_____
(SIGNATURE OF RESPONDENT)

Page 1 of 1

Form Approved for Optional Use
Judicial Council of California
FL-144 [Rev. January 1, 2007]

**STIPULATION AND WAIVER OF FINAL
DECLARATION OF DISCLOSURE**

Family Code, §§ 2102, 2104, 2105(d)
www.courtinfo.ca.gov

ATTORNEY OR PARTY WITHOUT ATTORNEY *(Name, State Bar number, and address):*	TELEPHONE NO.:

ATTORNEY FOR *(Name):*

SUPERIOR COURT OF CALIFORNIA, COUNTY OF

SHORT TITLE:

FORM INTERROGATORIES—FAMILY LAW	CASE NUMBER:
Asking Party:	
Answering Party:	
Set No.:	

Sec. 1. Instructions to Both Parties

The interrogatories on page 2 of this form are intended to provide for the exchange of relevant information without unreasonable expense to the answering party. They do not change existing law relating to interrogatories, nor do they affect the answering party's right to assert any privilege or make any objection. **Privileges must be asserted.**

Sec. 2. Definitions

Words in **boldface** in these interrogatories are defined as follows:

(a) **Person** includes a natural person; a partnership; any kind of business, legal, or public entity; and its agents or employees.

(b) **Document** means all written, recorded,or graphic materials, however stored, produced, or reproduced.

(c) **Asset** or **property** includes any interest in real estate or personal property. It includes any interest in a pension, profit-sharing, or retirement plan.

(d) **Debt** means any obligation, including debts paid since the date of separation.

(e) **Support** means any benefit or economic contribution to the living expenses of another person, including gifts.

(f) If asked to **identify a person,** give the person's name, last known residence and business addresses, telephone numbers, and company affiliation at the date of the transaction referred to.

(g) If asked to **identify a document,** attach a copy of the document unless you explain why not. If you do not attach the copy, describe the document, including its date and nature, and give the name, address, telephone number, and occupation of the person who has the document.

Sec. 3. Instructions to the Asking Party

Check the box next to each interrogatory you want the answering party to answer.

Sec. 4. Instructions to the Answering Party

You must answer these interrogatories under oath within 30 days, in accordance with Code of Civil Procedure section 2030.260.

You must furnish all information you have or can reasonably find out, including all information (not privileged) from your attorneys or under your control. If you don't know, say so.

If an interrogatory is answered by referring to a document, the document must be attached as an exhibit to the response and referred to in the response. If the document has more than one page, refer to the page and section where the answer can be found.

If a document to be attached to the response may also be attached to the *Schedule of Assets and Debts* (form FL-142), the document should be attached only to the response, and the form should refer to the response.

If an interrogatory cannot be answered completely, answer as much as you can, state the reason you cannot answer the rest, and state any information you have about the unanswered portion.

Sec. 5. Oath

Your answers to these interrogatories must be under oath, dated, and signed. Use the following statement **at the end of your answers:**

I declare under penalty of perjury under the laws of the State of California that the foregoing answers are true and correct.

▶

_____   _____
(DATE)   (SIGNATURE)

Form Approved for Optional Use
Judicial Council of California
FL-145 [Rev. January 1, 2006]

FORM INTERROGATORIES—FAMILY LAW

Code of Civil Procedure,
§§ 2030.010–2030.410, 2033.710
www.courtinfo.ca.gov

1. **Personal history**. State your full name, current residence address and work address, social security number, any other names you have used, and the dates between which you used each name.

2. **Agreements.** Are there any agreements between you and your spouse or domestic partner, made before or during your marriage or domestic partnership or after your separation, that affect the disposition of **assets, debts,** or **support** in this proceeding? If your answer is yes, for each agreement state the date made and whether it was written or oral, and attach a copy of the agreement or describe its contents.

3. **Legal actions.** Are you a party or do you anticipate being a party to any legal or administrative proceeding other than this action? If your answer is yes, state your role and the name, jurisdiction, case number, and a brief description of each proceeding.

4. **Persons sharing residence.** State the name, age, and relationship to you of each **person** at your present address.

5. **Support provided others.** State the name, age, address, and relationship to you of each **person** for whom you have provided **support** during the past 12 months and the amount provided per month for each.

6. **Support received for others.** State the name, age, address, and relationship to you of each **person** for whom you have received **support** during the past 12 months and the amount received per month for each.

7. **Current income.** List all income you received during the past 12 months, its source, the basis for its computation, and the total amount received from each. Attach your last three paycheck stubs.

8. **Other income.** During the past three years, have you received cash or other property from any source not identified in item 7? If so, list the source, the date, and the nature and value of the property.

9. **Tax returns.** Attach copies of all tax returns and tax schedules filed by or for you in any jurisdiction for the past three calendar years.

10. **Schedule of assets and debts.** Complete the *Schedule of Assets and Debts* (form FL-142) served with these interrogatories.

11. **Separate property contentions.** State the facts that support your contention that an asset or debt is separate property.

12. **Property valuations.** During the past 12 months, have you received written offers to purchase or had written appraisals of any of the assets listed on your completed *Schedule of Assets and Debts?* If your answer is yes, **identify the document.**

13. **Property held by others.** Is there any **property** held by any third party in which you have any interest or over which you have any control? If your answer is yes, indicate whether the property is shown on the *Schedule of Assets and Debts* completed by you. If it is not, describe and identify each such asset, state its present value and the basis for your valuation, and **identify the person** holding the asset.

14. **Retirement and other benefits.** Do you have an interest in any disability, retirement, profit-sharing, or deferred compensation plan? If your answer is yes, **identify** each plan and provide the name, address, and telephone number of the administrator and custodian of records.

15. **Claims of reimbursement.** Do you claim the legal right to be reimbursed for any expenditures of your separate or community property? If your answer is yes, state all supporting facts.

16. **Credits.** Have you claimed reimbursement credits for payments of community debts since the date of separation? If your answer is yes, **identify** the source of payment, the creditor, the date paid, and the amount paid. State whether you have added to the debt since the separation.

17. **Insurance. Identify** each health, life, automobile, and disability insurance policy or plan that you now own or that covers you, your children, or your assets. State the policy type, policy number, and name of the company. **Identify** the agent and give the address.

18. **Health.** Is there any physical or emotional condition that limits your ability to work? If your answer is yes, state each fact on which you base your answer.

19. **Children's needs.** Do you contend that any of your children have any special needs? If so, identify the child with the need, the reason for the need, its cost, and its expected duration.

20. **Attorney fees.** State the total amount of attorney fees and costs incurred by you in this proceeding, the amount paid, and the source of the money paid. Describe the billing arrangements.

21. **Gifts.** List any gifts you have made without the consent of your spouse or domestic partner in the past 24 months, their values, and the recipients.

FL-150

PARTY WITHOUT ATTORNEY OR ATTORNEY	STATE BAR NUMBER:	FOR COURT USE ONLY
NAME:		

FIRM NAME:

STREET ADDRESS:

CITY: STATE: ZIP CODE:

TELEPHONE NO.:   FAX NO.:

E-MAIL ADDRESS:

ATTORNEY FOR (name):

SUPERIOR COURT OF CALIFORNIA, COUNTY OF

STREET ADDRESS:

MAILING ADDRESS:

CITY AND ZIP CODE:

BRANCH NAME:

PETITIONER:

RESPONDENT:

OTHER PARTY/PARENT/CLAIMANT:

INCOME AND EXPENSE DECLARATION	CASE NUMBER:

1. **Employment** (*Give information on your current job or, if you're unemployed, your most recent job.*)

Attach copies of your pay stubs for last two months (black out Social Security numbers).	a. Employer:
	b. Employer's address:
	c. Employer's phone number:
	d. Occupation:
	e. Date job started:
	f. If unemployed, date job ended:
	g. I work about _____ hours per week.
	h. I get paid $ _____ gross (before taxes) ☐ per month ☐ per week ☐ per hour.

(If you have more than one job, attach an 8 1/2-by-11-inch sheet of paper and list the same information as above for your other jobs. Write "Question 1—Other Jobs" at the top.)

2. **Age and education**

   a. My age is (*specify*):

   b. I have completed high school or the equivalent: ☐ Yes ☐ No   If no, highest grade completed (*specify*):

   c. Number of years of college completed (*specify*): ☐ Degree(s) obtained (*specify*):

   d. Number of years of graduate school completed (*specify*): ☐ Degree(s) obtained (*specify*):

   e. I have: ☐ professional/occupational license(s) (*specify*):
   ☐ vocational training (*specify*):

3. **Tax information**

   a. ☐ I last filed taxes for tax year (*specify year*):

   b. My tax filing status is ☐ single ☐ head of household ☐ married, filing separately
   ☐ married, filing jointly with (*specify name*):

   c. I file state tax returns in ☐ California ☐ other (*specify state*):

   d. I claim the following number of exemptions (including myself) on my taxes (*specify*):

4. **Other party's income.** I estimate the gross monthly income (before taxes) of the other party in this case at (*specify*): $
   This estimate is based on (*explain*):

(If you need more space to answer any questions on this form, attach an 8 1/2-by-11-inch sheet of paper and write the question number before your answer.)   Number of pages attached: _____

I declare under penalty of perjury under the laws of the State of California that the information contained on all pages of this form and any attachments is true and correct.

Date:

▶

_____
(TYPE OR PRINT NAME)

_____
(SIGNATURE OF DECLARANT)

Page 1 of 4

Form Adopted for Mandatory Use
Judicial Council of California
FL-150 [Rev. January 1, 2019]

INCOME AND EXPENSE DECLARATION

Family Code, §§ 2030–2032, 2100–2113,
3552, 3620–3634, 4050–4076, 4300–4339
www.courts.ca.gov

0029

PETITIONER:	CASE NUMBER:
RESPONDENT:	
OTHER PARTY/PARENT/CLAIMANT:	

Attach copies of your pay stubs for the last two months and proof of any other income. Take a copy of your latest federal tax return to the court hearing. *(Black out your Social Security number on the pay stub and tax return.)*

5. **Income** *(For average monthly, add up all the income you received in each category in the last 12 months and divide the total by 12.)*

		Last month	Average monthly
a.	Salary or wages (gross, before taxes)...	$	
b.	Overtime (gross, before taxes)...	$	
c.	Commissions or bonuses..	$	
d.	Public assistance (for example: TANF, SSI, GA/GR) ☐ currently receiving	$	
e.	Spousal support ☐ from this marriage ☐ from a different marriage ☐ federally taxable*	$	
f.	Partner support ☐ from this domestic partnership ☐ from a different domestic partnership	$	
g.	Pension/retirement fund payments..	$	
h.	Social Security retirement (not SSI)...	$	
i.	Disability: ☐ Social Security (not SSI) ☐ State disability (SDI) ☐ Private insurance	$	
j.	Unemployment compensation...	$	
k.	Workers' compensation..	$	
l.	Other (military allowances, royalty payments) *(specify):*	$	

6. **Investment income** *(Attach a schedule showing gross receipts less cash expenses for each piece of property.)*

a.	Dividends/interest...	$	
b.	Rental property income..	$	
c.	Trust income..	$	
d.	Other *(specify):*	$	

7. **Income from self-employment, after business expenses for all businesses**........................ $ _____

I am the ☐ owner/sole proprietor ☐ business partner ☐ other *(specify):*
Number of years in this business *(specify):*
Name of business *(specify):*
Type of business *(specify):*

Attach a profit and loss statement for the last two years or a Schedule C from your last federal tax return. Black out your Social Security number. If you have more than one business, provide the information above for each of your businesses.

8. ☐ **Additional income.** I received one-time money (lottery winnings, inheritance, etc.) in the last 12 months *(specify source and amount):*

9. ☐ **Change in income.** My financial situation has changed significantly over the last 12 months because *(specify):*

10. **Deductions**

		Last month
a.	Required union dues..	$
b.	Required retirement payments (not Social Security, FICA, 401(k), or IRA).......................	$
c.	Medical, hospital, dental, and other health insurance premiums *(total monthly amount)*..........	$
d.	Child support that I pay for children from other relationships...	$
e.	Spousal support that I pay by court order from a different marriage ☐ federally tax deductible*.........	$
f.	Partner support that I pay by court order from a different domestic partnership..................	$
g.	Necessary job-related expenses not reimbursed by my employer *(attach explanation labeled "Question 10g")*.........	$

11. **Assets**

		Total
a.	Cash and checking accounts, savings, credit union, money market, and other deposit accounts..............	$
b.	Stocks, bonds, and other assets I could easily sell..	$
c.	All other property, ☐ real and ☐ personal *(estimate fair market value minus the debts you owe)*.....	$

* Check the box if the spousal support order or judgment was executed by the parties and the court before January 1, 2019, or if a court-ordered change maintains the spousal support payments as taxable income to the recipient and tax deductible to the payor.

PETITIONER:	CASE NUMBER:
RESPONDENT:	
OTHER PARTY/PARENT/CLAIMANT:	

12. **The following people live with me:**

Name	Age	How the person is related to me (ex: son)	That person's gross monthly income	Pays some of the household expenses?
a.				☐ Yes ☐ No
b.				☐ Yes ☐ No
c.				☐ Yes ☐ No
d.				☐ Yes ☐ No
e.				☐ Yes ☐ No

13. **Average monthly expenses** ☐ Estimated expenses ☐ Actual expenses ☐ Proposed needs

a. Home:
  (1) ☐ Rent or ☐ mortgage.......... $ _____
  If mortgage:
  (a) average principal: $ _____
  (b) average interest: $ _____
  (2) Real property taxes................................. $ _____
  (3) Homeowner's or renter's insurance (if not included above)............................. $ _____
  (4) Maintenance and repair.......................... $ _____
b. Health-care costs not paid by insurance........ $ _____
c. Child care.. $ _____
d. Groceries and household supplies................. $ _____
e. Eating out... $ _____
f. Utilities (gas, electric, water, trash)................ $ _____
g. Telephone, cell phone, and e-mail................ $ _____

h. Laundry and cleaning..................................... $ _____
i. Clothes... $ _____
j. Education.. $ _____
k. Entertainment, gifts, and vacation.................. $ _____
l. Auto expenses and transportation (insurance, gas, repairs, bus, etc.)................. $ _____
m. Insurance (life, accident, etc.; do not include auto, home, or health insurance)................... $ _____
n. Savings and investments............................... $ _____
o. Charitable contributions................................. $ _____
p. Monthly payments listed in item 14 (itemize below in 14 and insert total here)..... $ _____
q. Other (specify): $ _____

r. **TOTAL EXPENSES** (a–q) (do not add in the amounts in a(1)(a) and (b)) $ _____

s. **Amount of expenses paid by others** $ _____

14. **Installment payments and debts not listed above**

Paid to	For	Amount	Balance	Date of last payment
		$	$	
		$	$	
		$	$	
		$	$	
		$	$	
		$	$	

15. **Attorney fees** (This information is required if either party is requesting attorney fees):

a. To date, I have paid my attorney this amount for fees and costs (specify): $
b. The source of this money was (specify):
c. I still owe the following fees and costs to my attorney (specify total owed): $
d. My attorney's hourly rate is (specify):

I confirm this fee arrangement.

Date:

_____
(TYPE OR PRINT NAME)

▶

_____
(SIGNATURE OF DECLARANT)

0031

PETITIONER:	CASE NUMBER:
RESPONDENT:	
OTHER PARTY/PARENT/CLAIMANT:	

CHILD SUPPORT INFORMATION
(NOTE: Fill out this page only if your case involves child support.)

16. **Number of children**
    a. I have *(specify number):*   children under the age of 18 with the other parent in this case.
    b. The children spend   percent of their time with me and   percent of their time with the other parent.
       (If you're not sure about percentage or it has not been agreed on, please describe your parenting schedule here.)

17. **Children's health-care expenses**
    a. ☐ I do   ☐ I do not   have health insurance available to me for the children through my job.
    b. Name of insurance company:
    c. Address of insurance company:

    d. The monthly cost for the **children's** health insurance is or would be *(specify):* $
       (Do not include the amount your employer pays.)

18. **Additional expense for the children in this case**   Amount per month
    a. Childcare so I can work or get job training... $ _____
    b. Children's health care not covered by insurance... $ _____
    c. Travel expenses for visitation... $ _____
    d. Children's educational or other special needs *(specify below):*...................... $ _____

19. **Special hardships.** I ask the court to consider the following special financial circumstances
    (attach documentation of any item listed here, including court orders):   Amount per month   For how many months?
    a. Extraordinary health expenses not included in 18b................................. $ _____   _____
    b. Major losses not covered by insurance *(examples: fire, theft, other
       insured loss)*... $ _____   _____
    c. (1) Expenses for my minor children who are from other relationships and
           are living with me.. $ _____   _____
       (2) Names and ages of those children *(specify):*

       (3) Child support I receive for those children... $ _____
    The expenses listed in a, b, and c create an extreme financial hardship because *(explain):*

20. **Other information I want the court to know concerning support in my case** *(specify):*

0032

FL-155

Your name and address or attorney's name and address:	TELEPHONE NO.:	FOR COURT USE ONLY

ATTORNEY FOR *(Name):*

SUPERIOR COURT OF CALIFORNIA, COUNTY OF

STREET ADDRESS:

MAILING ADDRESS:

CITY AND ZIP CODE:

BRANCH NAME:

PETITIONER/PLAINTIFF:

RESPONDENT/DEFENDANT:

OTHER PARENT:

FINANCIAL STATEMENT (SIMPLIFIED)

CASE NUMBER:

NOTICE: Read page 2 to find out if you qualify to use this form and how to use it.

1. a. ☐ My only source of income is TANF, SSI, or GA/GR.
   b. ☐ I have applied for TANF, SSI, or GA/GR.
2. I am the parent of the following number of natural or adopted children from this relationship . . . . ___
3. a. The children from this relationship are with me this amount of time . . . . ___ %
   b. The children from this relationship are with the other parent this amount of time . . . . ___ %
   c. Our arrangement for custody and visitation is *(specify, using extra sheet if necessary):*
4. My tax filing status is: ☐ single ☐ married filing jointly ☐ head of household ☐ married filing separately.
5. My current gross income *(before taxes)* per month is . . . . $_____

   Attach 1 copy of pay stubs for last 2 months here (cross out social security numbers)

   This income comes from the following:
   ☐ Salary/wages: Amount before taxes per month. . . . . $_____
   ☐ Retirement: Amount before taxes per month. . . . . $_____
   ☐ Unemployment compensation: Amount per month . . . . $_____
   ☐ Workers' compensation: Amount per month . . . . $_____
   ☐ Social security: ☐ SSI ☐ Other Amount per month . . . . $_____
   ☐ Disability: Amount per month . . . . $_____
   ☐ Interest income (from bank accounts or other): Amount per month . . . . $_____
   I have no income other than as stated in this paragraph.

6. I pay the following monthly expenses for the children in this case:
   a. ☐ Day care or preschool to allow me to work or go to school . . . . $_____
   b. ☐ Health care not paid for by insurance . . . . $_____
   c. ☐ School, education, tuition, or other special needs of the child . . . . $_____
   d. ☐ Travel expenses for visitation . . . . $_____

7. ☐ There are *(specify number)* _____ other minor children of mine living with me. Their monthly expenses that I pay are . . . . $_____

8. I spend the following average monthly amounts *(please attach proof):*
   a. ☐ Job-related expenses that are not paid by my employer *(specify reasons for expenses on separate sheet)* $_____
   b. ☐ Required union dues . . . . $_____
   c. ☐ Required retirement payments (not social security, FICA, 401k or IRA) . . . . $_____
   d. ☐ Health insurance costs . . . . $_____
   e. ☐ Child support I am paying for other minor children of mine who are not living with me . . . . $_____
   f. ☐ Spousal support I am paying because of a court order for another relationship. . . . . $_____
   g. ☐ Monthly housing costs: ☐ rent or ☐ mortgage . . . . $_____
      If mortgage: interest payments $_____ real property taxes $_____

9. Information concerning ☐ my current employment ☐ my most recent employment:
   Employer:
   Address:
   Telephone number:
   My occupation:
   Date work started:
   Date work stopped *(if applicable):* What was your gross income *(before taxes)* before work stopped?:

Page 1 of 2

Form Approved for Optional Use
Judicial Council of California
FL-155 [Rev. January 1, 2004]

FINANCIAL STATEMENT (SIMPLIFIED)

Family Code, § 4068(b)
www.courtinfo.ca.gov

PETITIONER/PLAINTIFF:	CASE NUMBER:
RESPONDENT/DEFENDANT:	
OTHER PARENT:	

10. My estimate of the other party's gross monthly income *(before taxes)* is . . . . $ _____

11. My current spouse's monthly income *(before taxes)* is . . . . $ _____

12. Other information I want the court to know concerning child support in my case *(attach extra sheet with the information)*.

13. ☐ I am attaching a copy of page 3 of form FL-150, *Income and Expense Declaration* showing my expenses.

I declare under penalty of perjury under the laws of the State of California that the information contained on all pages of this form and any attachments is true and correct.

Date:

_____
(TYPE OR PRINT NAME)

▶

_____
(SIGNATURE OF DECLARANT)

☐ PETITIONER/PLAINTIFF ☐ RESPONDENT/DEFENDANT

INSTRUCTIONS

Step 1: Are you eligible to use this form? *If your answer is YES to any of the following questions, you may NOT use this form:*

• Are you asking for spousal support (alimony) or a change in spousal support?
• Is your spouse or former spouse asking for spousal support (alimony) or a change in spousal support?
• Are you asking the other party to pay your attorney fees?
• Is the other party asking you to pay his or her attorney fees?
• Do you receive money (income) from any source other than the following?

  • Welfare (such as TANF, GR, or GA)   • Interest
  • Salary or wages   • Workers' compensation
  • Disability   • Social security
  • Unemployment   • Retirement

• Are you self-employed?

If you are eligible to use this form and choose to do so, you do not need to complete the *Income and Expense Declaration* (form FL-150). Even if you are eligible to use this form, you may choose instead to use the *Income and Expense Declaration* (form FL-150).

Step 2: Make 2 copies of each of your pay stubs for the last two months. If you received money from other than wages or salary, include copies of the pay stub received with that money.
Privacy notice: If you wish, you may cross out your social security number if it appears on the pay stub, other payment notice or your tax return

Step 3: Make 2 copies of your most recent federal income tax form.

Step 4: Complete this form with the required information. Type the form if possible or complete it neatly and clearly in black ink. If you need additional room, please use plain or lined paper, 8½-by-11", and staple to this form.

Step 5: Make 2 copies of each side of this completed form and any attached pages.

Step 6: Serve a copy on the other party. Have someone other than yourself mail to the attorney for the other party, the other party, and the local child support agency, if they are handling the case, 1 copy of this form, 1 copy of each of your stubs for the last two months, and 1 copy of your most recent federal income tax return.

Step 7: File the original with the court. Staple this form with 1 copy of each of your pay stubs for the last two months. Take this document and give it to the clerk of the court. Check with your local court about how to submit your return.

Step 8: Keep the remaining copies of the documents for your file.

Step 9: Take the copy of your latest federal income tax return to the court hearing.

It is very important that you attend the hearings scheduled for this case. If you do not attend a hearing, the court may make an order without considering the information you want the court to consider.

FL-157

PETITIONER/PLAINTIFF:	CASE NUMBER:
RESPONDENT/DEFENDANT:	
OTHER PARTY:	

SPOUSAL OR PARTNER SUPPORT DECLARATION ATTACHMENT

☐ **Declaration for Default or Uncontested Judgment (form FL-170)**   ☐ **Supporting Declaration for Attorney's Fees and Costs Attachment (form FL-158)**

☐ **Other** (specify):

1. **Spousal or domestic partner support.** I request that the court (check all that apply):

   a. ☐ Enter a judgment for spousal or domestic partner support for ☐ Petitioner ☐ Respondent.

   b. ☐ Modify the judgment for spousal or domestic partner support for ☐ Petitioner ☐ Respondent.

   c. ☐ Deny the request to modify the judgment for spousal or domestic partner support.

   d. ☐ Terminate jurisdiction to award spousal or domestic partner support to ☐ Petitioner ☐ Respondent.

2. ☐ **Attorney fees and costs.** I request that the court (check one):

   a. ☐ Order my attorney fees and costs to be paid by ☐ my spouse or domestic partner ☐ a joined party (specify):

   b. ☐ Deny the request for attorney fees and costs.

3. The facts in support of my request are:

   a. **Family Code section 4320(a)(1)**

   (1) The supported party has the following training, job skills, and work history:

   (2) The current job market for the job skills of the supported party described in item 3a(1) is:

   (3) The supported party would need the following time and expense to acquire the education or training to develop the job skills described in item 3a(1):

   (4) To develop other, more marketable job skills or employment, the supported party would need the following retraining or education:

Form Approved for Optional Use
Judicial Council of California
FL-157 [New January 1, 2012]

**SPOUSAL OR PARTNERSHIP SUPPORT
DECLARATION ATTACHMENT**

Family Code, §§ 270, 2030, 2032, 4320, 6344, 7640
www.courts.ca.gov

PETITIONER/PLAINTIFF:	CASE NUMBER:
RESPONDENT/DEFENDANT:	
OTHER PARTY:	

3. Facts in support of request.

   b. **Family Code section 4320(a)(2)**

   Provide any facts that indicate the supported party's earning ability is, or is not, lower than it might be if he or she had not had periods of unemployment because of the time needed to attend to domestic duties *(explain)*:

   c. **Family Code section 4320(b)**

   Provide any facts that indicate that the supported party contributed to the education, training, career position, or license of the supporting party.

   d. **Family Code section 4320(c)**

   (1) The supporting party ☐ does ☐ does not   have the ability to pay spousal or domestic partner support.

   (2) The supporting party's current gross income from employment or self-employment is *(specify)*:

   (3) The supporting party's current income from investments, retirement, other sources is *(specify)*:

   (4) The supporting party's current assets and their values and balances are *(specify)*:

   (5) The supporting party's standard of living is *(describe, for example, type and frequency of vacations, value of home and other real estate, value of investments, type of vehicles owned, credit card use or nonuse)*:

**SPOUSAL OR PARTNERSHIP SUPPORT
DECLARATION ATTACHMENT**

0036

PETITIONER/PLAINTIFF:	CASE NUMBER:
RESPONDENT/DEFENDANT:	
OTHER PARTY:	

3. Facts in support of request.

   e. **Family Code section 4320(d)**

      The supported party ☐ does ☐ does not need support to maintain the standard of living we enjoyed during the marriage or domestic partnership.

   f. **Family Code Section 4320(e)**

      (1) The supported party's assets and obligations, including separate property, are *(list values and balances):*

      (2) The supporting party's assets and obligations, including separate property, are *(list values and balances):*

**SPOUSAL OR PARTNERSHIP SUPPORT
DECLARATION ATTACHMENT**

PETITIONER/PLAINTIFF:	CASE NUMBER:
RESPONDENT/DEFENDANT:	
OTHER PARTY:	

3. Facts in support of request.

g. **Family Code section 4320(f)**

Length of marriage or domestic partnership *(specify):*

h. **Family Code section 4320(g)**

Provide any facts indicating whether or not the supported party is able to work without unduly interfering with the interests of the children in his or her care *(describe):*

i. **Family Code section 4320(h)**

(1) Petitioner's age is *(specify):*   Respondent's age is *(specify):*

(2) Petitioner's current health condition is *(describe):*

(3) Respondent's current health condition is *(describe):*

j. **Additional factors (Family Code sections 4320(i)–(n))**

The court will also consider the following factors before making a judgment for spousal or domestic partner support:

(1) Any documented evidence of domestic violence between the parties as defined in Family Code section 6211.

(2) The immediate and specific tax consequences for each party;

(3) The balance of the hardships on each party;

(4) The criminal conviction of an abusive spouse in reducing or eliminating support in accordance with Family Code section 4325;

(5) The goal that the supported party will be self-supporting within a reasonable period of time; and

(6) Any other factors the court determines are just and equitable.

Describe below any additional information that will assist the court in considering the above factors:

**SPOUSAL OR PARTNERSHIP SUPPORT
DECLARATION ATTACHMENT**

0038

PETITIONER/PLAINTIFF:	CASE NUMBER:
RESPONDENT/DEFENDANT:	
OTHER PARTY:	

SUPPORTING DECLARATION FOR ATTORNEY'S FEES AND COSTS ATTACHMENT

To: ☐ *Request for Attorney's Fees and Costs Attachment* (form FL-319)

☐ *Responsive Declaration* (form FL-320)

1. I am
   a. ☐ the petitioner/plaintiff.
   b. ☐ the respondent/defendant.
   c. ☐ the other party.

2. I request that the court ☐ grant ☐ grant in part ☐ deny the request for attorney's fees and costs.

3. I am providing the following information ☐ in support of ☐ in opposition to the request for attorney's fees and costs.
   a. The ☐ petitioner/plaintiff ☐ respondent/defendant ☐ other party has the ability to pay
      (1) ☐ my attorney's fees and costs.
      (2) ☐ his or her own attorney's fees and costs.
      (3) ☐ both my and his or her own attorney's fees and costs.
      (4) ☐ other (specify):

   b. The attorney's fees and costs can be paid from the following sources:

   c. The court should consider the following facts in deciding whether to grant, grant in part, or deny the request for attorney's fees and costs (describe):
      ☐ See Attachment 3c.

   d. If appropriate, describe the reasons why a non-spouse party or domestic partner is involved in the case and whether he or she should or should not pay attorney's fees and costs:
      ☐ See Attachment 3d.

Form Approved for Optional Use
Judicial Council of California
FL-158 [New January 1, 2012]

**SUPPORTING DECLARATION FOR ATTORNEY'S FEES
AND COSTS ATTACHMENT
(Family Law)**

Family Code, §§ 270,
2030, 2032, 3121, 3557,
4320, 7605; Cal. Rules of
Court, rules 5.425, 5.93
www.courts.ca.gov

0039

PETITIONER/PLAINTIFF:	CASE NUMBER:
RESPONDENT/DEFENDANT:	
OTHER PARTY:	

4. Has an order already been made for payment of child support in this case?

    a. ☐ No.

    b. ☐ Yes. If so, describe the order:

        (1) The ☐ petitioner/plaintiff ☐ respondent/defendant ☐ other party must pay: $
        per month for child support.

        (a) This order has been in effect since (date):

        (b) The payments ☐ have been made ☐ have not been made ☐ have been made in part
        since the date of the order.

        (2) ☐ Additional information (specify):

5. Has an order already been made for payment of spousal, partner, or family support in this case?

    a. ☐ No.

    b. ☐ Yes. If so, describe the order:

        (1) The ☐ petitioner/plaintiff ☐ respondent/defendant ☐ other party must pay: $
        per month for ☐ spousal support ☐ partner support ☐ family support.

        (a) This order has been in effect since (date):

        (b) The payments ☐ have been made ☐ have not been made ☐ have been made in part
        since the date of the order.

        (2) ☐ Additional information (specify):

6. If you are or were married to, or in a domestic partnership with, the person you are seeking fees from, the court must consider the factors in Family Code section 4320 in determining whether it is just and reasonable under the relative circumstances to award attorney's fees and costs. Complete and attach *Spousal or Partner Support Declaration Attachment* (form FL-157) or a comparable declaration to provide the court with information about the factors described in section 4320.

7. You must complete, file, and serve a current *Income and Expense Declaration* (form FL-150). It is considered current if you have completed form FL-150 within the past three months and no facts have changed since the time of completion.

8. Number of pages attached to this *Supporting Declaration:* _____

I declare under penalty of perjury under the laws of the State of California that the information contained on all pages of this form and any attachments is true and correct.

Date:

_____ ▶ _____
(TYPE OR PRINT NAME)   (SIGNATURE)

**SUPPORTING DECLARATION FOR ATTORNEY'S FEES
AND COSTS ATTACHMENT
(Family Law)**

FL-160

PARTY WITHOUT ATTORNEY OR ATTORNEY	STATE BAR NUMBER:	
NAME:		
FIRM NAME:		
STREET ADDRESS:		
CITY:	STATE: ZIP CODE:	
TELEPHONE NO.:	FAX NO.:	
E-MAIL ADDRESS:		
ATTORNEY FOR (name):		

SUPERIOR COURT OF CALIFORNIA, COUNTY OF
STREET ADDRESS:
MAILING ADDRESS:
CITY AND ZIP CODE:
BRANCH NAME:

PETITIONER:
RESPONDENT:
OTHER PARENT/PARTY:

☐ **PETITIONER'S** ☐ **RESPONDENT'S**	CASE NUMBER:
☐ **COMMUNITY AND QUASI-COMMUNITY PROPERTY DECLARATION**	
☐ **SEPARATE PROPERTY DECLARATION**	

See *Instructions* on page 4 for information about completing this form. For additional space, use *Continuation of Property Declaration* (form FL-161).

A	B	C -	D =	E	F	
ITEM NO. BRIEF DESCRIPTION	DATE ACQUIRED	GROSS FAIR MARKET VALUE	AMOUNT OF DEBT	NET FAIR MARKET VALUE	PROPOSAL FOR DIVISION Award or Confirm to: PETITIONER	RESPONDENT
1. REAL ESTATE		$	$	$	$	$
2. HOUSEHOLD FURNITURE, FURNISHINGS, APPLIANCES						
3. JEWELRY, ANTIQUES, ART, COIN COLLECTIONS, etc.						
4. VEHICLES, BOATS, TRAILERS						
5. SAVINGS ACCOUNTS						
6. CHECKING ACCOUNTS						

Page 1 of 4

Form Approved for Mandatory Use
Judicial Council of California
FL-160 [Rev. July 1, 2016]

PROPERTY DECLARATION
(Family Law)

Family Code, §§ 115, 2104, 2500-2660
www.courts.ca.gov

A	B	C	-	D	=	E	F	
ITEM BRIEF DESCRIPTION NO.	DATE ACQUIRED	GROSS FAIR MARKET VALUE		AMOUNT OF DEBT		NET FAIR MARKET VALUE	PROPOSAL FOR DIVISION Award or Confirm to: PETITIONER	RESPONDENT
7. CREDIT UNION, OTHER DEPOSITORY ACCOUNTS		$		$		$	$	$
8. CASH								
9. TAX REFUND								
10. LIFE INSURANCE WITH CASH SURRENDER OR LOAN VALUE								
11. STOCKS, BONDS, SECURED NOTES, MUTUAL FUNDS								
12. RETIREMENT AND PENSIONS								
13. PROFIT-SHARING, IRAS, DEFERRED COMPENSATION, ANNUITIES								
14. ACCOUNTS RECEIVABLE, UNSECURED NOTES								
15. PARTNERSHIP, OTHER BUSINESS INTERESTS								
16. OTHER ASSETS								
17. ASSETS FROM CONTINUATION SHEET								
18. TOTAL ASSETS								

PROPERTY DECLARATION
(Family Law)

A	B	C	D		
ITEM DEBTS— NO. SHOW TO WHOM OWED	DATE INCURRED	TOTAL OWING	PROPOSAL FOR DIVISION Award or Confirm to:		
			PETITIONER	RESPONDENT	
19. STUDENT LOANS		$	$	$	
20. TAXES					
21. SUPPORT ARREARAGES					
22. LOANS—UNSECURED					
23. CREDIT CARDS					
24. OTHER DEBTS					
25. OTHER DEBTS FROM CONTINUATION SHEET					
26. TOTAL DEBTS					

[ ] A *Continuation of Property Declaration* (form FL-161) is attached and incorporated by reference.

I declare under penalty of perjury under the laws of the State of California that, to the best of my knowledge, the foregoing is a true and correct listing of assets and obligations and the amounts shown are correct.

Date:

▶

_____
(TYPE OR PRINT NAME)

_____
SIGNATURE

PROPERTY DECLARATION
(Family Law)

INFORMATION AND INSTRUCTIONS FOR COMPLETING FORM FL-160

Property Declaration (form FL-160) is a multipurpose form, which may be filed with the court as an attachment to a *Petition* or *Response* or served on the other party to comply with disclosure requirements in place of a *Schedule of Assets and Debts* (form FL-142). Courts may also require a party to file a *Property Declaration* as an attachment to a *Request to Enter Default* (form FL-165) or *Judgment* (form FL-180).

When filing a *Property Declaration* with the court, do not include private financial documents listed below.

Identify the type of declaration completed
1. Check "Community and Quasi-Community Property Declaration" on page 1 to use *Property Declaration* (form FL-160) to provide a combined list of community and quasi-community property assets and debts. Quasi-community property is property you own outside of California that would be community property if it were located in California.

2. Do not combine a separate property declaration with a community and quasi-community property declaration. Check "Separate Property Declaration" on page 1 when using *Property Declaration* to provide a list of separate property assets and debts.

Description of the Property Declaration chart
Pages 1 and 2
1. Column A is used to provide a brief description of each item of separate or community or quasi-community property.
2. Column B is used to list the date the item was acquired.
3. Column C is used to list the item's gross fair market value (an estimate of the amount of money you could get if you sold the item to another person through an advertisement).
4. Column D is used to list the amount owed on the item.
5. Column E is used to indicate the net fair market value of each item. The net fair market value is calculated by subtracting the dollar amount in column D from the amount in column C ("C minus D").
6. Column F is used to show a proposal on how to divide (or confirm) the item described in column A.
Page 3
1. Column A is used to provide a brief description of each separate or community or quasi-community property debt.
2. Column B is used to list the date the debt was acquired.
3. Column C is used to list the total amount of money owed on the debt.
4. Column D is used to show a proposal on how to divide (or confirm) the item of debt described in column A.

When using this form only as an attachment to a *Petition* or *Response*
1. Attach a *Separate Property Declaration* (form FL-160) to respond to item 9. Only columns A and F on pages 1 and 2 and columns A and D on page 3 are required.
2. Attach a *Community or Quasi-Community Declaration* (form FL-160) to respond to item 10, and complete column A on all pages.

When serving this form on the other party as an attachment to *Declaration of Disclosure* (form FL-140)
1. Complete columns A through E on pages 1 and 2, and columns A through C on page 3.
2. Copies of the following documents must be attached and served on the other party:
   (a) *For real estate* (item 1): deeds with legal descriptions and the latest lender's statement.
   (b) *For vehicles, boats, trailers* (item 4): the title documents.
   (c) *For all bank accounts* (item 5, 6, 7): the latest statement.
   (d) *For life insurance policies with cash surrender or loan value* (item 10): the latest declaration page.
   (e) *For stocks, bonds, secured notes, mutual funds* (item 11): the certificate or latest statement.
   (f) *For retirement and pensions* (item 12): the latest summary plan document and latest benefit statement.
   (g) *For profit-sharing, IRAs, deferred compensation, and annuities* (item 13): the latest statement.
   (h) *For each account receivable and unsecured note* (item 14): documentation of the account receivable or note.
   (i) *For partnerships and other business interests* (item 15): the most current K-1 and Schedule C.
   (j) *For other assets* (item 16): the most current statement, title document, or declaration.
   (k) *For support arrearages* (item 21): orders and statements.
   (l) *For credit cards and other debts* (items 23 and 24): the latest statement.
3. Do not file copies of the above private financial documents with the court.

When filing this form with the court as a attachment to *Request to Enter Default* (FL-165) or *Judgment* (FL-180)
Complete all columns on the form.

For more information about forms required to process and obtain a judgment in dissolution, legal separation, and nullity cases, see *http://www.courts.ca.gov/8218.htm.*

PROPERTY DECLARATION
(Family Law)

FL-161

PETITIONER:	CASE NUMBER:
RESPONDENT:	
OTHER PARENT/PARTY:	

☐ **PETITIONER'S**   ☐ **RESPONDENT'S**

☐ **COMMUNITY AND QUASI-COMMUNITY PROPERTY DECLARATION**

☐ **SEPARATE PROPERTY DECLARATION**

A		B	C -	D =	E	F	
ITEM NO.	BRIEF DESCRIPTION	DATE ACQUIRED (mm/dd/yyyy)	GROSS FAIR MARKET VALUE	AMOUNT OF DEBT	NET FAIR MARKET VALUE	PROPOSAL FOR DIVISION Award or Confirm to: PETITIONER	RESPONDENT
			$	$	$	$	$

Page 1 of 2

Form Approved for Mandatory Use
Judicial Council of California
FL-160 [Rev. July 1, 2013]

CONTINUATION OF PROPERTY DECLARATION
(Family Law)

Family Code, §§ 115, 2104, 2500-2660
www.courts.ca.gov

A	B	C	D	
ITEM NO.	DEBTS-- SHOW TO WHOM OWED	DATE INCURRED	AMOUNT OF DEBT	PROPOSAL FOR DIVISION Award or Confirm to:
				PETITIONER	RESPONDENT
			$	$	$

CONTINUATION OF PROPERTY DECLARATION
(Family Law)

FL-165

ATTORNEY OR PARTY WITHOUT ATTORNEY *(Name, State Bar number, and address):*	*FOR COURT USE ONLY*
TELEPHONE NO.: FAX NO. *(Optional):* E-MAIL ADDRESS *(Optional):* ATTORNEY FOR *(Name):*	

SUPERIOR COURT OF CALIFORNIA, COUNTY OF

STREET ADDRESS:

MAILING ADDRESS:

CITY AND ZIP CODE:

BRANCH NAME:

PETITIONER:

RESPONDENT:

REQUEST TO ENTER DEFAULT	CASE NUMBER:

1. **To the clerk:** Please enter the default of the respondent who has failed to respond to the petition.

2. A completed *Income and Expense Declaration* (form FL-150) or *Financial Statement (Simplified)* (form FL-155)
   ☐ is attached ☐ is not attached.
   A completed *Property Declaration* (form FL-160) ☐ is attached ☐ is not attached
   because *(check at least one of the following):*
   (a) ☐ there have been no changes since the previous filing.
   (b) ☐ the issues subject to disposition by the court in this proceeding are the subject of a written agreement.
   (c) ☐ there are no issues of child, spousal, or partner support or attorney fees and costs subject to determination by the court.
   (d) ☐ the petition does not request money, property, costs, or attorney fees. (Fam. Code, § 2330.5.)
   (e) ☐ there are no issues of division of community property.
   (f) ☐ this is an action to establish parental relationship.

Date:

_____ ▶ _____
(TYPE OR PRINT NAME)   (SIGNATURE OF [ATTORNEY FOR] PETITIONER)

3. **Declaration**
   a. ☐ No mailing is required because service was by publication or posting and the address of the respondent remains unknown.
   b. ☐ A copy of this *Request to Enter Default,* including any attachments and an envelope with sufficient postage, was provided to the court clerk, with the envelope addressed as follows *(address of the respondent's attorney or, if none, the respondent's last known address):*

I declare under penalty of perjury under the laws of the State of California that the foregoing is true and correct.

Date:

_____ ▶ _____
(TYPE OR PRINT NAME)   (SIGNATURE OF DECLARANT)

FOR COURT USE ONLY
☐ *Request to Enter Default* mailed to the respondent or the respondent's attorney on *(date):*
☐ Default entered as requested on *(date):*
☐ Default **not** entered. Reason:

Clerk, by _____ , Deputy

Page 1 of 2

Form Adopted for Mandatory Use
Judicial Council of California
FL-165 [Rev. January 1, 2005]

REQUEST TO ENTER DEFAULT
(Family Law—Uniform Parentage)

Code of Civil Procedure, §§ 585, 587;
Family Code, § 2335.5
www.courtinfo.ca.gov

0047

CASE NAME (Last name, first name of each party):	CASE NUMBER:

4. **Memorandum of costs**

   a. ☐ Costs and disbursements are waived.

   b. Costs and disbursements are listed as follows:

   (1) ☐ Clerk's fees .... $..............................

   (2) ☐ Process server's fees .... $..............................

   (3) ☐ Other (specify): .... $..............................

   .... $..............................

   .... $..............................

   .... $ _____

   TOTAL .... $..............................

   c. I am the attorney, agent, or party who claims these costs. To the best of my knowledge and belief, the foregoing items of cost are correct and have been necessarily incurred in this cause or proceeding.

I declare under penalty of perjury under the laws of the State of California that the foregoing is true and correct.

Date:

_____
(TYPE OR PRINT NAME)

▶ _____
(SIGNATURE OF DECLARANT)

5. **Declaration of nonmilitary status.** The respondent is not in the military service of the United States as defined in section 511 et seq. of the Servicemembers Civil Relief Act (50 U.S.C. Appen. § 501 et seq.), and is not entitled to the benefits of such act.

I declare under penalty of perjury under the laws of the State of California that the foregoing is true and correct.

Date:

_____
(TYPE OR PRINT NAME)

▶ _____
(SIGNATURE OF DECLARANT)

FL-170

ATTORNEY OR PARTY WITHOUT ATTORNEY *(Name, State Bar number, and address):*	*FOR COURT USE ONLY*
TELEPHONE NO.: FAX NO. *(Optional):* E-MAIL ADDRESS *(Optional):* ATTORNEY FOR *(Name):*	

SUPERIOR COURT OF CALIFORNIA, COUNTY OF

STREET ADDRESS:

MAILING ADDRESS:

CITY AND ZIP CODE:

BRANCH NAME:

PETITIONER:

RESPONDENT:

DECLARATION FOR DEFAULT OR UNCONTESTED ☐ **DISSOLUTION** ☐ **LEGAL SEPARATION**	CASE NUMBER:

(NOTE: Items 1 through 12 apply to both dissolution and legal separation proceedings.)

1. I declare that if I appeared in court and were sworn, I would testify to the truth of the facts in this declaration.

2. I agree that my case will be proven by this declaration and that I will not appear before the court unless I am ordered by the court to do so.

3. All the information in the ☐ amended ☐ *Petition* ☐ *Response* is true and correct.

4. **Type of case** *(check a, b, or c):*

     a. ☐   **Default without agreement**

          (1) No response has been filed and there is no written agreement or stipulated judgment between the parties;

          (2) The default of the respondent was entered or is being requested, and I am not seeking any relief not requested in the petition; and

          (3) The following statement is true *(check one):*

              (A) ☐   There are no assets or debts to be disposed of by the court.

              (B) ☐   The community and quasi-community assets and debts are listed on the **completed** current *Property Declaration* (form FL-160), which includes an estimate of the value of the assets and debts that I propose to be distributed to each party. The division in the proposed *Judgment* (form FL-180) is a fair and equal division of the property and debts, or if there is a negative estate, the debts are assigned fairly and equitably.

     b. ☐   **Default with agreement**

          (1) No response has been filed and the parties have agreed that the matter may proceed as a default matter without notice; and

          (2) The parties have entered into a written agreement regarding their property and their marriage or domestic partnership rights, including support, the original of which is being or has been submitted to the court. I request that the court approve the agreement.

     c. ☐   **Uncontested**

          (1) Both parties have appeared in the case; and

          (2) The parties have entered into a written agreement regarding their property and their marriage or domestic partnership rights, including support, the original of which is being or has been submitted to the court. I request that the court approve the agreement.

5. **Declaration of disclosure** *(check a, b, or c):*

     a. ☐   Both the petitioner and respondent have filed, or are filing concurrently, a *Declaration Regarding Service of Declaration of Disclosure* (form FL-141) and an *Income and Expense Declaration* (form FL-150).

     b. ☐   This matter is proceeding by default. I am the petitioner in this action and have filed a proof of service of the preliminary *Declaration of Disclosure* (form FL-140) with the court. I hereby waive receipt of the final *Declaration of Disclosure* (form FL-140) from the respondent.

     c. ☐   This matter is proceeding as an uncontested action. Service of the final *Declaration of Disclosure* (form FL-140) is mutually waived by both parties. A waiver provision executed by both parties under penalty of perjury is contained on the *Stipulation and Waiver of Final Declaration of Disclosure* (form FL-144), in the settlement agreement or proposed judgment or another, separate stipulation.

Form Adopted for Mandatory Use
 Judicial Council of California
 FL-170 [Rev. July 1, 2012]

**DECLARATION FOR DEFAULT OR UNCONTESTED
 DISSOLUTION OR LEGAL SEPARATION
 (Family Law)**

Family Code, § 2336 <br> www.courts.ca.gov

0049

PETITIONER:	CASE NUMBER:
RESPONDENT:	

6. ☐ **Child custody and visitation (parenting time)** should be ordered as set forth in the proposed *Judgment* (form FL-180).

    a. ☐ The information in *Declaration Under Uniform Child Custody Jurisdiction and Enforcement Act* (UCCJEA) (form FL-105)
        ☐ has ☐ has not changed since it was last filed with the court. *(If changed, attach updated form.)*

    b. ☐ There is an existing court order for custody/parenting time in another case in *(county):*
        The case number is *(specify):*

    c. ☐ The current custody and visitation (parenting time) previously ordered in this case, or current schedule is *(specify):*
        ☐ Contained on Attachment 6c.

    d. ☐ Facts in support of requested judgment (*In a default case, state your reasons below):*
        ☐ Contained on Attachment 6d.

7. ☐ **Child support** should be ordered as set forth in the proposed *Judgment* (form FL-180).

    a. If there are minor children, check and complete item (1) if applicable and item (2) or (3):

      (1) ☐ Child support is being enforced in another case in *(county):*
          The case number is *(specify):*

      (2) ☐ The information in the child support calculation attached to the proposed judgment is correct based on my personal knowledge.

      (3) ☐ I request that this order be based on the ☐ petitioner's ☐ respondent's earning ability. The facts in support of my estimate of earning ability are *(specify):*
          ☐ Continued on Attachment 7a(3).

    b. Complete items (1) and (2) regarding public assistance.

      (1) I ☐ am receiving ☐ am not receiving ☐ intend to apply for public assistance for the child or children listed in the proposed order.

      (2) To the best of my knowledge, the other party ☐ is ☐ is not receiving public assistance.

    c. ☐ The petitioner ☐ respondent is presently receiving public assistance, and all support should be made payable to the local child support agency at the address set forth in the proposed judgment. A representative of the local child support agency has signed the proposed judgment.

8. **Spousal, Partner, and Family Support** (*If a support order or attorney fees are requested, submit a completed* Income and Expense Declaration *(form FL-150) unless a current form is on file. Include your best estimate of the other party's income. Check at least one of the following.)*

    a. ☐ I knowingly give up forever any right to receive spousal or partner support.

    b. ☐ I ask the court to reserve jurisdiction to award spousal or partner support in the future to *(name):*

    c. ☐ I ask the court to terminate forever spousal or partner support for: ☐ petitioner ☐ respondent.

    d. ☐ Spousal support or domestic partner support should be ordered as set forth in the proposed *Judgment* (form FL-180) based on the factors described in:
        ☐ *Spousal or Partner Support Declaration Attachment* (form FL-157)
        ☐ written agreement
        ☐ attached declaration (Attachment 8d.)

    e. ☐ Family support should be ordered as set forth in the proposed *Judgment* (form FL-180).

    f. ☐ Other *(specify):*

DECLARATION FOR DEFAULT OR UNCONTESTED DISSOLUTION OR LEGAL SEPARATION (Family Law)

PETITIONER:	CASE NUMBER:
RESPONDENT:	

9. ☐ **Parentage** of the children of the petitioner and respondent born prior to their marriage or domestic partnership should be ordered as set forth in the proposed *Judgment* (form FL-180).

   a. ☐ A Voluntary Declaration of Paternity is attached.

   b. ☐ Parentage was previously established by the court in *(county)*:

   The case number is *(specify)*:

   ☐ Written agreement of the parties attached here or to the *Judgment* (form FL-180).

10. ☐ **Attorney fees** should be ordered as set forth in the proposed *Judgment* (form FL-180)

   ☐ facts in support in form FL-319

   ☐ other *(specify facts below)*:

11. ☐ The judgment should be entered nunc pro tunc for the following reasons *(specify)*:

12. ☐ The petitioner ☐ respondent requests restoration of his or her former name as set forth in the proposed *Judgment* (form FL-180).

13. There are irreconcilable differences that have led to the irremediable breakdown of the marriage or domestic partnership, and there is no possibility of saving the marriage or domestic partnership through counseling or other means.

14. This declaration may be reviewed by a commissioner sitting as a temporary judge, who may determine whether to grant this request or require my appearance under Family Code section 2336.

STATEMENTS IN THIS BOX APPLY ONLY TO DISSOLUTIONS

15. If this is a dissolution of marriage or of a domestic partnership created in another state, the petitioner and/or the respondent have been residents of this county for at least three months and of the state of California for at least six months continuously and immediately preceding the date of the filing of the petition for dissolution of marriage or domestic partnership.

16. I ask that the court grant the request for a judgment for dissolution of marriage or domestic partnership based on irreconcilable differences and that the court make the orders set forth in the proposed *Judgment* (form FL-180) submitted with this declaration.

17. ☐ This declaration is for the termination of **marital or domestic partner status only.** I ask the court to reserve jurisdiction over all issues whose determination is not requested in this declaration.

THIS STATEMENT APPLIES ONLY TO LEGAL SEPARATIONS

18. I ask that the court grant the request for a judgment for legal separation based on irreconcilable differences and that the court make the orders set forth in the proposed *Judgment* (form FL-180) submitted with this declaration.

   I understand that a judgment of legal separation does not terminate a marriage or domestic partnership and that I am still married or a partner in a domestic partnership.

---

19. ☐ Other *(specify)*:

I declare under penalty of perjury under the laws of the State of California that the foregoing is true and correct.

Date:

▶

_____
(TYPE OR PRINT NAME)

_____
(SIGNATURE OF DECLARANT)

**DECLARATION FOR DEFAULT OR UNCONTESTED
DISSOLUTION OR LEGAL SEPARATION**
(Family Law)

0051
(THIS FORM IS FOR COURT USE ONLY)

SUPERIOR COURT OF CALIFORNIA, COUNTY OF	FOR COURT USE ONLY
STREET ADDRESS:	
MAILING ADDRESS:	
CITY AND ZIP CODE:	
BRANCH NAME:	
PETITIONER/PLAINTIFF:	
RESPONDENT/DEFENDANT:	
OTHER PARTY:	
CASE INFORMATION—FAMILY LAW	CASE NUMBER:

1. **ASSIGNMENT** Case assigned to ☐ Judicial Officer *(name):* ☐ Dept. No.

2. **PETITION**

   The petition for ☐ dissolution ☐ legal separation ☐ nullity ☐ parentage ☐ other *(specify):*
   was filed on *(date):*

3. **BACKGROUND DATA**

   a. Date of marriage/registered domestic partnership:

   Date of separation on the petition: on the response *(if different):*

   Length of marriage or partnership:

   b. ☐ There is a dispute about the length of the marriage or partnership.

   c. ☐ Interpreter needed

       (1) ☐ Petitioner's Language:

       (2) ☐ Respondent's Language:

       (3) ☐ Other Party's Language:

4. **CHILDREN**

Name of child or children	Birthdate	Age	Gender

   ☐ Additional children listed on Attachment 4.

5. ☐ **RELATED CASES**

   One or both of the parties, or a child or children of the parties, has been involved in other related court cases. *(List county or district and case number, if known):*

   a. ☐ Custody or visitation (parenting time) for the children of this case:

   b. ☐ Juvenile delinquency:

   c. ☐ Juvenile dependency:

   d. ☐ Domestic violence/protective order:

   e. ☐ Bankruptcy:

   f. ☐ Criminal *(only if reasonably related to the issues of this case):*

   g. ☐ Other:

6. ☐ **JUDGMENT TERMINATING STATUS OF MARRIAGE OR DOMESTIC PARTNERSHIP HAS BEEN ENTERED**

   a. Date of termination:

   b. Date status judgment entered:

Page 1 of 2

PETITIONER:	CASE NUMBER:
RESPONDENT:	
OTHER PARTY:	

7. **SERVICE AND RESPONSE**

a. ☐ Respondent **was served** with the petition on *(date):* , by *(method):*

☐ personal service   ☐ substituted service   ☐ publication or posting   ☐ notice and acknowledgement

of receipt   ☐ other *(specify):*

b. ☐ Respondent **has not been served** with the petition.

c. ☐ Respondent **filed a response** on *(date):*

d. ☐ Respondent **has not filed a response** with the court.

e. ☐ Default has been entered against respondent.

f. ☐ Respondent appeared by filing an *Appearance, Stipulations, and Waivers* (form FL-130).

8. **DISCLOSURE**

Service of declarations of disclosure has been completed by:

a. Preliminary   ☐ Petitioner   ☐ Respondent

b. Final   ☐ Petitioner   ☐ Respondent

c. Final has been waived by   ☐ Petitioner   ☐ Respondent

d. Other (specify):   ☐ Petitioner   ☐ Respondent

9. **PROTECTIVE ORDERS**

☐ The parties have a restraining order that expires on *(date):*

a. ☐ Protected party *(name):*

b. ☐ Children are included as protected persons.

10. **DEPARTMENT OF CHILD SUPPORT SERVICES**

a. ☐ The Department of Child Support Services has a separate case open.

b. ☐ The Department of Child Support Services has intervened in this case.

11. **CUSTODY/PARENTING TIME (VISITATION)**

a. ☐ The parties have participated in child custody and visitation (parenting time) mediation.

b. ☐ An agreement has been reached.

c. ☐ Counsel has been appointed to represent the minor child or children.

d. ☐ A child custody evaluation   ☐ has been ordered   ☐ report has been filed.

12. **EXPERTS**

☐ The following experts have been appointed *(include issues):*

13. **OTHER**

0053

ATTORNEY OR PARTY WITHOUT ATTORNEY *(Name, State Bar number, and address):*

FOR COURT USE ONLY

TELEPHONE NO.:   FAX NO. *(Optional):*

E-MAIL ADDRESS *(Optional):*

ATTORNEY FOR *(Name):*

SUPERIOR COURT OF CALIFORNIA, COUNTY OF

STREET ADDRESS:

MAILING ADDRESS:

CITY AND ZIP CODE:

BRANCH NAME:

PETITIONER:

RESPONDENT:

OTHER PARTY:

FAMILY CENTERED CASE RESOLUTION ORDER

CASE NUMBER:

1. Conference date: Judicial Officer *(name):*   Dept. No.

   a. ☐ Petitioner present   ☐ Attorney present *(name):*

   b. ☐ Respondent present   ☐ Attorney present *(name):*

   c. ☐ Other party present   ☐ Attorney present *(name):*

2. **The next court dates.** Parties must attend the following court events:

   a. ☐ Next family centered case resolution conference   Date: Time: Dept./Room:

   b. ☐ Status conference

   c. ☐ Other *(specify):*

3. **Settlement**

   a. ☐ The case is settled. The judgment paperwork must be submitted to the court before the next family centered case resolution conference scheduled on the date in item 2a.

   b. ☐ The parties agree to participate in settlement discussions or other alternative dispute resolution services as follows:

   c. ☐ Separate sessions for domestic violence settlement discussions or other alternative dispute resolution (ADR) services must be provided because there is an issue of domestic violence in the case.

Page 1 of 3

FAMILY CENTERED CASE RESOLUTION ORDER
(Family Law)

Family Code, §§ 2450, 2451
www.courts.ca.gov

PETITIONER:	CASE NUMBER:
RESPONDENT:	
OTHER PARTY:	

4. **Declaration of disclosure**

   a. ☐ Petitioner must serve the other party with the *Preliminary Declaration of Disclosure* (form FL-140) and the *Declaration Regarding Service of Declaration of Disclosure and Income and Expense Declaration* (form FL-141) by *(date):*

   b. ☐ Respondent must serve the other party with the *Preliminary Declaration of Disclosure* (form FL-140) and the *Declaration Regarding Service of Declaration of Disclosure and Income and Expense Declaration* (form FL-141) by *(date):*

   c. ☐ The parties must submit *Declaration Regarding Service of Final Declaration of Disclosure* (form FL-141) or a waiver by *(date):*

5. **Income and expense declarations**

   a. ☐ Petitioner must serve and file a current *Income and Expense Declaration* (form FL-150) by *(date):*

   b. ☐ Respondent must serve and file a current *Income and Expense Declaration* (form FL-150) by *(date):*

6. **Other discovery**

   a. ☐ Discovery is completed.

   b. ☐ Discovery is suspended pending settlement discussions or other alternative dispute resolution services.

   c. ☐ The parties must complete the following discovery as follows:

   <u>Party</u>   <u>Description</u>   <u>By (date)</u>

7. **Experts**
   a. Pursuant to agreement of the parties, experts will be as follows:

   <u>Name</u>   <u>To address the issue of</u>

   b. Pursuant to agreement of the parties, the experts will be paid as follows:

FAMILY CENTERED CASE RESOLUTION ORDER
(Family Law)

0055

PETITIONER:	CASE NUMBER:
RESPONDENT:	

8. **Trial setting**

   a. ☐ A trial is set for *(date):*   Time: Dept. No.

   b. ☐ A mandatory settlement conference is set for *(date):*   Time: Dept. No.

   c. ☐ Settlement conference statement filed by *(date):*

   d. ☐ Estimated time for trial:

   e. ☐ Issues for trial:

   f. ☐ Other orders related to trial setting:

9. **Other family centered case resolution orders:**

10. **Total number of pages attached** *(if any):* _____

Date: _____

_____
JUDGE OF THE SUPERIOR COURT

FAMILY CENTERED CASE RESOLUTION ORDER
(Family Law)

0056

ATTORNEY OR PARTY WITHOUT ATTORNEY *(Name, State Bar number, and address):*

FOR COURT USE ONLY

TELEPHONE NO.:   FAX NO. *(Optional):*

E-MAIL ADDRESS *(Optional):*

ATTORNEY FOR *(Name):*

SUPERIOR COURT OF CALIFORNIA, COUNTY OF

STREET ADDRESS:

MAILING ADDRESS:

CITY AND ZIP CODE:

BRANCH NAME:

MARRIAGE OR PARTNERSHIP OF

PETITIONER:

RESPONDENT:

JUDGMENT

CASE NUMBER:

☐ **DISSOLUTION**   ☐ **LEGAL SEPARATION**   ☐ **NULLITY**

☐ **Status only**

☐ **Reserving jurisdiction over termination of marital or domestic partnership status**

☐ **Judgment on reserved issues**

Date marital or domestic partnership status ends:

1. ☐ This judgment ☐ contains personal conduct restraining orders ☐ modifies existing restraining orders. The restraining orders are contained on page(s)   of the attachment. They expire on *(date):*

2. This proceeding was heard as follows: ☐ Default or uncontested ☐ By declaration under Family Code section 2336
   ☐ Contested ☐ Agreement in court
   a. Date: Dept.:   Room:
   b. Judicial officer *(name):*   ☐ Temporary judge
   c. ☐ Petitioner present in court   ☐ Attorney present in court *(name):*
   d. ☐ Respondent present in court   ☐ Attorney present in court *(name):*
   e. ☐ Claimant present in court *(name):*   ☐ Attorney present in court *(name):*
   f. ☐ Other *(specify name):*

3. The court acquired jurisdiction of the respondent on *(date):*
   a. ☐ The respondent was served with process.
   b. ☐ The respondent appeared.

THE COURT ORDERS, GOOD CAUSE APPEARING

4. a. ☐ Judgment of dissolution is entered. Marital or domestic partnership status is terminated and the parties are restored to the status of single persons
      (1) ☐ on *(specify date):*
      (2) ☐ on a date to be determined on noticed motion of either party or on stipulation.
   b. ☐ Judgment of legal separation is entered.
   c. ☐ Judgment of nullity is entered. The parties are declared to be single persons on the ground of *(specify):*

   d. ☐ This judgment will be entered nunc pro tunc as of *(date):*
   e. ☐ Judgment on reserved issues.
   f. The ☐ petitioner's ☐ respondent's former name is restored to *(specify):*
   g. ☐ Jurisdiction is reserved over all other issues, and all present orders remain in effect except as provided below.
   h. ☐ This judgment contains provisions for child support or family support. Each party must complete and file with the court a *Child Support Case Registry Form* (form FL-191) within 10 days of the date of this judgment. The parents must notify the court of any change in the information submitted within 10 days of the change, by filing an updated form. The *Notice of Rights and Responsibilities—Health-Care Costs and Reimbursement Procedures and Information Sheet on Changing a Child Support Order* (form FL-192) is attached.

Page 1 of 2

Form Adopted for Mandatory Use
Judicial Council of California
FL-180 [Rev. July 1, 2012]

JUDGMENT
(Family Law)

Family Code, §§ 2024, 2340,
2343, 2346
www.courts.ca.gov

0057

CASE NAME (Last name, first name of each party):	CASE NUMBER:

4. i. ☐ The children of this marriage or domestic partnership are:

    (1) ☐ Name   Birthdate

    (2) ☐ Parentage is established for children of this relationship born prior to the marriage or domestic partnership

  j. ☐ Child custody and visitation (parenting time) are ordered as set forth in the attached

    (1) ☐ Settlement agreement, stipulation for judgment, or other written agreement which contains the information required by Family Code section 3048(a).

    (2) ☐ *Child Custody and Visitation Order Attachment* (form FL-341).

    (3) ☐ *Stipulation and Order for Custody and/or Visitation of Children* (form FL-355).

    (4) ☐ Previously established in another case. Case number: Court:

  k. ☐ Child support is ordered as set forth in the attached

    (1) ☐ Settlement agreement, stipulation for judgment, or other written agreement which contains the declarations required by Family Code section 4065(a).

    (2) ☐ *Child Support Information and Order Attachment* (form FL-342).

    (3) ☐ *Stipulation to Establish or Modify Child Support and Order* (form FL-350).

    (4) ☐ Previously established in another case. Case number: Court:

  l. ☐ Spousal, domestic partner, or family support is ordered:

    (1) ☐ Reserved for future determination as relates to ☐ petitioner ☐ respondent

    (2) ☐ Jurisdiction terminated to order spousal or partner support to ☐ petitioner ☐ respondent

    (3) ☐ As set forth in the attached *Spousal, Partner, or Family Support Order Attachment* (form FL-343).

    (4) ☐ As set forth in the attached settlement agreement, stipulation for judgment, or other written agreement.

    (5) ☐ Other (specify):

  m. ☐ Property division is ordered as set forth in the attached

    (1) ☐ Settlement agreement, stipulation for judgment, or other written agreement.

    (2) ☐ *Property Order Attachment to Judgment* (form FL-345).

    (3) ☐ Other (specify):

  n. ☐ Attorney fees and costs are ordered as set forth in the attached

    (1) ☐ Settlement agreement, stipulation for judgment, or other written agreement.

    (2) ☐ *Attorney Fees and Costs Order* (form FL-346).

    (3) ☐ Other (specify):

  o. ☐ Other (specify):

Each attachment to this judgment is incorporated into this judgment, and the parties are ordered to comply with each attachment's provisions. Jurisdiction is reserved to make other orders necessary to carry out this judgment.

Date:

5. Number of pages attached: _____

                                    JUDICIAL OFFICER

☐ SIGNATURE FOLLOWS LAST ATTACHMENT

NOTICE

Dissolution or legal separation may automatically cancel the rights of a spouse or domestic partner under the other spouse's or domestic partner's will, trust, retirement plan, power of attorney, pay-on-death bank account, transfer-on-death vehicle registration, survivorship rights to any property owned in joint tenancy, and any other similar property interest. It does not automatically cancel the rights of a spouse or domestic partner as beneficiary of the other spouse's or domestic partner's life insurance policy. You should review these matters, as well as any credit cards, other credit accounts, insurance policies, retirement plans, and credit reports, to determine whether they should be changed or whether you should take any other actions.

A debt or obligation may be assigned to one party as part of the dissolution of property and debts, but if that party does not pay the debt or obligation, the creditor may be able to collect from the other party.

An earnings assignment may be issued without additional proof if child, family, partner, or spousal support is ordered.

Any party required to pay support must pay interest on overdue amounts at the "legal rate," which is currently 10 percent.

FL-182

ATTORNEY OR PARTY WITHOUT ATTORNEY *(Name, State Bar number, and address):*

TELEPHONE NO.:
E-MAIL ADDRESS *(Optional)*:
ATTORNEY FOR *(Name)*:

FAX NO. *(Optional)*:

FOR COURT USE ONLY

SUPERIOR COURT OF CALIFORNIA, COUNTY OF

STREET ADDRESS:

MAILING ADDRESS:

CITY AND ZIP CODE:

BRANCH NAME:

PETITIONER:

RESPONDENT:

JUDGMENT CHECKLIST— DISSOLUTION/LEGAL SEPARATION	CASE NUMBER:

This judgment checklist is a list of documents that a court may require to complete a default or uncontested judgment. The checklist may be filed along with your judgment, but is not required. If the forms or other documents have already been filed, you should check the boxes indicating that they have been previously filed. Unless listed otherwise on this form, when you file a document with the court, you should submit an original and 2 copies. One copy is for you and one is for the other party. There are three types of default and uncontested judgments:

- **Default With No Agreement (no response and no written agreement)**
- **Default With Agreement (no response, but there is a written agreement)**
- **Uncontested Case (response filed, or other appearance by respondent, and a written agreement)**

1. ☐ **DEFAULT WITH NO AGREEMENT (no response and no written agreement)**

   (Please check the box by each document being filed)   Previously Filed

   a. ☐ *Proof of Service of Summons* (form FL-115) or other proof of service   ☐

   b. ☐ *Request to Enter Default* (form FL-165), with a stamped envelope addressed to respondent and the court   ☐
   clerk's address as the return address

   c. ☐ Petitioner's *Declaration Regarding Service of Declaration of Disclosure* (form FL-141)   ☐

   d. ☐ *Declaration for Default or Uncontested Dissolution or Legal Separation* (form FL-170)

   e. ☐ *Judgment* (form FL-180) *(5 copies)*

   f. ☐ *Notice of Entry of Judgment* (form FL-190)

   g. ☐ 2 stamped envelopes of sufficient size and with sufficient postage to return the *Judgment* and *Notice of Entry of Judgment*, one envelope addressed to petitioner and the other to respondent.

   If there are minor children of the marriage or domestic partnership:

   h. ☐ *Declaration Under Uniform Child Custody Jurisdiction and Enforcement Act (UCCJEA)* (form FL-105).   ☐
   (A new form must be filed if there have been any changes since the one most recently filed.)

   i. ☐ Petitioner's *Income and Expense Declaration* (form FL-150) or *Financial Statement (Simplified)* (form   ☐
   FL-155). *(Needed unless one has been filed within the past 90 days and there have been no changes since then.)*

   j. ☐ Computer printout of guideline child support *(optional)*

   k. ☐ *Notice of Rights and Responsibilities and Information Sheet on Changing a Child Support Order* (form FL-192). This may be attached by the petitioner or by the court.

Page 1 of 3

Form Approved for Optional Use
Judicial Council of California
FL-182 [New July 1, 2012]

**JUDGMENT CHECKLIST—
DISSOLUTION/LEGAL SEPARATION**

Cal. Rules of Court, rule 5.405
www.courts.ca.gov

PETITIONER:	CASE NUMBER:
RESPONDENT:	

Previously Filed

l. Child Support Order

    ☐ *Stipulation to Establish or Modify Child Support and Order* (form FL-350) *(attach to* Judgment*),* or

    ☐ *Child Support Information and Order Attachment* (form FL-342) *(attach to* Judgment*),* or

    ☐ Written agreement containing declarations required by Family Code section 4065(a) *(attach to* Judgment*)*

m. ☐ *Income Withholding for Support* (form FL-195/OMB No. 0970-0154)

n. ☐ *Child Custody and Visitation* (Parenting Time) *Order Attachment* (form FL-341) or other proposed written order containing the information required by Family Code 3048(a) *(attach to* Judgment*)*

If spousal/partner support is requested, the marriage/partnership is over 10 years in duration, or termination of spousal/partner support for the respondent is requested:

o. ☐ *Spousal or Partnership Support Declaration Attachment* (form FL-157)

p. ☐ *Income and Expense Declaration* (form FL-150) *(Needed unless a current financial declaration has been filed within the past 90 days and there have been no changes since then.)*   ☐

q. ☐ *Spousal, Partner, or Family Support Order Attachment* (form FL-343) or other proposed written order *(attach to* Judgment*)*

If assets or debts need to be divided or assigned:

r. ☐ *Property Declaration* (form FL-160)   ☐

s. ☐ *Property Order Attachment to Judgment* (form FL-345) or other proposed written order *(attach to* Judgment*)*

If attorney fees and costs are requested:

t. ☐ *Request for Attorney Fees and Costs* (form FL-319)

u. ☐ *Attorney Fees and Costs Order Attachment* (form FL-346) or other proposed written order *(attach to* Judgment*)*

2. ☐ **DEFAULT WITH AGREEMENT (no response and a written agreement)**

a. ☐ *Proof of Service of Summons* (form FL-115) or other proof of service   ☐

b. ☐ *Request to Enter Default* (form FL-165), with a stamped envelope addressed to respondent and the court clerk's address as the return address   ☐

c. ☐ Petitioner's *Declaration Regarding Service of Declaration of Disclosure* (form FL-141) (preliminary)   ☐

d. Declaration Regarding Service of Final Declaration of Disclosure   ☐

    ☐ Petitioner's *Declaration Regarding Service of Declaration of Disclosure* (form FL-141) (final) or

    ☐ *Stipulation and Waiver of Final Declaration of Disclosure* (form FL-144) or

    ☐ Separately filed waiver or waiver included in a written agreement under Family Code section 2105(d)

e. ☐ *Declaration for Default or Uncontested Dissolution or Legal Separation* (form FL-170)

f. ☐ Written agreement of the parties. Respondent's signature on the agreement must be notarized. *(attach to* Judgment.*)*

g. ☐ *Judgment* (form FL-180) *(5 copies)*

h. ☐ *Notice of Entry of Judgment* (form FL-190)

i. ☐ 2 stamped envelopes of sufficient size and with sufficient postage to return the *Judgment* and *Notice of Entry of Judgment*, one envelope addressed to petitioner and the other to respondent

If there are minor children of the marriage or domestic partnership:

j. ☐ *Declaration Under Uniform Child Custody Jurisdiction and Enforcement Act (UCCJEA)* (form FL-105). *(A new form must be filed if there have been any changes since the one most recently filed.)*   ☐

k. ☐ *Income and Expense Declaration* (form FL-150) or *Financial Statement (Simplified)* (form FL-155). *(Needed unless one has been filed within the past 90 days and there have been no changes since then.)*

**JUDGMENT CHECKLIST–
DISSOLUTION/LEGAL SEPARATION**

PETITIONER:	CASE NUMBER:
RESPONDENT:	

Previously Filed

    l. ☐ Computer printout of guideline child support *(optional).*

    m. ☐ *Notice of Rights and Responsibilities and Information Sheet on Changing a Child Support Order* (form FL-192). This may be attached by the petitioner or by the court.

    n. Child Support Order

        ☐ *Stipulation to Establish or Modify Child Support and Order* (form FL-350) *(attach to* Judgment*), or*

        ☐ *Child Support Information and Order Attachment* (form FL-342) *(attach to* Judgment*), or*

        ☐ *Written agreement containing declarations required by Family Code section 4065(a)* *(attach to* Judgment*)*

    o. ☐ *Income Withholding for Support* (form FL-195/OMB No. 0970-0154)

    p. ☐ *Child Custody and Visitation Order Attachment* (form FL-341) or written agreement containing the information required by Family Code section 3048(a) *(attach to* Judgment*)*

3. ☐ **UNCONTESTED CASE (Response filed, or other appearance by respondent, and a written agreement)**

    a. ☐ *Proof of Service of Summons* (form FL-115) or other proof of service if you want to use the date of service as the beginning of the six-month waiting period. ☐

    b. ☐ *Appearance, Stipulations, and Waivers* (form FL-130) ☐

    c. ☐ Respondent's filing fee, if first appearance, unless respondent has a fee waiver or is currently on active duty in the military ☐

    d. ☐ *Declaration Regarding Service of Declaration of Disclosure* (**both** petitioner's and respondent's preliminary) (form FL-141) ☐

    e. Declaration Regarding Service of Final Declaration of Disclosure ☐

        ☐ *Declaration Regarding Service of Declaration of Disclosure* (**both** petitioner's and respondent's final) (form FL-141), or

        ☐ *Stipulation and Waiver of Final Declaration of Disclosure* (form FL-144), or

        ☐ Separately filed waiver or waiver included in a written agreement under Family Code section 2105(d)

    f. ☐ *Declaration for Default or Uncontested Dissolution or Legal Separation* (form FL-170)

    g. ☐ Written agreement of the parties *(attach to* Judgment*)*

    h. ☐ *Judgment* (form FL-180) *(5 copies)*

    i. ☐ *Notice of Entry of Judgment* (form FL-190)

    j. ☐ 2 stamped envelopes of sufficient size and with sufficient postage to return the *Judgment* and *Notice of Entry of Judgment*, one envelope addressed to petitioner and the other to respondent

If there are minor children of the marriage or domestic partnership:

    k. ☐ *Declaration Under Uniform Child Custody Jurisdiction and Enforcement Act (UCCJEA)* (form FL-105). *(A new form must be filed if there have been any changes since the one most recently filed.)* ☐

    l. ☐ Computer printout of guideline child support *(optional)*

    m. ☐ *Notice of Rights and Responsibilities and Information Sheet on Changing a Child Support Order* (form FL-192). This may be attached by either party or by the court.

    n. Child Support Order

        ☐ *Stipulation to Establish or Modify Child Support and Order* (form FL-350) *(attach to* Judgment*)* or

        ☐ *Child Support Information and Order Attachment* (form FL-342) *(attach to* Judgment*), or*

        ☐ *Written agreement which includes declarations required by Family Code section 4065(a)* *(attach to* Judgment*)*

    o. ☐ *Income Withholding for Support* (form FL-195/OMB No. 0970-0154)

    p. ☐ *Child Custody and Visitation Order Attachment* (form FL-341) or written agreement containing the information required by Family Code section 3048(a) *(attach to* Judgment*)*

**JUDGMENT CHECKLIST–
DISSOLUTION/LEGAL SEPARATION**

0061

ATTORNEY OR PARTY WITHOUT ATTORNEY *(Name, State Bar number, and address):*

FOR COURT USE ONLY

TELEPHONE NO.:   FAX NO. *(Optional):*

E-MAIL ADDRESS *(Optional):*

ATTORNEY FOR *(Name):*

SUPERIOR COURT OF CALIFORNIA, COUNTY OF

STREET ADDRESS:

MAILING ADDRESS:

CITY AND ZIP CODE:

BRANCH NAME:

PETITIONER:

RESPONDENT:

NOTICE OF ENTRY OF JUDGMENT

CASE NUMBER:

You are notified that the following judgment was entered on *(date):*

1. ☐ Dissolution
2. ☐ Dissolution—status only
3. ☐ Dissolution—reserving jurisdiction over termination of marital status or domestic partnership
4. ☐ Legal separation
5. ☐ Nullity
6. ☐ Parent-child relationship
7. ☐ Judgment on reserved issues
8. ☐ Other *(specify):*

Date:

Clerk, by _____, Deputy

—NOTICE TO ATTORNEY OF RECORD OR PARTY WITHOUT ATTORNEY—

Under the provisions of Code of Civil Procedure section 1952, if no appeal is filed the court may order the exhibits destroyed or otherwise disposed of after 60 days from the expiration of the appeal time.

STATEMENT IN THIS BOX APPLIES ONLY TO JUDGMENT OF DISSOLUTION

Effective date of termination of marital or domestic partnership status *(specify):*

WARNING: Neither party may remarry or enter into a new domestic partnership until the effective date of the termination of marital or domestic partnership status, as shown in this box.

CLERK'S CERTIFICATE OF MAILING

I certify that I am not a party to this cause and that a true copy of the *Notice of Entry of Judgment* was mailed first class, postage fully prepaid, in a sealed envelope addressed as shown below, and that the notice was mailed

at *(place):* _____, California, on *(date):*

Date: Clerk, by _____, Deputy

┌─ Name and address of petitioner or petitioner's attorney ─┐   ┌─ Name and address of respondent or respondent's attorney ─┐

Page 1 of 1

Form Adopted for Mandatory Use
Judicial Council of California
FL-190 [Rev. January 1, 2005]

NOTICE OF ENTRY OF JUDGMENT
(Family Law—Uniform Parentage—Custody and Support)

Family Code, §§ 2338, 7636, 7637
www.courtinfo.ca.gov

0062

NOTICE OF RIGHTS AND RESPONSIBILITIES

Health-Care Costs and Reimbursement Procedures

IF YOU HAVE A CHILD SUPPORT ORDER THAT INCLUDES A PROVISION FOR THE REIMBURSEMENT OF A PORTION OF THE CHILD'S OR CHILDREN'S HEALTH-CARE COSTS AND THOSE COSTS ARE NOT PAID BY INSURANCE, THE LAW SAYS:

1. Notice. You must give the other parent an itemized statement of the charges that have been billed for any health-care costs not paid by insurance. You must give this statement to the other parent within a reasonable time, but no more than 30 days after those costs were given to you.

2. Proof of full payment. If you have already paid all of the uninsured costs, you must (1) give the other parent proof that you paid them and (2) ask for reimbursement for the other parent's court-ordered share of those costs.

3. Proof of partial payment. If you have paid only your share of the uninsured costs, you must (1) give the other parent proof that you paid your share, (2) ask that the other parent pay his or her share of the costs directly to the health-care provider, and (3) give the other parent the information necessary for that parent to be able to pay the bill.

4. Payment by notified parent. If you receive notice from a parent that an uninsured health-care cost has been incurred, you must pay your share of that cost within the time the court orders; or if the court has not specified a period of time, you must make payment (1) within 30 days from the time you were given notice of the amount due, (2) according to any payment schedule set by the health-care provider, (3) according to a schedule agreed to in writing by you and the other parent, or (4) according to a schedule adopted by the court.

5. Disputed charges. If you dispute a charge, you may file a motion in court to resolve the dispute, but only if you pay that charge before filing your motion. If you claim that the other party has failed to reimburse you for a payment, or the other party has failed to make a payment to the provider after proper notice has been given, you may file a motion in court to resolve the dispute. The court will presume that if uninsured costs have been paid, those costs were reasonable. The court may award attorney fees and costs against a party who has been unreasonable.

6. Court-ordered insurance coverage. If a parent provides health-care insurance as ordered by the court, that insurance must be used at all times to the extent that it is available for health-care costs.

a. Burden to prove. The party claiming that the coverage is inadequate to meet the child's needs has the burden of proving that to the court.

b. Cost of additional coverage. If a parent purchases health-care insurance in addition to that ordered by the court, that parent must pay all the costs of the additional coverage. In addition, if a parent uses alternative coverage that costs more than the coverage provided by court order, that parent must pay the difference.

7. Preferred health providers. If the court-ordered coverage designates a preferred health-care provider, that provider must be used at all times consistent with the terms of the health insurance policy. When any party uses a health-care provider other than the preferred provider, any health-care costs that would have been paid by the preferred health provider if that provider had been used must be the sole responsibility of the party incurring those costs.

Form Approved for Optional Use
Judicial Council of California
FL-192 [Rev. January 1, 2015]

NOTICE OF RIGHTS AND RESPONSIBILITIES
Health-Care Costs and Reimbursement Procedures

Family Code, §§ 4062, 4063
www.courts.ca.gov

INFORMATION SHEET ON CHANGING A CHILD SUPPORT ORDER

General Information
The court has just made a child support order in your case. This order will remain the same unless a party to the action requests that the support be changed (modified). An order for child support can be modified only by filing a motion to change child support and serving each party involved in your case. If both parents and the local child support agency (if it is involved) agree on a new child support amount, you can complete, have all parties sign, and file with the court a *Stipulation to Establish or Modify Child Support and Order* (form FL-350) or *Stipulation and Order (Governmental)* (form FL-625).

When a Child Support Order May Be Modified
The court takes several things into account when ordering the payment of child support. First, the number of children is considered. Next, the net incomes of both parents are determined, along with the percentage of time each parent has physical custody of the children. The court considers both parties' tax filing status and may consider hardships, such as a child of another relationship. An existing order for child support may be modified when the net income of one of the parents changes significantly, the parenting schedule changes significantly, or a new child is born.

Examples
- You have been ordered to pay $500 per month in child support. You lose your job. You will continue to owe $500 per month, plus 10 percent interest on any unpaid support, unless you file a motion to modify your child support to a lower amount and the court orders a reduction.
- You are currently receiving $300 per month in child support from the other parent, whose net income has just increased substantially. You will continue to receive $300 per month unless you file a motion to modify your child support to a higher amount and the court orders an increase.
- You are paying child support based upon having physical custody of your children 30 percent of the time. After several months it turns out that you actually have physical custody of the children 50 percent of the time. You may file a motion to modify child support to a lower amount.

How to Change a Child Support Order
To change a child support order, you must file papers with the court. *Remember:* You must follow the order you have now.

What forms do I need?
If you are asking to change a child support order open with the local child support agency, you must fill out one of these forms:
- FL-680, *Notice of Motion (Governmental)* **or** FL-683 *Order to Show Cause (Governmental)* **and**
- FL-684, *Request for Order and Supporting Declaration (Governmental)*

If you are asking to change a child support order that is **not** open with the local child support agency, you must fill out one of these forms:
- FL-300, *Request for Order* **or**
- FL-390, *Notice of Motion and Motion for Simplified Modification of Order for Child, Spousal, or Family Support*

You must also fill out one of these forms:
- FL-150, *Income and Expense Declaration* **or** FL-155, *Financial Statement (Simplified)*

What if I am not sure which forms to fill out?
Talk to the family law facilitator at your court.

After you fill out the forms, file them with the court clerk and ask for a hearing date. Write the hearing date on the form.
The clerk will ask you to pay a filing fee. If you cannot afford the fee, fill out these forms, too:
- Form FW-001, *Request to Waive Court Fees*
- Form FW-003, *Order on Court Fee Waiver (Superior Court)*

You must serve the other parent. If the local child support agency is involved, serve it too.

This means someone 18 or over—**not you**—must serve the other parent copies of your filed court forms at least **16 court days** before the hearing. Add **5 calendar days** if you serve by mail within California (see Code of Civil Procedure section 1005 for other situations). **Court days** are weekdays when the court is open for business (Monday through Friday except court holidays). **Calendar days** include all days of the month, including weekends and holidays. To find court holidays, go to *www.courts.ca.gov/holidays.htm*.

The server must also serve blank copies of these forms:
- FL-320, *Responsive Declaration to Request for Order* **and** FL-150, *Income and Expense Declaration,* **or**
- FL-155, *Financial Statement (Simplified)*
Then the server fills out and signs a *Proof of Service* (form FL-330 or FL-335). Take this form to the clerk and file it.

Go to your hearing and ask the judge to change the support. Bring your tax returns from the last two years and your last two months' pay stubs. The judge will look at your information, listen to both parents, and make an order. After the hearing, fill out:
- FL-340, *Findings and Order After Hearing* **and**
- FL-342, *Child Support Information and Order Attachment*

Need help?
Contact the family law facilitator in your county or call your county's bar association and ask for an experienced family lawyer.

INCOME WITHHOLDING FOR SUPPORT

☐ **INCOME WITHHOLDING ORDER/NOTICE FOR SUPPORT (IWO)**
☐ **AMENDED IWO**
☐ **ONE-TIME ORDER/NOTICE FOR LUMP SUM PAYMENT**
☐ **TERMINATION OF IWO**

Date: _____

☐ Child Support Enforcement (CSE) Agency ☐ Court ☐ Attorney ☐ Private Individual/Entity (Check One)

NOTE: This IWO must be regular on its face. Under certain circumstances you must reject this IWO and return it to the sender (see IWO instructions **www.acf.hhs.gov/css/resource/income-withholding-for-support-instructions**). If you receive this document from someone other than a state or tribal CSE agency or a court, a copy of the underlying support order must be attached.

State/Tribe/Territory _____   Remittance ID (include w/payment) _____
City/County/Dist./Tribe _____   Order ID _____
Private Individual/Entity _____   Case ID _____

_____   RE: _____
Employer/Income Withholder's Name   Employee/Obligor's Name (Last, First, Middle)

_____
Employer/Income Withholder's Address   Employee/Obligor's Social Security Number

_____
                                          Employee/Obligor's Date of Birth

_____
                                          Custodial Party/Obligee's Name (Last, First, Middle)

Employer/Income Withholder's FEIN _____

Child(ren)'s Name(s) (Last, First, Middle)   Child(ren)'s Birth Date(s)

_____   _____
_____   _____
_____   _____
_____   _____
_____   _____
_____   _____

ORDER INFORMATION: This document is based on the support order from _____ (State/Tribe).
You are required by law to deduct these amounts from the employee/obligor's income until further notice.
$ _____ Per _____ current child support
$ _____ Per _____ past-due child support - **Arrears greater than 12 weeks?** ☐ Yes ☐ No
$ _____ Per _____ current cash medical support
$ _____ Per _____ past-due cash medical support
$ _____ Per _____ current spousal support
$ _____ Per _____ past-due spousal support
$ _____ Per _____ other (must specify) _____ .
for a **Total Amount to Withhold** of $ _____ per _____ .

AMOUNTS TO WITHHOLD: You do not have to vary your pay cycle to be in compliance with the *Order Information*. If your pay cycle does not match the ordered payment cycle, withhold one of the following amounts:
$ _____ per weekly pay period $ _____ per semimonthly pay period (twice a month)
$ _____ per biweekly pay period (every two weeks)$ _____ per monthly pay period
$ _____ **Lump Sum Payment:** Do not stop any existing IWO unless you receive a termination order.

Document Tracking ID _____

Employer's Name: _____ **0065** Employer FEIN: _____

Employee/Obligor's Name: _____ SSN: _____

Case Identifier: _____ Order Identifier: _____

REMITTANCE INFORMATION: If the employee/obligor's principal place of employment is _____ (State/Tribe), you must begin withholding no later than the first pay period that occurs _____ days after the date of _____ . Send payment within _____ business days of the pay date. If you cannot withhold the full amount of support for any or all orders for this employee/obligor, withhold _____ % of disposable income for all orders. If the obligor is a non-employee, obtain withholding limits from Supplemental Information. If the employee/obligor's principal place of employment is _____ (State/Tribe), obtain withholding limitations, time requirements, and any allowable employer fees from the jurisdiction of the employee/obligor's principal place of employment. State-specfic withholding limit information is available at ***www.acf.hhs.gov/css/resource/state-income-withholding-contacts-and-program-requirements***. For tribe-specific contacts, payment addresses, and withholding limitations, please contact the tribe at ***www.acf.hhs.gov/sites/default/files/programs/css/tribal_agency_contacts_printable_pdf.pdf*** or https://www.bia.gov/tribalmap/DataDotGovSamples/tld_map.html.

For electronic payment requirements and centralized payment collection and disbursement facility information [State Disbursement Unit (SDU)], see www.acf.hhs.gov/css/employers/employer-responsibilities/payments.

Include the Remittance ID with the payment and if necessary this locator code: _____ .

Remit payment to	California State Disbursement Unit	(SDU/Tribal Order Payee)
at	P.O. Box 989067, West Sacramento, CA 95798-9067	(SDU/Tribal Payee Address)

☐ **Return to Sender (Completed by Employer/Income Withholder).** Payment must be directed to an SDU in accordance with sections 466(b)(5) and (6) of the Social Security Act or Tribal Payee (see Payments to SDU below). If payment is not directed to an SDU/Tribal Payee or this IWO is not regular on its face, you *must* check this box and return the IWO to the sender.

If Required by State or Tribal Law:
Signature of Judge/Issuing Official: _____
Print Name of Judge/Issuing Official: _____
Title of Judge/Issuing Official: _____
Date of Signature: _____

If the employee/obligor works in a state or for a tribe that is different from the state or tribe that issued this order, a copy of this IWO must be provided to the employee/obligor.

☐ If checked, the employer/income withholder must provide a copy of this form to the employee/obligor.

ADDITIONAL INFORMATION FOR EMPLOYERS/INCOME WITHHOLDERS

State-specific contact and withholding information can be found on the Federal Employer Services website located at www.acf.hhs.gov/css/resource/state-income-withholding-contacts-and-program-requirements.

Employers/income withholders may use OCSE's Child Support Portal (https://ocsp.acf.hhs.gov/csp/) to provide information about employees who are eligible to receive a lump sum payment, have terminated employment, and to provide contacts, addresses, and other information about their company.

Priority: Withholding for support has priority over any other legal process under State law against the same income (section 466(b)(7) of the Social Security Act). If a federal tax levy is in effect, please notify the sender.

Combining Payments: When remitting payments to an SDU or tribal CSE agency, you may combine withheld amounts from more than one employee/obligor's income in a single payment. You must, however, separately identify each employee/obligor's portion of the payment.

Payments To SDU: You must send child support payments payable by income withholding to the appropriate SDU or to a tribal CSE agency. If this IWO instructs you to send a payment to an entity other than an SDU (e.g., payable to the custodial party, court, or attorney), you must check the box above and return this notice to the sender. Exception: If this IWO was sent by a court, attorney, or private individual/entity and the initial order was entered before January 1, 1994 or the order was issued by a tribal CSE agency, you must follow the "Remit payment to" instructions on this form.

Employer's Name: _____ Employer FEIN: _____

Employee/Obligor's Name: _____ SSN: _____

Case Identifier: _____ Order Identifier: _____

Reporting the Pay Date: You must report the pay date when sending the payment. The pay date is the date on which the amount was withheld from the employee/obligor's wages. You must comply with the law of the state (or tribal law if applicable) of the employee/obligor's principal place of employment regarding time periods within which you must implement the withholding and forward the support payments.

Multiple IWOs: If there is more than one IWO against this employee/obligor and you are unable to fully honor all IWOs due to federal, state, or tribal withholding limits, you must honor all IWOs to the greatest extent possible, giving priority to current support before payment of any past-due support. Follow the state or tribal law/procedure of the employee/obligor's principal place of employment to determine the appropriate allocation method.

Lump Sum Payments: You may be required to notify a state or tribal CSE agency of upcoming lump sum payments to this employee/obligor such as bonuses, commissions, or severance pay. Contact the sender to determine if you are required to report and/or withhold lump sum payments.

Liability: If you have any doubts about the validity of this IWO, contact the sender. If you fail to withhold income from the employee/obligor's income as the IWO directs, you are liable for both the accumulated amount you should have withheld and any penalties set by state or tribal law/procedure.

Anti-discrimination: You are subject to a fine determined under state or tribal law for discharging an employee/obligor from employment, refusing to employ, or taking disciplinary action against an employee/obligor because of this IWO.

Withholding Limits: You may not withhold more than the lesser of: 1) the amounts allowed by the Federal Consumer Credit Protection Act (CCPA) [15 USC §1673 (b)]; or 2) the amounts allowed by the law of the state of the employee/obligor's principal place of employment, if the place of employment is in a state; or the tribal law of the employee/obligor's principal place of employment if the place of employment is under tribal jurisdiction. Disposable income is the net income after mandatory deductions such as: state, federal, local taxes; Social Security taxes; statutory pension contributions; and Medicare taxes. The federal limit is 50% of the disposable income if the obligor is supporting another family and 60% of the disposable income if the obligor is not supporting another family. However, those limits increase 5% --to 55% and 65% --if the arrears are greater than 12 weeks. If permitted by the state or tribe, you may deduct a fee for administrative costs. The combined support amount and fee may not exceed the limit indicated in this section.

Depending upon applicable state or tribal law, you may need to consider amounts paid for health care premiums in determining disposable income and applying appropriate withholding limits.

Arrears Greater Than 12 Weeks? If the *Order Information* section does not indicate that the arrears are greater than 12 weeks, then the employer should calculate the CCPA limit using the lower percentage.

Supplemental Information:

Employer's Name: _____ Employer FEIN: _____

Employee/Obligor's Name: _____ SSN: _____

Case Identifier: _____ Order Identifier: _____

NOTIFICATION OF EMPLOYMENT TERMINATION OR INCOME STATUS: If this employee/obligor never worked for you or you are no longer withholding income for this employee/obligor, you must promptly notify the CSE agency and/or the sender by returning this form to the address listed in the contact information below:

☐ This person has never worked for this employer nor received periodic income.

☐ This person no longer works for this employer nor receives periodic income.

Please provide the following information for the employee/obligor:

Termination date: _____ Last known telephone number: _____

Last known address: _____

_____

Final payment date to SDU/Tribal Payee: _____ Final payment amount: _____

New employer's name: _____

New employer's address: _____

_____

CONTACT INFORMATION:

To Employer/Income Withholder: If you have questions, contact _____ (issuer name)

by telephone: _____ , by fax: _____ , by email or website: _____ .

Send termination/income status notice and other correspondence to:

_____ (issuer address).

To Employee/Obligor: If the employee/obligor has questions, contact _____ (issuer name)

by telephone: _____ , by fax: _____ , by email or website: _____ .

IMPORTANT: The person completing this form is advised that the information may be shared with the employee/obligor.

Encryption Requirements:
When communicating this form through electronic transmission, precautions must be taken to ensure the security of the data. Child support agencies are encouraged to use the electronic applications provided by the federal Office of Child Support Enforcement. Other electronic means, such as encrypted attachments to emails, may be used if the encryption method is compliant with Federal Information Processing Standard (FIPS) Publication 140-2 (FIPS PUB 140-2).

The Paperwork Reduction Act of 1995
This information collection and associated responses are conducted in accordance with 45 CFR 303.100 of the Child Support Enforcement Program. This form is designed to provide uniformity and standardization. Public reporting for this collection of information is estimated to average two to five minutes per response. An agency may not conduct or sponsor, and a person is not required to respond to, a collection of information unless it displays a currently valid OMB control number.

INCOME WITHHOLDING FOR SUPPORT - Instructions

FL-196

The Income Withholding for Support (IWO) is the OMB-approved form used for income withholding in:
- tribal, intrastate, and interstate cases enforced under Title IV-D of the Social Security Act
- all child support orders initially issued in the state on or after January 1, 1994, and
- all child support orders initially issued (or modified) in the state before January 1, 1994 if arrearages occur.

This form is the standard format prescribed by the Secretary in accordance with section 466(b)(6)(a)(ii) of the Social Security Act. **Except as noted, the following information is required and must be included.**

Please note:
- For the purpose of this IWO form and these instructions, "state" is defined as a state or territory.
- Dos and don'ts on using this form are found at www.acf.hhs.gov/css/resource/using-the-income-withholding-for-support-form-dos-and-donts .

COMPLETED BY SENDER:

1a.   **Income Withholding Order/Notice for Support (IWO).** Check the box if this is an initial IWO.

1b.   **Amended IWO.** Check the box to indicate that this form amends a previous IWO. Any changes to an IWO must be done through an amended IWO.

1c.   **One-Time Order/Notice For Lump Sum Payment.** Check the box when this IWO is to attach a one-time collection of a lump sum payment after receiving notification from an employer/income withholder or other source. When this box is checked, enter the amount in field 14, Lump Sum Payment, in the *Amounts to Withhold* section. Additional IWOs must be issued to collect subsequent lump sum payments.

1d.   **Termination of IWO.** Check the box to stop income withholding on a child support order. Complete all applicable identifying information to aid the employer/income withholder in terminating the correct IWO.

1e.   **Date.** Date this form is completed and/or signed.

1f.   **Child Support Enforcement (CSE) Agency, Court, Attorney, Private Individual/Entity (Check One).** Check the appropriate box to indicate which entity is sending the IWO. If this IWO is **not** completed by a state or tribal CSE agency, the sender should contact the CSE agency (see www.acf.hhs.gov/programs/css/resource/state-income-withholding-contacts-and-program-requirements) to determine if the CSE agency needs a copy of this form to facilitate payment processing.

NOTE TO EMPLOYER/INCOME WITHHOLDER:

This IWO must be regular on its face. The IWO must be rejected and returned to sender under the following circumstances:
- IWO instructs the employer/income withholder to send a payment to an entity other than a state disbursement unit (for example, payable to the custodial party, court, or attorney). Each state is required to operate a state disbursement unit (SDU), which is a centralized facility for collection and disbursement of child support payments. Exception: If this IWO is issued by a court, attorney, or private individual/entity and the initial child support order was entered before January 1, 1994 or the order was issued by a tribal CSE agency, the employer/income withholder must follow the payment instructions on the form.
- Form does not contain all information necessary for the employer to comply with the withholding.
- Form is altered or contains invalid information.

- Amount to withhold is not a dollar amount.
- Sender has not used the OMB-approved form for the IWO.
- A copy of the underlying order is required and not included.

If you receive this document from an attorney or private individual/entity, a copy of the underlying support order containing a provision authorizing income withholding must be attached.

COMPLETED BY SENDER:

1g.   **State/Tribe/Territory.** Name of state or tribe sending this form. This must be a governmental entity of the state or a tribal organization authorized by a tribal government to operate a CSE program. If you are a tribe submitting this form on behalf of another tribe, complete field 1i.

1h.   **Remittance ID (include w/payment).** Identifier that employers/income withholders must include when sending payments for this IWO. The Remittance ID is entered as the case identifier on the electronic funds transfer/electronic data interchange (EFT/EDI) record.

NOTE TO EMPLOYER/INCOME WITHHOLDER:

The employer/income withholder must use the Remittance ID when remitting payments so the SDU or tribe can identify and apply the payment correctly. The Remittance ID is entered as the case identifier on the EFT/EDI record.

COMPLETED BY SENDER:

1i.   **City/County/Dist./Tribe. Optional** field for the name of the city, county, or district sending this form. If entered, this must be a government entity of the state or the name of the tribe authorized by a tribal government to operate a CSE program for which this form is being sent. If a tribe is submitting this form on behalf of another tribe, enter the name of that tribe.

1j.   **Order ID.** Unique identifier associated with a specific child support obligation. It could be a court case number, docket number, or other identifier designated by the sender.

1k.   **Private Individual/Entity.** Name of the private individual/entity or non-IV-D tribal CSE organization sending this form.

1l.   **Case ID.** Unique identifier assigned to a state or tribal CSE case. In a state IV-D case as defined at 45 Code of Federal Regulations (CFR) 305.1, this is the identifier reported to the Federal Case Registry (FCR). One IWO must be issued for each IV-D case and must use the unique CSE Agency Case ID. For tribes, this would be either the FCR identifier or other applicable identifier.

Fields 2 and 3 refer to the employee/obligor's employer/income withholder and specific case information.

2a.   **Employer/Income Withholder's Name.** Name of employer or income withholder.

2b.   **Employer/Income Withholder's Address.** Employer/income withholder's mailing address including street/PO box, city, state, and zip code. (This may differ from the employee/obligor's work site.) If the employer/income withholder is a federal government agency, the IWO should be sent to the address listed under Federal Agency Income Withholding Contacts and Program Information at www.acf.hhs.gov/css/resource/federal-agency-iwo-and-medical-contact-information.

2c.   **Employer/Income Withholder's FEIN.** Employer/income withholder's nine-digit Federal Employer Identification Number (if available).

3a.   **Employee/Obligor's Name.** Employee/obligor's last name and first name. A middle name is **optional.**

3b.   **Employee/Obligor's Social Security Number.** Employee/obligor's Social Security number or other taxpayer identification number.

3c.   **Employee/Obligor's Date of Birth.** Employee/obligor's date of birth is **optional.**

3d.   **Custodial Party/Obligee's Name.** Custodial party/obligee's last name and first name. A middle name is **optional.** Enter one custodial party/obligee's name on each IWO form. Multiple custodial parties/obligees are not to be entered on a single IWO. Issue one IWO per state IV-D case as defined at 45 CFR 305.1.

3e.   **Child(ren)'s Name(s).** Child(ren)'s last name(s) and first name(s). A middle name(s) is **optional.** (Note: If there are more than six children for this IWO, list additional children's names and birth dates in the **Supplemental Information** section). Enter the child(ren) associated with the custodial party/obligee and employee/obligor only. Child(ren) of multiple custodial parties/obligees is not to be entered on an IWO.

3f.   **Child(ren)'s Birth Date(s).** Date of birth for each child named.

3g.   **Blank box.** Space for court stamps, bar codes, or other information.

ORDER INFORMATION – Field 4 identifies which state or tribe issued the order. Fields 5 through 12 identify the dollar amounts for specific kinds of support (taken directly from the support order) and the total amount to withhold for specific time periods.

4.   **State/Tribe.** Name of the state or tribe that issued the support order.

5a-b.   **Current Child Support.** Dollar amount to be withheld **per** the time period (for example, week, month) specified in the underlying support order.

6a-b.   **Past-due Child Support.** Dollar amount to be withheld **per** the time period (for example, week, month) specified in the underlying support order.

6c.   **Arrears Greater Than 12 Weeks?** The appropriate box (Yes/No) must be checked indicating whether arrears are greater than 12 weeks.

7a-b.   **Current Cash Medical Support.** Dollar amount to be withheld **per** the time period (for example, week, month) specified in the underlying support order.

8a-b.   **Past-due Cash Medical Support.** Dollar amount to be withheld **per** the time period (for example, week, month) specified in the underlying support order.

9a-b.   **Current Spousal Support.** (Alimony) Dollar amount to be withheld **per** the time period (for example, week, month) specified in the underlying support order.

10a-b.   **Past-due Spousal Support.** (Alimony) Dollar amount to be withheld **per** the time period (for example, week, month) specified in the underlying order.

11a-c.   **Other.** Miscellaneous obligations dollar amount to be withheld **per** the time period (for example, week, month) specified in the underlying order. **Must specify** a description of the obligation (for example, court fees).

12a-b.   **Total Amount to Withhold.** The total amount of the deductions **per** the corresponding time period. Fields 5a, 6a, 7a, 8a, 9a, 10a, and 11a should total the amount in 12a.

NOTE TO EMPLOYER/INCOME WITHHOLDER:

An acceptable method of determining the amount to be paid on a weekly or biweekly basis is to multiply the monthly amount due by 12 and divide that result by the number of pay periods in a year. Additional information about this topic is available in Action Transmittal 16-04, Correctly Withholding Child Support from Weekly and Biweekly Pay Cycles (https://www.acf.hhs.gov/css/resource/correctly-withholding-child-support-from-weekly-and-biweekly-pay-cycles).

COMPLETED BY SENDER:

AMOUNTS TO WITHHOLD - Fields 13a through 13d specify the dollar amount to be withheld for this IWO if the employer/income withholder's pay cycle does not correspond with field 12b.

13a. **Per Weekly Pay Period.** Total amount an employer/income withholder should withhold if the employee/obligor is paid weekly.

13b. **Per Semimonthly Pay Period.** Total amount an employer/income withholder should withhold if the employee/obligor is paid twice a month.

13c. **Per Biweekly Pay Period.** Total amount an employer/income withholder should withhold if the employee/obligor is paid every two weeks.

13d. **Per Monthly Pay Period.** Total amount an employer/income withholder should withhold if the employee/obligor is paid once a month.

14. **Lump Sum Payment.** Dollar amount withheld when the IWO is used to attach a lump sum payment. This field should be used when field 1c is checked.

15. **Document Tracking ID. Optional** unique identifier for this form assigned by the sender.

Please Note: Employer's Name, FEIN, Employee/Obligor's Name and SSN, Case ID, and Order ID must appear in the header on page two and subsequent pages.

REMITTANCE INFORMATION - Payments are forwarded to the SDU in each state, unless the initial child support order was entered by a state before January 1, 1994 and never modified, accrued arrears, or was enforced by a child support agency or by a tribal CSE agency. If the order was issued by a tribal CSE agency, the employer/income withholder must follow the remittance instructions on the form.

16. **State/Tribe.** Name of the state or tribe sending this document.

17. **Days.** Number of days after the effective date noted in field 18 in which withholding must begin according to the state or tribal laws/procedures for the employee/obligor's principal place of employment.

18. **Date.** Effective date of this IWO.

19. **Business Days.** Number of business days within which an employer/income withholder must remit amounts withheld pursuant to the state or tribal laws/procedures of the principal place of employment.

20. **Percentage of Disposable Income.** The percentage of disposable income that may be withheld from the employee/obligor's paycheck. It is the sender's responsibility to determine the percentage an employer/income withholder is required to withhold.

NOTE TO EMPLOYER/INCOME WITHHOLDER:

The employer/income withholder may not withhold more than the lesser of: the amounts allowed by the Federal Consumer Credit Protection Act [15 USC §1673(b)]; or 2) the amounts allowed by the jurisdiction of the employee/obligor's principal place of employment (i.e., the amounts allowed by state law if the employee/obligor's principal place of employment is in a state; or the amounts allowed by tribal law if the employee/obligor's principal place of employment is under tribal jurisdiction). State-specific withholding limitations, time requirements, and any allowable employer fees are available at http://www.acf.hhs.gov/css/resource/state-income-withholding-contacts-and-program-requirements. For tribe- specific contacts, payment addresses, and withholding limitations, please contact the tribe at www.acf.hhs.gov/sites/default/files/programs/css/tribal_agency_contacts_printable_pdf.pdf or https://www.bia.gov/tribalmap/DataDotGovSamples/tld_map.html.

A federal government agency may withhold from a variety of incomes and forms of payment, including voluntary separation incentive payments (buy-out payments), incentive pay, and cash awards. For a more complete list, see 5 CFR 581.103.

COMPLETED BY SENDER:

21. **State/Tribe.** Name of the state or tribe sending this document.

22. **Locator Code.** Geographic Locator Codes are standard codes for states, counties, and cities issued by the National Institute of Standards and Technology. These were formerly known as Federal Information Processing Standards (FIPS) codes.

23. **SDU/Tribal Order Payee.** Name of SDU (or payee specified in the underlying tribal support order) to which payments must be sent.

24. **SDU/Tribal Payee Address.** Address of the SDU (or payee specified in the underlying tribal support order) to which payments must be sent.

COMPLETED BY EMPLOYER/INCOME WITHHOLDER:

25. **Return to Sender Checkbox.** The employer/income withholder should check this box and return the IWO to the sender if this IWO is not payable to an SDU or Tribal Payee or this IWO is not regular on its face as indicated on page 1 of these instructions.

COMPLETED BY SENDER IF REQUIRED BY STATE OR TRIBAL LAW:

26. **Signature of Judge/Issuing Official.** Signature of the official authorizing this IWO.

27. **Print Name of Judge/Issuing Official.** Name of the official authorizing this IWO.

28. **Title of Judge/Issuing Official.** Title of the official authorizing this IWO.

29. **Date of Signature.** Date the judge/issuing official signs this IWO.

30. **Copy of IWO checkbox.** Check this box for all intergovernmental IWOs. If checked, the employer/income withholder is required to provide a copy of the IWO to the employee/obligor.

ADDITIONAL INFORMATION FOR EMPLOYERS/INCOME WITHHOLDERS

The following fields refer to federal, state, or tribal laws that apply to issuing an IWO to an employer/income withholder. State- or tribal-specific information may be included only in the fields below.

COMPLETED BY SENDER:

31. **Liability.** Additional information on the penalty and/or citation of the penalty for an employer/income withholder who fails to comply with the IWO. The state or tribal law/procedures of the employee/obligor's principal place of employment govern the penalty.

32. **Anti-discrimination.** Additional information on the penalty and/or citation of the penalty for an employer/income withholder who discharges, refuses to employ, or disciplines an employee/obligor as a result of the IWO. The state or tribal law/procedures of the employee/obligor's principal place of employment govern the penalty.

33. **Supplemental Information.** Any state-specific information needed, such as maximum withholding percentage for nonemployees/independent contractors, fees the employer/income withholder may charge the obligor for income withholding, or children's names and DOBs if there are more than six children on this IWO. Additional information must be consistent with the requirements of the form and the instructions.

COMPLETED BY EMPLOYER/INCOME WITHHOLDER:

NOTIFICATION OF EMPLOYMENT TERMINATION OR INCOME STATUS

The employer must complete this section when the employee/obligor's employment is terminated, income withholding ceases, or if the employee/obligor has never worked for the employer.

34a-b. **Employment/Income Status Checkbox.** Check the employment/income status of the employee/obligor.

35. **Termination Date.** If applicable, date employee/obligor was terminated.

36. **Last Known Telephone Number.** Last known (home/cell/other) telephone number of the employee/obligor.

37. **Last Known Address.** Last known home/mailing address of the employee/obligor.

38. **Final Payment Date.** Date employer sent final payment to SDU/Tribal Payee.

39. **Final Payment Amount.** Amount of final payment sent to SDU/Tribal Payee.

40. **New Employer's Name.** Name of employee's/obligor's new employer (if known).

41. **New Employer's Address.** Address of employee's/obligor's new employer (if known).

COMPLETED BY SENDER:

CONTACT INFORMATION

42. **Issuer Name (Employer/Income Withholder Contact).** Name of the contact person that the employer/income withholder can call for information regarding this IWO.

43. **Issuer Telephone Number.** Telephone number of the contact person.

44. **Issuer Fax Number. Optional** fax number of the contact person.

45. **Issuer Email/Website. Optional** email or website of the contact person.

46. **Issuer Address (Termination/Income Status and Correspondence Address).** Address to

which the employer should return the Employment Termination or Income Status notice. It is also the address that the employer should use to correspond with the issuing entity.

47.   **Issuer Name (Employee/Obligor Contact).** Name of the contact person that the employee/ obligor can call for information.

48.   **Issuer Telephone Number.** Telephone number of the contact person.

49.   **Issuer Fax Number. Optional** fax number of the contact person.

50.   **Issuer Email/Website. Optional** email or website of the contact person.

Encryption Requirements:

When communicating the Income Withholding for Support (IWO) through electronic transmission, precautions must be taken to ensure the security of the data. Child support agencies are encouraged to use the electronic applications provided by the federal Office of Child Support Enforcement. Other electronic means, such as encrypted attachments to emails, may be used if the encryption method is compliant with Federal Information Processing Standard (FIPS) Publication 140-2 (FIPS PUB 140-2).

The Paperwork Reduction Act of 1995

This information collection and associated responses are conducted in accordance with 45 CFR 303.100 of the Child Support Enforcement Program. This form is designed to provide uniformity and standardization. Public reporting burden for this collection of information is estimated to average 5 minutes per response for Non-IV-D CPs; 2 minutes per response for employers; 3 seconds for e-IWO employers, including the time for reviewing instructions, gathering and maintaining the data needed, and reviewing the collection of information.

An agency may not conduct or sponsor, and a person is not required to respond to, a collection of information unless it displays a currently valid OMB control number.

0075

ATTORNEY OR PARTY WITHOUT ATTORNEY *(Name, state bar number, and address):*	FOR COURT USE ONLY
TELEPHONE NO. *(Optional):* FAX NO. *(Optional):*	
E–MAIL ADDRESS *(Optional):*	
ATTORNEY FOR *(Name):*	

SUPERIOR COURT OF CALIFORNIA, COUNTY OF

STREET ADDRESS:

MAILING ADDRESS:

CITY AND ZIP CODE:

BRANCH NAME:

PETITIONER:

RESPONDENT:

PETITION TO ESTABLISH PARENTAL RELATIONSHIP ☐ **Child Support** ☐ **Child Custody** ☐ **Visitation** ☐ **Other** *(specify):*	CASE NUMBER:

1. Petitioner is
   a. ☐ the mother.
   b. ☐ the father.
   c. ☐ the child or the child's personal representative *(specify court and date of appointment):*
   d. ☐ other *(specify):*

2. The children are
   a. Child's name   Date of birth   Age   Sex

   b. ☐ a child who is not yet born.

3. The court has jurisdiction over the respondent because the respondent
   a. ☐ resides in this state.
   b. ☐ had sexual intercourse in this state, which resulted in conception of the children listed in item 2.
   c. ☐ other *(specify):*

4. The action is brought in this county because *(you must check one or more to file in this county):*
   a. ☐ the child resides or is found in the county.
   b. ☐ a parent is deceased and proceedings for administration of the estate have been or could be started in this county.

5. Petitioner claims *(check all that apply):*
   a. ☐ respondent is the child's mother.
   b. ☐ respondent is the child's father.
   c. ☐ parentage has been established by Voluntary Declaration of Paternity *(attach copy).*
   d. ☐ respondent who is child's parent has failed to support the child.
   e. ☐ *(name):*   has furnished or is furnishing the following reasonable expenses
   of pregnancy and birth for which the respondent as parent of the child is obligated:
   Amount   Payable to   For *(specify):*

   f. ☐ public assistance is being provided to the child.
   g. ☐ other *(specify):*

6. A completed *Declaration Under Uniform Child Custody Jurisdiction and Enforcement Act (UCCJEA))* (form FL-105) is attached.

Form Approved for Optional Use
Judicial Council of California
FL-200 [Rev. January 1, 2003]

PETITION TO ESTABLISH PARENTAL RELATIONSHIP
(Uniform Parentage)

Family Code, § 7630
www.courtinfo.ca.gov

PETITIONER:	CASE NUMBER:
RESPONDENT:	

Petitioner requests the court to make the determinations indicated below.

7. PARENT-CHILD RELATIONSHIP
   a. ☐ Respondent   b. ☐ Petitioner
   c. ☐ Other (specify):   is the parent of the children listed in item 2.

8. CHILD CUSTODY AND VISITATION

	Petitioner	Respondent	Joint	Other
a. Legal custody of children to	☐	☐	☐	☐
b. Physical custody of children to	☐	☐	☐	☐

   c. Visitation of children:
      (1) ☐ None
      (2) ☐ Reasonable visitation.
      (3) ☐ Petitioner   ☐ Respondent   should have the right to visit the children as follows:

      (4) ☐ Visitation with the following restrictions (specify):

   d. Facts in support of the requested custody and visitation orders are (specify):
      ☐ Contained in the attached declaration.
   e. ☐ I request mediation to work out a parenting plan.

9. REASONABLE EXPENSES OF PREGNANCY AND BIRTH:

	Petitioner	Respondent	Joint
Reasonable expenses of pregnancy and birth be paid by as follows:	☐	☐	☐

10. FEES AND COSTS OF LITIGATION

	Petitioner	Respondent	Joint
a. Attorney fees to be paid by	☐	☐	☐
b. Expert fees, guardian ad litem fees, and other costs of the action or pretrial proceedings to be paid by	☐	☐	☐

11. NAME CHANGE
    ☐ Children's names be changed, according to Family Code section 7638, as follows (specify):

12. CHILD SUPPORT
    The court may make orders for support of the children and issue an earnings assignment without further notice to either party.

13. I have read the restraining order on the back of the *Summons* (FL-210) and I understand it applies to me when this Petition is filed.

I declare under penalty of perjury under the laws of the State of California that the foregoing is true and correct.

Date:

▶

_____   _____
(TYPE OR PRINT NAME)   (SIGNATURE OF PETITIONER)

A blank *Response to Petition to Establish Parental Relationship* (form FL-220) must be served on the Respondent with this Petition.

NOTICE: If you have a child from this relationship, the court is required to order child support based upon the income of both parents. Support normally continues until the child is 18. You should supply the court with information about your finances. Otherwise, the child support order will be based upon information supplied by the other parent.
Any party required to pay child support must pay interest on overdue amounts at the "legal" rate, which is currently 10 percent.

PETITION TO ESTABLISH PARENTAL RELATIONSHIP
(Uniform Parentage)

0077

SUMMONS
(Parentage—Custody and Support)

CITACIÓN *(Paternidad—Custodia y Manutención)*

NOTICE TO RESPONDENT *(Name):*

AVISO AL DEMANDADO (Nombre):

FOR COURT USE ONLY
(SOLO PARA USO DE LA CORTE)

You have been sued. Read the information below and on the next page.
Lo han demandado. Lea la información a continuación y en la página siguiente.

Petitioner's name:
El nombre del demandante:

CASE NUMBER: *(Número de caso)*

You have **30 calendar days** after this *Summons* and *Petition* are served on you to file a *Response* (form FL-220 or FL-270) at the court and have a copy served on the petitioner. A letter, phone call, or court appearance will not protect you.	*Tiene **30 días de calendario** después de habir recibido la entrega legal de esta Citación y Petición para presentar una Respuesta (formulario FL-220 o FL-270) ante la corte y efectuar la entrega legal de una copia al demandante. Una carta o llamada telefónica o una audiencia de la corte no basta para protegerlo.*
If you do not file your *Response* on time, the court may make orders affecting your right to custody of your children. You may also be ordered to pay child support and attorney fees and costs.	*Si no presenta su Respuesta a tiempo, la corte puede dar órdenes que afecten la custodia de sus hijos. La corte también le puede ordenar que pague manutención de los hijos, y honorarios y costos legales.*
For legal advice, contact a lawyer immediately. Get help finding a lawyer at the California Courts Online Self-Help Center *(www.courts.ca.gov/selfhelp)*, at the California Legal Services website *(www.lawhelpca.org)*, or by contacting your local bar association.	*Para asesoramiento legal, póngase en contacto de inmediato con un abogado. Puede obtener información para encontrar un abogado en el Centro de Ayuda de las Cortes de California (www.sucorte.ca.gov), en el sitio web de los Servicios Legales de California (www.lawhelpca.org), o poniéndose en contacto con el colegio de abogados de su condado.*
NOTICE: *The restraining order on page 2 remains in effect against each parent until the petition is dismissed, a judgment is entered, or the court makes further orders. This order is enforceable anywhere in California by any law enforcement officer who has received or seen a copy of it.*	**AVISO:** *La órden de protección que aparecen en la pagina 2 continuará en vigencia en cuanto a cada parte hasta que se emita un fallo final, se despida la petición o la corte dé otras órdenes. Cualquier agencia del orden público que haya recibido o visto una copia de estas orden puede hacerla acatar en cualquier lugar de California.*
FEE WAIVER: If you cannot pay the filing fee, ask the clerk for a fee waiver form. The court may order you to pay back all or part of the fees and costs that the court waived for you or the other party.	*EXENCIÓN DE CUOTAS: Si no puede pagar la cuota de presentación, pida al secretario un formulario de exención de cuotas. La corte puede ordenar que usted pague, ya sea en parte o por completo, las cuotas y costos de la corte previamente exentos a petición de usted o de la otra parte.*

[SEAL]

1. The name and address of the court are: *(El nombre y dirección de la corte son:)*

2. The name, address, and telephone number of petitioner's attorney, or petitioner without an attorney, are: *(El nombre, la dirección y el número de teléfono del abogado del demandante, o del demandante si no tiene abogado, son:)*

Date (Fecha): _____ Clerk, by (Secretario, por) _____ , Deputy (Asistente)

Page 1 of 2

Form Adopted for Mandatory Use
Judicial Council of California
FL-210 [Rev. January 1, 2015]

SUMMONS
(Parentage—Custody and Support)

Family Code, §§ 232, 233, 7700;
Cal. Rules of Court, rule 5.50
www.courts.ca.gov

STANDARD RESTRAINING ORDER
(Parentage—Custody and Support)

ORDEN DE RESTRICCIÓN ESTÁNDAR
(Paternidad—Custodia y Manutención)

Starting immediately, you and every other party are restrained from removing from the state, or applying for a passport for, the minor child or children for whom this action seeks to establish a parent-child relationship or a custody order without the prior written consent of every other party or an order of the court.

This restraining order takes effect against the petitioner when he or she files the petition and against the respondent when he or she is personally served with the *Summons* and *Petition* OR when he or she waives and accepts service.

This restraining order remains in effect until the judgment is entered, the petition is dismissed, or the court makes other orders.

This order is enforceable anywhere in California by any law enforcement officer who has received or seen a copy of it.

En forma inmediata, usted y cada otra parte tienen prohibido llevarse del estado a los hijos menores para quienes esta acción judicial procura establecer una relación entre hijos y padres o una orden de custodia, ni pueden solicitar un pasaporte para los mismos, sin el consentimiento previo por escrito de cada otra parte o sin una orden de la corte.

Esta orden de restricción entrará en vigencia para el demandante una vez presentada la petición, y para el demandado una vez que éste reciba la notificación personal de la Citación y Petición, o una vez que renuncie su derecho a recibir dicha notificación y se dé por notificado.

Esta orden de restricción continuará en vigencia hasta que se emita un fallo final, se despida la petición o la corte dé otras órdenes.

Cualquier agencia del orden público que haya recibido o visto una copia de esta orden puede hacerla acatar en cualquier lugar de California.

NOTICE—ACCESS TO AFFORDABLE HEALTH INSURANCE Do you or someone in your household need affordable health insurance? If so, you should apply for Covered California. Covered California can help reduce the cost you pay toward high-quality, affordable health care. For more information, visit *www.coveredca.com.* Or call Covered California at 1-800-300-1506.

AVISO—ACCESO A SEGURA DE SALUD MÁS ECONOMICO Necessita seguro de salud a un costo asequible, ya sea para usted o alguien en su hogar? Si es asi, puede presentar una solicitud con Covered California. Covered California lo puede ayudar a reducir al costo que paga por seguro de salud asequible y de alta calidad. Para obtener más información, visite www.coveredca.com. O llame a Covered California al 1-800-300-0213.

0079

ATTORNEY OR PARTY WITHOUT ATTORNEY *(Name, State Bar number, and address):*	FOR COURT USE ONLY

TELEPHONE NO.:   FAX NO. *(Optional):*

E-MAIL ADDRESS *(Optional):*

ATTORNEY FOR *(Name):*

SUPERIOR COURT OF CALIFORNIA, COUNTY OF

STREET ADDRESS:

MAILING ADDRESS:

CITY AND ZIP CODE:

BRANCH NAME:

PETITIONER:

RESPONDENT:

RESPONSE TO PETITION TO ESTABLISH PARENTAL RELATIONSHIP (Uniform Parentage)	CASE NUMBER:

1. The children are *(name each):*

    a. <u>Child's name</u>   <u>Date of birth</u>   <u>Age</u>   <u>Sex</u>

    b. ☐ A child who is not yet born

2. The petitioner is

    a. ☐ the mother of the children listed above.

    b. ☐ the father of the children listed above.

    c. ☐ not certain whether he or she is the biological parent of the children listed above.

    d. ☐ the child or child's representative *(specify court and date of appointment):*

    e. ☐ other *(specify):*

3. The respondent

    a. ☐ lives in the State of California.

    b. ☐ was in California when the listed children were conceived.

    c. ☐ neither a nor b

    d. ☐ other *(specify):*

4. The children

    a. ☐ live or are in this county.

    b. ☐ are children of a parent who is deceased, and proceedings for administration of the estate have been or could be started in this county.

5. The respondent is

    a. ☐ the father of the children listed in item 1 above.

    b. ☐ the mother of the children listed in item 1 above.

    c. ☐ not certain if he or she is the parent of the children listed in item 1 above.

    d. ☐ not the parent of the children listed in item 1 above.

    e ☐ other *(specify):*

6. Additional statements

    a. ☐ Parentage has been established by a Voluntary Declaration of Paternity *(attach copy).*

    b. ☐ Parentage has been established in another case ☐ governmental child support ☐ other *(specify):*

    c. ☐ Public assistance is being provided to the children.

Form Approved for Optional Use
Judicial Council of California
FL-220 [Rev. January 1, 2006]

RESPONSE TO PETITION TO ESTABLISH PARENTAL RELATIONSHIP
(Uniform Parentage)

Family Code, § 7600
www.courtinfo.ca.gov

0080

PETITIONER:	CASE NUMBER:
RESPONDENT:	

The respondent requests that the court make the orders listed below.

7. **Parent-child relationship** *(check all that apply)*:

   a. ☐ Respondent ☐ Petitioner ☐ Other *(specify):*   is the parent of the children listed in item 1.

   b. ☐ Respondent ☐ Petitioner ☐ Other *(specify):*   is not the parent of the children listed in item 1.

   c. ☐ Respondent requests genetic (blood) tests to determine whether the ☐ petitioner ☐ respondent   is the parent of the children listed.

8. **Child custody and visitation**

   a. If ☐ Petitioner ☐ Respondent ☐ Other   is found to be the parent of the children in listed in item 1:

	Petitioner	Respondent	Joint	Other
b. Legal custody of the children should go to	☐	☐	☐	☐
c. Physical custody of the children should go to	☐	☐	☐	☐

   d. Visitation of the children should be as follows:

   (1) ☐ None

   (2) ☐ Reasonable visitation

   (3) ☐ Petitioner ☐ Respondent   should have the right to visit the children as follows *(specify):*

   (4) ☐ Visitation should occur with the following restrictions *(specify):*

   (5) ☐ I request mediation to work out a parenting plan.

9. **Reasonable expenses of pregnancy and birth**

	Petitioner	Respondent	Both
Reasonable expenses of pregnancy and birth should be paid by	☐	☐	☐

10. **Fees and costs of litigation**

	Petitioner	Respondent	Both
a. Attorney fees should be paid by	☐	☐	☐
b. Expert fees, guardian ad litem fees, and other costs of the action or pretrial proceedings should be paid by	☐	☐	☐

11. **Name change.** ☐ The children's names should be changed, according to Family Code section 7638, as follows *(specify old and new names):*

12. **Other orders requested** *(specify):*

13. **Child support.** The court may make orders for support of the children and issue an earnings assignment without further notice to either party.

I have read the restraining order on the back of the *Summons* (form FL-210) and I understand it applies to me.

I declare under penalty of perjury under the laws of the State of California that the foregoing is true and correct.

Date:

▶

_____
(TYPE OR PRINT NAME)

_____
(SIGNATURE OF RESPONDENT)

NOTICE: If you have a child from this relationship, the court is required to order child support based upon the income of both parents. Support normally continues until the child is 18. You should supply the court with information about your finances. Otherwise, the child support order will be based upon information supplied by the other parent. Any party required to pay child support must pay interest on overdue amounts at the "legal" rate, which is currently 10 percent.

0081

ATTORNEY OR PARTY WITHOUT ATTORNEY *(Name, state bar number, and address):*	FOR COURT USE ONLY
TELEPHONE NO.: FAX NO.:	
ATTORNEY FOR *(Name):*	

SUPERIOR COURT OF CALIFORNIA, COUNTY OF

STREET ADDRESS:

MAILING ADDRESS:

CITY AND ZIP CODE:

BRANCH NAME:

PETITIONER:

RESPONDENT:

DECLARATION FOR DEFAULT OR UNCONTESTED JUDGMENT	CASE NUMBER:

1. I declare that if I appeared in court and were sworn, I would testify to the truth of the facts in this declaration.
2. I request that proof will be by this declaration and that I will not appear before the court unless I am ordered by the court to appear.
3. All the information in the ☐ *Petition or Complaint to Establish Parental Relationship* ☐ *Response or Answer*
   ☐ *Petition to Establish Custody and Support* ☐ *Response* is true and correct.
4. ☐ Respondent and/or ☐ Petitioner is/are the parent(s) of the minor child(ren).
5. A Voluntary Declaration of Paternity form ☐ has ☐ has not been signed regarding this child *(attach a copy if available).*
6. DEFAULT OR UNCONTESTED *(Check a or b)*
   a. ☐ The default of the respondent was entered or is being requested, and I am not seeking any relief not requested in the petition. **OR**
   b. ☐ The parties have stipulated that the matter may proceed as an uncontested matter without notice, and the stipulation is attached.
7. ☐ CHILD SUPPORT should be ordered as set forth in the proposed *Judgment* (form FL-250).
   a. ☐ Petitioner ☐ Respondent is presently receiving public assistance (TANF); thus all support should be made payable to the local child support agency at *(specify address):*

   b. **NOTE: If a support order is requested, submit a completed *Income and Expense Declaration* (form FL-150), or *Financial Statement (Simplified)* (form FL-155), unless a current form is on file. Include your best estimate of the other party's gross monthly income.**
8. ☐ ATTORNEY FEES should be ordered as set forth in the proposed *Judgment* (form FL-250).
9. ☐ CHILD CUSTODY should be ordered as set forth in the proposed *Judgment* (form FL-250).
10. ☐ CHILD VISITATION should be ordered as set forth in the proposed *Judgment* (form FL-250).
11. ☐ REASONABLE EXPENSES OF PREGNANCY AND BIRTH should be ordered as set forth in the proposed *Judgment* (form FL-250).
12. ☐ NAMES OF THE CHILDREN should be changed as set forth in the proposed *Judgment* (form FL-250).

13. This declaration may be reviewed by a commissioner sitting as a temporary judge who may determine whether to grant this request or require my appearance.
14. I have read and understand the *Advisement and Waiver of Rights Re: Establishment of Parental Relationship* (form FL-235), which is signed and attached to this declaration.
15. ☐ Other *(specify):*

I declare under penalty of perjury under the laws of the State of California that the foregoing is true and correct.

Date:

▶

_____
(TYPE OR PRINT NAME)

_____
(SIGNATURE OF DECLARANT)

Page 1 of 1

Form Adopted for Mandatory Use
Judicial Council of California
FL-230 [Rev. January 1, 2003]

DECLARATION FOR DEFAULT OR UNCONTESTED JUDGMENT
(Uniform Parentage, Custody and Support)

Family Code, §§ 7600, 3120,
3900 et seq
www.courtinfo.ca.gov.

FL-235

PETITIONER:	CASE NUMBER:
RESPONDENT:	

ADVISEMENT AND WAIVER OF RIGHTS RE: ESTABLISHMENT OF PARENTAL RELATIONSHIP

1. **RIGHT TO BE REPRESENTED BY A LAWYER.** I understand that I have the right to be represented by a lawyer of my own choice at my own expense. If I cannot afford a lawyer, I can contact the Lawyer Referral Association of the local bar association or the Family Law Facilitator for assistance.

2. **RIGHT TO A TRIAL.** I understand that I have a right to have a judge determine whether I am the parent of the children named in this action.

3. **RIGHT TO CONFRONT AND CROSS-EXAMINE WITNESSES.** I understand that in a trial I have the right to confront and cross-examine the witnesses against me and to present evidence and witnesses in my own defense.

4. **RIGHT TO HAVE PARENTAGE TESTS.** I understand that, where the law permits, I have the right to have the court order parentage tests. The court will decide who pays for the tests. The court could order that I pay none, some, or all of the costs of the tests.

5. **OBLIGATIONS.** I understand that if I admit that I am the parent of the children in this action that those children will be my children for legal purposes.

6. **WAIVER.** I understand that I am admitting that I am the parent of the children named in the stipulation and am giving up the rights stated above (except the right to an attorney if I have an attorney).

7. **CHILD SUPPORT.** I understand that I will have the duty to contribute to the support of the children named in this action and that this duty of support will continue for each child until the obligation is terminated by law.

8. **CRIMINAL NON-SUPPORT.** I understand that if I willfully fail to support the children, criminal proceedings may be initiated against me.

9. **UNDERSTANDING.**
   a. ☐ I have read and understand the *Judgment (Uniform Parentage—Custody and Support)* (form FL-250) and this *Advisement and Waiver of Rights.*
   b. ☐ I understand the translation.

> **IF I AM REPRESENTED BY AN ATTORNEY, I ACKNOWLEDGE THAT MY ATTORNEY HAS READ AND EXPLAINED TO ME THE CONTENTS OF THE STIPULATION, RECITALS, AND WAIVERS, AND I ACKNOWLEDGE THAT I UNDERSTAND THEM.**

Date:

▶

_____
(TYPE OR PRINT NAME)

_____
(SIGNATURE OF DECLARANT)

INTERPRETER'S DECLARATION

1. The ☐ Petitioner ☐ Respondent   is unable to read or understand the *Judgment (Uniform Parentage—Custody and Support)* (form FL-250) and this *Advisement and Waiver of Rights* because:
   a. ☐ his/her primary language is *(specify):*
   b. ☐ other *(specify):*

2. I certify under penalty of perjury under the laws of the State of California that I have, to the best of my ability, read or translated for the ☐ Petitioner ☐ Respondent the *Judgment (Uniform Parentage—Custody and Support)* (form FL-250) and this *Advisement and Waiver of Rights.* ☐ Petitioner ☐ Respondent said he or she understood the *Judgment (Uniform Parentage—Custody and Support)* (form FL-250) and this *Advisement and Waiver of Rights* before signing them.

Date:

▶

_____
(TYPE OR PRINT NAME)

_____
(SIGNATURE OF INTERPRETER)

Page 1 of 1

Form Approved for Optional Use
Judicial Council of California
FL-235 [Rev. January 1, 2003]

**ADVISEMENT AND WAIVER OF RIGHTS RE:
ESTABLISHMENT OF PARENTAL RELATIONSHIP
(Uniform Parentage)**

Family Code, § 7600 et seq.
www.courtinfo.ca.gov

FL-240

ATTORNEY OR PARTY WITHOUT ATTORNEY (Name, State Bar number, and address):

TELEPHONE NO.:   FAX NO. :
E-MAIL ADDRESS:
ATTORNEY FOR (Name):

FOR COURT USE ONLY

SUPERIOR COURT OF CALIFORNIA, COUNTY OF
  STREET ADDRESS:
  MAILING ADDRESS:
  CITY AND ZIP CODE:
  BRANCH NAME:

PETITIONER:
RESPONDENT:
OTHER PARENT/PARTY:

STIPULATION FOR ENTRY OF JUDGMENT RE: ESTABLISHMENT
OF PARENTAL RELATIONSHIP

CASE NUMBER:

THE PARTIES STIPULATE THAT

1. ☐ The parties have read and understand the *Advisement and Waiver of Rights Re: Establishment of Parental Relationship* (form FL-235), which is submitted with this *Stipulation for Entry of Judgment.* The parties give up those rights and freely agree that a judgment may be entered in accordance with this stipulation.

2. Name: ☐ Mother   ☐ Father
   Name: ☐ Mother   ☐ Father

   are the parents of the following children:
   Name   Date of Birth

3. ☐ Child custody and visitation shall be ordered as set forth in the proposed *Judgment (Uniform Parentage)* (form FL-250).
4. ☐ Child support shall be ordered as set forth in the proposed *Judgment (Uniform Parentage)* (form FL-250).
5. ☐ Attorney fees shall be ordered as set forth in the proposed *Judgment (Uniform Parentage)* (form FL-250).
6. ☐ Names of the children shall be changed as set forth in the proposed *Judgment (Uniform Parentage)* (form FL-250).
7. ☐ Reasonable costs of pregnancy and birth shall be paid as ordered in the proposed *Judgment (Uniform Parentage)* (form FL-250).
8. ☐ Other orders shall be as set forth in the proposed *Judgment (Uniform Parentage)* (form FL-250).
9. ☐ The parties further agree that the court make the following orders:

☐ See attachment 9.

Date: _____
_____
(TYPE OR PRINT NAME)

Date: _____
_____
(TYPE OR PRINT NAME)

Date: _____
_____
(TYPE OR PRINT NAME)

Date: _____
_____
(TYPE OR PRINT NAME)

Date: _____
_____
(TYPE OR PRINT NAME)

▶ _____
(SIGNATURE OF PETITIONER)

▶ _____
(SIGNATURE OF RESPONDENT)

▶ _____
(SIGNATURE OF ATTORNEY FOR PETITIONER)

▶ _____
(SIGNATURE OF ATTORNEY FOR RESPONDENT)

▶ _____
(SIGNATURE OF OTHER PARTY OR ATTORNEY)

Page 1 of 1

Form Adopted for Mandatory Use
Judicial Council of California
FL-240 [Rev. January 1, 2015]

**STIPULATION FOR ENTRY OF JUDGMENT RE:
ESTABLISHMENT OF PARENTAL RELATIONSHIP**
(Parentage)

Family Code, § 7600 et seq.
www.courts.ca.gov

FL-250

ATTORNEY OR PARTY WITHOUT ATTORNEY *(Name, State Bar number, and address)*:	*FOR COURT USE ONLY*

TELEPHONE NO.:   FAX NO.:

ATTORNEY FOR *(Name)*:

SUPERIOR COURT OF CALIFORNIA, COUNTY OF

STREET ADDRESS:

MAILING ADDRESS:

CITY AND ZIP CODE:

BRANCH NAME:

PETITIONER:

RESPONDENT:

JUDGMENT	CASE NUMBER:

1. ☐ This judgment ☐ contains personal conduct restraining orders ☐ modifies existing restraining orders.
   The restraining orders are contained in item(s):   of the attachment.
   They expire on *(date)*:   A CLETS form must be attached.

2. a. This matter proceeded as follows: ☐ Default or uncontested ☐ By declaration ☐ Contested
   b. Date: Dept.:   Room:
   c. Judicial officer *(name)*:   ☐ Temporary judge
   d. ☐ Petitioner present ☐ Attorney present *(name)*:
   e. ☐ Respondent present ☐ Attorney present *(name)*:
   f. **Petitioner** (1) ☐ The petitioner appeared without counsel and was advised of relevant rights.
         (2) ☐ The petitioner signed *Advisement and Waiver of Rights Re: Establishment of Parental Relationship* (form FL-235).
         (3) ☐ The petitioner is married to the Respondent, and no other action is pending.
         (4) ☐ The petitioner signed a Voluntary Declaration of Paternity.
         (5) ☐ There is a prior judgment of parentage in a family support, juvenile, or adoption court case.
   g. **Respondent** (1) ☐ The respondent appeared without counsel and was advised of relevant rights.
         (2) ☐ The respondent signed *Advisement and Waiver of Rights Re: Establishment of Parental Relationship* (form FL-235).
         (3) ☐ The respondent is married to the Petitioner, and no other action is pending.
         (4) ☐ The respondent signed a Voluntary Declaration of Paternity.
         (5) ☐ There is a prior judgment of parentage in a family support, juvenile or adoption court case.
   h. Other parties or attorneys present *(specify)*:

3. **THE COURT FINDS**
   Name: ☐ Mother ☐ Father
   Name: ☐ Mother ☐ Father
   are the parents of the following children:

Child's name	Date of birth

4. **THE COURT ORDERS**
   a. ☐ Child custody and visitation are as specified in one or more of the attached forms:
         (1) ☐ *Child Custody and Visitation Order Attachment* (form FL-341)
         (2) ☐ *Stipulation for Order for Child Custody and/or Visitation of Children* (form FL-355)
         (3) ☐ Other *(specify)*:

Form Adopted for Mandatory Use
Judicial Council of California
FL-250 [Rev. January 1, 2004]

JUDGMENT
(Uniform Parentage—Custody and Support)

Family Code, §§ 3120, 3900, 7600 et seq.
www.courtinfo.ca.gov

PETITIONER:	CASE NUMBER:
RESPONDENT:	

5. **THE COURT FURTHER ORDERS**

    a. ☐ Child support is as stated in one or more of the attached:

        (1) ☐ *Child Support Information and Order Attachment* (form FL-342)

        (2) ☐ *Stipulation to Establish or Modify Child Support and Order* (form FL-350)

        (3) ☐ Other *(specify):*

    b. Both parties must complete and file with the court a *Child Support Case Registry Form* (form FL-191) within 10 days of the date of this judgment. Thereafter, the parents must notify the court of any change in the information submitted, within 10 days of the change.

    c. The form *Notice of Rights and Responsibilities—Health Care Costs and Reimbursement Procedures* and *Information Sheet on Changing a Child Support Order* (form FL-192) is attached.

    d. ☐ The last names of the children are changed to *(specify):*

    e. ☐ The birth certificates must be amended to conform to this court order by

        (1) ☐ adding the father's name.

        (2) ☐ changing the last name of the children.

    f. ☐ Attorney fees and costs are as stated in the attachment.

    g. ☐ Reasonable expenses of pregnancy and birth are as stated in the attachment.

    h. ☐ Other *(specify):*

    ☐ Continued on Attachment 3h.

6. Number of pages attached: _____

Date: _____

_____

JUDICIAL OFFICER

☐ SIGNATURE FOLLOWS LAST ATTACHMENT

NOTICE: Any party required to pay child support must pay interest on overdue amounts at the "legal" rate, which is currently 10 percent.

JUDGMENT
(Uniform Parentage—Custody and Support)

0086

ATTORNEY OR PARTY WITHOUT ATTORNEY *(Name, State Bar number, and address):*

FOR COURT USE ONLY

TELEPHONE NO. *(Optional):*   FAX NO. *(Optional):*

E–MAIL ADDRESS *(Optional):*

ATTORNEY FOR *(Name):*

SUPERIOR COURT OF CALIFORNIA, COUNTY OF

STREET ADDRESS:

MAILING ADDRESS:

CITY AND ZIP CODE:

BRANCH NAME:

PETITIONER:

RESPONDENT:

PETITION FOR CUSTODY AND SUPPORT OF MINOR CHILDREN	CASE NUMBER:

NOTICE: This action will not terminate a marriage or establish a parental relationship.

1. **Jurisdiction for bringing action**
   a. Petitioner is the ☐ mother ☐ father of the minor children.
   b. Respondent is the ☐ mother ☐ father of the minor children.

2. a. ☐ Petitioner is married to the respondent, and no action is pending in any court for dissolution, legal separation, or nullity.

   b. ☐ Petitioner and respondent have signed a *Voluntary Declaration of Paternity* regarding the minor children, and no action regarding the children has been filed in any other court. *(Attach a copy of declaration)*

   c. ☐ Petitioner and respondent are not married and have legally adopted a child together.

   d. ☐ Petitioner and respondent have been determined to be the parents in juvenile or governmental child support case number _____.

   County _____ State _____ Country (if not the United States) _____

3. The following minor children are the subject of this action:

   Child's name   Date of birth   Age   Sex

   ☐ Continued on Attachment 3.

4. A completed *Declaration Under Uniform Child Custody Jurisdiction and Enforcement Act (UCCJEA)* (form FL-105) is attached.

5. **Child custody and visitation.** I request the following orders:

	Petitioner	Respondent	Joint	Other
a. Legal custody of children to	☐	☐	☐	☐
b. Physical custody of children to	☐	☐	☐	☐
c. Visitation of children with:	☐	☐	☐	☐

   (1) The proposed schedule for visitation is as follows:

   ☐ See the attached form FL-311, *Child Custody and Visitation Attachment.*

Form Approved for Optional Use
Judicial Council of California
FL-260 [Rev. January 1, 2004]

**PETITION FOR CUSTODY
AND SUPPORT OF MINOR CHILDREN**

Family Code, §§ 3120, 3400, 3900
www.courtinfo.ca.gov

0087

5. d. ☐ I request that visitation be supervised for the following persons, with the following restrictions:

☐ Continued on Attachment 5d.

e. ☐ I request that the child abduction prevention orders requested on form FL-312 be approved.

f. ☐ I request that the proposed holiday schedule set out in ☐ form FL-341(C) ☐ other be approved.

g. ☐ I request that additional orders regarding child custody set out in ☐ form FL-341(D) ☐ other be approved.

h. ☐ I request that joint legal custody orders set out in ☐ form FL-341(E) ☐ other be approved.

6. **Fees and cost of litigation**
   a. Attorney fees will be paid by ☐ petitioner ☐ respondent.
   b. ☐ Each party will pay own fees.

7. **Child support.** The court may make orders for support of the children and issue an earnings assignment without further notice to either party. *A completed Income and Expense Declaration* (form FL-150) *or Financial Statement (Simplified)* (form FL-155) *is attached.*

8. Other *(specify):*

9. **I have read the restraining order on the back of the** *Summons (Uniform Parentage—Petition for Custody and Support)* **(form FL-210) that is being filed with this petition, and I understand that it applies to me when this petition is filed.**

I declare under penalty of perjury under the laws of the State of California that the foregoing is true and correct.

Date:

_____
(TYPE OR PRINT NAME)

▶

_____
(SIGNATURE OF PETITIONER)

A blank *Response to Petition for Custody and Support of Minor Children* (form FL-270) must be served on the respondent with this *Petition.*

NOTICE: If you have a child from this relationship, the court is required to order child support based on the incomes of both parents. You should supply the court with information about your income. Otherwise, the child support order will be based on information supplied by the other parent. Any party required to pay child support must pay interest on overdue amounts at the "legal rate," which is currently 10 percent.

0088

ATTORNEY OR PARTY WITHOUT ATTORNEY *(Name, State Bar number, and address)*:	FOR COURT USE ONLY
TELEPHONE NO. *(Optional)*: FAX NO. *(Optional)*: E–MAIL ADDRESS *(Optional)*: ATTORNEY FOR *(Name)*:	

SUPERIOR COURT OF CALIFORNIA, COUNTY OF
STREET ADDRESS:
MAILING ADDRESS:
CITY AND ZIP CODE:
BRANCH NAME:

PETITIONER:

RESPONDENT:

RESPONSE TO PETITION FOR CUSTODY AND SUPPORT **OF MINOR CHILDREN**	CASE NUMBER:

NOTICE: This action will not terminate a marriage or establish a parental relationship.

1. **Jurisdiction for bringing action**
   a. Petitioner is the ☐ mother ☐ father of the minor children.
   b. Respondent is the ☐ mother ☐ father of the minor children.

2. a. ☐ Petitioner is married to the respondent, and no action is pending in any court for dissolution, legal separation, or nullity.

   b. ☐ Petitioner and respondent have signed a Voluntary Declaration of Paternity regarding the minor children, and no other action is pending in any other court. *(Attach a copy of declaration)*

   c. ☐ Petitioner and respondent are not married and have legally adopted a child together.

   d. ☐ Petitioner and respondent have been determined to be the parents in a juvenile or governmental child support case number _____.

   County _____ State _____ Country (if not the United States) _____

3. The following minor children are the subject of this action:

Child's name	Date of birth	Age	Sex

   ☐ Continued on Attachment 3.

4. A completed *Declaration Under Uniform Child Custody Jurisdiction and Enforcement Act (UCCJEA)* (form FL-105) is attached.

5. **Child custody and visitation.** I request the following orders:

	Petitioner	Respondent	Joint	Other
a. Legal custody of children to	☐	☐	☐	☐
b. Physical custody of children to	☐	☐	☐	☐
c. Visitation of children with	☐	☐		☐

   (1) The proposed schedule for visitation is as follows:

   ☐ See the attached form FL-311, *Child Custody and Visitation Attachment.*

Form Approved for Optional Use
Judicial Council of California
FL-270 [Rev. January 1, 2004]

RESPONSE TO PETITION FOR CUSTODY
AND SUPPORT OF MINOR CHILDREN

Family Code, §§ 3120, 3400, 3900
www.courtinfo.ca.gov

0089

5. d. ☐ I request that visitation be supervised with the following persons, with the following restrictions:

☐ Continued on Attachment 5d.

e. ☐ I request that the child abduction prevention orders requested on form FL-312 be approved.

f. ☐ I request that the proposed holiday schedule set out in ☐ form FL-341(C) ☐ other be approved.

g. ☐ I request that additional orders regarding child custody set out in ☐ form FL-341(D) ☐ other be approved.

h. ☐ I request that joint legal custody orders set out in ☐ form FL-341(E) ☐ other be approved.

6. **Fees and cost of litigation**

a. Attorney fees will be paid by ☐ petitioner ☐ respondent.

b. ☐ Each party will pay own fees.

7. **Child support.** The court may make orders for support of the children and issue an earnings assignment without further notice to either party. *A completed Income and Expense Declaration* (form FL-150) *or Financial Statement (Simplified)* (form FL-155) *is attached.*

8. Other *(specify):*

I declare under penalty of perjury under the laws of the State of California that the foregoing is true and correct.

Date:

_____ ▶ _____
(TYPE OR PRINT NAME)   (SIGNATURE OF RESPONDENT)

NOTICE: Any party required to pay child support must pay interest on overdue amounts at the "legal rate," which is currently 10 percent.

0090

ATTORNEY OR PARTY WITHOUT ATTORNEY OR GOVERNMENTAL AGENCY (under Family Code, §§ 17400, 17406) (Name, State Bar number, and address):	FOR COURT USE ONLY

TELEPHONE NO.:   FAX NO. (Optional):

E-MAIL ADDRESS (Optional):

ATTORNEY FOR (Name):

SUPERIOR COURT OF CALIFORNIA, COUNTY OF

STREET ADDRESS:

MAILING ADDRESS:

CITY AND ZIP CODE:

BRANCH NAME:

PETITIONER/PLAINTIFF:

RESPONDENT/DEFENDANT:

OTHER PARENT:

NOTICE OF MOTION TO SET ASIDE JUDGMENT OF PATERNITY	CASE NUMBER:

1. TO (name):   ☐ Petitioner   ☐ Respondent

☐ Local Child Support Agency   ☐ Other (specify):

2. A hearing on the motion for the relief requested will be held as follows:

a. Date: Time: ☐ Dept: ☐ Rm.:

b. Address of court ☐ same as noted above ☐ other (specify):

ORDER

3. ☐ Time for ☐ service ☐ hearing   is shortened. Service must be on or before (date):

4. Any responsive declaration must be served on or before (date):

Date:

_____
JUDICIAL OFFICER

5. I declare and request as follows (List the legal names of all children on the paternity judgment. Also list the date of birth, home address and county of residence for each child for whom relief is requested on Declaration in Support of Motion to Set Aside Judgment of Paternity (form FL-273):

Name of child	No relief required	Order genetic testing	Paternity Judgment entered	Date/County filed	Declaration of Paternity signed
a.	☐	☐	☐		☐ Yes ☐ No
b.	☐	☐	☐		☐ Yes ☐ No
c.	☐	☐	☐		☐ Yes ☐ No
d.	☐	☐	☐		☐ Yes ☐ No
e.	☐	☐	☐		☐ Yes ☐ No
f.	☐	☐	☐		☐ Yes ☐ No
g.	☐	☐	☐		☐ Yes ☐ No
h.	☐	☐	☐		☐ Yes ☐ No

i. ☐ Additional children are listed on a page attached to this notice.

Page 1 of 3

Form Adopted for Mandatory Use Judicial Council of California FL-272 [New January 1, 2006]	**NOTICE OF MOTION TO SET ASIDE JUDGMENT OF PATERNITY** (Family Law—Governmental)	Family Code, §§ 7646, 7575 www.courtinfo.ca.gov

FL-272

PETITIONER/PLAINTIFF:	CASE NUMBER:
RESPONDENT/DEFENDANT:	
OTHER PARENT:	

6. I request that the court find the previously established father is not the biological father of the children for whom genetic testing is requested.

7. I request that the court set aside any voluntary declaration of paternity or judgment of paternity, set aside all child support and unpaid arrearage orders concerning any children listed above for whom genetic testing is being requested, and enter a judgment of nonpaternity as to those children.

8. ☐ A local child support agency is providing services in this case (specify county, if known):

9. ☐ The judgment of paternity has been registered in the following states and counties (specify):

      State   County   Court Case Number

10. The marital presumption contained in Family Code section 7540 does not apply.

11. A *Declaration in Support of Motion to Set Aside Judgment of Paternity* (form FL-273) is attached for each child in this action.

12. ☐ I request that the court appoint a guardian ad litem for each child subject to this motion.

13. Other (specify):

14. Number of pages attached: _____

I declare under penalty of perjury under the laws of the State of California that the foregoing is true and correct.

Date:

_____
(TYPE OR PRINT NAME)

▶

_____
(SIGNATURE OF PERSON REQUESTING THESE ORDERS)

NOTICE FOR CASES INVOLVING A LOCAL CHILD SUPPORT AGENCY

This case may be referred to a court commissioner for hearing. By law, court commissioners do not have the authority to issue final orders and judgments in contested cases unless they are acting as temporary judges. The court commissioner in your case will act as a temporary judge unless, *before the hearing,* you or any other party objects to the commissioner acting as a temporary judge. The court commissioner may still hear your case to make findings and a recommended order. If you do not like the recommended order, you must object to it within 10 court days; otherwise, the recommended order will become a final order of the court. If you object to the recommended order, a judge will make a temporary order and set a new hearing.

NOTICE OF MOTION TO SET ASIDE JUDGMENT OF PATERNITY
(Family Law—Governmental)

PETITIONER/PLAINTIFF:	CASE NUMBER:
RESPONDENT/DEFENDANT:	
OTHER PARENT:	

PROOF OF SERVICE BY MAIL

1. I am at least 18 years of age, not a party to this case, and a resident of, or an employee in, the county where the mailing took place.

2. My residence or business address is *(specify):*

3. I served a copy of this *Notice of Motion to Set Aside Judgment of Paternity,* a copy of the *Declaration in Support of Motion to Set Aside Judgment of Paternity* (form FL-273), and a blank *Response to Notice of Motion to Set Aside Judgment of Paternity* (form FL-276) by enclosing them in a sealed envelope with first-class postage fully prepaid and depositing it in the United States mail as follows:

    a. Date of deposit: c. Place of deposit *(city and state):*

    b. Addressed as follows:

I declare under penalty of perjury under the laws of the State of California that the foregoing is true and correct.

Date:

_____ ▶ _____
(TYPE OR PRINT NAME)   (SIGNATURE OF DECLARANT)

NOTICE OF MOTION TO SET ASIDE JUDGMENT OF PATERNITY
(Family Law—Governmental)

0093

PETITIONER/PLAINTIFF:	CASE NUMBER:
RESPONDENT/DEFENDANT:	
OTHER PARENT:	

DECLARATION IN SUPPORT OF MOTION TO SET ASIDE JUDGMENT OF PATERNITY
(Attach a copy of this declaration for each child for whom relief is requested.)

1. The orders requested are for the following child. The legal name, home address, date of birth, and county of residence are *(specify if known, write "unknown" if unknown):*

   a. Child's name: d. Date of birth:

   b. Address:

   c. County of residence:

2. The name, mailing address, and county of residence, or, if deceased, the date and place of death, of the following persons are *(if unknown, write "unknown"):*

   a. **Previously Established Father**

   Name:
   Address:
   County of residence:
   ☐ Deceased   Date of death:
   Place of death:

   b. **Previously Established Mother**

   Name:
   Address:
   County of residence:
   ☐ Deceased   Date of death:
   Place of death:

   c. **Biological Father**   ☐ Same as above

   Name:
   Address:
   County of residence:
   ☐ Deceased   Date of death:
   Place of death:

   d. **Biological Mother**   ☐ Same as above

   Name:
   Address:
   County of residence:
   ☐ Deceased   Date of death:
   Place of death:

   e. **Guardian of the child**

   Name:
   Address:
   County of residence:
   ☐ Deceased   Date of death:
   Place of death:

   f. **Person with physical custody of the child**

   Name:
   Address:
   County of residence:
   ☐ Deceased   Date of death:
   Place of death:

   g. **Guardian Ad Litem of the child**

   Name:
   Address:
   County of residence:
   ☐ Deceased   Date of death:
   Place of death:

   h. **Other *(specify):***

   Name:
   Address:
   County of residence:
   ☐ Deceased   Date of death:
   Place of death:

3. In support of this request, I declare:

   a. I believe the previously established father is not the biological father of the child. The specific reasons for this belief are *(specify):*

   ☐ included in the attached page(s).

Form Adopted for Mandatory Use
Judicial Council of California
FL-273 [New January 1, 2006]

**DECLARATION IN SUPPORT OF MOTION
TO SET ASIDE JUDGMENT OF PATERNITY
(Family Law—Governmental)**

www.courtinfo.ca.gov

PETITIONER/PLAINTIFF:	CASE NUMBER:
RESPONDENT/DEFENDANT:	
OTHER PARENT:	

3. b. There ☐ is ☐ is not   another judgment of paternity in a different case for the same previously established father and child. The other court case is *(specify case number, state, and county of court):*

A copy of the other judgment ☐ is ☐ is not   attached. *(If not attached, explain why.)*

c. Other *(specify):*

COMPLETE THIS SECTION ONLY IF THERE IS A VOLUNTARY DECLARATION OF PATERNITY

4. ☐   The previously established father has signed a voluntary declaration of paternity for the child involved.

a. A copy of the voluntary declaration of paternity ☐ is ☐ is not   attached. *(If not attached, explain why not.)*

b. ☐ There ☐ is ☐ is not   an order for child support, custody, or visitation based on the voluntary declaration of paternity, initially filed on *(date):*   in *(specify state and county):*

A copy of the order ☐ is ☐ is not   attached. *(If not attached, explain why not.)*

c. The grounds for setting aside the voluntary declaration of paternity are *(check all boxes that apply):*

(1) ☐   No more than two years have passed since the date of birth of the child.

(2) ☐   No more than six months have passed since the date of the initial order for child support, custody, or visitation based on the voluntary declaration of paternity, and there is a mistake of fact or law, inadvertence, surprise, or excusable neglect regarding the signing of the voluntary declaration of paternity.

(3) ☐   No more than one year has passed since the date fraud or perjury regarding the signing of the voluntary declaration of paternity was discovered or should have been discovered.

(4) ☐   Other *(specify):*

I declare under penalty of perjury under the laws of the State of California that the foregoing is true and correct.

Date:

_____
(TYPE OR PRINT NAME)

▶

_____
(SIGNATURE OF PERSON REQUESTING THESE ORDERS)

**DECLARATION IN SUPPORT OF MOTION
TO SET ASIDE JUDGMENT OF PATERNITY
(Family Law—Governmental)**

INFORMATION SHEET FOR COMPLETING
NOTICE OF MOTION TO SET ASIDE JUDGMENT OF PATERNITY (FORMS FL-272 AND FL-273)

NOTICE
YOU MUST CONTINUE PAYING SUPPORT WHILE THIS ACTION IS PENDING.

Use forms FL-272, *Notice of Motion to Set Aside Judgment of Paternity,* and FL-273, *Declaration in Support of Motion to Set Aside Judgment of Paternity,* to set aside (vacate) an existing paternity judgment. If there is also a corresponding voluntary declaration of paternity, this motion may also be used to set aside the voluntary declaration of paternity. The voluntary declaration of paternity and/or judgment of paternity may be set aside only if the previously established father is determined by genetic testing not to be the biological father of the child. (Even if the motion can be brought as described below, there may be other grounds to set aside the paternity judgment or other related relief may be available. You may wish to consult with an attorney or the family law facilitator.) In addition to this motion, you may file a separate motion to modify child support and set arrears. For information on changing the support order, see the *Information Sheet on Changing a Child Support Order* on pages 3-5 of form FL-192.

The following persons may bring this motion:

A previously established mother;

A previously established father;

A child;

A legal representative of any of the above persons; or

A Local Child Support Agency (LCSA).

This motion must be brought within the following time frames:

(1) Within a two-year period commencing with the date:

   (a) on which the previously established father knew or should have known of a judgment that established him as the father of the child (for example, the date a wage garnishment was served), or

   (b) on which the previously established father knew or should have known of the existence of an action to adjudicate the issue of paternity (for example, the date of service of a summons),

   whichever is first, except as provided in paragraph (2) or (3) below.

(2) Within a two-year period commencing with the date of the child's birth if paternity was established by a voluntary declaration of paternity.

(3) In the case of any previously established father who is the legal father as a result of a default judgment as of January 1, 2005, within a two-year period after the enactment of Assembly Bill 252.

This motion *may not* be brought if any of the following conditions apply:

The paternity judgment resulted from a marital dissolution, legal separation, or nullity action.

The marital presumption contained in Family Code section 7540 applies.

There is a voluntary declaration of paternity, and there is no basis to set aside the voluntary declaration of paternity.

There is another California judgment of paternity in a different case for the same previously established father and child, unless both paternity judgments qualify for this motion and you filed a motion in each case.

The paternity judgment was not issued in California.

The paternity judgment is based on genetic tests that were conducted before the judgment and that indicated the previously established father is the biological father of the child.

The judgment is based on an adoption.

The child was conceived by artificial insemination, and the judgment is based on Family Code section 7613.

The child was conceived under a surrogacy agreement.

Page 1 of 2

INFORMATION SHEET FOR COMPLETING NOTICE OF MOTION
TO SET ASIDE JUDGMENT OF PATERNITY
(Family Law—Governmental)

Family Code, §§ 7646,7575
www.courtinfo.ca.gov

The completed motion and a blank *Response to Notice of Motion to Set Aside Judgment of Paternity* (form FL-276) must be served on the following, if applicable:

A previously established mother;

A previously established father;

The child's guardian ad litem, if any; and

The Local Child Support Agency (LCSA) if it is providing services.

GENETIC TESTING

In most cases, genetic tests will be required. If the LCSA is providing services, the LCSA will pay for and coordinate the genetic testing.

If you receive an administrative order for genetic testing from the LCSA, you may file a motion with the court seeking relief from the LCSA genetic testing order. However, the court may order participation in genetic testing.

If any person refuses to submit to genetic testing after receipt of the LCSA order for genetic testing, or fails to seek relief from the court before the scheduled test date or within 10 days after the scheduled test date, the court may resolve the question of paternity against that person or enforce the LCSA order if the rights of others or the interest of justice so require.

The moving party is not required to present evidence of a paternity test indicating that the previously established father is not the biological father of the child in order to bring this motion.

ADDITIONAL INFORMATION

An adult child may be included when completing forms FL-272 and FL-273.

A guardian ad litem may be appointed by the court to represent the best interest of the child.

If the previously established father is found not to be the biological father of the child, the court may still deny this motion if it determines it is in the best interest of the child to do so.

If the court grants this motion to set aside the paternity judgment, the previously established father has no right of reimbursement of any support paid before the granting of the motion.

To obtain information about or a copy of a declaration of paternity in your case, contact:

California Department of Child Support Services—POP Unit, at:

P.O. Box 419064

Rancho Cordova, CA 95741-9064

Telephone (toll-free): 866-249-0773

Your Local Child Support Agency (LCSA)

A family law facilitator

If you need additional assistance with these forms, contact an attorney or the court's family law facilitator.

INFORMATION SHEET FOR COMPLETING NOTICE OF MOTION TO SET ASIDE JUDGMENT OF PATERNITY (Family Law—Governmental)

0097

ATTORNEY OR PARTY WITHOUT ATTORNEY OR GOVERNMENTAL AGENCY *(under Family Code, §§ 17400, 17406)* *(Name, State Bar number, and address):*	FOR COURT USE ONLY
TELEPHONE NO.: FAX NO. *(Optional):*	
E-MAIL ADDRESS *(Optional):*	
ATTORNEY FOR *(Name):*	

SUPERIOR COURT OF CALIFORNIA, COUNTY OF

STREET ADDRESS:

MAILING ADDRESS:

CITY AND ZIP CODE:

BRANCH NAME:

PETITIONER/PLAINTIFF:

RESPONDENT/DEFENDANT:

OTHER PARENT:

**RESPONSE TO NOTICE OF MOTION
TO SET ASIDE JUDGMENT OF PATERNITY**

HEARING DATE:	TIME:	DEPT., ROOM, OR DIVISION:	CASE NUMBER:

1. My position on the facts regarding paternity as alleged in the motion to set aside the judgment and voluntary declaration of paternity, if a declaration was filed regarding the following children, is:

<u>Name of child</u>   <u>Date of birth</u>

   a. ☐ Agree ☐ Disagree
   b. ☐ Agree ☐ Disagree
   c. ☐ Agree ☐ Disagree
   d. ☐ Agree ☐ Disagree
   e. ☐ Agree ☐ Disagree
   f. ☐ Agree ☐ Disagree
   g. ☐ Agree ☐ Disagree
   h. ☐ Agree ☐ Disagree
   i. ☐ Additional children are listed on a page attached to this response.

2. My position on genetic testing of each of the following children is:

<u>Name of child</u>   <u>Date of birth</u>

   a. ☐ Agree ☐ Disagree
   b. ☐ Agree ☐ Disagree
   c. ☐ Agree ☐ Disagree
   d. ☐ Agree ☐ Disagree
   e. ☐ Agree ☐ Disagree
   f. ☐ Agree ☐ Disagree
   g. ☐ Agree ☐ Disagree
   h. ☐ Agree ☐ Disagree
   i. ☐ Additional children are listed on a page attached to this response.

3. I ☐ agree ☐ disagree with the request to appoint a guardian ad litem for each of the children subject to this request.

4. ☐ The motion is not complete because *(specify):*

5. ☐ The motion is not timely because *(specify):*

6. ☐ The motion is not proper because *(specify):*

Form Adopted for Mandatory Use
Judicial Council of California
FL-276 [New January 1, 2006]

**RESPONSE TO NOTICE OF MOTION
TO SET ASIDE JUDGMENT OF PATERNITY
(Family Law—Governmental)**

Family Code, §§ 7646, 7575
www.courtinfo.ca.gov

FL-276

PETITIONER/PLAINTIFF:	CASE NUMBER:
RESPONDENT/DEFENDANT:	
OTHER PARENT:	

7. ☐ The facts in support of this response are:

a. ☐ The paternity judgment resulted from a marital dissolution, legal separation, or nullity action.

b. ☐ The marriage presumption contained in Family Code section 7540 applies.

c. ☐ The paternity judgment was not issued in California.

d. ☐ There is another California judgment of paternity in a different case for the same previously established father and child.

e. ☐ There is a voluntary declaration of paternity, and there is no basis to set it aside.

f. ☐ Genetic tests were conducted before the judgment that indicated the previously established father is the biological father of the child.

g. ☐ The paternity judgment is based on an adoption.

h. ☐ The child was conceived by artificial insemination, and the paternity judgment is based on Family Code section 7613.

i. ☐ The child was conceived under a surrogacy agreement.

j. ☐ The motion is not in the best interest of the child because *(specify):*

k. ☐ Other *(specify):*

☐ Contained in the attached declaration.

8. Number of pages attached: _____

I declare under the penalty of perjury under the laws of the State of California that the foregoing is true and correct.

Date:

▶

_____
(TYPE OR PRINT NAME)

_____
(SIGNATURE OF DECLARANT)

**RESPONSE TO NOTICE OF MOTION
TO SET ASIDE JUDGMENT OF PATERNITY
(Family Law—Governmental)**

FL-276

	CASE NUMBER:
PETITIONER/PLAINTIFF:	
RESPONDENT/DEFENDANT:	
OTHER PARENT:	

PROOF OF SERVICE BY MAIL

1. I am at least 18 years of age, not a party to this case, and a resident of, or an employee in, the county where the mailing took place.

2. My residence or business address is *(specify):*

3. I served a copy of this response by enclosing it in a sealed envelope with first-class postage fully prepaid and depositing it in the United States mail as follows:

   a. Date of deposit:

   b. Addressed as follows:

   c. Place of deposit *(city and state):*

I declare under penalty of perjury under the laws of the State of California that the foregoing is true and correct.

Date:

_____
(TYPE OR PRINT NAME)

▶

_____
(SIGNATURE OF DECLARANT)

**RESPONSE TO NOTICE OF MOTION
TO SET ASIDE JUDGMENT OF PATERNITY
(Family Law—Governmental)**

0100

ATTORNEY OR PARTY WITHOUT ATTORNEY OR GOVERNMENTAL AGENCY *(under Family Code, §§ 17400 and 17406)* *(Name, State Bar number, and address):*	FOR COURT USE ONLY

TELEPHONE NO.:   FAX NO. *(Optional)*:

E-MAIL ADDRESS *(Optional)*:

ATTORNEY FOR *(Name)*:

SUPERIOR COURT OF CALIFORNIA, COUNTY OF

STREET ADDRESS:

MAILING ADDRESS:

CITY AND ZIP CODE:

BRANCH NAME:

PETITIONER/PLAINTIFF:

RESPONDENT/DEFENDANT:

OTHER PARENT:

ORDER AFTER HEARING ON MOTION TO SET ASIDE JUDGMENT OF PATERNITY	CASE NUMBER:

1. This matter proceeded as follows: ☐ Uncontested ☐ By stipulation ☐ Contested

    a. Date: Dept.:   Judicial officer:

    b. ☐ Petitioner/plaintiff present   ☐ Attorney present *(name)*:

    c. ☐ Respondent/defendant present   ☐ Attorney present *(name)*:

    d. ☐ Other parent present   ☐ Attorney present *(name)*:

    e. ☐ Children present *(name)*:   ☐ Attorney present *(name)*:

    f. ☐ Guardian ad litem present *(name)*:

    g. ☐ Attorney for local child support agency *(name)*:

    h. ☐ Other *(specify)*:

2. For purposes of this order

    a. the previously established father is *(name)*:

    b. the previously established mother is *(name)*:

THE COURT FINDS

3. The following facts exist regarding the previously established father and the children listed below:

Name of child	Date of birth	Biological Father	Paternity Judgment	Signed Voluntary Declaration of Paternity
a.		☐ Yes ☐ No	☐ Yes ☐ No	☐ Yes ☐ No
b.		☐ Yes ☐ No	☐ Yes ☐ No	☐ Yes ☐ No
c.		☐ Yes ☐ No	☐ Yes ☐ No	☐ Yes ☐ No
d.		☐ Yes ☐ No	☐ Yes ☐ No	☐ Yes ☐ No
e.		☐ Yes ☐ No	☐ Yes ☐ No	☐ Yes ☐ No
f.		☐ Yes ☐ No	☐ Yes ☐ No	☐ Yes ☐ No
g.		☐ Yes ☐ No	☐ Yes ☐ No	☐ Yes ☐ No
h.		☐ Yes ☐ No	☐ Yes ☐ No	☐ Yes ☐ No

    i. ☐ Additional children are listed on a page attached to this order.

Form Adopted for Mandatory Use Judicial Council of California FL-278 [New January 1, 2006]	**ORDER AFTER HEARING ON MOTION** **TO SET ASIDE JUDGMENT OF PATERNITY** **(Family Law—Governmental)**	Family Code, §§ 7646, 7575 *www.courtinfo.gov*

FL-278

PETITIONER/PLAINTIFF:	CASE NUMBER:
RESPONDENT/DEFENDANT:	
OTHER PARENT:	

4. Other *(specify):*

THE COURT ORDERS

5. All orders previously made in this action will remain in full force and effect except as specifically modified below.

Name of child	Date of birth	Judgment of Paternity Set Aside		Voluntary Declaration of Paternity Set Aside		
a.		☐ Yes ☐ No		☐ Yes ☐ No		☐ N/A
b.		☐ Yes ☐ No		☐ Yes ☐ No		☐ N/A
c.		☐ Yes ☐ No		☐ Yes ☐ No		☐ N/A
d.		☐ Yes ☐ No		☐ Yes ☐ No		☐ N/A
e.		☐ Yes ☐ No		☐ Yes ☐ No		☐ N/A
f.		☐ Yes ☐ No		☐ Yes ☐ No		☐ N/A
g.		☐ Yes ☐ No		☐ Yes ☐ No		☐ N/A
h.		☐ Yes ☐ No		☐ Yes ☐ No		☐ N/A

i. ☐ Additional children are listed on a page attached to this order.

All child support and arrearage orders concerning each child for whom a previous judgment of paternity has been set aside are vacated. The previously established father has no right to reimbursement for any child support paid before the set-aside of the judgment of paternity or voluntary declaration of paternity.

j. ☐ A judgment of nonpaternity is granted with respect to the following children *(specify):*

k. ☐ The motion is denied, based upon the best interest of the child, with regard to the following children *(specify):*

6. For the children named in item 5k, the court denies the motion to set aside because of *(check all that apply):*

a. ☐ The age of the child *(specify):*

b. ☐ The length of time since the entry of the judgment establishing paternity *(specify time period):*

c. ☐ The nature, duration, and quality of the relationship between the previously established father and the child, including the duration and frequency of any time periods during which the child and the previously established father resided in the same household or enjoyed a parent-child relationship *(specify):*

d. ☐ The fact that the previously established father has requested that the parent-child relationship continue.

e. ☐ The fact that the biological father of the child does not oppose preservation of the relationship between the previously established father and the child.

f. ☐ The fact that there would be a detriment to the child if biological parentage was established *(explain):*

**ORDER AFTER HEARING ON MOTION
TO SET ASIDE JUDGMENT OF PATERNITY
(Family Law—Governmental)**

0102

FL-278

PETITIONER/PLAINTIFF:	CASE NUMBER:
RESPONDENT/DEFENDANT:	
OTHER PARENT:	

7. g. ☐ The fact that the previously established father has hindered the ability to discover the identity of, or get support from, the biological father *(specify):*

   h. ☐ Other factors concerning the best interest of the child *(specify):*

8. ☐ If this order vacates or sets aside a voluntary declaration of paternity, the court clerk must send a copy of this order to the California Department of Child Support Services at *(specify address):*

9. ☐ The court further orders *(specify):*

Date:

_____
JUDICIAL OFFICER

Number of pages attached: _____

☐ SIGNATURE FOLLOWS LAST ATTACHMENT

Approved as conforming to court order:
Date:
▶
SIGNATURE OF ATTORNEY FOR *(specify):*
☐ PETITIONER/PLAINTIFF ☐ RESPONDENT/DEFENDANT ☐ OTHER
Approved as conforming to court order:
Date:
▶
SIGNATURE OF ATTORNEY FOR *(specify):*
☐ PETITIONER/PLAINTIFF ☐ RESPONDENT/DEFENDANT ☐ OTHER
Approved as conforming to court order:
Date:
▶
SIGNATURE OF ATTORNEY FOR *(specify):*
☐ PETITIONER/PLAINTIFF ☐ RESPONDENT/DEFENDANT ☐ OTHER
Approved as conforming to court order:
Date:
▶
SIGNATURE OF ATTORNEY FOR *(specify):*
☐ PETITIONER/PLAINTIFF ☐ RESPONDENT/DEFENDANT ☐ OTHER

FL-278 [New January 1, 2006]

**ORDER AFTER HEARING ON MOTION
TO SET ASIDE JUDGMENT OF PATERNITY
(Family Law—Governmental)**

Page 3 of 3

0103

PARTY WITHOUT ATTORNEY OR ATTORNEY	STATE BAR NUMBER:	FOR COURT USE ONLY
NAME:		
FIRM NAME:		
STREET ADDRESS:		
CITY: STATE: ZIP CODE:		
TELEPHONE NO.: FAX NO.:		
E-MAIL ADDRESS:		
ATTORNEY FOR (name):		

SUPERIOR COURT OF CALIFORNIA, COUNTY OF
STREET ADDRESS:
MAILING ADDRESS:
CITY AND ZIP CODE:
BRANCH NAME:

PETITIONER:
RESPONDENT:
OTHER PARENT/PARTY:

REQUEST FOR ORDER ☐ **CHANGE** ☐ **TEMPORARY EMERGENCY ORDERS**	CASE NUMBER:
☐ Child Custody ☐ Visitation (Parenting Time) ☐ Spousal or Partner Support ☐ Child Support ☐ Domestic Violence Order ☐ Attorney's Fees and Costs ☐ Property Control ☐ Other (specify):	

NOTICE OF HEARING

1. TO (name(s)): _____
   ☐ Petitioner ☐ Respondent ☐ Other Parent/Party ☐ Other (specify):

2. **A COURT HEARING WILL BE HELD AS FOLLOWS:**

   a. Date: Time: ☐ Dept.: ☐ Room.:
   b. Address of court ☐ same as noted above ☐ other (specify):

3. **WARNING to the person served with the Request for Order:** The court may make the requested orders without you if you do not file a Responsive Declaration to Request for Order (form FL-320), serve a copy on the other parties at least nine court days before the hearing (unless the court has ordered a shorter period of time), and appear at the hearing. (See form FL-320-INFO for more information.)

   (Forms FL-300-INFO and DV-400-INFO provide information about completing this form.)

COURT ORDER

It is ordered that: (FOR COURT USE ONLY)

4. ☐ Time ☐ for service ☐ until the hearing is shortened. Service must be on or before (date):

5. ☐ A Responsive Declaration to Request for Order (form FL-320) must be served on or before (date):

6. ☐ The parties must attend an appointment for child custody mediation or child custody recommending counseling as follows (specify date, time, and location):

7. ☐ The orders in Temporary Emergency (Ex Parte) Orders (form FL-305) apply to this proceeding and must be personally served with all documents filed with this Request for Order.

8. ☐ Other (specify):

Date: _____

_____
JUDICIAL OFFICER

Page 1 of 4

Form Adopted for Mandatory Use
Judicial Council of California
FL-300 [Rev. July 1, 2016]

REQUEST FOR ORDER

Family Code, §§ 2045, 2107, 6224,
6226, 6320–6326, 6380–6383;
Government Code, § 26826
Cal. Rules of Court, rule 5.92
www.courts.ca.gov

PETITIONER:	CASE NUMBER:
RESPONDENT:	
OTHER PARENT/PARTY:	

REQUEST FOR ORDER

Note: Place a mark ⊠ in front of the box that applies to your case or to your request. If you need more space, mark the box for "Attachment." For example, mark "Attachment 2a" to indicate that the list of children's names and birth dates continues on a paper attached to this form. Then, on a sheet of paper, list each attachment number followed by your request. At the top of the paper, write your name, case number, and "FL-300" as a title. (You may use *Attached Declaration* (form MC-031) for this purpose.)

1. ☐ **RESTRAINING ORDER INFORMATION**
   One or more domestic violence restraining/protective orders are now in effect between *(specify)*:
   ☐ Petitioner ☐ Respondent ☐ Other Parent/Party *(Attach a copy of the orders if you have one.)*
   The orders are from the following court or courts *(specify county and state)*:
   a. ☐ Criminal: County/state *(specify)*:   Case No. *(if known)*:
   b. ☐ Family: County/state *(specify)*:   Case No. *(if known)*:
   c. ☐ Juvenile: County/state *(specify)*:   Case No. *(if known)*:
   d. ☐ Other: County/state *(specify)*:   Case No. *(if known)*:

2. ☐ **CHILD CUSTODY**   ☐ I request temporary emergency orders
   ☐ **VISITATION (PARENTING TIME)**
   a. I request that the court make orders about the following children *(specify)*:

Child's Name	Date of Birth	☐ Legal Custody to *(person who decides: health, education, etc)*:	☐ Physical Custody to *(person with whom child lives)*:

   ☐ Attachment 2a.

   b. ☐ The orders I request for ☐ child custody ☐ visitation (parenting time) are:
       (1) ☐ Specified in the attached forms:
            ☐ Form FL-305   ☐ Form FL-311   ☐ Form FL-312   ☐ Form FL-341(C)
            ☐ Form FL-341(D)   ☐ Form FL-341(E)   ☐ Other *(specify)*:
       (2) ☐ As follows *(specify)*:   ☐ Attachment 2b.

   c. The orders that I request are in the best interest of the children because *(specify)*:   ☐ Attachment 2c.

   d. ☐ This is a change from the current order for ☐ child custody ☐ visitation (parenting time).
       (1) ☐ The order for legal or physical custody was filed on *(date)*:   . The court ordered *(specify)*:

       (2) ☐ The visitation (parenting time) order was filed on *(date)*:   . The court ordered *(specify)*:

   ☐ Attachment 2d.

0105

PETITIONER: RESPONDENT: OTHER PARENT/PARTY:	CASE NUMBER:

3. ☐ CHILD SUPPORT

(Note: An earnings assignment may be issued. See *Income Withholding for Support* (form FL-195)

    a. I request that the court order child support as follows:

        Child's name and age   ☐ I request support for each child   Monthly amount ($) requested
                                      based on the child support guideline. (if not by guideline)

                                                                             ☐ Attachment 3a.

    b. ☐ I want to change a current court order for child support filed on *(date):*
        The court ordered child support as follows *(specify):*

    c. I have completed and filed with this *Request for Order* a current *Income and Expense Declaration* (form FL-150) or I filed
       a current *Financial Statement (Simplified)* (form FL-155) because I meet the requirements to file form FL-155.

    d. The court should make or change the support orders because *(specify):*   ☐ Attachment 3d.

4. ☐ SPOUSAL OR DOMESTIC PARTNER SUPPORT

(Note: An *Earnings Assignment Order For Spousal or Partner Support* (form FL-435) may be issued.)

    a. ☐ Amount requested *(monthly):* $

    b. ☐ I want the court to ☐ change ☐ end the current support order filed on *(date):*
        The court ordered $ per month for support.

    c. ☐ This request is to modify (change) spousal or partner support after entry of a judgment.
        I have completed and attached *Spousal or Partner Support Declaration Attachment* (form FL-157) or a declaration
        that addresses the same factors covered in form FL-157.

    d. I have completed and filed a current *Income and Expense Declaration* (form FL-150) in support of my request.

    e. The court should should make, change, or end the support orders because *(specify):*   ☐ Attachment 4e.

5. ☐ PROPERTY CONTROL   ☐ I request temporary emergency orders

    a. The ☐ petitioner ☐ respondent ☐ other parent/party be given exclusive temporary use, possession, and
        control of the following property that we ☐ own or are buying ☐ lease or rent *(specify):*

    b. The ☐ petitioner ☐ respondent ☐ other parent/party be ordered to make the following payments on debts
        and liens coming due while the order is in effect:

        Pay to: _____ For: _____ Amount: $ _____ Due date: _____

        Pay to: _____ For: _____ Amount: $ _____ Due date: _____

        Pay to: _____ For: _____ Amount: $ _____ Due date: _____

        Pay to: _____ For: _____ Amount: $ _____ Due date: _____

    c. ☐ This is a change from the current order for property control filed on *(date):*

    d. Specify in Attachment 5d the reasons why the court should make or change the property control orders.

PETITIONER: RESPONDENT: OTHER PARENT/PARTY:	CASE NUMBER:

6. [ ] ATTORNEY'S FEES AND COSTS

I request attorney's fees and costs, which total *(specify amount):* $. I filed the following to support my request:

    a. A current *Income and Expense Declaration* (form FL-150).

    b. A *Request for Attorney's Fees and Costs Attachment* (form FL-319) or a declaration that addresses the factors covered in that form.

    c. A *Supporting Declaration for Attorney's Fees and Costs Attachment* (form FL-158) or a declaration that addresses the factors covered in that form.

7. [ ] DOMESTIC VIOLENCE ORDER

> • Do not use this form to ask for domestic violence restraining orders! Read form DV-505-INFO, *How Do I Ask for a Temporary Restraining Order,* for forms and information you need to ask for domestic violence restraining orders.
>
> • Read form DV-400-INFO, *How to Change or End a Domestic Violence Restraining Order* for more information.

    a. The *Restraining Order After Hearing* (form DV-130) was filed on *(date):*

    b. I request that the court [ ] change [ ] end the personal conduct, stay-away, move-out orders, or other protective orders made in *Restraining Order After Hearing* (form DV-130). *(If you want to change the orders, complete 7c.)*

    c. [ ] I request that the court make the following changes to the restraining orders *(specify):*   [ ] Attachment 7c.

    d. I want the court to change or end the orders because *(specify):*   [ ] Attachment 7d.

8. [ ] OTHER ORDERS REQUESTED *(specify):*   [ ] Attachment 8.

9. [ ] TIME FOR SERVICE / TIME UNTIL HEARING   I urgently need:

    a. [ ] To serve the *Request for Order* no less than *(number):*   court days before the hearing.

    b. [ ] The hearing date and service of the the *Request for Order* to be sooner.

    c. I need the order because *(specify):*   [ ] Attachment 9c.

10. [ ] FACTS TO SUPPORT the orders I request are listed below. The facts that I write in support and attach to this request cannot be longer than 10 pages, unless the court gives me permission.   [ ] Attachment 10.

I declare under penalty of perjury under the laws of the State of California that the information provided in this form and all attachments is true and correct.

Date:

_____
(TYPE OR PRINT NAME)

▶ _____
(SIGNATURE OF APPLICANT)

Requests for Accommodations

Assistive listening systems, computer-assisted real-time captioning, or sign language interpreter services are available if you ask at least five days before the proceeding. Contact the clerk's office or go to *www.courts.ca.gov/forms* for *Request for Accommodations by Persons With Disabilities and Response* (form MC-410). (Civ. Code, § 54.8.)

FL-300-INFO Information Sheet for Request for Order

(1) USE *Request for Order* (form FL-300):
- To schedule a court hearing and ask the court to make new orders or to change orders in your case. The request can be about child custody, visitation (parenting time), child support, spousal or partner support, property, finances, attorney's fees and costs, or other matters.
- To change or end the domestic violence restraining orders granted by the court in *Restraining Order After Hearing* (form DV-130). See *How Do I Ask to Change or End a Domestic Violence Restraining Order* (form DV-400-INFO) for more information.

(2) DO NOT USE *Request for Order* (form FL-300):
- Before you have filed a Petition to start your case (form FL-300 may be filed with the Petition).
- If you and the other party have an agreement. For information about how to write up your agreement, get it approved by the court, and filed in your case, see http://www.courts.ca.gov/selfhelp-agreeFL, speak with an attorney, or get help at your court's Self-Help Center or Family Law Facilitator's Office.
- When specific Judicial Council forms must be used to ask the court for orders. For example, to ask:
  –For a domestic violence restraining order, use forms DV-100, DV-109, and DV-110.
  –For an order for contempt, use form FL-410.
  –To set aside a child support order, use form FL-360 or form FL-640.
  –To set aside a voluntary declaration of paternity, use form FL-280.

(3) Forms checklist

a. Form FL-300, *Request for Order,* is the basic form you need to file with the court. Depending on your request, you may need these additional forms:

b. To request child custody or visitation (parenting time) orders, you may need to complete some of these forms:
- ☐ FL-105, *Declaration Under Uniform Child Custody Jurisdiction and Enforcement Act*
- ☐ FL-311, *Child Custody and Visitation (Parenting Time) Application Attachment*
- ☐ FL-312, *Request for Child Abduction Prevention Orders*
- ☐ FL-341(C), *Children's Holiday Schedule Attachment*
- ☐ FL-341(D), *Additional Provisions—Physical Custody Attachment*
- ☐ FL-341(E), *Joint Legal Custody Attachment*

c. If you want child support, you need this form:
- ☐ A current FL-150, *Income and Expense Declaration.* You may use form FL-155, *Financial Statement (Simplified)* instead of form FL-150 if you meet the requirements listed on page 2 of form FL-155.

d. If you want spousal or partner support or orders about your finances, you need:
- ☐ A current FL-150, *Income and Expense Declaration*
- ☐ FL-157, *Spousal or Partner Support Declaration Attachment* (if the request is to change a support judgment)

e. If you want attorney's fees and costs, you need these forms:
- ☐ A current FL-150, *Income and Expense Declaration*
- ☐ FL-319, *Request for Attorney's Fees and Costs Attachment* (or provide the information in a declaration)
- ☐ FL-158, *Supporting Declaration for Attorney's Fees and Costs* (or provide the information in a declaration)

f. To request temporary emergency (ex parte) orders, you need:
- ☐ FL-305, *Temporary Emergency Orders* to serve as the proposed temporary emergency orders.
- ☐ Your declaration describing how and when you gave notice about the request for temporary emergency orders. You may use form FL-303, *Declaration Regarding Notice and Service of Request for Temporary Emergency (Ex Parte) Orders.*
- ☐ Other forms required by local courts. See item 9 on page 3 of this form for more information.

g. If you plan to have witnesses testify at the hearing, you need form:
- ☐ FL-321, *Witness List*

h. If you want to request a separate trial (bifurcation) on an issue, you need form:
- ☐ FL-315, *Request or Response to Request for Separate Trial*

Form Approved for Optional Use
Judicial Council of California
www.courts.ca.gov
Revised July 1, 2016

Information Sheet for Request for Order
(Family Law)

FL-300-INFO, Page 1 of 4
→

FL-300-INFO Information Sheet for Request for Order

4 Complete form FL-300 (Page 1)

Caption: Complete the top portion with your name, address, and telephone number, and the court address. Next, write the name of the Petitioner, Respondent, or Other Parent/Party (You must use the party names as they appear in the petition that was originally filed with the court). Then, write the case number.

In the next section, check "CHANGE" if you want to change an existing order. Check "TEMPORARY EMERGENCY (EX PARTE) ORDER" if you are asking that the court make emergency orders that will be effective until the hearing date. Then, check all the boxes that apply to the orders you are requesting.

Item 1: List the name(s) of the other person(s) in your case who will receive your request. In some cases, this might include a grandparent who is joined as a party in the case, a local child support agency, or a lawyer who represents a child in the case.

Item 2: Leave this blank. The court clerk will fill in the date, time, and location of the hearing.

Item 3: This is a notice to all other parties.

Items 4–5: Leave these blank. The court will complete them if the orders are granted.

Item 6: In some counties, the court clerk will check item 6 and provide the details for your required child custody mediation or recommending counseling appointment. Other courts require the party or the party's lawyer to make the appointment and then complete item 6 before filing form FL-300.

Ask your court's Family Law Facilitator or Self-Help Center to find out what your court requires.

Items 7–8: Leave these blank. The court will complete them, if needed.

5 Complete form FL-300 (pages 2–4)

6 Complete additional forms and make copies

Complete any additional forms that you need to file with the *Request for Order*. Make at least two copies of your full packet.

Note: You may file one form FL-150 to respond to items 3, 4, and 6.

7 File your documents

Give your paperwork and the copies you made to the court clerk to process. You may take them to the clerk's office in person, mail them, or, in some counties, you can e-file them.

The clerk will keep the original and give you back the copies you made with a court date and time stamped on the first page of the *Request for Order*. The procedure may be different in some courts if you are requesting temporary emergency orders.

8 Pay filing fees

A fee is due at the time of filing.

If you cannot afford to pay the filing fee, and you do not already have a valid fee waiver order in this case, you can ask the court to waive the fee by completing and filing form FW-001, *Request to Waive Court Fees* and form FW-003, *Order on Court Fee Waiver*.

FL-300-INFO — Information Sheet for Request for Order

(9) **Temporary Emergency (Ex Parte) Orders**
(nondomestic violence restraining orders)

Courts can make temporary orders in your family law case to respond to emergencies that cannot wait to be heard on the court's regular hearing calendar.

The emergency must involve an immediate danger or irreparable harm to a party or children in the case, or an immediate loss or damage to property.

To request these orders:

- Complete form FL-300. Describe the emergency and explain why you need the temporary emergency orders before the hearing.
- Complete form FL-305 to serve as your proposed temporary orders.
- Include a declaration describing how and when you notified the other parties (or why you could not give notice) about your request and the hearing (see form FL-303).
- Complete other forms if required by your local court rules.
- Follow your court's local procedures for reserving the day for the hearing, submitting your paperwork, and paying filing fees.

(10) **General information about "service"**

"Service" is the act of giving your legal papers to all persons named as parties in the case so that they know what orders you are asking for and have information about the hearing.

If the other parties are NOT properly served, the judge cannot make the orders you requested on the date of the hearing.

(11) **Serve the Request for Order and blank forms**

The other party must be "served" with a:

- Copy of the *Request for Order* and all the other forms and attachments filed with the court clerk.
- Copy of any temporary emergency orders granted.
- Blank form FL-320, *Responsive Declaration to Request for Order.*
- Blank form FL-150, *Income and Expense Declaration* (if you served form FL-150 or FL-155).

(12) **Who can be a "server"**

You cannot serve the papers. Have someone else (who is at least 18 years old) do it. The "server" can be a friend, a relative who is not involved in your case, a sheriff, or a professional process server.

(13) **"Personal Service"**

Personal service means that your "server" walks up to each person to be served, makes sure he or she is the right person, and then hand-delivers a copy of all the papers (and the blank forms) to him or her. The server may leave the papers near the person if he or she will not take them.

Note: Sometimes the papers may be personally served on the other party's lawyer (if he or she has one) in the family law case.

(14) **"Service by mail"**

means that your "server" places copies of all the documents (and blank forms) in a sealed envelope and mails them to the address of each party being served (or to the party's lawyer, if he or she has one).

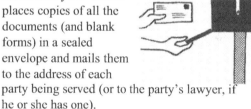

The server must be 18 years of age or over and live or work in the county where the mailing took place.

> ***Important!*** For questions about personal service or service by mail, talk with a lawyer or check with your court's Family Law Facilitator or Self-Help Center at *http://www.courts.ca.gov/1083.htm*.

FL-300-INFO Information Sheet for Request for Order

(15) When to use personal service or service by mail

Personal Service

Personal service is the best way to make sure the other adults in your case are correctly served. Sometimes you **must** use personal service.

You **must** use personal service when the court:

☑ Ordered personal service;

☑ Granted temporary emergency orders;

☑ Does not yet have the power to make orders that apply to the other party because he or she has either NOT previously:
- Been served with a *Summons* and *Petition;* *

  OR
- Appeared in the case by filing a:
  a. *Response* to a *Petition;*
  b. *Appearance, Stipulations, and Waivers;*
  c. Written notice of appearance;
  d. Request to strike all or part of the *Petition;* or
  e. Request to transfer the case.

  *Note: A *Request for Order* may be served at the same time as the family law *Summons* and *Petition.*

1. After serving, the server must fill out a *Proof of Personal Service* (form FL-330) and give it to you. If the server needs instructions, give him or her form FL-330-INFO, *Information Sheet for Proof of Personal Service.*
2. Take the completed *Proof of Personal Service* form to the clerk's office (or e-file it, if available in your court) at least 5 court days before your hearing.

Deadline: The deadline for personal service is **16 court days** before the hearing date, unless the court orders a different deadline.

Service by Mail

If you are not required to use personal service, you may use service by mail.

Important! Check with your court's Family Law Facilitator's Office or Self-Help Center, or ask a lawyer to be sure you are allowed to use service by mail in your case.

A *Request for Order* to change a judgment or final order on the issue of child custody, visitation (parenting time), or child support may be served by mail if:

☑ The documents do not include temporary emergency orders;

☑ The court did not order personal service; and

☑ You have verified the other party's current residence or office address. (You may use *Address Verification* (form FL-334).)

To change a judgment or final order on any other issue, including spousal or domestic partner support, the *Request for Order* may need to be personally served on the other party.

1. After serving, the server must fill out a *Proof of Service by Mail* (form FL-335) and give it to you. If the server needs instructions, give him or her an *Information Sheet for Proof of Service by Mail* (form FL-335-INFO).
2. Take the completed *Proof of Personal Service* form to the clerk's office (or e-file it, if available in your court) at least 5 court days before your hearing.

Deadline: Unless the court orders a different time, service by mail must be completed at least **16 court days *PLUS* 5 calendar days** before the hearing date (if service is in California). Other time lines apply for service outside of California.

(16) Get ready for your hearing
- Take at least two copies of your documents and filed forms to the hearing. Include a filed *Proof of Service* form.
- Find more information about preparing for your hearing at http://www.courts.ca.gov/1094.htm.
- For information about having the other party testify in court, go to http://www.courts.ca.gov/29283.htm.

(17) **After the hearing,** the order made on form FL-340, *Findings and Order After Hearing,* must be filed and served.

(18) Do you have questions or need help?
- Find a lawyer through your local bar association, the State Bar of California at http://calbar.ca.gov, or the Lawyer Referral Service at 1-866-442-2529.
- For free and low-cost legal help (if you qualify), go to http://www.lawhelpca.org.
- Contact the Family Law Facilitator or Self-Help Center for information and assistance, and referrals to local legal services providers. Go to http://www.courts.ca.gov/selfhelp-courtresources.htm.

FL-303

PARTY WITHOUT ATTORNEY OR ATTORNEY	STATE BAR NUMBER:	FOR COURT USE ONLY
NAME:		
FIRM NAME:		
STREET ADDRESS:		
CITY: STATE: ZIP CODE:		
TELEPHONE NO.: FAX NO.:		
E-MAIL ADDRESS:		
ATTORNEY FOR (name):		

SUPERIOR COURT OF CALIFORNIA, COUNTY OF
  STREET ADDRESS:
  MAILING ADDRESS:
  CITY AND ZIP CODE:
  BRANCH NAME:

PETITIONER:
RESPONDENT:
OTHER PARENT/PARTY:

DECLARATION REGARDING NOTICE AND SERVICE OF REQUEST FOR TEMPORARY EMERGENCY (EX PARTE) ORDERS	CASE NUMBER:

NOTICE: Do not use this form to ask for domestic violence restraining orders. Before completing this form, read your court's local procedures for requesting temporary emergency orders and obtaining the information needed to complete item 2 of this form. Courts may grant temporary emergency orders with or without an emergency hearing. Find local rules at courts.ca.gov/3027.htm.

1. I am (specify) ☐ attorney for ☐ petitioner ☐ respondent ☐ other parent/party
   ☐ not a party in the case (name and title/relationship to party):

2. I ☐ did ☐ did not give notice that
   ☐ there will be an emergency court hearing on a request for temporary emergency (ex parte) orders.
   ☐ papers will be submitted to the court asking a judicial officer to grant temporary emergency orders without a hearing.
   on the date, time, and location indicated below:

   a. Date: Time: ☐ Dept.: ☐ Room:
   b. Address of court: ☐ same as noted above ☐ other (specify):

3. **NOTICE** (If you gave notice, complete item 3a. If you did not give notice complete item 3b or 3c.)
   a. ☐ I gave notice as described in items (1) through (5):
      (1) I gave notice to (select all that apply)
         ☐ petitioner   ☐ petitioner's attorney
         ☐ respondent   ☐ respondent's attorney
         ☐ other parent/party ☐ other parent's/party's attorney
         ☐ child's attorney   ☐ Other (specify):
      (2) I gave notice
         ☐ personally on (date):   at (location):   , California; at ☐ a.m. ☐ p.m.
         ☐ by telephone on (date):   telephone no.:   at ☐ a.m. ☐ p.m.
         ☐ by voicemail on (date):   voicemail no.:   at ☐ a.m. ☐ p.m.
         ☐ by fax on (date):   fax no.:   at ☐ a.m. ☐ p.m.
      (3) I gave notice (select one):
         ☐ by 10 a.m. the court day before this emergency hearing.
         ☐ after 10 a.m. the court day before this emergency hearing because of the following exceptional circumstances (specify):

Form Approved for Optional Use
Judicial Council of California
FL-303 [Rev. September 1, 2017]

DECLARATION REGARDING NOTICE AND SERVICE OF REQUEST FOR TEMPORARY EMERGENCY (EX PARTE) ORDERS

Family Law, §§ 2045, 3062–3064, 4620, 7710
Cal. Rules of Court, rules 5.151–5.169
www.courts.ca.gov

FL-303

PETITIONER: RESPONDENT: OTHER PARENT/PARTY:	CASE NUMBER:

3. a. (4) I notified the person in 3a(1) that the following temporary emergency orders are being requested *(specify):*

    (5) The person in 3a(1) responded as follows: ☐ Attachment 3a(5)

    (6) I ☐ do ☐ do not   believe that the person in 3a(1) will oppose the request for temporary emergency orders.

  b. ☐ **Request for waiver of notice.** I did not give notice about the request for temporary emergency orders. I ask that the court waive notice to the other party to help prevent an immediate *(identify the exceptional circumstances)*

    (1) ☐ danger or irreparable harm to myself (or my client) or to the children in the case.

    (2) ☐ risk that the children in the case will be removed from the state of California.

    (3) ☐ loss or damage to property subject to disposition in the case.

    (4) ☐ Other exceptional circumstances *(specify):*

    Facts in support of the request to waive notice *(specify):*   ☐ Attachment 3b.

  c. ☐ **Unable to provide notice.** I did not give notice about the request for temporary emergency orders. I used my best efforts to tell the opposing party when and where this hearing would take place but was unable to do so. The efforts I made to inform the other person were *(specify below):*   ☐ Attachment 3c.

4. ☐ **SERVICE OF FORMS**

  a. An unfiled copy of *Request for Order* (form FL-300) for temporary emergency orders, *Temporary Emergency (Ex Parte) Orders* (form FL-305), and related documents were served on

    ☐ petitioner ☐ petitioner's attorney ☐ other parent/party ☐ other parent/party's attorney

    ☐ respondent ☐ respondent's attorney ☐ child's attorney

    ☐ Other*(specify):*

  b. Method of service:

    ☐ Personal service on *(date):*   at *(location):*   , California; at   ☐ a.m. ☐ p.m.

    ☐ Fax on *(date):*   fax no.:   at   ☐ a.m. ☐ p.m.

    ☐ Overnight mail or other overnight carrier

  c. ☐ **Documents were not served on the opposing party** due to the exceptional circumstances specified in

    ☐ 3b, above ☐ 3c, above ☐ Attachment 4c.

I declare under penalty of perjury under the laws of the State of California that the foregoing is true and correct.

Date:

_____
(TYPE OR PRINT NAME)

▶ _____
(SIGNATURE)

DECLARATION REGARDING NOTICE AND SERVICE OF REQUEST FOR TEMPORARY EMERGENCY (EX PARTE) ORDERS

0113

FL-305

ATTORNEY OR PARTY WITHOUT ATTORNEY	STATE BAR NUMBER:	FOR COURT USE ONLY

NAME:

FIRM NAME:

STREET ADDRESS:

CITY: STATE: ZIP CODE:

TELEPHONE NO.: FAX NO.:

E-MAIL ADDRESS:

ATTORNEY FOR (name):

SUPERIOR COURT OF CALIFORNIA, COUNTY OF

STREET ADDRESS:

MAILING ADDRESS:

CITY AND ZIP CODE:

BRANCH NAME:

PETITIONER:

RESPONDENT:

OTHER PARENT/PARTY:

TEMPORARY EMERGENCY (EX PARTE) ORDERS	CASE NUMBER:
☐ Child Custody ☐ Visitation (Parenting Time) ☐ Property Control ☐ Other (specify):	

1. **TO (name(s)):** _____

☐ Petitioner ☐ Respondent ☐ Other Parent/Party ☐ Other (specify):

A court hearing will be held on the *Request for Order* (form FL-300) served with this order, as follows:

a. Date: Time: ☐ Dept.: ☐ Room:

b. Address of court ☐ same as noted above ☐ other (specify):

2. **Findings:** Temporary emergency (ex parte) orders are needed to: (a) help prevent an immediate loss or irreparable harm to a party or to children in the case, (b) help prevent immediate loss or damage to property subject to disposition in the case, or (c) set or change procedures for a hearing or trial.

COURT ORDERS: The following temporary emergency orders expire on the date and time of the hearing scheduled in (1), unless extended by court order:

3. ☐ **CHILD CUSTODY**

Temporary physical custody, care, and control to:

a. Child's name	Date of Birth	Petitioner	Respondent	Other Party/Parent
		☐	☐	☐
		☐	☐	☐
		☐	☐	☐
		☐	☐	☐
		☐	☐	☐

☐ Continued on Attachment 3(a)

b. ☐ **Visitation (Parenting Time)** The temporary orders for physical custody, care, and control of the minor children in (3) are subject to the other party's or parties' rights of visitation (parenting time) as follows (specify):

☐ See Attachment 3(b)

Page 1 of 2

THIS IS A COURT ORDER.

Form Adopted for Mandatory Use
Judicial Council of California
FL-305 [Rev. July 1, 2016]

TEMPORARY EMERGENCY (EX PARTE) ORDERS

Family Code, §§ 2045, 3062–3064,
Cal. Rules of Court, rules 5.151–5.169
www.courts.ca.gov

0114

PETITIONER: RESPONDENT: OTHER PARENT/PARTY:	CASE NUMBER:

3. ☐ **CHILD CUSTODY (continued)**

   c. **Travel restrictions**

      (1) The party or parties with temporary physical custody, care, and control of minor children **must not remove the minor children from the state of California unless the court allows it after a noticed hearing.**

      (2) ☐ Petitioner ☐ Respondent ☐ Other Parent/Party must not remove their minor children *(specify):*

         (a) ☐ from the state of California.

         (b) ☐ from the following counties *(specify):*

         (c) ☐ other *(specify):*

   d. ☐ **Child abduction prevention orders** are attached (see form FL-341(B)).

   e. (1) **Jurisdiction:** This court has jurisdiction to make child custody orders in this case under the Uniform Child Custody Jurisdiction and Enforcement Act (part 3 of the California Family Code, commencing with section 3400).

      (2) **Notice and opportunity to be heard:** The responding party was given notice and an opportunity to be heard as provided by the laws of the State of California.

      (3) **Country of habitual residence:** The country of habitual residence of the child or children is *(specify):*

         ☐ The United States of America ☐ Other *(specify):*

      (4) **If you violate this order, you may be subject to civil or criminal penalties, or both.**

4. ☐ **PROPERTY CONTROL**

   a. ☐ Petitioner ☐ Respondent ☐ Other Parent/Party is given exclusive temporary use, possession, and control of the following property that the parties ☐ own or are buying ☐ lease or rent

   b. ☐ Petitioner ☐ Respondent ☐ Other Parent/Party is ordered to make the following payments on the liens and encumbrances coming due while the order is in effect:

     Pay to: For: Amount: $ Due date:

     Pay to: For: Amount: $ Due date:

     Pay to: For: Amount: $ Due date:

     Pay to: For: Amount: $ Due date:

5. ☐ All other existing orders, not in conflict with these temporary emergency orders, remain in full force and effect.

6. ☐ **OTHER ORDERS** *(specify):*   ☐ Additional orders are listed in Attachment 6.

Date:

_____
JUDGE OF THE SUPERIOR COURT

THIS IS A COURT ORDER.

0115

PARTY WITHOUT ATTORNEY OR ATTORNEY	STATE BAR NUMBER:	FOR COURT USE ONLY
NAME:		
FIRM NAME:		
STREET ADDRESS:		
CITY: STATE: ZIP CODE:		
TELEPHONE NO.: FAX NO.:		
E-MAIL ADDRESS:		
ATTORNEY FOR (name):		

SUPERIOR COURT OF CALIFORNIA, COUNTY OF
STREET ADDRESS:
MAILING ADDRESS:
CITY AND ZIP CODE:
BRANCH NAME:

PETITIONER/PLAINTIFF:

RESPONDENT/DEFENDANT:

OTHER PARENT/PARTY:

ORDER ON REQUEST TO CONTINUE HEARING	CASE NUMBER:

Complete items 1, 2, 3, and 4.

1. The hearing is currently scheduled for *(date):*

2. Name of party who filed the *Request for Order, Order to Show Cause,* or other matter is *(specify):*

3. Name of party asking to continue the hearing is *(specify):*

4. The request to continue ☐ includes ☐ does not include temporary emergency (ex parte) orders previously issued.

The court will complete the rest of this form.

5. ☐ **Order denying request to continue hearing**
   The request to continue the hearing is DENIED for the reasons specified ☐ below ☐ on Attachment 5.

6. ☐ **Order granting request to continue hearing and notice of new hearing**
   a. The court hearing is continued to the date, time, and location shown below:

New Hearing Date:	Time:	Dept.:	Room:

   Address of court: ☐ Same as noted above ☐ Other *(specify):*

   b. ☐ By granting the continuance, any temporary emergency (ex parte) orders previously issued remain in effect until
      (1) ☐ the end of the new hearing in 6a.
      (2) ☐ *(date):*

7. **Reason for the continuance**
   a. The continuance is needed because
      (1) ☐ the papers could not be served as required before the hearing date.
      (2) ☐ the parties need to attend child custody mediation or child custody recommending counseling before the hearing.
      (3) ☐ the responding party asked for a first continuance in a matter involving temporary emergency (ex parte) orders.
      (4) ☐ Other good cause as stated ☐ below ☐ on Attachment 7(a)(4)

   b. ☐ The court finds good cause and orders a continuance in its discretion.

Page 1 of 2

Form Adopted for Mandatory Use
Judicial Council of California
FL-307 [New September 1, 2017]

ORDER ON REQUEST TO CONTINUE HEARING
(Family Law—Governmental—Uniform Parentage—Custody and Support)

Family Code, § 245
Cal. Rules of Court, rule 5.94
www.courts.ca.gov

FL-307

PETITIONER/PLAINTIFF: RESPONDENT/DEFENDANT: OTHER PARENT/PARTY:	CASE NUMBER:

8. **Temporary emergency (ex parte) orders**

a. ☐ No temporary emergency (ex parte) orders were changed.

b. ☐ The temporary emergency (ex parte) orders are MODIFIED as of this date. The new orders are stated in the attached

    (1) ☐ *Request for Order* (form FL-300)

    (2) ☐ *Temporary Emergency (Ex Parte) Orders* (form FL-305)

    (3) ☐ *Order to Show Cause* ☐ Contempt ☐ Seek Work ☐ Other *(specify):*

    (4) ☐ Other *(specify):*

c. ☐ The temporary emergency (ex parte) orders are TERMINATED for the reasons stated ☐ on Attachment 8c
    ☐ in this section:

9. **Service of order**

a. ☐ No further service is required. Both parties were present at the hearing when the court granted this order.

b. ☐ The documents listed in 10 must be served by *(date):*   on *(specify)*

    (1) ☐ petitioner/plaintiff

    (2) ☐ respondent/defendant

    (3) ☐ other parent/party

    (4) ☐ Other *(specify):*

c. ☐ All documents must be ☐ personally served ☐ served by mail.

d. ☐ Other orders regarding service *(specify):*

10. **Documents for service**

A filed copy of this order (form FL-307) must be presented as the cover page to the following documents when served:

a. ☐ A copy of the previously filed *Request for Order, Order to Show Cause,* or other moving paper

b. ☐ A copy of the extended or modified *Temporary Emergency (Ex Parte) Orders* (form FL-305)

c. ☐ Other *(specify):*

11. ☐ A *Responsive Declaration to Request for Order* form FL-320 must be filed and served on or before *(date):*

12. ☐ Other orders:

Date: _____

▶ _____
                            JUDICIAL OFFICER

ORDER ON REQUEST TO CONTINUE HEARING
(Family Law—Governmental—Uniform Parentage—Custody and Support)

0117

PARTY WITHOUT ATTORNEY OR ATTORNEY	STATE BAR NUMBER:	FOR COURT USE ONLY
NAME:		
FIRM NAME:		
STREET ADDRESS:		
CITY: STATE: ZIP CODE:		
TELEPHONE NO.: FAX NO.:		
E-MAIL ADDRESS:		
ATTORNEY FOR (name):		

SUPERIOR COURT OF CALIFORNIA, COUNTY OF
STREET ADDRESS:
MAILING ADDRESS:
CITY AND ZIP CODE:
BRANCH NAME:

PETITIONER/PLAINTIFF:

RESPONDENT/DEFENDANT:

OTHER PARENT/PARTY:

REQUEST TO CONTINUE HEARING	CASE NUMBER:
☐ And Extend Temporary Emergency (Ex Parte) Orders	

Notice: Do not use this form to ask to change the date of a domestic violence restraining order hearing. Read DV-115-INFO, *How to Ask for a New Hearing Date*, for more information.

1. Name of person seeking a continuance *(specify):*

2. I ask that the court reschedule (continue) the hearing date for the *(select one)*
   a. ☐ *Request for Order* regarding *(specify issues):*
   b. ☐ *Order to Show Cause for* ☐ Contempt ☐ Seek Work
   c. ☐ Other *(specify):*

3. The item in 2 was filed on *(date):*

4. The hearing is currently set for *(date):*

5. I ask that the court reschedule (continue) the hearing to another date because *(check all boxes that apply)*
   a. ☐ the papers could not be served as required before the hearing date.
   b. ☐ the parties have not been able to meet with a child custody mediator or child custody recommending counselor as ordered by the court.
   c. ☐ I am entitled, as a matter of course, to one continuance for a reasonable period to respond to the request for temporary emergency (ex parte) orders. This is my first request for a continuance. *(The responding party must complete item 5d if requesting more than one continuance of the hearing.)*
   d. ☐ Other good cause as stated ☐ below ☐ on Attachment 5(d):

6. The request to continue ☐ includes ☐ does not include temporary emergency (ex parte) orders previously issued. *Notice: If the court grants the continuance, the expiration date of any temporary emergency (ex parte) orders will be extended to the end of the new hearing, unless otherwise ordered by the court.*

7. I have completed the required sections of *Order on Request to Continue Hearing* (form FL-307). *(Note: Form FL-307 must be submitted to the court with this form.)*

I declare under penalty of perjury under the laws of the State of California that the foregoing is true and correct.

Date:

_____
(TYPE OR PRINT NAME)

▶

_____
SIGNATURE

Page 1 of 1

Form Adopted for Mandatory Use
Judicial Council of California
FL-306 [New September 1, 2017]

REQUEST TO CONTINUE HEARING
(Family Law—Governmental—Uniform Parentage—Custody and Support)

Family Code, § 245
Cal. Rules of Court, rule 5.94
www.courts.ca.gov

0118

PETITIONER: RESPONDENT: OTHER PARENT/PARTY:	CASE NUMBER:

CHILD CUSTODY AND VISITATION (PARENTING TIME) APPLICATION ATTACHMENT
—This is not a court order—

TO ☐ **Petition** ☐ **Response** ☐ **Request for Order** ☐ **Responsive Declaration to Request for Order**
☐ **Other** *(specify):*

1. ☐ **Custody.** Custody of the minor children of the parties is requested as follows:

Child's Name	Date of Birth	Legal Custody to *(person who decides about health, education, etc.)*	Physical Custody to *(person with whom the child lives)*

2. ☐ **Visitation (Parenting Time).**
   Note: Unless specifically ordered, a child's holiday schedule order has priority over the regular parenting time.
   a. ☐ Reasonable right of parenting time (visitation) to the party without physical custody **(not appropriate in cases involving domestic violence).**
   b. ☐ See the attached _____ -page document dated *(specify date):*
   c. ☐ The parties will go to child custody mediation or child custody recommending counseling at *(specify date, time, and location):*

   d. ☐ No visitation (parenting time).
   e. ☐ Visitation (parenting time). *(Specify start and ending date and time. If applicable, check "start of" OR "after school.")*
      ☐ **Petitioner's** ☐ **Respondent's** ☐ **Other Parent's/Party's** parenting time (visitation) will be as follows:
      (1) ☐ **Weekends starting** *(date):*
          (Note: The first weekend of the month is the first weekend with a Saturday.)
          ☐ 1st ☐ 2nd ☐ 3rd ☐ 4th ☐ 5th weekend of the month
          from _____ at _____ ☐ a.m. ☐ p.m./ if applicable, specify: ☐ start of school ☐ after school
          _____(day of week)_____ ___(time)___
          to _____ at _____ ☐ a.m. ☐ p.m./ if applicable, specify: ☐ start of school ☐ after school
          _____(day of week)_____ ___(time)___
          (a) ☐ The parties will alternate the fifth weekends, with the ☐ petitioner ☐ respondent ☐ other parent/party having the initial fifth weekend, which starts *(date):*
          (b) ☐ The ☐ petitioner ☐ respondent ☐ other parent/party will have the fifth weekend in ☐ odd ☐ even numbered months.
      (2) ☐ **Alternate weekends starting** *(date):*
          from _____ at _____ ☐ a.m. ☐ p.m./ if applicable, specify: ☐ start of school ☐ after school
          _____(day of week)_____ ___(time)___
          to _____ at _____ ☐ a.m. ☐ p.m./ if applicable, specify: ☐ start of school ☐ after school
          _____(day of week)_____ ___(time)___
      (3) ☐ **Weekdays starting** *(date):*
          from _____ at _____ ☐ a.m. ☐ p.m./ if applicable, specify: ☐ start of school ☐ after school
          _____(day of week)_____ ___(time)___
          to _____ at _____ ☐ a.m. ☐ p.m./ if applicable, specify: ☐ start of school ☐ after school
          _____(day of week)_____ ___(time)___
      (4) ☐ Other visitation (parenting time) days and restrictions are: ☐ listed in Attachment 2e(4)
          ☐ as follows:

Form Approved for Optional Use
Judicial Council of California
FL-311 [Rev. July 1, 2016]

**CHILD CUSTODY AND VISITATION (PARENTING TIME)
APPLICATION ATTACHMENT**

Family Code, § 6200 et seq.
www.courts.ca.gov

0119

PETITIONER: RESPONDENT: OTHER PARENT/PARTY:	CASE NUMBER:

3. ☐ **Supervised visitation (parenting time).**

    a. **If item 3 is checked, you must attach a declaration that shows why unsupervised visitation (parenting time) would be bad for your children. The judge is required to consider supervised visitation if one parent or party is alleging domestic violence and is protected by a restraining order.**

    b. ☐ The person who supervises the visitation (parenting time) must meet the requirements listed in *Declaration of Supervised Visitation Provider* (form FL-324) under Family Code § 3200.5.

    c. I request that *(name):*   have supervised visitation (parenting time) with the minor children according to the schedule set out on page 1.

    d. I request that the visitation (parenting time) be supervised by *(name):*

    who is a ☐ professional ☐ nonprofessional supervisor.
The supervisor's phone number is *(specify):*

    e. I request that any costs of supervision be paid as follows: petitioner: percent; respondent: percent; other parent/party: percent.

4. ☐ **Transportation for visitation (parenting time) and place of exchange.**

    a. The children will be driven only by a licensed and insured driver. The car or truck must have legal child restraint devices.

    b. ☐ Transportation **to** begin the visits will be provided by *(name):*

    c. ☐ Transportation **from** the visits will be provided by *(name):*

    d. ☐ The exchange point at the beginning of the visit will be *(address):*

    e. ☐ The exchange point at the end of the visit will be *(address):*

    f. ☐ During the exchanges, the party driving the children will wait in the car and the other party will wait in his or her home (or exchange location) while the children go between the car and the home (or exchange location).

    g. ☐ Other *(specify):*

5. ☐ **Travel with children.** The ☐ petitioner ☐ respondent ☐ other parent/party **must** have written permission from the other parent or party, or a court order, to take the children out of the following places:

    a. ☐ the state of California.

    b. ☐ the following counties *(specify):*

    c. ☐ other places *(specify):*

6. ☐ **Child abduction prevention.** There is a risk that one of the parties will take the children out of California without the other party's permission. I request the orders set out on attached form FL-312.

7. ☐ **Children's holiday schedule.** I request the holiday and vacation schedule set out on the attached ☐ form FL-341(C) ☐ Other *(specify):*

8. ☐ **Additional custody provisions.** I request the additional orders regarding custody set out on the attached ☐ form FL-341(D) ☐ Other *(specify):*

9. ☐ **Joint legal custody provisions.** I request joint legal custody and want the additional orders set out on the attached ☐ form FL-341(E) ☐ Other *(specify):*

10. ☐ **Other.** I request the following additional orders *(specify):*

0120

PETITIONER: RESPONDENT: OTHER PARENT/PARTY:	CASE NUMBER:

REQUEST FOR CHILD ABDUCTION PREVENTION ORDERS
—This is not a court order—

TO ☐ **Petition** ☐ **Response** ☐ **Request for Order** ☐ **Responsive Declaration to Request for Order**
☐ Other *(specify):*

1. Your name:

2. **I request orders to prevent child abduction by** *(specify):* ☐ **Petitioner** ☐ **Respondent** ☐ **Other Parent/Party**

3. **I think that he or she might take the children without my permission to** *(check all that apply):*

    a. ☐ another county in California *(specify the county):*

    b. ☐ another state *(specify the state):*

    c. ☐ a foreign country *(specify the foreign country):*

        (1) ☐ He or she is a citizen of that country.

        (2) ☐ He or she has family or emotional ties to that country *(explain):*

4. **I think that he or she might take the children without my permission because he or she** *(check all that apply):*

    a. ☐ has violated—or threatened to violate—a custody or visitation (parenting time) order in the past.
        Explain:

    b. ☐ does not have strong ties to California.
        Explain any work, financial, social, or family situation that makes it easy for the party to leave California.

    c. ☐ has recently done things that make it easy for him or her to take the children away without permission. He or she has *(check all that apply):*

        ☐ quit his or her job.   ☐ sold his or her home.

        ☐ closed a bank account.   ☐ ended a lease.

        ☐ sold or gotten rid of assets.   ☐ hidden or destroyed documents.

        ☐ applied for a passport, birth certificate, or school or medical records.

        ☐ Other *(specify):*

    d. ☐ has a history of *(check all that apply and explain your answers in the space provided in this section):*

        ☐ domestic violence.   ☐ child abuse.   ☐ not cooperating with me in parenting.

        ☐ taking the children without my permission.

        Explain your answers to item d.

    e. ☐ has a criminal record. *Explain:*

Form Adopted for Mandatory Use
Judicial Council of California
FL-312 [Rev. July 1, 2016]
REQUEST FOR CHILD ABDUCTION PREVENTION ORDERS
Family Code, § 3048
www.courts.ca.gov

0121

PETITIONER: RESPONDENT: OTHER PARENT/PARTY:	CASE NUMBER:

I REQUEST THE FOLLOWING ORDERS AGAINST *(specify)*: ☐ **Petitioner** ☐ **Respondent** ☐ **Other Parent/Party**

5. ☐ **Supervised Visitation (Parenting Time)**
   I ask the court to order supervised visitation (parenting time). I understand that the person I request to supervise the visits must meet the qualifications listed in *Declaration of Supervised Visitation Provider* (form FL-324)
   The specific terms are attached *(check one):* ☐ form FL-311 ☐ as follows:

6. ☐ **Post a Bond**
   I ask the court to order the posting of a bond for $ _____ . If the party takes the children without my permission, I can use this money to bring the children back.

7. ☐ **Do Not Move Without My Permission or Court Order**
   I ask for a court order preventing the party from moving with the children without my written permission or a court order.

8. ☐ **No Travel Without My Permission or Court Order**
   I ask for a court order preventing the party from traveling with the children outside *(check all that apply):*
   ☐ this county ☐ the United States
   ☐ California ☐ Other *(specify):*
   without my written permission or a court order.

9. ☐ **Notify Other State of Travel Restrictions**
   I ask the court to order the party to register this order in the state of _____ and provide the court with proof of the registration before the children can travel to that state for child visitation (parenting time).

10. ☐ **Turn In and Do Not Apply for Passports or Other Vital Documents**
    I ask for a court order *(check all that apply):*
    ☐ requiring the party to turn in all the children's passports and other documents (such as visas, birth certificates, and other documents used for travel) that are in his or her possession and control.
    ☐ preventing the party from applying for passports or other documents (such as visas or birth certificates) that can be used to travel with the children.

11. ☐ **Provide Itinerary and Other Travel Documents**
    If the party is allowed to travel with the children, I ask the court to order the party to give me before leaving *(specify):*
    ☐ the children's travel itinerary.
    ☐ copies of round-trip airline tickets.
    ☐ addresses and telephone numbers where the children can be reached at all times.
    ☐ an open airline ticket for me in case the children are not returned.
    ☐ other *(specify):*

12. ☐ **Notify Foreign Embassy or Consulate of Passport Restrictions**
    I ask the court to order the party to notify the embassy or consulate of _____ of this order and to provide the court with proof of that notification within _____ calendar days.

13. ☐ **Foreign Custody and Visitation (Parenting Time) Order**
    I ask the court to order the party to get a custody and visitation (parenting time) order in a foreign country equal to the most recent United States order before the children can travel to that country for visits. I understand that foreign orders may be changed or enforced depending on the laws of that country.

14. ☐ **Other** *(specify):*

I declare under penalty of perjury under the laws of the State of California that the information on this form is true and correct.

Date: _____

▶ _____
(SIGNATURE)

FL-312 [Rev. July 1, 2016]   **REQUEST FOR CHILD ABDUCTION PREVENTION ORDERS**   Page 2 of 2

FL-313-INFO   Child Custody Information Sheet—Recommending Counseling

Parents who come to court about child custody and parenting time (visitation) face decisions about parenting plans for their children. This information sheet provides general information about child custody and parenting time matters, how to get help resolving a custody dispute or making a parenting plan, where to find an attorney, and where to find other resources.

What is a parenting plan?

A parenting plan describes how the parents will divide their responsibilities for taking care of their child.

The plan may include a general or specific schedule of days, times, weekends, holidays, vacations, transportation, pick-up/drop-off, limits on travel, counseling, and treatment services, and other details.

What are legal and physical custody?

A parenting plan usually includes:

- *Legal custody:* how parents make major decisions about the child's health, education, and welfare;

- *Physical custody:* where the child lives; and

- *Parenting time, time-share, or visitation:* when the child spends time with each parent.

Legal custody and *physical custody* may each be specified as *joint* (both parents have certain responsibilities) or *sole* (one parent has the responsibility alone).

Can we make our own parenting plan?

Yes. You have a right to make a parenting plan agreement on your own. This agreement may be called a *stipulation, time-share plan,* or *parenting plan.*

If both parents can agree on a parenting plan, the judge will probably approve it. The agreement becomes a court order after it is signed by both parents and the judge, and filed with the court.

What if there is domestic violence or a protective order?

If there is domestic violence or a protective order, talk with an attorney, counselor, or child custody recommending counselor before making a parenting plan.

For domestic violence help, call the National Domestic Violence Hotline at 1-800-799-7233 (TDD:1-800-787-3224) or call 211 if available in your area.

What if we don't have a parenting plan?

If you can't reach an agreement, the court will refer you to family court services (FCS) for child custody mediation also called "child custody recommending counseling." At the appointment, you will meet with an FCS professional also called a "child custody recommending counselor." He or she will help you and the other parent reach an agreement about a parenting plan.

What is child custody recommending counseling with family court services?

Family court services (FCS) provides child custody recommending counseling (sometimes referred to as child custody mediation) to help parents resolve disagreements about the care of their child. The child custody recommending counselor will meet with you and the other parent to try to help you both make a parenting plan. There may be an orientation provided that offers additional information about the process.

If you are unable to reach an agreement after meeting with family court services, the child custody recommending counselor will make a written recommendation to the court about a parenting plan. You and the other parent and the attorneys (if any) will get a copy of the recommendation before the court hearing.

If you are concerned about meeting with the other parent, or there is a domestic violence issue or a protective order involving the other parent, you may

FL-313-INFO Child Custody Information Sheet—Recommending Counseling

ask to meet alone with the child custody recommending counselor without the other parent. You may also request to have a support person with you. The support person may not speak for you.

Do we have to agree to a parenting plan when we meet?

No. You do not have to come to an agreement. When the parents can't agree, the judge will decide. For legal advice, contact an attorney. For other information, ask the self-help center or family court services about how the process works in your court.

Are there other ways to resolve our dispute?

Yes. You may try other alternative dispute resolution (ADR) options, including:

1. Meet and Confer: Parents and their attorneys (if any) may meet at any time and as often as necessary to work out a parenting plan without a court hearing. If there is a protective order limiting the contact between the parents, then the "meet and confer" can be through attorneys or a mediator in separate sessions.

2. Settlement Conference: In some courts, parents may meet with a judge, neutral evaluators, or family law attorneys not involved in the case to discuss settlement. Check with the local court to find out if this is an option. If there is a protective order, the settlement discussion can be through attorneys or a mediator in separate sessions.

3. Private Mediation: Parents may hire a private mediator to help them resolve their dispute.

4. Collaborative Law Process: Each parent hires a lawyer and agrees to resolve the dispute without going to court. The parents may also hire other experts.

Court Hearing

When the parents cannot agree to a parenting plan on their own, in child custody recommending

counseling, or in any other ADR process, the judge will decide.

If there is domestic violence or a protective order, a parent may be able to bring a support person with him or her to the court hearing, but the support person may not speak for that person.

Where can I get help?

This information sheet gives only basic information on the child custody process and is not legal advice. If you want legal advice, ask an attorney for assistance. For other information, you may want to:

1. Contact family court services.

2. Contact the family law facilitator or self-help center for information, local rules and court forms, and referrals to local legal services providers.

3. Find an attorney through your local bar association, the State Bar of California at *http://calbar.ca.gov*, or the Lawyer Referral Service at 1-866-442-2529.

4. Hire a private mediator for help with your parenting agreement. A mediator may be an attorney or counselor. Contact your local bar association, court ADR program, or family court services for a referral to local resources.

5. Find information on the Online Self-Help Center website at *www.courts.ca.gov/selfhelp*.

6. For free and low-cost legal help (if you qualify), go to *www.lawhelpcalifornia.org*.

7. Find information at your local law library or ask at your public library.

8. Ask for a court hearing and let the judge decide what is best for your child.

Requests for Accommodations
Assistive listening systems, computer-assisted real-time captioning, or sign language interpreter services are available if you ask at least five days before the proceeding. Contact the clerk's office or go to *www.courts.ca.gov/forms* for *Request for Accommodations by Persons with Disabilities and Response* (form MC-410). (Civil Code, § 54.8.)

FL-314-INFO Child Custody Information Sheet—Child Custody Mediation

Parents who come to court about child custody and parenting time (visitation) face decisions about parenting plans for their children. This information sheet provides general information about child custody and parenting time matters, how to get help resolving a custody dispute or making a parenting plan, where to find an attorney, and where to find other resources.

What is a parenting plan?

A parenting plan describes how the parents will divide their responsibilities for taking care of their child.

The plan may include a general or specific schedule of days, times, weekends, holidays, vacations, transportation, pick-up/drop-off, limits on travel, counseling and treatment services, and other details.

What are legal and physical custody?

A parenting plan usually includes:

- *Legal custody:* how parents make major decisions about the child's health, education, and welfare;

- *Physical custody:* where the child lives; and

- *Parenting time, time-share, or visitation:* when the child spends time with each parent.

Legal custody and *physical custody* may each be specified as *joint* (both parents have certain responsibilities) or *sole* (one parent has the responsibility alone).

Can we make our own parenting plan?

Yes. You have a right to make a parenting plan agreement on your own. This agreement may be called a *stipulation, time-share plan,* or *parenting plan.*

If both parents can agree on a parenting plan, the judge will probably approve it. The agreement becomes a court order after it is signed by both parents and the judge, and filed with the court.

What if there is domestic violence or a protective order?

If there is domestic violence or a protective order, talk with an attorney, counselor, or mediator before making a parenting plan.

For domestic violence help, call the National Domestic Violence Hotline at 1-800-799-7233 (TDD:1-800-787-3224) or call 211 if available in your area.

What if we don't have a parenting plan?

If you can't reach an agreement, the court will refer you to mediation with family court services (FCS) to try to work out a parenting plan.

What is mediation with family court services?

Family court services (FCS) provides mediation to help parents resolve disagreements about the care of their child. The mediator will meet with you and the other parent to try to help you both make a parenting plan. An orientation may be provided that offers additional information about the process.

If you are concerned about meeting with the other parent in mediation, or there is a domestic violence issue or a protective order involving the other parent, you may ask to meet alone with the mediator without the other parent. You may also request to have a support person with you at mediation. The support person may not speak for you.

Do we have to agree to a parenting plan in mediation?

No. You do not have to come to an agreement in mediation. When the parents can't agree, the judge will decide. For legal advice, contact an attorney. For other information, ask the self-help center or family court services about how the process works in your court.

FL-314-INFO   Child Custody Information Sheet—Child Custody Mediation

Are there other ways to resolve our dispute?

Yes. You may try other alternative dispute resolution (ADR) options, including:

1. Meet and Confer: Parents and their attorneys (if any) may meet at any time and as often as necessary to work out a parenting plan without a court hearing. If there is a protective order limiting the contact between the parents, then the "meet and confer" can be through attorneys or a mediator in separate sessions.

2. Settlement Conference: In some courts, parents may meet with a judge, neutral evaluators, or family law attorneys not involved in the case to discuss settlement. Check with the local court to find out if this is an option. If there is a protective order, the settlement discussion can be through attorneys or a mediator in separate sessions.

3. Private Mediation: Parents may hire a private mediator to help them resolve their dispute.

4. Collaborative Law Process: Each parent hires a lawyer and agrees to resolve the dispute without going to court. The parents may also hire other experts.

Court Hearing

When the parents cannot agree to a parenting plan on their own, in mediation, or in any other ADR process, the judge will decide.

If there is domestic violence or a protective order, a parent may be able to bring a support person with him or her to the court hearing, but the support person may not speak for that person.

Where can I get help?

This information sheet gives only basic information on the child custody process and is not legal advice. If you want legal advice, ask an attorney for assistance. For other information, you may want to:

1. Contact family court services.

2. Contact the family law facilitator or self-help center for information, local rules and court forms, and referrals to local legal services providers.

3. Find an attorney through your local bar association, the State Bar of California at *http://calbar.ca.gov*, or the Lawyer Referral Service at 1-866-442-2529.

4. Hire a private mediator for help with your parenting agreement. A mediator may be an attorney or counselor. Contact your local bar association, court ADR program, or family court services for a referral to local resources.

5. Find information on the Online Self-Help Center website at *www.courts.ca.gov/selfhelp*.

6. For free and low-cost legal help (if you qualify), go to *www.lawhelpcalifornia.org*.

7. Find information at your local law library or ask at your public library.

8. Ask for a court hearing and let the judge decide what is best for your child.

Requests for Accommodations

Assistive listening systems, computer-assisted real-time captioning, or sign language interpreter services are available if you ask at least five days before the proceeding. Contact the clerk's office or go to *www.courts.ca.gov/forms* for *Request for Accommodations by Persons with Disabilities and Response* (form MC-410). (Civil Code, § 54.8.)

0126

PETITIONER:	CASE NUMBER:
RESPONDENT:	

☐ **REQUEST FOR SEPARATE TRIAL**   OR   ☐ **RESPONSE TO REQUEST FOR SEPARATE TRIAL**

Attachment to ☐ *Request for Order*   ☐ *Responsive Declaration to Request for Order*
            (form FL-300)   *(form FL-320)*

1. I am the ☐ petitioner ☐ respondent and ☐ request ☐ oppose the request that the court sever (bifurcate) and grant an early and separate trial on the following issue or issues:

   a. ☐ Permanent custody and visitation of the children of the marriage of domestic partnership

   b. ☐ Date of separation of the parties

   c. ☐ Alternate valuation date for property

   d. ☐ Validity of agreement entered into before or during the marriage or domestic partnership

   e. ☐ Dissolution of the status of the marriage or domestic partnership

      (1) I will serve with this application or response my preliminary *Declaration of Disclosure* (form FL-140) and completed *Schedule of Assets* and *Debts* (form FL-142) *and Income and Expense Declaration* (FL-150) unless they have been previously served or the parties have stipulated in writing to defer service.

      (2) All pension or retirement plans in which the community has an interest are listed below or on attachment 1e(2):

      (3) All pension or retirement plans listed in 1e(2) have been joined as a party to this proceeding, unless joinder is precluded or made unnecessary as a matter of law. *(See* Retirement Plan Joinder—Information Sheet (form FL-318-INFO) *to determine if a joinder is required.)*

      (4) I understand that the court may make the orders specified or requested on pages 2 and 3 if the request is granted to bifurcate the status of the marriage or domestic partnership and the marriage or partnership is ended.

      (5) ☐ I request that the court make the orders indicated on pages 2 and 3 and any attachments.

   NOTE: A request for an early termination of your marital or partnership status may have a significant impact on your rights or responsibilities in your case. If you do not understand this form, you should speak with an attorney.

   f. ☐ Other *(specify)*:

2. a. ☐ I request that the court conduct this separate trial on the hearing date.

   b. ☐ I will, at the hearing, ask the court to set a date for this separate trial.

3. The reasons in support of this request are *(specify)*:

   ☐ Memorandum attached.   ☐ Supporting declarations attached.

Form Adopted for Mandatory Use
Judicial Council of California
FL-315 [January 1, 2018]

REQUEST OR RESPONSE TO REQUEST FOR SEPARATE TRIAL
(Family Law)

Family Code § 2337
www.courts.ca.gov

PETITIONER:	CASE NUMBER:
RESPONDENT:	

4. Conditions relating to bifurcation of the status of the marriage or partnership:

   a. I understand that the court must enter an order to preserve the claims of each spouse or domestic partner in all retirement plan benefits upon entry of judgment granting a dissolution of the status of the marriage or domestic partnership.

   b. I request that the court order the following as a condition of granting the bifurcation and ending the marriage or partnership upon an early and separate trial:

   (1) ☐ **Division of property**

   The ☐ petitioner ☐ respondent and his or her estate must indemnify and hold me harmless from any taxes, reassessments, interest, and penalties that I have to pay in connection with the division of the community estate that I would not have had to pay if we were still married or in a domestic partnership at the time the division was made.

   (2) ☐ **Health insurance**

   Until judgment has been entered on all remaining issues and has become final ☐ petitioner ☐ respondent must maintain all existing health and medical insurance coverage for me and any minor children as named dependents as long as he or she is eligible to do so. If at any time during this period, he or she is not eligible to maintain that coverage, he or she must, at his or her sole expense, provide and maintain health and medical insurance coverage that is comparable to the existing health and medical insurance coverage to the extent it is available.

   To the extent that coverage is not available, the ☐ petitioner ☐ respondent must be responsible for paying, and demonstrate to the court's satisfaction the ability to pay, for health and medical care for me and the minor children to the extent that care would have been covered by the existing insurance coverage but for the dissolution of marital status or domestic partnership, and must otherwise indemnify and hold me harmless from any adverse consequences resulting from the loss or reduction of the existing coverage.

   (3) ☐ **Probate homestead**

   Until judgment has been entered on all remaining issues and has become final, the ☐ petitioner ☐ respondent must indemnify and hold me harmless from any adverse consequences if the bifurcation results in a termination of my right to a probate homestead in the residence in which I am residing at the time the severance is granted.

   (4) ☐ **Probate family allowance**

   Until judgment has been entered on all remaining issues and has become final, the ☐ petitioner ☐ respondent must indemnify and hold me harmless from any adverse consequences if the bifurcation results in the loss of my right to a probate family allowance as the surviving spouse or surviving domestic partner.

   (5) ☐ **Retirement benefits**

   Until judgment has been entered on all remaining issues and has become final, the ☐ petitioner ☐ respondent must indemnify and hold me harmless from any adverse consequences if the bifurcation results in the loss of my rights with respect to any retirement, survivor, or deferred compensation benefits under any plan, fund, or arrangement, or to any elections or options associated those benefits, to the extent that I would have been entitled to those benefits or elections as the spouse or surviving spouse or the domestic partner or surviving domestic partner.

   (6) ☐ **Social security benefits**

   The ☐ petitioner ☐ respondent must indemnify and hold me harmless from any adverse consequences if the bifurcation results in the loss of rights to social security benefits or elections to the extent that I would have been entitled to those benefits or elections as the surviving spouse or surviving domestic partner.

   (7) ☐ **Beneficiary designation—nonprobate transfer**

   The ☐ petitioner ☐ respondent must maintain the beneficiary designation specified for each Nonprobate Transfer Asset (Probate Code section 5000) identified on the attached list in the percentage indicated. *(See Attachment 7 (not a form), which lists each asset and proposed percentage.)* This designation must stay in effect until judgment has been entered with respect to the community ownership of that asset and until my interest in it has been distributed to me.

REQUEST OR RESPONSE TO REQUEST FOR SEPARATE TRIAL
(Family Law)

PETITIONER:	CASE NUMBER:
RESPONDENT:	

(8) ☐ **Individual Retirement Accounts**

To preserve the ability of the nonowner to defer the distribution of an Individual Retirement Account (IRA) or annuity upon the death of the owner, the court should make the attached orders assigning and transferring the community interest of ☐ petitioner ☐ respondent in each listed IRA to that party. *(See Attachment 8 (not a form), which lists names of IRAs, account numbers, and amount to be awarded.)*

(9) ☐ **Enforcement of community property rights**

Because it will be difficult to enforce either of our community property rights if one of us dies before the division and distribution or compliance with any court-ordered payment of any community property interest, the court should make the attached order to provide enforcement security for ☐ petitioner ☐ respondent. *(See attachment 9 (not a form), which specifies the security interest to be ordered as provided by Family Code section 2337(c)(9).)*

(10) ☐ **Other conditions that are just and equitable**

I request that the court make the following additional orders:

5. Number of pages attached after this page:

I declare under penalty of perjury under the laws of the State of California that the foregoing is true and correct.

Date:

▶

_____
(TYPE OR PRINT NAME)

_____
(SIGNATURE OF DECLARANT)

REQUEST OR RESPONSE TO REQUEST FOR SEPARATE TRIAL
(Family Law)

0129

PETITIONER:	CASE NUMBER:
RESPONDENT:	

REQUEST FOR ORDERS REGARDING NONCOMPLIANCE
WITH DISCLOSURE REQUIREMENTS

Attachment to *Request for Order* (form FL-300)

1. ☐ Petitioner ☐ Respondent   has complied with mandatory disclosure requirements (you must attach a copy of your filed *Declaration Regarding Service of Declaration of Disclosure and Income and Expense Declaration* (form FL-141)), and requests an order that

☐ petitioner ☐ respondent

a. ☐ provide a

   (1) ☐ preliminary declaration of disclosure under Family Code section 2104 as directed by court order.

   (2) ☐ final declaration of disclosure under Family Code section 2105 as directed by court order.

b. ☐ provide a further response to his or her ☐ preliminary ☐ final declaration of disclosure under Family Code section 2107(b)(1).

c. ☐ has failed to comply with disclosure requirements and is prevented from presenting evidence on the issues that should have been covered in the declaration of disclosure under Family Code section 2107(b)(2).

d. ☐ be granted for good cause his or her request for voluntary waiver of receipt of ☐ preliminary ☐ final declaration of disclosure under Family Code section 2107(b)(3).

e. ☐ for the reasons described below, be ordered to pay money sanctions for failure to comply with disclosure requirements. The amount of the money sanctions should be in an amount sufficient to deter him or her from repeating the conduct or comparable conduct, including reasonable attorney fees, costs incurred, or both, unless the court finds that the noncomplying party acted with substantial justification or that other circumstances make the imposition of the sanction unjust. (Family Code, § 2107(c).)

f. ☐ be granted his or her request to set aside the judgment under Family Code section 2107(d).

g. ☐ be ordered to comply with other, or alternative, relief, requested *(specify)*:

2. ☐ FACTS IN SUPPORT of relief requested are *(specify)*:

☐ Contained in the attached declaration. (You may use *Attached Declaration* (form MC-031) for this purpose).

I declare under penalty of perjury under the laws of the State of California that the foregoing is true and correct.

Date:

▶

_____
(TYPE OR PRINT NAME)

_____
(SIGNATURE OF APPLICANT)

Page 1 of 1

**REQUEST FOR ORDERS REGARDING NONCOMPLIANCE
WITH DISCLOSURE REQUIREMENTS**

0130

RETIREMENT PLAN JOINDER—INFORMATION SHEET

Type of Retirement Plan	Examples	Joinder Required
Governmental plan of a state, county, public school or university, or other public agency	California Public Employees' Retirement System (CalPERS), California State Teachers' Retirement System (CalSTRS), and University of California Retirement System (UCRS) (includes both qualified plans and nonqualified plans, such as Int. Rev. Code, § 457(b) or (f) deferral plans or Int. Rev. Code, § 403(b) Tax Sheltered Annuity (TSA)	Yes
Federal government plan	Federal government plans including all military branches, Civil Service Retirement System (CSRS), Federal Employees Retirement System (FERS), Foreign Service Pension System (FSPS)	No
Funded plan (whether or not qualified) covering employees working for private-industry employer (includes collectively bargained plans)	Int. Rev. Code, § 401(k) plan, defined benefit pension plan (traditional or cash balance), profit-sharing plan, money purchase or target benefit pension plan, Employee Stock Ownership Plan (ESOP), Tax Sheltered Annuity (TSA)	No (ERISA covered)
Unfunded nonqualified plan covering employees working for private-industry or tax-exempt employer (other than excess benefit plans)	Supplemental executive retirement plan, Int. Rev. Code, § 457(f) deferral plan, Stock Appreciation Right (SAR) or phantom stock plan, severance plan	No (ERISA covered)
Plan (qualified or nonqualified) covering only business owners and spouses or employees of a church	Int. Rev. Code, § 401(k) plan, defined benefit pension plan (traditional or cash balance), profit-sharing plan, money purchase or target benefit pension plan, Keogh, Tax Sheltered Annuity (TSA)	Yes
Individual Retirement Account or annuity	Individual Retirement Account (IRA), Roth IRA	No (not true retirement plans; Qualified Domestic Relations Orders (QDROs) do not apply). May be divided by judgment or order
All others		Generally yes

For domestic partnerships and same-sex marriages, please consult an attorney as federal laws apply and rules may vary.

Form Approved for Optional Use
Judicial Council of California
FL-318-INFO [New January 1, 2009]

RETIREMENT PLAN JOINDER—INFORMATION SHEET
(Family Law)

Family Code, § 2337
www.courtinfo.ca.gov

0131

PETITIONER/PLAINTIFF:	CASE NUMBER:
RESPONDENT/DEFENDANT:	
OTHER PARTY:	

REQUEST FOR ATTORNEY'S FEES AND COSTS ATTACHMENT

1. I am completing this form because:
   a. I need to have enough money for attorney's fees and costs to present my case adequately;
      ☐ I am receiving free legal services from an attorney at a nonprofit legal services agency or a volunteer attorney.
   b. I have less money or limited access to funds to retain or maintain an attorney compared to the party that I am requesting pay for my attorney's fees and costs; and
   c. the party that I want the court to order to pay for my attorney's fees and costs has or is reasonably likely to have the ability to pay for attorney's fees and costs for me and himself or herself.

2. I am asking the court to order that (check all that apply): ☐ petitioner/plaintiff ☐ respondent/defendant
   ☐ other party (specify): _____ pay for my attorney's fees and costs in this legal proceeding as follows:
   a. ☐ Fees: $
   b. ☐ Costs: $

3. The requested amount includes (check all that apply):
   a. ☐ a fee in the amount of: $ _____ to hire an attorney in a timely manner before the proceedings in the matter go forward.
   b. ☐ attorney's fees and costs incurred from the beginning of representation until now in the amount of: $
   c. ☐ estimated attorney's fees and costs in the amount of: $
   d. ☐ attorney's fees and costs for limited scope representation in the amount of: $

4. Have attorney's fees and costs been ordered in this case before?
   a. ☐ No.
   b. ☐ Yes. If so, describe the order:
      (1) The ☐ petitioner/plaintiff ☐ respondent/defendant ☐ other party must pay: $ _____ for attorney's fees and costs.
         (a) This order was made on (date):
         (b) From the payment sources of (if known):

         (c) The payments ☐ have been made ☐ have not been made ☐ have been made in part since the date of the order.
      (2) ☐ Additional information (specify):

5. Along with this Request form, you must complete, file and serve:
   a. A current Income and Expense Declaration (form FL-150). It is considered current if you have completed form FL-150 within the past three months and no facts have changed since the time of completion; and

Form Approved for Optional Use
Judicial Council of California
FL-319 [New January 1, 2012]

**REQUEST FOR ATTORNEY'S FEES AND
COSTS ATTACHMENT
(Family Law)**

Family Code, §§ 270, 2030, 2032, 3121, 3557,
7605; Cal. Rules of Court, rules 5.425, 5.93
www.courts.ca.gov

0132

PETITIONER/PLAINTIFF: RESPONDENT/DEFENDANT: OTHER PARTY:	CASE NUMBER:

5. b. A personal declaration in support of your request for attorney's fees and costs that explains why you need an award of attorney's fees and costs (either *Supporting Declaration for Attorney's Fees and Costs Attachment (*form FL-158) or a comparable declaration that addresses the factors covered in form FL-158).

6. The party requesting attorney's fees and costs must provide the court with sufficient information about the following factors:
   a. The attorney's hourly billing rate;
   b. The nature of the litigation, its difficulty, and the skill required and employed in handling the litigation;
   c. Fees and costs incurred until now; anticipated attorney's fees and costs; and why the fees and costs are just, necessary, and reasonable;
   d. The attorney's experience in the particular type of work demanded; and
   e. If it is a limited scope fee arrangement, the scope of representation.

Notice to Responding Party

7. To respond to this request, you must complete, file, and serve:
   a. A *Responsive Declaration* (form FL-320);
   b. A current *Income and Expense Declaration* (form FL-150). It is considered current if you have completed form FL-150 within the past three months and no facts have changes since the time of completion; and
   c. A personal declaration explaining why the court should grant or deny the request for attorney's fees and costs (either *Supporting Declaration for Attorney's Fees and Costs Attachment* (form FL-158) or a comparable declaration that addresses the factors covered in form FL-158).

8. Number of pages attached to this *Request* form: _____

I declare under penalty of perjury under the laws of the State of California that the information contained on all pages of this form and any attachments is true and correct.

Date:

_____
(TYPE OR PRINT NAME)

▶ _____
(SIGNATURE)

REQUEST FOR ATTORNEY'S FEES AND COSTS ATTACHMENT
(Family Law)

0133

FL-320

PARTY WITHOUT ATTORNEY OR ATTORNEY	STATE BAR NUMBER:	FOR COURT USE ONLY
NAME:		
FIRM NAME:		
STREET ADDRESS:		
CITY:	STATE: ZIP CODE:	
TELEPHONE NO.:	FAX NO.:	
E-MAIL ADDRESS:		
ATTORNEY FOR (name):		

SUPERIOR COURT OF CALIFORNIA, COUNTY OF
  STREET ADDRESS:
  MAILING ADDRESS:
CITY AND ZIP CODE:
  BRANCH NAME:

PETITIONER:
RESPONDENT:
OTHER PARENT/PARTY:

RESPONSIVE DECLARATION TO REQUEST FOR ORDER	CASE NUMBER:
HEARING DATE: TIME: DEPARTMENT OR ROOM:	

Read *Information Sheet: Responsive Declaration to Request for Order* (form FL-320-INFO) for more information about this form.

1. [   ] RESTRAINING ORDER INFORMATION
    a. [   ] No domestic violence restraining/protective orders are now in effect between the parties in this case.
    b. [   ] I agree that one or more domestic violence restraining/ protective orders are now in effect between the parties in this case.

2. [   ] CHILD CUSTODY
   [   ] VISITATION (PARENTING TIME)
    a. [   ] I consent to the order requested for child custody (legal and physical custody).
    b. [   ] I consent to the order requested for visitation (parenting time).
    c. [   ] I do not consent to the order requested for [   ] child custody [   ] visitation (parenting time)
       [   ] but I consent to the following order:

3. [   ] CHILD SUPPORT
    a. I have completed and filed a current *Income and Expense Declaration* (form FL-150) or, if eligible, a current *Financial Statement (Simplified)* (form FL-155) to support my responsive declaration.
    b. [   ] I consent to the order requested.
    c. [   ] I consent to guideline support.
    d. [   ] I do not consent to the order requested [   ] but I consent to the following order:

4. [   ] SPOUSAL OR DOMESTIC PARTNER SUPPORT
    a. I have completed and filed a current *Income and Expense Declaration* (form FL-150) to support my responsive declaration.
    b. [   ] I consent to the order requested.
    c. [   ] I do not consent to the order requested [   ] but I consent to the following order:

Form Adopted for Mandatory Use
Judicial Council of California
FL-320 [Rev. July 1, 2016]
RESPONSIVE DECLARATION TO REQUEST FOR ORDER
Code of Civil Procedure, § 1005
Cal. Rules of Court, rule 5.92
www.courts.ca.gov

0134

PETITIONER: RESPONDENT: OTHER PARENT/PARTY:	CASE NUMBER:

5. ☐ PROPERTY CONTROL
    a. ☐ I consent to the order requested.
    b. ☐ I do not consent to the order requested ☐ but I consent to the following order:

6. ☐ ATTORNEY'S FEES AND COSTS
    a. I have completed and filed a current *Income and Expense Declaration* (form FL-150) to support my responsive declaration.
    b. I have completed and filed with this form a *Supporting Declaration for Attorney's Fees and Costs Attachment* (form FL-158) or a declaration that addresses the factors covered in that form.
    c. ☐ I consent to the order requested.
    d. ☐ I do not consent to the order requested ☐ but I consent to the following order:

7. ☐ DOMESTIC VIOLENCE ORDER
    a. ☐ I consent to the order requested.
    b. ☐ I do not consent to the order requested ☐ but I consent to the following order:

8. ☐ OTHER ORDERS REQUESTED
    a. ☐ I consent to the order requested.
    b. ☐ I do not consent to the order requested ☐ but I consent to the following order:

9. ☐ TIME FOR SERVICE / TIME UNTIL HEARING
    a. ☐ I consent to the order requested.
    b. ☐ I do not consent to the order requested ☐ but I consent to the following order:

10. ☐ FACTS TO SUPPORT my responsive declaration are listed below. The facts that I write and attach to this form cannot be longer than 10 pages, unless the court gives me permission. ☐ Attachment 10.

I declare under penalty of perjury under the laws of the State of California that the information provided in this form and all attachments is true and correct.

Date:

▶

_____
(TYPE OR PRINT NAME)

_____
(SIGNATURE OF DECLARANT)

FL-323-INFO Attorney for Child in a Family Law Case—Information Sheet

In some cases, the family court judge will appoint a private attorney to represent a child in a custody or parenting time (visitation) case. These attorneys are often called "minor's counsel."

Why might the court appoint an attorney for a child?

The court might appoint an attorney for a child for many different reasons. For example, if parents significantly disagree about issues of parenting time and a child is experiencing stress, the court might appoint an attorney to represent the child in the case.

What will minor's counsel do?

Minor's counsel will:
- Gather and present evidence about the best interests of the child;
- If the child wants, present the child's wishes to the court; and
- Inform the court if the child wants to address the court.

Generally, minor's counsel will also:
- Interview the child; and
- Review court files and records available to the parties and make additional investigation.

Minor's counsel:
- Cannot be called as a witness but can bring witnesses for the child's case;
- Can see a child's mental health, medical, dental, and other health-care records, and school and educational records;
- Has the right to interview school personnel, caretakers, health-care providers, mental health professionals, and others who have assessed the child or provided care to the child; and
- Must be served with all documents in the case once appointed.

Who pays for minor's counsel?

In general, the parties pay for the attorney for their child, but sometimes the court will cover the cost of minor's counsel. The court must determine the reasonable amount for the attorney. The court must also decide about the ability of the parties to pay all or some of that amount. The court will review the parties' financial information to make this decision. If the parties do not pay when they are required to, the attorney or the court could bring a case against them to collect the money. If the court finds that the parties are not able to pay all or some of the cost, the court must pay the part the parties can't pay.

Who can ask that minor's counsel be appointed?

Parties and their attorneys, other types of attorneys, the child or a relative of the child, or a child custody mediator, recommending counselor, or evaluator may ask the court to appoint minor's counsel for the child. The court may also decide to appoint minor's counsel without a request.

What will a court order for minor's counsel include?

The court must make written orders when appointing and relieving counsel for a child.

Appointment orders must include the appointed counsel's name, address, and telephone number; the name of the child for whom counsel is appointed; and the child's date of birth.

Orders might also include:
- The child's address, if appropriate;
- Issues to be addressed in the case;
- Case-related tasks that would benefit from the services of counsel for the child;
- Responsibilities and rights of the child's counsel;
- Counsel's rate or amount of compensation;
- Allocation of fees payable by each party or the court;
- Source of funds and manner of reimbursement for costs and attorney fees;
- Allocation of payment of attorney fees to one party subject to reimbursement by the other party;
- The terms and amount of any progress or installment payments; and

Judicial Council of California, *www.courts.ca.gov*
New July 1, 2017, Optional Form
Family Code, §§ 3150–3152
Cal. Rules of Court, rules 5.240, 5.241, 5.242

**Attorney for Child in a Family Law Case—
Information Sheet**

FL-323-INFO, Page 1 of 2
→

FL-323-INFO Attorney for Child in a Family Law Case—Information Sheet

- The ability of the court to change the order on fees and payment.

When does the minor's counsel stop representing the child?

Generally, the attorney keeps representing the child until the court decides otherwise or when the child turns 18 years.

Does the court have a list of attorneys who might be appointed?

The court may or may not maintain a list or panel of attorneys meeting the minimum qualifications to be appointed. The court may also appoint attorneys not on a list and may take into consideration factors including language, culture, and the special needs of the child.

What do I do if I have a complaint about minor's counsel?

Look in the court's local rules or ask the court about its complaint procedures.

What kind of qualifications must attorneys have to be appointed?

An attorney must:
- Be an active member in good standing of the State Bar of California;
- Have professional liability insurance or demonstrate to the court that he or she is adequately self-insured;
- Have completed at least 12 hours of education and training on specific topics (see California Rules of Court, rule 5.242); and
- Have a certain amount of experience before being appointed and also receive at least 8 hours of additional training each year.

How does the attorney tell the court he or she is qualified?

The attorney must file a declaration with the court indicating compliance with all requirements no later than 10 days after being appointed and before beginning work on the case.

0137

SUPERIOR COURT OF CALIFORNIA, COUNTY OF

STREET ADDRESS:

MAILING ADDRESS:

CITY AND ZIP CODE:

BRANCH NAME:

FOR COURT USE ONLY

PETITIONER/PLAINTIFF:

RESPONDENT/DEFENDANT:

OTHER PARENT/PARTY:

ORDER APPOINTING COUNSEL FOR A CHILD	CASE NUMBER:

1. The proceeding was heard:

   On *(date)*:   at *(time)*:   in Dept.:   Room:

   Judge *(name)*:   ☐ Temporary Judge

   ☐ Petitioner/Plaintiff present   ☐ Attorney present *(name)*:
   ☐ Respondent/Defendant present   ☐ Attorney present *(name)*:
   ☐ Other parent/party present   ☐ Attorney present *(name)*:
   ☐ On the request for order, order to show cause, or motion filed *(date)*:   by *(name)*:

2. **THE COURT FINDS** it is in the best interest of the child to appoint counsel to represent the child under Family Code section 3150(a).

   a. Counsel appointed for the child *(name of counsel)*:

   b. Address:

   c. Phone number: d. E-mail address *(optional)*:

3. **CHILD OR CHILDREN FOR WHOM COUNSEL IS APPOINTED**

   Name   Date of birth   Address(es) *(if appropriate)*

4. **REASON FOR APPOINTMENT** *(specify)*:

5. **DUTIES OF COUNSEL FOR A CHILD**

   a. Counsel for a child must:

   (1) Represent the child's best interests.

   (2) Gather evidence that bears on the best interest of the child and present that admissible evidence to the court in any manner appropriate for the counsel of a party.

   (3) Present the child's wishes to the court if the child so desires.

   (4) Serve notices and pleadings on all parties consistent with rules and laws applicable to parties.

   (5) Unless under the circumstances it is inappropriate to exercise the duty:

   (A) Interview the child;

   (B) Review the court files and all accessible relevant records available to both parties; and

   (C) Make any further investigations child's counsel considers necessary to ascertain evidence relevant to the custody or visitation hearings.

   b. Counsel may introduce and examine witnesses, present arguments to the court concerning the child's welfare, and participate further in the proceeding to the degree necessary to represent the child adequately.

Page 1 of 3

Form Approved for Optional Use
Judicial Council of California
FL-323 [Rev. January 1, 2012]

ORDER APPOINTING COUNSEL FOR A CHILD

Family Code, §§ 3150, 3151, 3151.5, 3152;
Government Code, § 77003;
Cal. Rules of Court, rules 5.240, 5.241, 5.242
www.courts.ca.gov

FL-323

PETITIONER/PLAINTIFF:	CASE NUMBER:
RESPONDENT/DEFENDANT:	
OTHER PARENT/PARTY:	

6. **COUNSEL FOR A CHILD HAS THE FOLLOWING RIGHTS:**

   a. To have reasonable access to the child;

   b. To have standing to seek affirmative relief on behalf of the child;

   c. To receive notice of any proceeding, and all phases of that proceeding, including a request for examination affecting the child;

   d. To be heard in the proceeding and take any action available to a party in the proceeding;

   e. To have access to the child's medical, dental, mental health, and other health-care records;

   f. To have access to the child's school and educational records;

   g. To interview school personnel, caretakers, health-care providers, mental health professionals, and others who have assessed the child or provided care to the child;

   h. To interview mediators subject to the provisions of Family Code sections 3177 and 3182;

   i. To assert or waive any privilege on behalf of the child;

   j. To receive reasonable advance notice of and the right to refuse any physical or psychological examination or evaluation that has not been ordered by the court;

   k. On approval of the court, to seek independent psychological or physical examination or evaluation of the child for purposes of the pending proceeding;

   l. On noticed motion to all parties and the local child protective services agency, to request the court to authorize the relevant local child protective services agency to release relevant reports or files concerning the child represented by the counsel as provided by Family Code section 3152; and

   m. Not to be called as a witness in the proceeding. (Fam. Code, §§ 3151(b), 3151.5)

7. **DETERMINATION OF FEES AND PAYMENT**

   a. Counsel for the child will be compensated as follows:
      (1) *(Specify amount or rate and terms):*

      (2) ☐ The court reserves jurisdiction to determine compensation payable to counsel for the child.

      (3) The court reserves jurisdiction to retroactively modify the compensation payable to counsel for the child.

   b. The court finds that the parties are able to pay the compensation and expenses for the child's counsel.
      The parties are ordered to pay counsel for the child as follows:
      (1) ☐ Petitioner/Plaintiff: % ☐ Respondent/Defendant: % ☐ Other parent/party: %
         (a) ☐ Petitioner/Plaintiff must make installment payments of $ per month until paid or modified by court order.
         (b) ☐ Respondent/Defendant must make installment payments of $ per month until paid or modified by court order.
         (c) ☐ Other parent/party must make installment payments of $ per month until paid or modified by court order.
      (2) The court reserves jurisdiction to reallocate attorney's fees and costs between the parties.

   c. The court finds that the parties are unable to pay ☐ all ☐ a portion of the costs for child's counsel.
      The child's counsel must be paid as follows:
      (1) ☐ The court will pay all the fees and expenses for the child's attorney.
      (2) ☐ Petitioner/Plaintiff: % ☐ Respondent/Defendant: % ☐ Other parent/party: %
         ☐ Payable by court: %
         (a) ☐ Petitioner/Plaintiff must make installment payments of $ per month until paid or modified by court order.
         (b) ☐ Respondent/Defendant must make installment payments of $ per month until paid or modified by court order.
         (c) ☐ Other parent/party must make installment payments of $ per month until paid or modified by court order.
      (3) The court reserves jurisdiction to reallocate attorney fees and costs between the parties.
      (4) The court may seek reimbursement from the parties if the court pays all or a portion of the compensation for the child's counsel.

   d. Other:

PETITIONER/PLAINTIFF:	CASE NUMBER:
RESPONDENT/DEFENDANT:	
OTHER PARENT/PARTY:	

8. ADDITIONAL ORDERS

a. No later than 10 court days after being appointed by the court and before beginning work on the case, counsel for a child must file a declaration with the court indicating compliance with the requirements of rule 5.242 of the California Rules of Court. *Declaration of Counsel for a Child Regarding Qualifications* (form FL-322) or other local court forms may be used for this purpose.

b. The parties and their counsel are ordered to cooperate with counsel for the child to permit the performance of his or her duties.

c. Counsel for the child must be provided with complete copies of all relevant documents and records filed in the proceeding within 10 days of the appointment.

d. The parties must provide complete information concerning the child's school, medical, psychological, psychiatric, and other pertinent records to the child's counsel on request. The parties must execute such waivers and releases necessary to facilitate the child's counsel in securing access to records for the child.

e. The parties and/or their counsel must not compromise, settle, dismiss, or otherwise remove from the court's calendar all or any portion of the issues, claims, or proceedings concerning which the child's counsel has been appointed, without participation of the child's counsel or advance notice to the child's counsel.

f. Counsel must continue to represent the child until the appointment terminates, as provided in rule 5.240(f) of the California Rules of Court, or as stated below in item 9.

9. OTHER ORDERS:

THE COURT SO ORDERS.

Date:

_____
JUDICIAL OFFICER

0140

EVALUATOR (Name and address):

FOR COURT USE ONLY

TELEPHONE NO.:   FAX NO. (Optional):
E-MAIL ADDRESS (Optional):

SUPERIOR COURT OF CALIFORNIA, COUNTY OF
    STREET ADDRESS:
    MAILING ADDRESS:
    CITY AND ZIP CODE:
    BRANCH NAME:

PETITIONER/PLAINTIFF:

RESPONDENT/DEFENDANT:

DECLARATION OF PRIVATE CHILD CUSTODY EVALUATOR REGARDING QUALIFICATIONS	CASE NUMBER:

1. I, (name): _____ , declare that if I appeared in court and were sworn, I would testify to the truth of the facts in this declaration.

2. On (date): _____ , I was appointed by the court to perform a child custody evaluation in this case.

3. I submit this form to indicate compliance with all applicable requirements for a private child custody evaluator under rule 5.225 of the California Rules of Court at the time of my appointment to this case.

LICENSING REQUIREMENTS

4. a. ☐ I am licensed as a psychologist, marriage and family therapist, or clinical social worker;

   b. ☐ I am licensed as a physician and I am a board-certified psychiatrist, or I have completed a residency in psychiatry; or

   c. ☐ I am not licensed as indicated in 4a or 4b.

     NOTICE: If item 4c is checked the court may not appoint the person to perform a child custody evaluation in this case unless, under Family Code section 3110.5(d) and rule 5.225(c)(2)(B) of the California Rules of Court, all the following criteria have been met:

     (1) The court determined that there are no evaluators who meet the licensing requirements who are willing and available, within a reasonable period of time, to perform child custody evaluations;

     (2) The parties have stipulated that the person may conduct the child custody evaluation; and

     (3) The court approves the person's appointment.

EDUCATION AND TRAINING REQUIREMENTS

5. I have completed:

   a. ☐ The basic and advanced domestic violence training requirements under rule 5.225(e); and

   b. ☐ The 40 hours of education and training requirements under rule 5.225(d).

CONTINUING EDUCATION AND TRAINING REQUIREMENTS

6. a. ☐ I have recently completed the initial education and training in item 5. I am required to complete the continuing education requirements of rule 5.225(i) by (specify): _____ (within 18 months after completing the initial education and training described in item 5); or

   b. ☐ I have completed the continuing education and training requirements under rule 5.225(i) within the 12-month period immediately preceding my appointment to this case:

     (1) ☐ 8 hours of update training requirements covering the subjects described in rule 5.225(d)

     (2) ☐ 4 hours of domestic violence update training under rule 5.230

Page 1 of 2

Form Adopted for Mandatory Use
Judicial Council of California
FL-326 [Rev. January 1, 2011]

DECLARATION OF PRIVATE CHILD CUSTODY
EVALUATOR REGARDING QUALIFICATIONS

Family Code, §§ 1816, 3110.5;
Cal. Rules of Court, rules 5.225, 5.230
www.courts.ca.gov

EVALUATOR'S NAME:	CASE NUMBER:
PETITIONER/PLAINTIFF:	
RESPONDENT/DEFENDANT:	

7. ☐ I have complied with the experience requirements for a private child custody evaluator specified in rule 5.225(g) because I participated in the completion of four court-appointed child custody evaluations in the preceding three years.

    a. ☐ I independently conducted and completed the child custody evaluations as required in rule 5.225(g)(1)(A); or

    b. ☐ I materially assisted another evaluator as stated in rule 5.225(g)(1)(B).

8. ☐ I have not complied with the experience requirements for child custody evaluators stated in rule 5.225(g)(1).

    NOTICE: If item 8 is checked, the court may not appoint an evaluator to perform a child custody evaluation unless, under rule 5.225(g)(2), all the following criteria have been met:

    1. **The court determined that there are no child custody evaluators who meet the experience requirements for child custody evaluators who are willing and available, within a reasonable period of time, to perform child custody evaluations;**

    2. **The parties have stipulated that the person may conduct the evaluation; and**

    3. **The court approves the person's appointment.**

USE OF INTERNS

9. ☐ I intend to use interns to assist with the child custody evaluation in the manner disclosed and agreed to by the parties and attorneys in the case. Each intern will have complied with the criteria of rule 5.225(m) and will work under my supervision at all times.

NOTICE
Private child custody evaluators must complete this form and file it with the clerk's office no later than 10 days after notification of each appointment and before beginning any work on the child custody evaluation. (Cal. Rules of Court, rule 5.225(l)(1)(B).)

I declare under penalty of perjury under the laws of the State of California that the foregoing is true and correct.

Date:

_____
(TYPE OR PRINT NAME)

▶ _____
(SIGNATURE OF DECLARANT)

**DECLARATION OF PRIVATE CHILD CUSTODY
EVALUATOR REGARDING QUALIFICATIONS**

FL–327

ATTORNEY OR PARTY WITHOUT ATTORNEY *(Name, State Bar number, and address):*	*FOR COURT USE ONLY*

TELEPHONE NO. *(Optional):*   FAX NO. *(Optional):*

E-MAIL ADDRESS *(Optional):*

ATTORNEY FOR *(Name):*

SUPERIOR COURT OF CALIFORNIA, COUNTY OF

STREET ADDRESS:

MAILING ADDRESS:

CITY AND ZIP CODE:

BRANCH NAME:

PETITIONER/PLAINTIFF:

RESPONDENT/DEFENDANT:

OTHER PARTY:

ORDER APPOINTING CHILD CUSTODY EVALUATOR	CASE NUMBER:

THE COURT ORDERS AS FOLLOWS:

1. The court appoints:

   a. ☐ a local court-connected child custody evaluation service *(specify):*

   b. ☐ a private child custody evaluator *(specify):*

   c. ☐ family court services

   d. ☐ other *(specify):*

   in this matter to perform *(check one):*

   e. ☐ a full child custody evaluation

   f. ☐ a partial child custody evaluation

   under the statutory authority of:

   g. ☐ Family Code section 3111.

   h. ☐ Family Code section 3118.

   i. ☐ Evidence Code section 730.

   j. ☐ Chapter 15 (commencing with section 2032.010) of title 4, part 4 of the Code of Civil Procedure.

2. The names and dates of birth of the children are *(specify):*

   ☐ See attachment.

Name	Date of birth

3. The purpose and scope of the evaluation is *(specify):*

   ☐ See attachment.

Page 1 of 2

Form Adopted for Mandatory Use
Judicial Council of California
FL-327 [Rev. January 1, 2010]

ORDER APPOINTING CHILD CUSTODY EVALUATOR

Family Code, §§ 3110.5, 3111;
Cal.Rules of Court, rule 5.220
www.courtinfo.ca.gov

0143

PETITIONER/PLAINTIFF:	CASE NUMBER:
RESPONDENT/DEFENDANT:	
OTHER PARTY:	

4. **DETERMINATION OF FEES AND PAYMENT**

    ☐ See attached order on fees and costs.

  a. The evaluator will be compensated as follows:
     (Specify amount or rate and terms):

     ☐ The court reserves jurisdiction to determine the amount of the fees and costs for the evaluation.

  b. The court finds that the parties are able to pay the cost of the child custody evaluation. The parties are ordered to pay as follows:
    (1) ☐ Petitioner/plaintiff must pay   % of the cost. ☐ Respondent/defendant must pay   % of the cost.
    (2) ☐ The court reserves jurisdiction to reallocate the cost of the evaluation between the parties.
    (3) ☐ Other:

  c. Payment will be made as follows:
    (1) ☐ Petitioner/plaintiff must make installment payments of $ per month until the cost of the evaluation is
       paid or modified by court order.
    (2) ☐ Respondent/defendant must make installment payments of $ per month until the cost of the evaluation is
       paid or modified by court order.
    (3) ☐ Other:

5. **NOTICE TO EVALUATOR**

  Within 10 court days of receipt of this order and before the evaluation, the child custody evaluator must file a *Declaration of Private Child Custody Evaluator Regarding Qualifications* (form FL-326) with the court unless the person is a court-connected employee who must annually file the *Declaration of Court-Connected Child Custody Evaluator Regarding Qualifications* (FL-325).

6. **NOTICE REGARDING CONFIDENTIALITY OF EVALUATION REPORT**

  The child custody evaluation report is confidential. You must not make an unwarranted disclosure of the contents of the child custody evaluation report. By law, a court can order a penalty for the unwarranted disclosure of the child custody evaluation report, which can include an order that the disclosing party pay a fine and attorney fees and costs.

  For more information, read Family Code section 3111 and obtain *Child Custody Evaluation Information Sheet* (form FL-329-INFO). This form is available from the office of the court clerk or online at *www.courtinfo.ca.gov/forms.*

7. **INSTRUCTIONS FOR INITIAL CONTACT**

  a. ☐ The evaluator will contact each party.
  b. ☐ Each party must contact the evaluator.
  c. ☐ Additional instructions *(specify):*

8. **OTHER**

9. ☐ Additional orders attached.

Number of pages attached: _____

Date: _____

_____
JUDGE OF THE SUPERIOR COURT

..

FL-329-INFO   Child Custody Evaluation Information Sheet

We can't agree on a parenting plan. So how will the court make a custody order?

Parents in family court need to have a plan that shows how their child will be cared for after they separate. When parents can't agree on a parenting plan on their own or with the help of a mediator, the judge will make a decision about child custody at a hearing. The judge may order a child custody evaluation to assist in this process. A parent can also ask for an evaluation. This information sheet provides general information in cases where the judge appoints a child custody evaluator.

What is a child custody evaluation?

It is an investigation and analysis of the health, safety, welfare, and best interest of the child. In cases where the court has determined there is an allegation of child sexual abuse, state law requires that the evaluator conduct a detailed investigation if the court is considering permanent child custody or visitation orders. The evaluation is usually completed by a licensed psychologist, marriage and family therapist, clinical social worker, or psychiatrist. The evaluator may be a private professional, a court employee, or a professional under contract with the court.

What kind of evaluation will be done?

The evaluator will follow the court order by investigating and making recommendations that address the issues raised in your case. For example, the court might order the evaluator to make a recommendation about these and other issues:

- *Legal custody:* Who makes major decisions about the child's health, education, and welfare;
- *Physical custody:* Whom the child lives with;
- *Parenting plan or visitation:* The schedule of when the child spends time with each parent;
- *Supervised visitation:* Whether visitation should be supervised and, if so, by what type of program and for how long;
- *Safety issues:* The protection needs of the child in cases involving allegations of domestic violence or child sexual abuse.
- *Child custody modification:* Whether an existing child custody order should be changed.

What if there has been domestic violence or a protective order?

The evaluator must consider any history of domestic violence before interviewing the parents or the child. The parties may request separate interviews with the evaluator. *Give the evaluator copies of any restraining or protective orders.*

For help, call the National Domestic Violence Hotline at 1-800-799-7233 (TDD: 1-800-787-3224) or call 211 (if available in your area).

- *Counseling:* If, and for how long, either parent should be required to attend parenting, coparenting, domestic violence, substance abuse, rehabilitation, or other programs.

What will the evaluator do?

The evaluator will conduct a full or limited-scope investigation. He or she may do all the following as part of the investigation:

- Review documents related to custody, including local police reports and juvenile court records;
- Review the child's medical, dental, mental health, and other health-care records and school and educational records;
- Observe parent-child interaction and interview parents, the child, the child's family members, and others who have had contact with the child;
- Interview professionals who have provided care for the child; and
- Consult with other experts.

Will the evaluator speak with our child?

Depending on the child's age and maturity, the evaluator may consider observing and talking with your child.

How long will the evaluation take?

This varies depending on the kinds of issues the evaluator must investigate. The evaluator will give you a written explanation of the process, which will describe the time frame for gathering and analyzing information for the evaluation.

Judicial Council of California, *www.courtinfo.ca.gov*
New January 1, 2010, Optional Form
Family Code, §§ 3111-3118, 3025.5;
Cal. Rules of Court, rule 5.220

Child Custody Evaluation Information Sheet

FL-329-INFO   Page 1 of 2

→

FL-329-INFO   Child Custody Evaluation Information Sheet

What do I need to do after the court orders the evaluation?

1. Follow the court order about initial contact with the evaluator.
2. Promptly provide documents and information to the evaluator and to the other party at the same time.
3. If needed, sign release forms to allow the evaluator access to documents and the child's care providers.
4. Fully cooperate with the evaluation.

Will I have to pay for the evaluation?

Fees and costs for the evaluation are often paid by the parents; however, sometimes evaluations are paid for by the courts. Your order should say who is responsible for paying for the evaluation.

What happens after the evaluator completes the investigation?

If the court orders it, the evaluator may prepare a verbal or written report about the issues investigated in your case. The report may include recommendations about child custody and visitation. If the court orders the evaluator to file a written, confidential report about the evaluation, you or your attorney and any attorney appointed for the child will receive a copy of the confidential report 10 days before any hearing about custody of the child. The court may consider the report and receive it as evidence. The report will go in the confidential portion of the court's file.

Is the report confidential, or can I share it with others?

The child custody evaluation report is confidential. You must not make an unwarranted disclosure of the contents of the child custody evaluation report. By law, a court can order a fine for an unwarranted disclosure of the child custody evaluation report in an amount that is large enough to prevent the person from disclosing information in the future. The fine can include an order to pay the other party's attorney fees or costs or both.

What if I disagree with the evaluator's report?

You may object to the evaluator's report and request a hearing to explain your concerns to the court. If you do not have an attorney, you may wish to get legal help with this matter. Read the local rules of the family law court in your county to find out how to request a hearing.

What if I have an issue about how the evaluation was conducted?

- Discuss your concern with the evaluator or the evaluator's supervisor to try to resolve the issue.
- Contact the clerk of the court to find out the court's procedures for making and responding to complaints about an evaluator.
- Follow any complaint procedures posted in the evaluator's office.
- Submit your complaint to the court so the court can respond to your concern.
- Contact your court's self-help center or facilitator program for more information.
- Consult with an attorney about raising your concern as part of your case. See information below about where to find legal help.

Does my court have special rules or forms?

Courts in most counties have local rules and forms for cases involving child custody evaluations. Courts generally provide online access to their local rules and forms. See *www.courtinfo.ca.gov/rules/localrules/htm*. You may also contact the family law facilitator or self-help center at the superior court in your county.

Where can I get more information about child custody evaluations?

1. Visit the California Courts Online Self-Help Center Web site: *www.courtinfo.ca.gov/selfhelp*.
2. Ask at your local law library or public library.
3. Read Family Code sections 3110–3118 and 3025.5.
4. Read rules 5.220 and 5.225 of the California Rules of Court.

Where can I get information or legal advice?

1. Talk to your lawyer if you have one.
2. Contact the family law facilitator or self-help center for referrals to local legal services providers and lawyer referral services.
3. Find a lawyer through your local bar association or the State Bar of California at *http://calbar.ca.gov*. Or call the Lawyer Referral Service at 866-442-2529 or 415-538-2250.
4. Seek free and low-cost legal help (if you qualify): *www.lawhelpcalifornia.org*.

0146

ATTORNEY OR PARTY WITHOUT ATTORNEY OR GOVERNMENTAL AGENCY (under Family Code, §§ 17400,17406 (Name, State Bar number, and address):

FOR COURT USE ONLY

TELEPHONE NO.:   FAX NO.:

ATTORNEY FOR (Name):

SUPERIOR COURT OF CALIFORNIA, COUNTY OF

STREET ADDRESS:

MAILING ADDRESS:

CITY AND ZIP CODE:

BRANCH NAME:

PETITIONER/PLAINTIFF:

RESPONDENT/DEFENDANT:

OTHER PARENT/PARTY:

CASE NUMBER:

(If applicable, provide):

HEARING DATE:

HEARING TIME:

PROOF OF PERSONAL SERVICE

DEPT.:

1. I am at least 18 years old, not a party to this action, and not a protected person listed in any of the orders.
2. Person served (name):
3. I served copies of the following documents (specify):

4. By personally delivering copies to the person served, as follows:
   a. Date: b. Time:
   c. Address:

5. I am
   a. ☐ not a registered California process server.
   b. ☐ a registered California process server.
   c. ☐ an employee or independent contractor of a registered California process server.
   d. ☐ exempt from registration under Business & Profession Code section 22350(b).
   e. ☐ a California sheriff or marshal.

6. My name, address, and telephone number, and, if applicable, county of registration and number (specify):

7. ☐ I declare under penalty of perjury under the laws of the State of California that the foregoing is true and correct.
8. ☐ I am a California sheriff or marshal and I certify that the foregoing is true and correct.

Date:

▶

_____
(TYPE OR PRINT NAME OF PERSON WHO SERVED THE PAPERS)

_____
(SIGNATURE OF PERSON WHO SERVED THE PAPERS)

Page 1 of 1

Form Approved for Optional Use
Judicial Council of California
FL-330 [Rev. January 1, 2012]

PROOF OF PERSONAL SERVICE

Code of Civil Procedure, § 1011
www.courts.ca.gov

FL-330-INFO

INFORMATION SHEET FOR PROOF OF PERSONAL SERVICE

Use these instructions to complete the *Proof of Personal Service* (form FL-330).

A person at least 18 years of age or older must serve the documents. There are two ways to serve documents: (1) personal delivery and (2) by mail. See the *Proof of Service by Mail* (form FL-335) if the documents are being served by mail. The person who serves the documents must complete a proof of service form for the documents being served. **You cannot serve documents if you are a party to the action.**

INSTRUCTIONS FOR THE PERSON WHO SERVES THE DOCUMENTS (TYPE OR PRINT IN BLACK INK)

You must complete a proof of service for each package of documents you serve. For example, if you serve the respondent and the other parent, you must complete two proofs of service; one for the respondent and one for the other parent.

Complete the top section of the proof of service forms as follows:
First box, left side: In this box print the name, address, and phone number of the person for whom you are serving the documents.
Second box, left side: Print the name of the county in which the legal action is filed and the court's address in this box. Use the same address for the court that is on the documents you are serving.
Third box, left side: Print the names of the petitioner/plaintiff, respondent/defendant, and other parent in this box. Use the same names listed on the documents you are serving.
First box, top of form, right side: Leave this box blank for the court's use.
Second box, right side: Print the case number in this box. This number is also stated on the documents you are serving.
Third box, right side: Print the hearing date, time, and department. Use the same information that is on the documents you are serving.

1. You are stating that you are over the age of 18 and that you are neither a party of this action nor a protected person listed in any of the orders.
2. Print the name of the party to whom you handed the documents.
3. List the name of each document that you delivered to the party.
4. a. Write in the date that you delivered the documents to the party.
   b. Write in the time of day that you delivered the documents to the party.
   c. Print the address where you delivered the documents.
5. Check the box that applies to you. If you are a private person serving the documents for a party, check box "a."
6. Print your name, address, and telephone number. If applicable, include the county in which you are registered as a process server and your registration number.
7. You must check this box if you are not a California sheriff or marshal. You are stating under penalty of perjury that the information you have provided is true and correct.
8. Do not check this box unless you are a California sheriff or marshal.

Print your name, fill in the date, and sign the form.

If you need additional assistance with this form, contact the family law facilitator in your county.

FL-330-INFO [New January 1, 2012]   INFORMATION SHEET FOR PROOF OF PERSONAL SERVICE   Code of Civil Procedure, § 1011
www.courts.ca.gov

FL-335

ATTORNEY OR PARTY WITHOUT ATTORNEY *(Name, State Bar number, and address)*:	*FOR COURT USE ONLY*
TELEPHONE NO.: FAX NO. *(Optional)*: E-MAIL ADDRESS *(Optional)*: ATTORNEY FOR *(Name)*:	

SUPERIOR COURT OF CALIFORNIA, COUNTY OF
    STREET ADDRESS:
    MAILING ADDRESS:
    CITY AND ZIP CODE:
    BRANCH NAME:

PETITIONER/PLAINTIFF:	CASE NUMBER:
RESPONDENT/DEFENDANT:	*(If applicable, provide):* HEARING DATE:
OTHER PARENT/PARTY:	HEARING TIME:
PROOF OF SERVICE BY MAIL	DEPT.:

NOTICE: To serve temporary restraining orders you must use personal service (see form FL-330).

1. I am at least 18 years of age, not a party to this action, and I am a resident of or employed in the county where the mailing took place.

2. My residence or business address is:

3. I served a copy of the following documents *(specify)*:

   by enclosing them in an envelope AND
   a. ☐ **depositing** the sealed envelope with the United States Postal Service with the postage fully prepaid.
   b. ☐ **placing** the envelope for collection and mailing on the date and at the place shown in item 4 following our ordinary business practices. I am readily familiar with this business's practice for collecting and processing correspondence for mailing. On the same day that correspondence is placed for collection and mailing, it is deposited in the ordinary course of business with the United States Postal Service in a sealed envelope with postage fully prepaid.

4. The envelope was addressed and mailed as follows:
   a. Name of person served:
   b. Address:

   c. Date mailed:
   d. Place of mailing *(city and state)*:

5. ☐ I served a request to modify a child custody, visitation, or child support judgment or permanent order which included an address verification declaration. *(Declaration Regarding Address Verification—Postjudgment Request to Modify a Child Custody, Visitation, or Child Support Order* (form FL-334) may be used for this purpose.)

6. I declare under penalty of perjury under the laws of the State of California that the foregoing is true and correct.

Date:

▶

_____
(TYPE OR PRINT NAME)

_____
(SIGNATURE OF PERSON COMPLETING THIS FORM)

Page 1 of 1

Form Approved for Optional Use
Judicial Council of California
FL-335 [Rev. January 1, 2012]

PROOF OF SERVICE BY MAIL

Code of Civil Procedure, §§ 1013, 1013a
www.courts.ca.gov

FL-340

ATTORNEY OR PARTY WITHOUT ATTORNEY *(Name, State Bar number, and address):*

FOR COURT USE ONLY

TELEPHONE NO.:   FAX NO. *(Optional):*

E-MAIL ADDRESS *(Optional):*

ATTORNEY FOR *(Name):*

SUPERIOR COURT OF CALIFORNIA, COUNTY OF

STREET ADDRESS:

MAILING ADDRESS:

CITY AND ZIP CODE:

BRANCH NAME:

PETITIONER/PLAINTIFF:

RESPONDENT/DEFENDANT:

OTHER PARTY:

FINDINGS AND ORDER AFTER HEARING

CASE NUMBER:

1. This proceeding was heard

on *(date):*   at *(time):*   in Dept.:   Room:

by Judge *(name):*   ☐ Temporary Judge

On the order to show cause, notice of motion or request for order filed *(date):*   by *(name):*

a. ☐ Petitioner/plaintiff present   ☐ Attorney present *(name):*

b. ☐ Respondent/defendant present   ☐ Attorney present *(name):*

c. ☐ Other party present   ☐ Attorney present *(name):*

THE COURT ORDERS

2. Custody and visitation/parenting time: As attached ☐ on form FL-341   ☐ Other   ☐ Not applicable

3. Child support: As attached ☐ on form FL-342   ☐ Other   ☐ Not applicable

4. Spousal or family support: As attached ☐ on form FL-343   ☐ Other   ☐ Not applicable

5. Property orders: As attached ☐ on form FL-344   ☐ Other   ☐ Not applicable

6. Attorney's fees: As attached ☐ on form FL-346   ☐ Other   ☐ Not applicable

7. Other orders: ☐ As attached   ☐ Not applicable

8. All other issues are reserved until further order of court.

9. ☐ This matter is continued for further hearing on *(date):*   at *(time):*   in Dept.:

on the following issues:

Date:

▶ _____

JUDICIAL OFFICER

Approved as conforming to court order.

▶ _____

SIGNATURE OF ATTORNEY FOR ☐ PETITIONER / PLAINTIFF ☐ RESPONDENT/DEFENDANT ☐ OTHER PARTY

Page 1 of 1

Form Adopted for Mandatory Use
Judicial Council of California
FL-340 [Rev. January 1, 2012]

FINDINGS AND ORDER AFTER HEARING
(Family Law—Custody and Support—Uniform Parentage)

www.courts.ca.gov

FL-341

PETITIONER:	CASE NUMBER:
RESPONDENT:	
OTHER PARENT/PARTY:	

CHILD CUSTODY AND VISITATION (PARENTING TIME) ORDER ATTACHMENT

TO ☐ *Findings and Order After Hearing* (form FL-340) ☐ *Judgment* (form FL-180) ☐ *Judgment* (form FL-250)
☐ *Stipulation and Order fo Custody and/or Visitation of Children* (form FL-355)
☐ Other *(specify):*

1. **Jurisdiction.** This court has jurisdiction to make child custody orders in this case under the Uniform Child Custody Jurisdiction and Enforcement Act (Fam. Code, §§ 3400–3465).

2. **Notice and opportunity to be heard.** The responding party was given notice and an opportunity to be heard, as provided by the laws of the State of California.

3. **Country of habitual residence.** The country of habitual residence of the child or children in this case is
   ☐ the United States ☐ Other *(specify):*

4. **Penalties for violating this order.** If you violate this order, you may be subject to civil or criminal penalties, or both.

5. ☐ **Child Custody.** Custody of the minor children of the parties is awarded as follows:

Child's Name	Birth Date	Legal custody to: *(person who makes decisions about health, education, etc.)*	Physical custody to: *(person with whom child lives)*

6. ☐ **Child abduction prevention.** There is a risk that one of the parties will take the children out of California without the other party's permission. (*Child Abduction Prevention Orders Attachment* (form FL-341(B)) must be attached and must be obeyed.)

7. ☐ **Visitation (Parenting Time)**

   a. ☐ Reasonable right of visitation to the party without physical custody **(not appropriate in cases involving domestic violence)**

   b. ☐ See the attached _____ -page document

   c. ☐ The parties will go to child custody mediation or child custody recommending counseling at *(specify date, time, and location):*

   d. ☐ No Visitation (Parenting Time)

   e. ☐ Visitation (Parenting Time) for the ☐ petitioner ☐ respondent ☐ other *(name):* will be as follows:

   (1) ☐ **Weekends starting** *(date):*

   (Note: The first weekend of the month is the first weekend with a Saturday.)

   ☐ 1st ☐ 2nd ☐ 3rd ☐ 4th ☐ 5th weekend of the month

   from _____ at _____ ☐ a.m. ☐ p.m./ if applicable, specify: ☐ start of school
   (day of week) *(time)* ☐ after school

   to _____ at _____ ☐ a.m. ☐ p.m./ if applicable, specify: ☐ start of school
   (day of week) *(time)* ☐ after school

   (a) ☐ The parties will alternate the fifth weekends, with the ☐ petitioner ☐ respondent ☐ other parent/party having the initial fifth weekend, which starts *(date):*

   (b) ☐ The ☐ petitioner ☐ respondent ☐ other parent/party will have the fifth weekend in ☐ odd ☐ even numbered months.

THIS IS A COURT ORDER.

Form Approved for Optional Use
Judicial Council of California
FL-341 [Rev. July 1, 2016]

CHILD CUSTODY AND VISITATION (PARENTING TIME) ORDER ATTACHMENT

Family Code, §§ 3020, 3022, 3025, 3040–3043, 3048, 3100, 6340, 7604
www.courts.ca.gov

FL-341

PETITIONER: RESPONDENT: OTHER PARENT/PARTY:	CASE NUMBER:

7. **Visitation (Parenting Time)** (continued)

    e. (2) ☐ **Alternate weekends starting** *(date):*

        from _____ at _____ ☐ a.m. ☐ p.m./ if applicable, specify: ☐ start of school ☐ after school
              (day of week)   *(time)*

        to _____ at _____ ☐ a.m. ☐ p.m./ if applicable, specify: ☐ start of school ☐ after school
            (day of week)   *(time)*

    (3) ☐ **Weekdays starting** *(date):*

        from _____ at _____ ☐ a.m. ☐ p.m./ if applicable, specify: ☐ start of school ☐ after school
              (day of week)   *(time)*

        to _____ at _____ ☐ a.m. ☐ p.m./ if applicable, specify: ☐ start of school ☐ after school
            (day of week)   *(time)*

    (4) ☐ **Other visitation (parenting time) days and restrictions are:** ☐ listed in Attachment 7e(4) *(form MC-025 may be used for this purpose)* ☐ as follows:

8. ☐ **Supervised visitation (parenting time).** Until ☐ further order of the court ☐ other *(specify):*
    The ☐ petitioner ☐ respondent ☐ other *(name):*
    will have supervised visitation (parenting time) with the minor children according to the schedule set forth on page 1.
    (You must attach *Supervised Visitation Order* (form FL-341(A).)

9. ☐ **Transportation for visitation (parenting time)**
    a. The children must be driven only by a licensed and insured driver. The car or truck must have legal child restraint devices.
    b. ☐ Transportation **to** begin the visits will be provided by the ☐ petitioner ☐ respondent ☐ other *(specify):*
    c. ☐ Transportation **from** the visits will be provided by the ☐ petitioner ☐ respondent ☐ other *(specify):*
    d. ☐ The exchange point at the beginning of the visit will be at *(address):*
    e. ☐ The exchange point at the end of the visit will be at *(address):*
    f. ☐ During the exchanges, the party driving the children will wait in the car and the other party will wait in his or her home (or exchange location) while the children go between the car and the home (or exchange location).
    g. ☐ Other *(specify):*

10. ☐ **Travel with children.** The ☐ petitioner ☐ respondent ☐ other parent/party *(name):*
    must have written permission from the other parent or a court order to take the children out of
    a. ☐ the state of California.
    b. ☐ the following counties *(specify):*
    c. ☐ other places *(specify):*

THIS IS A COURT ORDER.

0152

PETITIONER: RESPONDENT: OTHER PARENT/PARTY:	CASE NUMBER:

11. [ ] **Holiday schedule.** The children will spend holiday time as listed [ ] below [ ] in the attached schedule (*Children's Holiday Schedule Attachment* (form FL-341(C)) may be used for this purpose.)

12. [ ] **Additional custody provisions.** The parties will follow the additional custody provisions listed [ ] below [ ] in the attached schedule. (*Additional Provisions—Physical Custody Attachment* (form FL-341(D)) may be used for this purpose.)

13. [ ] **Joint legal custody.** The parties will share joint legal custody as listed [ ] below [ ] in the attached schedule. (*Joint Legal Custody Attachment* (form FL-341(E)) may be used for this purpose.)

14. **Access to children's records.** Both the custodial and noncustodial parent have the right to access records and information about their minor children (including medical, dental, and school records) and consult with professionals who are providing services to the children.

15. [ ] **Other** (*specify*):

THIS IS A COURT ORDER.

**CHILD CUSTODY AND VISITATION (PARENTING TIME)
ORDER ATTACHMENT**

0153

PETITIONER: RESPONDENT: OTHER PARENT/PARTY:	CASE NUMBER:

CHILDREN'S HOLIDAY SCHEDULE ATTACHMENT

TO ☐ Petition ☐ Response ☐ Request for Order ☐ Responsive Declaration to Request for Order
☐ Stipulation and Order for Custody and/or Visitation of Children ☐ Findings and Order After Hearing or Judgment
☐ Visitation Order—Juvenile ☐ Other *(specify):*

1. **Holiday parenting.** The following table shows the holiday parenting schedules. Write "Petitioner," "Respondent," "Other Parent," or "Other Party" to specify each parent's (or party's) years—odd or even numbered years or both ("every year")—and under "Times," specify the starting and ending days and times.

   Note: Unless specifically ordered, a child's holiday schedule order has priority over the regular parenting time.

Holidays	Times (from when to when) *(Unless noted below, all single-day holidays start at ____ a.m. and end at ____ p.m.)*	Every Year *Petitioner/ Respondent/ Other Parent/Party*	Even Numbered Years *Petitioner/ Respondent/ Other Parent/Party*	Odd Numbered Years *Petitioner/ Respondent/ Other Parent/Party*
December 31 (New Year's Eve)				
January 1 (New Year's Day)				
Martin Luther King's Birthday (weekend)				
February 12 (Lincoln's Birthday)				
President's Day (Weekend)				
President's Week Recess, first half				
President's Week Recess, second half				
Spring Break, first half				
Spring Break, second half				
Mother's Day				
Memorial Day (weekend)				
Father's Day				
July 4th				
Summer Break:				
Labor Day (weekend)				
Columbus Day (weekend)				
Halloween				
November 11 (Veterans Day)				
Thanksgiving Day				
Thanksgiving weekend				
December/January School Break				
Child's birthday *(date):*				
Child's birthday *(date):*				
Child's birthday *(date):*				
Mother's birthday *(date):*				
Father's birthday *(date):*				
Other Parent's/Party's birthday *(date):*				
Breaks for year-round schools:				

Form Approved for Optional Use
Judicial Council of California
FL-341(C) [Rev. July 1, 2016]

CHILDREN'S HOLIDAY SCHEDULE ATTACHMENT

Page 1 of 2
Family Code, §§ 3003, 3083
www.courts.ca.gov

0154

PETITIONER:	CASE NUMBER:
RESPONDENT:	
OTHER PARENT/PARTY:	

1. Holiday parenting *(continued)*

Other Holidays	Times (from when to when) *(Unless noted below, all single-day holidays start at _____ a.m. and end at _____ p.m.)*	Every Year *Petitioner/ Respondent/ Other Parent/Party*	Even Numbered Years *Petitioner/ Respondent/ Other Parent/Party*	Odd Numbered Years *Petitioner/ Respondent/ Other Parent/Party*

☐ Any three-day weekend not specified in item 1 will be spent with the parent or party who would normally have that weekend.

☐ Other *(specify):*

2. Vacations

The ☐ Petitioner ☐ Respondent ☐ Other Parent/Party:

a. May take vacation with the children of up to *(specify number):* ☐ days ☐ weeks the following number of times per year *(specify):*

b. Must notify the other parent or party in writing of vacation plans a minimum of *(specify number):* _____ days in advance and provide the other parent or party with a basic itinerary that includes dates of leaving and returning, destinations, flight information, and telephone numbers for emergency purposes.

   (1) ☐ The other parent or party has *(number):* _____ days to respond if there is a problem with the vacation schedule.

   (2) ☐ If the parties cannot agree on the vacation plans *(check all that apply):*

      (A) ☐ They must confer to try to resolve any disagreement before filing for a court hearing.

      (B) ☐ In even-numbered years, the parties will follow the suggestions of ☐ Petitioner ☐ Respondent ☐ Other Parent/Party for resolving the disagreement.

      (C) ☐ In odd-numbered years, the parties will follow the suggestions of ☐ Petitioner ☐ Respondent ☐ Other Parent/Party for resolving the disagreement.

      (D) ☐ Other *(specify):*

c. ☐ This vacation may be outside the state of California.

d. ☐ Any vacation outside ☐ California ☐ the United States requires prior written consent of the other parent or a court order.

e. ☐ Other *(specify):*

CHILDREN'S HOLIDAY SCHEDULE ATTACHMENT

0155

PETITIONER: RESPONDENT: OTHER PARENT/PARTY:	CASE NUMBER:

ADDITIONAL PROVISIONS—PHYSICAL CUSTODY ATTACHMENT

TO ☐ Petition ☐ Response ☐ Request for Order ☐ Responsive Declaration to Request for Order
☐ Stipulation and Order for Custody and/or Visitation of Children ☐ Findings and Order After Hearing or Judgment
☐ Custody Order—Juvenile—Final Judgment ☐ Other *(specify):*

The additional provisions to physical custody apply to *(specify parties):* ☐ Petitioner ☐ Respondent ☐ Other Parent/Party

1. ☐ **Notification of parties' current address.** ☐ Petitioner ☐ Respondent ☐ Other Parent/Party
   must notify all parties within *(specify number):* days of any change in his or her
   a. address for ☐ residence ☐ mailing ☐ work ☐ e-mail
   b. telephone/message number at ☐ home ☐ cell phone ☐ work ☐ the children's schools
   The parties may not use such information for the purpose of harassing, annoying, or disturbing the peace of the other or invading the other's privacy. No residence or work address is needed if a party has an address with the State of California's Safe at Home confidential address program.

2. ☐ **Notification of proposed move of child.** Each party must notify the other *(specify number):* days before any planned change in residence of the children. The notification must state, to the extent known, the planned address of the children, including the county and state of the new residence. The notification must be sent by certified mail, return receipt requested.

3. ☐ **Child care.**
   a. ☐ The children must not be left alone without age-appropriate supervision.
   b. ☐ The parties must let each other know the name, address, and phone number of the children's regular child-care providers.

4. ☐ **Right of first option of child care.** In the event any party requires child care for *(specify number):* hours or more while the children are in his or her custody, the other party or parties must be given first opportunity, with as much prior notice as possible, to care for the children before other arrangements are made. Unless specifically agreed or ordered by the court, this order does not include regular child care needed when a party is working.

5. ☐ **Canceled visitation (parenting time).**
   a. ☐ If the noncustodial party fails to arrive at the appointed time and fails to notify the custodial party that he or she will be late, then the custodial party need wait for only *(specify number):* minutes before considering the visitation (parenting time) canceled.
   b. ☐ If the noncustodial party is unable to exercise visitation (parenting time) on a given occasion, he or she must notify the custodial party *(specify):*
      ☐ at the earliest possible opportunity.
      ☐ Other *(specify):*
   c. ☐ If the children are ill and unable to participate in the scheduled visitation (parenting time), the custodial party must give the noncustodial party *(specify):*
      ☐ as much notice as possible.
      ☐ A doctor's excuse.
      ☐ Other *(specify):*

6. ☐ **Phone contact between parties and children.**
   a. ☐ The children may have telephone access to the parties ☐ and the parties may have telephone access to the children at reasonable times, for reasonable durations.
   b. ☐ The custodial parent must make the child available for the following scheduled telephone contact *(specify child's telephone contact with each party):*

   c. ☐ No party or any other third party may listen to, monitor, or interfere with the calls.

Form Approved for Optional Use
Judicial Council of California
FL-341(D) [Rev. July 1, 2016]

ADDITIONAL PROVISIONS—PHYSICAL CUSTODY ATTACHMENT

Family Code, §§ 3003, 3024, 3083
www.courts.ca.gov

0156

PETITIONER: RESPONDENT: OTHER PARENT/PARTY:	CASE NUMBER:

7. ☐ **No negative comments.** The parties will not make or allow others to make negative comments about each other or about their past or present relationships, family, or friends within hearing distance of the children.

8. ☐ **Discussion of court proceedings with children.** Other than age-appropriate discussion of the parenting plan and the children's role in mediation or other court proceedings, the parties will not discuss with the children any court proceedings relating to custody or visitation (parenting time).

9. ☐ **No use of children as messengers.** The parties will communicate directly with each other on matters concerning the children and may not use the children as messengers between them.

10. ☐ **Alcohol or substance abuse.** The ☐ petitioner ☐ respondent ☐ other parent/party may not consume alcoholic beverages, narcotics, or restricted dangerous drugs (except by prescription) within *(specify number):* hours before or during periods of time with the children ☐ and may not permit any third party to do so in the presence of the children.

11. ☐ **No exposure to cigarette or medical marijuana smoke.** The parties will not expose the children to secondhand cigarette or medical marijuana smoke.

12. ☐ **No interference with schedule of any party without that party's consent.** The parties will not schedule activities for the children during the other party's scheduled visitation (parenting time) without the other party's prior agreement.

13. ☐ **Third-party contact.**
   a. ☐ The children will have no contact with *(specify name):*
   b. ☐ The children must not be left alone in the presence of *(specify name):*

14. ☐ **Children's clothing and belongings.**
   a. ☐ Each party will maintain clothing for the children so that the children do not have to make the exchanges with additional clothing.
   b. ☐ The children will be returned to the other party with the clothing and other belongings they had when they arrived.

15. ☐ **Log book.** The parties will maintain a "log book" and make sure that the book is sent with the children between their homes. Using businesslike notes (no personal comments), parties will record information related to the health, education, and welfare issues that arise during the time the children are with them.

16. ☐ **Terms and conditions of order may be changed.** The terms and conditions of this order may be added to or changed as the needs of the children and parties change. Such changes will be in writing, dated and signed by the parties; each party will retain a copy. If the parties want a change to be a court order, it must be filed with the court in the form of a court document.

17. ☐ **Other** *(specify):*

0157

PETITIONER:	CASE NUMBER:
RESPONDENT:	
OTHER PARENT/PARTY:	

JOINT LEGAL CUSTODY ATTACHMENT

TO ☐ **Petition** ☐ **Response** ☐ **Request for Order** ☐ **Responsive Declaration to Request for Order**
☐ **Stipulation and Order for Custody and/or Visitation of Children** ☐ **Findings and Order After Hearing or Judgment**
☐ **Custody Order—Juvenile—Final Judgment** ☐ **Other** *(specify):*

> **NOTICE!** In exercising joint legal custody, the parties may act alone, as long as the action does not conflict with any orders about the physical custody of the children. **Use this form only if you want to ask the court to make orders specifying when the consent of both parties is required to exercise legal control of the children and the consequences for failing to obtain mutual consent.**

1. The parties *(specify):* ☐ Petitioner ☐ Respondent ☐ Other Parent/Party will have joint legal custody of the children.

2. In exercising joint legal custody, the parties will share in the responsibility and discuss in good faith matters concerning the health, education, and welfare of the children. The parties must discuss and consent in making decisions on the following matters:

   a. ☐ Enrollment in or leaving a particular private or public school or daycare center

   b. ☐ Beginning or ending of psychiatric, psychological, or other mental health counseling or therapy

   c. ☐ Participation in extracurricular activities

   d. ☐ Selection of a doctor, dentist, or other health professional (except in emergency situations)

   e. ☐ Participation in particular religious activities or institutions

   f. ☐ Out-of-country or out-of-state travel

   g. ☐ Other *(specify):*

3. If a party does not obtain the consent of the other party to those items in 2, which are granted as court orders:

   a. He or she may be subject to civil or criminal penalties.

   b. The court may change the legal and physical custody of the minor children.

   c. ☐ Other consequences *(specify):*

4. ☐ **Special decision making designation and access to children's records**

   a. The ☐ petitioner ☐ respondent ☐ other parent/party will be responsible for making decisions regarding the following issues *(specify):*

   b. Both the custodial and noncustodial parent have the right to access records and information about their minor children (including medical, dental, and school records) and consult with professionals who are providing services to the children.

5. ☐ **Health-care notification.**

   a. ☐ Each party must notify the other of the name and address of each health practitioner who examines or treats the children; such notification must be made within *(specify number):* days of the first treatment or examination.

   b. ☐ Each party is authorized to take any and all actions necessary to protect the health and welfare of the children, including but not limited to consent to emergency surgical procedures or treatment. The party authorizing such emergency treatment must notify the other party as soon as possible of the emergency situation and of all procedures or treatment administered to the children.

   c. ☐ The parties are required to administer any prescribed medications for the children.

6. ☐ **School notification.** Each party will be designated as a person the children's school will contact in the event of an emergency.

7. ☐ **Name.** The parties will not change the last name of the children or have a different name used on the children's medical, school, or other records without the written consent of the other party.

8. ☐ **Other** *(specify):*

Form Approved for Optional Use
Judicial Council of California
FL-341(E) [Rev. July 1, 2016]

JOINT LEGAL CUSTODY ATTACHMENT

Family Code, §§ 3003, 3025, 3083
www.courts.ca.gov

0158

PETITIONER/PLAINTIFF:	CASE NUMBER:
RESPONDENT/DEFENDANT:	
OTHER PARENT/PARTY:	

CHILD SUPPORT INFORMATION AND ORDER ATTACHMENT

TO ☐ **Findings and Order After Hearing (form FL-340)** ☐ **Judgment (form FL-180)**
☐ **Restraining Order After Hearing (CLETS-OAH) (form DV-130)**
☐ **Other** *(specify):*

THE COURT USED THE FOLLOWING INFORMATION IN DETERMINING THE AMOUNT OF CHILD SUPPORT:

1. ☐ A printout of a computer calculation and findings is attached and incorporated in this order for all required items not filled out below.

2. ☐ **Income**

	Gross monthly income	Net monthly income	Receiving TANF/CalWORKS
a. Each parent's monthly income is as follows:			
Petitioner/plaintiff: $	$		☐
Respondent/defendant: $	$		☐
Other parent/party: $	$		☐

   b. Imputation of income. The court finds that the ☐ Petitioner/plaintiff ☐ Respondent/defendant
☐ Other parent/party has the capacity to earn:

   $ per   and has based the support order upon this imputed income.

3. ☐ **Children of this relationship**

   a. Number of children who are the subjects of the support order *(specify):*

   b. Approximate percentage of time spent with petitioner/plaintiff: %
                   Respondent/defendant: %
                   Other parent/party: %

4. ☐ **Hardships**

Hardships for the following have been allowed in calculating child support:

		Petitioner/ plaintiff	Respondent/ defendant	Other parent/ party	Approximate ending time for the hardship
a.	☐ Other minor children:	$	$	$	
b.	☐ Extraordinary medical expenses:	$	$	$	
c.	☐ Catastrophic losses:	$	$	$	

THE COURT ORDERS

5. ☐ **Low-income adjustment**

   a. ☐ The low-income adjustment applies.

   b. ☐ The low-income adjustment does not apply because *(specify reasons):*

6. ☐ **Child support**

   a. **Base child support**

   ☐ Petitioner/plaintiff ☐ Respondent/defendant ☐ Other parent/party must pay child support beginning *(date):* and continuing until further order of the court, or until the child marries, dies, is emancipated, reaches age 19, or reaches age 18 and is not a full-time high school student, whichever occurs first, as follows:

Child's name	Date of birth	Monthly amount	Payable to *(name):*

Payable ☐ on the 1st of the month ☐ one-half on the 1st and one-half on the 15th of the month
☐ other *(specify):*

THIS IS A COURT ORDER.

Page 1 of 3

Form Adopted for Mandatory Use
Judicial Council of California
FL-342 [Rev. January 1, 2017]

CHILD SUPPORT INFORMATION AND ORDER ATTACHMENT

Family Code, §§ 4055–4069
www.courts.ca.gov

PETITIONER/PLAINTIFF:	CASE NUMBER:
RESPONDENT/DEFENDANT:	
OTHER PARENT/PARTY:	

THE COURT FURTHER ORDERS

6. b. ☐ **Mandatory additional child support**

    (1) Child-care costs related to employment or reasonably necessary job training

        (a) ☐ Petitioner/plaintiff must pay: _____ % of total or ☐ $ _____ per month child-care costs.

        (b) ☐ Respondent/defendant must pay: _____ % of total or ☐ $ _____ per month child-care costs.

        (c) ☐ Other parent/party must pay: _____ % of total or ☐ $ _____ per month child-care costs.

        (d) ☐ Costs to be paid as follows *(specify)*:

c. **Mandatory additional child support**

    (2) Reasonable uninsured health-care costs for the children

        (a) ☐ Petitioner/plaintiff must pay: _____ % of total or ☐ $ _____ per month.

        (b) ☐ Respondent/defendant must pay: _____ % of total or ☐ $ _____ per month.

        (c) ☐ Other parent/party must pay: _____ % of total or ☐ $ _____ per month.

        (d) ☐ Costs to be paid as follows *(specify)*:

d. ☐ **Additional child support**

    (1) ☐ Costs related to the educational or other special needs of the children

        (a) ☐ Petitioner/plaintiff must pay: _____ % of total or ☐ $ _____ per month.

        (b) ☐ Respondent/defendant must pay: _____ % of total or ☐ $ _____ per month.

        (c) ☐ Other parent/party must pay: _____ % of total or ☐ $ _____ per month.

        (d) ☐ Costs to be paid as follows *(specify)*:

    (2) ☐ Travel expenses for visitation

        (a) ☐ Petitioner/plaintiff must pay: _____ % of total or ☐ $ _____ per month.

        (b) ☐ Respondent/defendant must pay: _____ % of total or ☐ $ _____ per month.

        (c) ☐ Other parent/party must pay: _____ % of total or ☐ $ _____ per month.

        (d) ☐ Costs to be paid as follows *(specify)*:

e. ☐ **Non-Guideline Order**

    This order does not meet the child support guideline set forth in Family Code section 4055. *Non-Guideline Child Support Findings Attachment* (form FL-342(A)) is attached.

Total child support per month: $

f. **Child Support Order Suspension**

When a person who has been ordered to pay child support is in jail or prison or is involuntarily institutionalized for any period of more than 90 days in a row, the child support order is temporarily stopped. However, the child support order will not be stopped if the person who owes support has the financial ability to pay that support while in jail, prison, or an institution. It will also not be stopped if the reason the person is in jail, prison, or an institution is because the person didn't pay court ordered child support or committed domestic violence against the supported person or child. The child support order starts again on the first day of the month after the person is released from jail, prison, or an institution.

7. **Health-care expenses**

a. Health insurance coverage for the minor children of the parties must be maintained by the

☐ petitioner/plaintiff ☐ respondent/defendant ☐ other parent/party if available at no or reasonable cost through their respective places of employment or self-employment. Both parties are ordered to cooperate in the presentation, collection, and reimbursement of any health-care claims. The parent ordered to provide health insurance must seek continuation of coverage for the child after the child attains the age when the child is no longer considered eligible for coverage as a dependent under the insurance contract, if the child is incapable of self-sustaining employment because of a physically or mentally disabling injury, illness, or condition and is chiefly dependent upon the parent providing health insurance for support and maintenance.

THIS IS A COURT ORDER.

CHILD SUPPORT INFORMATION AND ORDER ATTACHMENT

0160

PETITIONER/PLAINTIFF:	CASE NUMBER:
RESPONDENT/DEFENDANT:	
OTHER PARENT/PARTY:	

7. b. ☐ Health insurance is not available to the ☐ petitioner/plaintiff ☐ respondent/defendant ☐ other parent/party at a reasonable cost at this time.

   c. ☐ The party providing coverage must assign the right of reimbursement to the other party.

8. **Earnings assignment**

   An earnings assignment order is issued. **Note:** The payor of child support is responsible for the payment of support directly to the recipient until support payments are deducted from the payor's wages and for payment of any support not paid by the assignment.

9. In the event that there is a contract between a party receiving support and a private child support collector, the party ordered to pay support must pay the fee charged by the private child support collector. This fee must not exceed 33 1/3 percent of the total amount of past due support nor may it exceed 50 percent of any fee charged by the private child support collector. The money judgment created by this provision is in favor of the private child support collector and the party receiving support, jointly.

10. ☐ **Employment search order (Family Code § 4505)**

   ☐ Petitioner/plaintiff ☐ Respondent/defendant ☐ Other parent/party is ordered to seek employment with the following terms and conditions:

11. **Other orders** *(specify):*

12. **Notices**

   a. *Notice of Rights and Responsibilities (Health-Care Costs and Reimbursement Procedures) and Information Sheet on Changing a Child Support Order* (form FL-192) must be attached and is incorporated into this order.

   b. If this form is attached to *Restraining Order After Hearing* (form DV-130), the support orders issued on this form (form FL-342) remain in effect after the restraining orders issued on form DV-130 end.

13. **Child Support Case Registry Form**

   Both parties must complete and file with the court a *Child Support Case Registry Form* (form FL-191) within 10 days of the date of this order. Thereafter, the parties must notify the court of any change in the information submitted within 10 days of the change by filing an updated form.

NOTICE: Any party required to pay child support must pay interest on overdue amounts at the legal rate, which is currently 10 percent per year.

THIS IS A COURT ORDER.

FL-342(A)

PETITIONER/PLAINTIFF:	CASE NUMBER:
RESPONDENT/DEFENDANT:	

NON-GUIDELINE CHILD SUPPORT FINDINGS ATTACHMENT

Attachment to ☐ Child Support Information and Order Attachment (form FL-342)
☐ Judgment (Family Law) (form FL-180) ☐ Other *(specify):*

The court makes the following findings required by Family Code sections 4056, 4057, and 4065:

1. STIPULATION TO NON-GUIDELINE ORDER

☐ The child support agreed to by the parties is ☐ below or ☐ above the statewide child support guidelines. The amount of support that would have been ordered under the guideline formula is: $ per month. The parties have been fully informed of their rights concerning child support. Neither party is acting out of duress or coercion. Neither party is receiving public assistance and no application for public assistance is pending. The needs of the children will be adequately met by this agreed-upon amount of child support. If the order is below the guideline, no change of circumstances will be required to modify this order. If the order is above the guideline, a change of circumstances will be required to modify this order.

OTHER REBUTTAL FACTORS

2. ☐ **Support calculation**

 a. The guideline amount of child support calculated is: $
  per month **payable** by ☐ petitioner/plaintiff ☐ respondent/defendant

 b. The court finds by a preponderance of the evidence that rebuttal factors exist. The rebuttal factors result in an ☐ increase ☐ decrease in child support. The revised amount of support is: $ per month.

 c. The court finds the child support amount revised by these factors to be in the best interest of the child and that application of the formula would be unjust or inappropriate in this case.
  These changes remain in effect ☐ until *(date):*
  ☐ until further order

 d. **The factors are:**

  (1) ☐ The sale of the family residence is deferred under Family Code section 3800, and the rental value of the family residence in which the children reside exceeds the mortgage payments, homeowners insurance, and property taxes by: $ per month. (Fam. Code, § 4057(b)(2).)

  (2) ☐ The parent paying support has extraordinarily high income, and the amount determined under the guideline would exceed the needs of the child. (Fam. Code, § 4057(b)(3).)

  (3) ☐ The ☐ petitioner/plaintiff ☐ respondent/defendant is not contributing to the needs of the children at a level commensurate with that party's custodial time. (Fam. Code, § 4057(b)(4).)

  (4) ☐ Special circumstances exist in this case. The special circumstances are:
   (i) ☐ The parents have different timesharing arrangements for different children.
    (Fam. Code, § 4057(b)(5) (A).)
   (ii) ☐ The parents have substantially equal custody of the children and one parent has a much lower or higher percentage of income used for housing than the other parent.
    (Fam. Code, § 4057(b)(5)(B).)
   (iii) ☐ The child has special medical or other needs that require support greater than the formula amount. These needs are (Fam. Code, § 4057(b)(5)(C)) *(specify):*

   (iv) ☐ Other (Fam. Code, § 4057(b)(5)) *(specify):*

Form Adopted for Mandatory Use
Judicial Council of California
FL-342(A) [Rev. January 1, 2008]

NON-GUIDELINE CHILD SUPPORT FINDINGS ATTACHMENT

Family Code, § 4056
www.courtinfo.ca.gov

0162

PETITIONER/PLAINTIFF:	CASE NUMBER:
RESPONDENT/DEFENDANT:	
OTHER PARENT:	

SPOUSAL, PARTNER, OR FAMILY SUPPORT ORDER ATTACHMENT

TO ☐ *Findings and Order After Hearing* **(form FL-340)** ☐ **Judgment** *(form FL-180)*

☐ *Restraining Order After Hearing (CLETS-OAH)* **(form DV-130)** ☐ **Other** *(specify):*

☐ **Stipulation of Parties**

THE COURT FINDS

1. **Net income.** The parties' monthly income and deductions are as follows *(complete a, b, or both)*:

	Total gross monthly income	Total monthly deductions	Total hardship deductions	Net monthly disposable income
a. Petitioner: ☐ receiving TANF/CalWORKS	$	$	$	$
b. Respondent: ☐ receiving TANF/CalWORKS	$	$	$	$

2. ☐ A printout of a computer calculation of the parties' financial circumstances is attached for all required items not filled out above *(for temporary support only)*.

3. **Judgment for spousal or partner support**

   a. ☐ Modifies a judgment or order entered on *(date):*

   b. ☐ The parties were married for *(specify numbers):* _____ years _____ months.

   c. ☐ The parties were registered as domestic partners or the equivalent for *(specify numbers):*_____ years _____ months.

   d. ☐ The parties are both self-supporting, as shown on the *Declaration for Default or Uncontested Dissolution or Legal Separation* (form FL-170).

   e. ☐ The marital standard of living was *(describe):*

   ☐ See Attachment 3d.

THE COURT ORDERS

4. ☐ The issue of spousal or partner support for the ☐ petitioner ☐ respondent is reserved for a later determination.

5. ☐ The court terminates jurisdiction over the issue of spousal or partner support for the ☐ petitioner ☐ respondent.

6. a. The ☐ petitioner ☐ respondent must pay to the ☐ petitioner ☐ respondent
   as ☐ temporary ☐ spousal support ☐ family support ☐ partner support
   $ _____ per month, beginning *(date):* _____, payable through *(specify end date):*

   ☐ payable on the *(specify):* _____ day of each month.
   ☐ Other *(specify):*

   b. ☐ Support must be paid by check, money order, or cash. The support payor's obligation to pay support will terminate on the death of either party, remarriage, or registration of a new domestic partnership of the support payee.

   c. ☐ An earnings assignment for the foregoing support will issue. (**Note:** The payor of spousal, family, or partner support is responsible for the payment of support directly to the recipient until support payments are deducted from the payor's earnings, and for any support not paid by the assignment.)

   d. ☐ Service of the earnings assignment is stayed provided the payor is not more than *(specify number):* _____ days late in the payment of spousal, family, or partner support.

THIS IS A COURT ORDER.

Page 1 of 2

Form Approved for Optional Use
Judicial Council of California
FL-343 [Rev. July 1, 2012]

SPOUSAL, PARTNER, OR FAMILY SUPPORT ORDER ATTACHMENT
(Family Law)

Family Code, §§ 150, 299, 3651,
3653, 3654, 4320, 4330, 4337
www.courts.ca.gov

0163

PETITIONER/PLAINTIFF:	CASE NUMBER:
RESPONDENT/DEFENDANT:	
OTHER PARENT:	

7. [ ] The [ ] petitioner [ ] respondent should make reasonable efforts to assist in providing for his or her support needs.

8. [ ] The parties must promptly inform each other of any change of employment, including the employer's name, address, and telephone number.

9. [ ] This order is for family support. Both parties must complete and file with the court a *Child Support Case Registry Form* (form FL-191) within 10 days of the date of this order. The parents must notify the court of any change of information submitted within 10 days of the change by filing an updated form. A *Notice of Rights and Responsibilities (Health-Care Costs and Reimbursement Procedures) and Information Sheet on Changing a Child Support Order* (form FL-192) is attached.

10. [ ] Notice: If this form is attached to *Restraining Order After Hearing (CLETS-OAH) (Order of Protection)* (form DV-130), the orders issued on this form (FL-343) do not expire upon termination of the restraining orders issued on form DV-130.

11. [ ] Other orders (*specify*):

> **NOTICE: Any party required to pay support must pay interest on overdue amounts at the "legal" rate, which is currently 10 percent.**

THIS IS A COURT ORDER.

0164

PETITIONER :	CASE NUMBER:
RESPONDENT:	

PROPERTY ORDER ATTACHMENT
TO FINDINGS AND ORDER AFTER HEARING

THE COURT ORDERS

1. ☐ **Property restraining orders**

   a. The ☐ petitioner ☐ respondent ☐ claimant is restrained from transferring, encumbering, hypothecating, concealing, or in any way disposing of any property, real or personal, whether community, quasi-community, or separate, except in the usual course of business or for the necessities of life.

   b. The ☐ petitioner ☐ respondent must notify the other party of any proposed extraordinary expenses at least five business days before incurring such expenses, and make an accounting of such to the court.

   c. The ☐ petitioner ☐ respondent is restrained from cashing, borrowing against, cancelling, transferring, disposing of, or changing the beneficiaries of any insurance or other coverage, including life, health, automobile, and disability, held for the benefit of the parties or their minor child or children.

   d. The ☐ petitioner ☐ respondent must not incur any debts or liabilities for which the other may be held responsible, other than in the ordinary course of business or for the necessities of life.

2. ☐ **Possession of property.** The exclusive use, possession, and control of the following property that the parties own or are buying is given as specified:

   Property   Given to

   ☐ See Attachment 2.

3. ☐ **Payment of debts.** Payments on the following debts that come due while this order is in effect must be paid as follows:

Total debt	Amount of payments	Pay to	Paid by
$	$		
$	$		
$	$		
$	$		

   ☐ See Attachment 3.

4. ☐ These are temporary orders only. The court will make final orders at the time of judgment.

5. ☐ Other *(specify):*

Form Adopted for Mandatory Use
Judicial Council of California
FL-344 [Rev. January 1, 2007]

**PROPERTY ORDER ATTACHMENT
TO FINDINGS AND ORDER AFTER HEARING**
(Family Law)

Family Code, §§ 2045, 6324
www.courtinfo.ca.gov

0165

| PETITIONER: | CASE NUMBER: |
| RESPONDENT: | |

PROPERTY ORDER ATTACHMENT TO JUDGMENT

1. **Division of community property assets**
   a. ☐ There are no community property assets.
   b. ☐ The court finds that the net value of the community estate is less than $5,000 and that the ☐ petitioner ☐ respondent cannot be found. Under Family Code section 2604, the entire community estate is awarded to the ☐ petitioner ☐ respondent.
   c. ☐ The petitioner will receive the following assets: *(Attach additional page if necessary.)*

   d. ☐ The respondent will receive the following assets: *(Attach additional page if necessary.)*

   e. The ☐ petitioner ☐ respondent will be responsible for preparing and filing a *Qualified Domestic Relations Order* (QDRO) to divide the following plan or retirement account(s) *(specify):*

   The fee for preparation of the QDRO shall be shared as follows *(specify):*

   f. ☐ Other orders:

   g. ☐ Each spouse will receive the assets listed above as his or her sole and separate property. The parties must execute any and all documents required to carry out this division.
   h. The court reserves jurisdiction to divide any community assets not listed here and enforce the terms of this order.

2. **Division of community property debts**
   a. ☐ There are no community debts.
   b. ☐ All community debts have been paid by the ☐ petitioner ☐ respondent.
      The ☐ petitioner ☐ respondent must reimburse the other party: $
      The payment plan is as follows:

   c. ☐ The petitioner will be responsible for the following debts: *(Attach additional page if necessary.)*

   d. ☐ The respondent will be responsible for the following debts: *(Attach additional page if necessary.)*

Form Approved for Optional Use
Judicial Council of California
FL-345 [Rev. January 1, 2007]

PROPERTY ORDER ATTACHMENT TO JUDGMENT
(Family Law)

Family Code, §§ 299, 2500–2660
www.courtinfo.ca.gov

FL-345

PETITIONER:	CASE NUMBER:
RESPONDENT:	

e. ☐ Other orders:

f. Each party will be solely responsible for paying the debts assigned to him or her and will hold the other harmless from those debts. The parties understand that the creditors are not bound by this judgment. If a creditor seeks payment from the party who is not listed as responsible for the debt, that party can file a motion to seek reimbursement from the defaulting party.

g. The court reserves jurisdiction to divide any community debts not listed here.

3. ☐ **Equalization of division of property and debt orders.** To equalize the division of the community property assets and debts, the ☐ petitioner ☐ respondent must pay to the other the sum of: $, payable as follows *(specify):*

4. **Separate property**

a. ☐ The court confirms the following assets or debts as the sole separate property, or sole responsibility, of the petitioner:

b. ☐ The court confirms the following assets or debts as the sole separate property, or sole responsibility, of the respondent:

5. ☐ The settlement agreement between the parties dated *(date):* is attached and made a part of this judgment.

6. ☐ **Sale of property.** The following property will be offered for sale and sold for the fair market value as soon as a willing buyer can be found, and the net proceeds from the sale will be ☐ divided equally ☐ other *(specify):*

7. ☐ Other orders *(specify):*

PROPERTY ORDER ATTACHMENT TO JUDGMENT
(Family Law)

FL-346

PETITIONER/PLAINTIFF:	CASE NUMBER:
RESPONDENT/DEFENDANT:	
OTHER PARTY:	

ATTORNEY'S FEES AND COSTS ORDER ATTACHMENT

Attached to:

☐ *Findings and Orders After Hearing* (form FL-340)

☐ *Judgment (Uniform Parentage—Custody and Support)* (form FL-250)

☐ *Judgment* (form FL-180)

☐ Other *(specify):*

THE COURT FINDS

1. ☐ An award of attorney's fees and costs is appropriate because there is a demonstrated disparity between the parties in access to funds to retain or maintain counsel and in the ability to pay for legal representation.

  a. ☐ The party requested to pay attorney's fees and costs has or is reasonably likely to have the ability to pay for legal representation for both parties.

  b. ☐ The requested attorney's fees and costs are reasonable and necessary.

2. ☐ An award of attorney's fees and costs is not appropriate because *(check all that apply):*

  a. ☐ there is not a demonstrated disparity between the parties in access to funds to retain or maintain counsel or in the ability to pay for legal representation.

  b. ☐ the party requested to pay attorney's fees and costs does not have or is not reasonably likely to have the ability to pay for legal representation for both parties.

  c. ☐ the requested attorney's fees and costs are not reasonable or necessary.

3. ☐ Other *(specify):*

THE COURT ORDERS

4. a. The ☐ petitioner/plaintiff ☐ respondent/defendant ☐ other party to pay attorney's fees and costs in this legal proceeding

  b. in the amount of:

  (1) ☐ Fees: $

  (2) ☐ Costs: $

  (3) ☐ Interest is not included and is not waived.

  c. Payable to ☐ petitioner/plaintiff ☐ respondent/defendant ☐ other party

  d. ☐ From the payment sources of *(if specified):*

Form Approved for Optional Use
Judicial Council of California
FL-346 [New January 1, 2012]

**ATTORNEY'S FEES AND COSTS ORDER ATTACHMENT
(Family Law)**

Family Code, §§ 270, 2030, 3121, 3557,
7605; Cal. Rules of Court, rules 5.425, 5.93
www.courts.ca.gov

PETITIONER/PLAINTIFF:	CASE NUMBER:
RESPONDENT/DEFENDANT:	
OTHER PARTY:	

4. e.   With a payment schedule of *(specify):*

(1) ☐ Due in full, on or before *(date):*

(2) ☐ Due in installments, with monthly payments of *(specify):* $, on the *(specify):*   day of each month, beginning *(date):*   until paid in full.

(3) ☐ If any payment is not timely made and more than   days overdue, the entire unpaid balance will immediately become due with interest at the legal rate, which is currently 10 percent per year, from the date of default to the date payment is finally made.

(4) ☐ No interest will accrue as long as payments are timely made.

(5) ☐ Other *(specify):*

5. ☐ This amount includes *(check all that apply):*

a. ☐ a fee in the amount of *(specify)* $ to hire an attorney in a timely manner before the proceedings in the matter go forward.

b. ☐ attorney's fees and costs incurred to date in the amount of *(specify):* $

c. ☐ estimated attorney's fees and costs in the amount of *(specify):* $

d. ☐ attorney's fees and costs for limited scope representation in the amount of *(specify):* $

e. ☐ any amounts previously ordered that have not yet been paid *(specify):* $

f. ☐ Other *(specify):*

6. ☐ Other orders *(specify):*

NOTICE: Any party required to pay attorney's fees and costs must pay interest on overdue amounts at the legal rate, which is currently 10 percent per year.

PETITIONER:	CASE NUMBER:
RESPONDENT:	

BIFURCATION OF STATUS OF MARRIAGE OR DOMESTIC PARTNERSHIP

ATTACHMENT TO ☐ **JUDGMENT (FL-180)** ☐ **FINDINGS AND ORDER AFTER HEARING (FL-340)**

The court grants the request of ☐ petitioner ☐ respondent to bifurcate and grant a separate trial on the issue of the dissolution of the status of the marriage or domestic partnership apart from other issues.

Date marital or domestic partnership status ends (specify):

THE COURT FINDS

1. A preliminary declaration of disclosure with a completed schedule of assets and debts and income and expense declaration has been served on the nonmoving party, or the parties have stipulated in writing to defer service of the preliminary declaration of disclosure until a later time.

2. Each retirement or pension plan of the parties has been joined as a party to the proceeding for dissolution unless joinder is precluded or made unnecessary by applicable law.

THE COURT ORDERS

3. a. To preserve the claims of each party in all retirement plan benefits on entry of judgment granting a dissolution of the status of the marriage or domestic partnership, the court makes one of the following orders for each retirement plan in which either party is a participant:

   (1) A final domestic relations order or qualified domestic relations order under Family Code section 2610 disposing of each party's interest in retirement plan benefits, including survivor and death benefits.

   (2) An interim order preserving the nonemployee party's right to retirement plan benefits, including survivor and death benefits, pending entry of judgment on all remaining issues.

   (3) A provisional order on *Pension Benefits—Attachment to Judgment* (form FL-348) incorporated as an attachment to the judgment of dissolution of the status of marriage or domestic partnership (*Judgment (Family Law)* (form FL-180)). This order provisionally awards to each party a one-half interest in all retirement benefits attributable to employment during the marriage or domestic partnership.

   b. Name of plan:

	Type of order attached	
3a(1)	3a(2)	3a(3)
☐	☐	☐
☐	☐	☐
☐	☐	☐

   ☐ See attachment 3b for additional plans.

   c. The moving party must promptly serve on the retirement or pension plan administrator a copy of any order entered under items a and b above and a copy of the judgment granting dissolution of the status of the marriage or domestic partnership (form FL-180).

4. Jurisdiction is reserved for later determination of all other pending issues in this case.

5. The court makes the following additional orders as conditions for granting the severance on the issue of dissolution of the status of marriage or domestic partnership. In the case of the moving party's death, the order continues to be binding on that moving party's estate and will be enforceable against any asset, including the proceeds thereof, to the same extent that these obligations would have been enforceable before the person's death.

   a. ☐ **Division of property**

   The ☐ petitioner ☐ respondent must indemnity and hold the other party harmless from any ☐ taxes, ☐ reassessments, ☐ interest, and ☐ penalties payable by the other party in connection with the division of the community estate that would not have been payable if the parties were still married or domestic partners at the time the division was made.

Form Adopted for Mandatory Use
Judicial Council of California
FL-347 [January 1, 2018]

**BIFURCATION OF STATUS OF MARRIAGE
OR DOMESTIC PARTNERSHIP—ATTACHMENT
(Family Law)**

Family Code, §§ 2337, 2610;
Probate Code, §§ 160 et seq., 5000 et seq.
www.courts.ca.gov

PETITIONER:	CASE NUMBER:
RESPONDENT:	

5. b. ☐ **Health insurance**

Until judgment has been entered on all remaining issues and has become final, the ☐ petitioner ☐ respondent must maintain all existing health and medical insurance coverage for the other party, and that party must also maintain any minor children as named dependents, as long as that party is eligible to do so. If at any time during this period the ☐ petitioner ☐ respondent is not eligible to maintain that coverage, that party must, at his or her sole expense, provide and maintain health and medical insurance coverage that is comparable to the existing health and medical insurance coverage to the extent it is available.

If that coverage is not available, the ☐ petitioner ☐ respondent is responsible for paying the health and medical care for the other party and the minor children to the extent that care would have been covered by the existing insurance coverage but for the dissolution of marital status or domestic partnership, and will otherwise indemnify and hold the other party harmless from any adverse consequences resulting from the loss or reduction of the existing coverage. "Health and medical insurance coverage" includes any coverage under any group or individual health or other medical plan, fund, policy, or program.

c. ☐ **Probate homestead**

Until judgment has been entered on all remaining issues and has become final, the ☐ petitioner ☐ respondent must indemnify and hold the other party harmless from any adverse consequences to the other party if the bifurcation results in a termination of the other party's right to a probate homestead in the residence in which the other party resides at the time the severance is granted.

d. ☐ **Probate family allowance**

Until judgment has been entered on all remaining issues and has become final, the ☐ petitioner ☐ respondent must indemnify and hold the other party harmless from any adverse consequences to the other party if the bifurcation results in the loss of the rights of the other party to a probate family allowance as the surviving spouse or surviving domestic partner.

e. ☐ **Retirement benefits**

Except for any retirement plan, fund, or arrangement identified in any order issued and attached as set out in paragraph 3, until judgment has been entered on all remaining issues and has become final, the ☐ petitioner ☐ respondent must indemnify and hold the other party harmless from any adverse consequences to the other party if the bifurcation results in the loss of the other party's rights with respect to any retirement, survivor, or deferred compensation benefits under any plan, fund, or arrangement, or to any elections or options associated with them, to the extent that the other party would have been entitled to those benefits or elections as the spouse or surviving spouse or the domestic partner or surviving domestic partner of the moving party.

f. ☐ **Social security benefits**

The moving party must indemnify and hold the other party harmless from any adverse consequences if the bifurcation results in the loss of rights to social security benefits or elections to the extent the other party would have been entitled to those benefits or elections as the surviving spouse or surviving domestic partner of the moving party.

g. ☐ **Beneficiary designation—nonprobate transfer**

Attachment 5(g), Order Re: Beneficiary Designation for Nonprobate Transfer Assets, will remain in effect for each covered asset until the division of any community interest therein has been completed.

h. ☐ **Individual Retirement Accounts**

Attachment 5(h), Order Re: Division of IRA Under Internal Revenue Code Section 408(d)(6), has been issued to preserve the ability of ☐ petitioner ☐ respondent to defer distribution of his or her community interest on the death of the IRA owner.

**BIFURCATION OF STATUS OF MARRIAGE
OR DOMESTIC PARTNERSHIP—ATTACHMENT
(Family Law)**

PETITIONER:	CASE NUMBER:
RESPONDENT:	

5. i. ☐ **Enforcement of community property rights**

Good cause exists to make additional orders as set out in Family Code section 2337(c)(9). See Attachment 5(i).

j. ☐ **Other conditions that are just and equitable**

Other:

6. Number of pages attachments:

WARNING: *Judgment (Family Law)* (form FL-180) (status only) must be completed in addition to this form for the status of the marriage or domestic partnership to be ended.

**BIFURCATION OF STATUS OF MARRIAGE
OR DOMESTIC PARTNERSHIP—ATTACHMENT
(Family Law)**

0172

PETITIONER/PLAINTIFF:	CASE NUMBER:
RESPONDENT/DEFENDANT:	

PENSION BENEFITS—ATTACHMENT TO JUDGMENT
(Attach to form FL-180)

This order concerns the division of retirement and survivor benefits between the following two parties:

Name of petitioner: Name of respondent:

Address of petitioner: Address of respondent:

Date of marriage or registration of domestic partnership: Date of separation:

TO THE EMPLOYER/PLAN ADMINISTRATOR OF EACH PLAN IDENTIFIED BELOW:

Each party identified above is provisionally awarded without prejudice, and subject to adjustment by a later domestic relations order, a separate interest equal to one-half of all benefits accrued or to be accrued under any retirement plan in which one party has accrued a benefit, including but not limited to the plans listed below, as a result of employment of the other party during the marriage or domestic partnership and before the date of separation. In addition, pending further notice, the plan must, as allowed by law, or as allowed by the terms of the plan in the case of a governmental plan, continue to treat the parties as married persons or domestic partners for purposes of any survivor rights and benefits available under the plan to the extent necessary to provide for payment to the surviving spouse or domestic partner of an amount equal to that separate interest or of all of the survivor benefits if at the time of death of the participant there is no other eligible recipient of the survivor benefit.

TO THE PARTIES:

Each party must provide the information and take the required actions listed below to protect the other party's interest in retirement benefits:

1. List below (or on a page attached) the name and address of each employer for which you or the other party work or worked where either of you participated in a retirement plan during the marriage and before your separation. Include the name (or a description if you do not have the name) of each of these plans.

          ☐ See Attached

2. For each plan you listed under item 1, promptly deliver a copy of this order to the plan's administrator. You can deliver a copy of this order in person or by mail. Provide a proof of service to the court and the other party.
   If you do not know the plan's administrator, deliver a copy to
   • the employer or plan sponsor, or, if unknown,
   • the trustee or custodian of any assets of the plan.

3. Each party who is a participant in a plan listed under item 1 must join that plan as a party to this case when joinder is required by law. (See Retirement Plan Joinder—Information Sheet [form FL-318-INFO].)

4. If you are not the party who participated in a plan listed in item 1 and are concerned that you have not received proof that notice of your interest has been delivered to that plan, you are encouraged to deliver a copy of this order to the appropriate plan administrator as described in item 2. You also have a right to join any plan that requires joinder in the event that no joinder documents have been filed with the court or served on the plan's administrator.

5. Each party must promptly let each plan representative know of any change in that party's mailing address until all benefits due that party under the plan have been paid.

Page 1 of 1

Form Approved for Optional Use
Judicial Council of California
FL-348 [New January 1, 2009]

PENSION BENEFITS—ATTACHMENT TO JUDGMENT

www.courtinfo.ca.gov
Family Code, §§ 2337, 2610

FL-350

ATTORNEY OR PARTY WITHOUT ATTORNEY:	STATE BAR NO:	FOR COURT USE ONLY

ATTORNEY OR PARTY WITHOUT ATTORNEY: STATE BAR NO:

NAME:

FIRM NAME:

STREET ADDRESS:

CITY: STATE: ZIP CODE:

TELEPHONE NO.:   FAX NO.:

E-MAIL ADDRESS:

ATTORNEY FOR (name):

SUPERIOR COURT OF CALIFORNIA, COUNTY OF

STREET ADDRESS:

MAILING ADDRESS:

CITY AND ZIP CODE:

BRANCH NAME:

PETITIONER/PLAINTIFF:

RESPONDENT/DEFENDANT:

OTHER PARENT/PARTY:

STIPULATION TO ESTABLISH OR MODIFY CHILD SUPPORT AND ORDER	CASE NUMBER:

1.   a. ☐ Mother's net monthly disposable income: $

       ☐ Father's net monthly disposable income: $

     -OR-

     b. ☐ A printout of a computer calculation of the parents' financial circumstances is attached.

2. ☐ Percentage of time each parent has primary responsibility for the children: Mother: %   Father: %

3.   a. ☐ A hardship is being experienced by the mother: $ per month because of (specify):

     The hardship will last until (date):

     b. ☐ A hardship is being experienced by the father: $ per month because of (specify):

     The hardship will last until (date):

4. The amount of child support payable by (name):   , referred to as "the parent ordered to pay support," as calculated under the guideline is: $ per month.

5. ☐ We agree to guideline support.

6. ☐ The guideline amount should be rebutted because of the following:

     a. ☐ We agree to child support in the amount of $ per month; the agreement is in the best interest of the children; the needs of the children will be adequately met by the agreed amount; and application of the guideline would be unjust or inappropriate in this case.

     b. ☐ Other rebutting factors (specify):

7. The parent ordered to pay support must pay child support as follows beginning (date):

     a. BASIC CHILD SUPPORT

Child's name	Monthly amount	Payable to (name):

     Total: $ payable ☐ on the first of the month   ☐ other (specify):

     b. ☐ In addition, the parent ordered to pay support must pay the following:

       (1) ☐ $ per month for child care costs to (name):   on (date):

       (2) ☐ $ per month for health-care costs not covered by insurance to (name):   on (date):

       (3) ☐ $ per month for special educational or other needs of the children to (name):   on (date):

       (4) ☐ other (specify):

     c. **Total monthly child support** payable by the parent ordered to pay support will be: $

       payable ☐ on the first of the month   ☐ other (specify):

     d. When a person who has been ordered to pay child support is in jail or prison or is involuntarily institutionalized for any period of more than 90 days in a row, the child support order is temporarily stopped. However, the child support order will not be stopped if the person who owes support has the financial ability to pay that support while in jail, prison, or an institution. It will also not be stopped if the reason the person is in jail, prison, or an institution is because the person didn't pay court ordered child support or committed domestic violence against the supported person or child. The child support order starts again on the first day of the month after the person is released from jail, prison, or an institution.

Page 1 of 2

Form Adopted for Mandatory Use
Judicial Council of California
FL-350 [Rev. January 1, 2017]

**STIPULATION TO ESTABLISH OR MODIFY
CHILD SUPPORT AND ORDER**

Family Code, § 4065
www.court.ca.gov

0174

PETITIONER/PLAINTIFF:	CASE NUMBER:
RESPONDENT/DEFENDANT:	
OTHER PARENT/PARTY:	

8. a. Health insurance will be maintained by *(specify name):*

The parent ordered to provide health insurance must seek continuation of coverage for the child after the child attains the age when the child is no longer considered eligible for coverage as a dependent under the insurance contract, if the child is incapable of self-sustaining employment because of a physically or mentally disabling injury, illness, or condition and is chiefly dependent upon the parent providing health insurance for support and maintenance.

b. ☐ A health insurance coverage assignment will issue if health insurance is available through employment or other group plan or otherwise is available at reasonable cost. Both parents are ordered to cooperate in the presentation, collection, and reimbursement of any medical claims.

c. Any health expenses not paid by insurance will be shared: Mother: %   Father: %

9. a. An earnings assignment order is issued.

b. ☐ We agree that service of the earnings assignment be stayed because we have made the following alternative arrangements to ensure payment *(specify):*

10. In the event that there is a contract between a party receiving support and a private child support collector, the party ordered to pay support must pay the fee charged by the private child support collector. This fee must not exceed 33 1/3 percent of the total amount in arrears nor may it exceed 50 percent of any fee charged by the private child support collector. The money judgment created by this provision is in favor of the private child support collector and the party receiving support, jointly.

11. ☐ Travel expenses for visitation will be shared: Mother: %   Father: %

12. ☐ We agree that we will promptly inform each other of any change of residence or employment, including the employer's name, address, and telephone number.

13. ☐ Other *(specify):*

14. We agree that we are fully informed of our rights under the California child support guidelines.

15. We make this agreement freely without coercion or duress.

16. The right to support

a. ☐ has not been assigned to any county, and no application for public assistance is pending.

b. ☐ has been assigned or an application for public assistance is pending in *(county name):*

If you checked b., an attorney for the local child support agency must sign below, joining in this agreement.

Date:

_____ ▶ _____
(TYPE OR PRINT NAME)   (SIGNATURE OF ATTORNEY FOR LOCAL CHILD SUPPORT AGENCY)

Notice: If the amount agreed to is less than the guideline amount, no change of circumstances need be shown to obtain a change in the support order to a higher amount. If the order is above the guideline, a change of circumstances will be required to modify this order. This form must be signed by the court to be effective.

Date:

_____ ▶ _____
(TYPE OR PRINT NAME)   (SIGNATURE OF PETITIONER)

Date:

_____ ▶ _____
(TYPE OR PRINT NAME)   (SIGNATURE OF RESPONDENT)

Date:

_____ ▶ _____
(TYPE OR PRINT NAME)   (SIGNATURE OF ATTORNEY FOR PETITIONER)

Date:

_____ ▶ _____
(TYPE OR PRINT NAME)   (SIGNATURE OF ATTORNEY FOR RESPONDENT)

THE COURT ORDERS

17. a. ☐ The guideline child support amount in item 4 is rebutted by the factors stated in item 6.

b. Items 7 through 13 are ordered. All child support payments must continue until further order of the court, or until the child marries, dies, is emancipated, or reaches age 18. The duty of support continues as to an unmarried child who has attained the age of 18 years, is a full-time high school student, and resides with a parent, until the time the child completes the 12th grade or attains the age of 19 years, whichever first occurs. Except as modified by this stipulation, all provisions of any previous orders made in this action will remain in effect.

Date:

_____
JUDGE OF THE SUPERIOR COURT

NOTICE: Any party required to pay child support must pay interest on overdue amounts at the "legal" rate, which is currently 10 percent per year. This can be a large added amount.

FL-350 [Rev. January 1, 2017]   **STIPULATION TO ESTABLISH OR MODIFY CHILD SUPPORT AND ORDER**   Page 2 of 2

FL-355

ATTORNEY OR PARTY WITHOUT ATTORNEY *(Name, State Bar number, and address)*:

TELEPHONE NO:　　　　　　　　　FAX NO. *(Optional)*:
E-MAIL ADDRESS *(Optional)*:
ATTORNEY FOR *(Name)*:

FOR COURT USE ONLY

SUPERIOR COURT OF CALIFORNIA, COUNTY OF
STREET ADDRESS:
MAILING ADDRESS:
CITY AND ZIP CODE:
BRANCH NAME:

PETITIONER:
RESPONDENT:
OTHER:

STIPULATION AND ORDER FOR CUSTODY AND/OR VISITATION OF CHILDREN [ ] MODIFICATION	CASE NUMBER:

The parties signing this stipulation agree that:

1. This court has jurisdiction over the minor children because California is the children's home state.

2. The habitual residence of the children is the United States of America.

3. **The parties acknowledge they were advised that any violation of this order may result in civil or criminal penalties, or both.**

4. a. The parties stipulate that the attached document, dated *(specify)*:　　　and consisting of *(number)*:　　　pages is their custody and visitation agreement and request that it be made an order of the court, or

   b. The parties stipulate that the attached forms

   [ ] FL-341　[ ] FL-341(A)　[ ] FL-341(B)　[ ] FL-341(C)　[ ] FL-341(D)　[ ] FL-341(E)

   are their agreement regarding custody and/or visitation of their children and request that they be made an order of the court.

Each party declares under penalty of perjury under the laws of the State of California that the foregoing is true and correct.

Date:

Date: _____ ▶ _____
　　　　(TYPE OR PRINT NAME)　　　　　　　　　(SIGNATURE OF PETITIONER)

Date: _____ ▶ _____
　　　　(TYPE OR PRINT NAME)　　　　　　　　　(SIGNATURE OF RESPONDENT)

Date: _____ ▶ _____
　　　　(TYPE OR PRINT NAME)　　　　　　(SIGNATURE OF ATTORNEY FOR PETITIONER)

Date: _____ ▶ _____
　　　　(TYPE OR PRINT NAME)　　　　　　(SIGNATURE OF ATTORNEY FOR RESPONDENT)

Date: _____ ▶ _____
　　　　(TYPE OR PRINT NAME)　　　　　　　　　(SIGNATURE OF OTHER)

_____ _____
　　　　(TYPE OR PRINT NAME)　　　　　　(SIGNATURE OF ATTORNEY FOR OTHER)

FINDINGS AND ORDER

THE COURT FINDS:

1. This court has jurisdiction over the minor children because California is the children's home state.
2. The habitual residence of the children is the United States of America.
3. Both parties have been advised that any violation of this order may result in civil or criminal penalties, or both.

THE COURT ORDERS:

1. The agreement of the parties regarding custody and visitation [ ] as set forth in the attached document dated *(specify)*:
   and consisting of *(number)*:　　　pages or [ ] set forth in the attached forms:

   [ ] FL-341　[ ] FL-341(A)　[ ] FL-341(B)　[ ] FL-341(C)　[ ] FL-341(D)　[ ] FL-341(E)

   is adopted as the order of the court and fully incorporated by reference herein.

Date: _____

_____
JUDICIAL OFFICER

Page 1 of 1

Form Approved for Optional Use
Judicial Council of California
FL-355 [New January 1, 2004]

**STIPULATION AND ORDER FOR CUSTODY
AND/OR VISITATION OF CHILDREN**

www.courtinfo.ca.gov

ATTORNEY OR PARTY WITHOUT ATTORNEY OR GOVERNMENTAL AGENCY *(Name, State Bar number, and address):*	**FOR COURT USE ONLY**

TELEPHONE NO.:   FAX NO. *(Optional):*

E-MAIL ADDRESS *(Optional):*

ATTORNEY FOR *(Name):*

SUPERIOR COURT OF CALIFORNIA, COUNTY OF

STREET ADDRESS:

MAILING ADDRESS:

CITY AND ZIP CODE:

BRANCH NAME:

PETITIONER/PLAINTIFF:

RESPONDENT/DEFENDANT:

OTHER PARENT:

REQUEST FOR HEARING AND APPLICATION TO SET ASIDE SUPPORT ORDER UNDER FAMILY CODE SECTION 3691	CASE NUMBER:

1. To ☐ petitioner *(specify name):*   ☐ respondent *(specify name):*

      ☐ local child support agency   ☐ other parent *(specify name):*

      ☐ other *(specify):*

      A hearing on this application will be held as follows:

a. Date:	Time:	Dept.:	Div.:	Room:

      b. The address of the court where the hearing will be held is ☐ same as above ☐ other *(specify):*

2. An order was entered in this case on *(date):*   requiring ☐ petitioner *(specify name):*

      ☐ respondent *(specify name):*   ☐ other parent *(specify name):*

      to pay support. I request that the order be set aside.

3. Grounds for this request are *(check all that apply):*
      a. ☐ Fraud
      b. ☐ Perjury
      c. ☐ Lack of notice

4. ☐ I have complied with the time limits for filing this request to set aside the order *(check one):*
      a. ☐ Request brought within six months after the date I discovered or reasonably should have discovered the fraud.
      b. ☐ Request brought within six months after the date I discovered or reasonably should have discovered the perjury.
      c. ☐ Request brought within six months after the date:
           (1) ☐ I obtained or reasonably should have obtained notice of the support order **or**
           (2) ☐ my income and assets were subject to attachment under the support order.

Form Adopted for Mandatory Use
Judicial Council of California
FL-360 [Rev. January 1, 2007]

REQUEST FOR HEARING AND APPLICATION TO SET ASIDE SUPPORT ORDER UNDER FAMILY CODE SECTION 3691
(Family Law—Governmental)

Family Code, §§ 3690–3693
www.courtinfo.ca.gov

FL-360

PETITIONER/PLAINTIFF:	CASE NUMBER:
RESPONDENT/DEFENDANT:	
OTHER PARENT:	

5. ☐ FACTS IN SUPPORT of relief requested are *(specify):*

☐ Contained in the attached declaration.

I declare under penalty of perjury under the laws of the State of California that the foregoing is true and correct.

Date:

_____
(TYPE OR PRINT NAME)

▶

_____
(SIGNATURE OF DECLARANT)

NOTICE FOR CASES INVOLVING A LOCAL CHILD SUPPORT AGENCY

This case may be referred to a court commissioner for hearing. By law, court commissioners do not have the authority to issue final orders and judgments in contested cases unless they are acting as temporary judges. The court commissioner in your case will act as a temporary judge unless, *before the hearing,* you or any other party objects to the commissioner acting as a temporary judge. The court commissioner may still hear your case to make findings and a recommended order. If you do not like the recommended order, you must object to it within 10 court days; otherwise, the recommended order will become a final order of the court. If you object to the recommended order, a judge will make a temporary order and set a new hearing.

Request for Accommodations
Assistive listening systems, computer-assisted real-time captioning, or sign language interpreter services are available if you ask at least five days before the proceeding. Contact the clerk's office or go to *www.courtinfo.ca.gov/forms* for *Request for Accommodations by Persons With Disabilities and Response* (form MC-410). (Civil Code, § 54.8)

**REQUEST FOR HEARING AND APPLICATION
TO SET ASIDE SUPPORT ORDER
(Family Law—Governmental)**

0178

ATTORNEY OR PARTY WITHOUT ATTORNEY *(Name, state bar number, and address)*:	*FOR COURT USE ONLY*
TELEPHONE NO.: FAX NO. *(Optional)*: E–MAIL ADDRESS *(Optional)*: ATTORNEY FOR *(Name)*:	

SUPERIOR COURT OF CALIFORNIA, COUNTY OF
STREET ADDRESS:
MAILING ADDRESS:
CITY AND ZIP CODE:
BRANCH NAME:

MARRIAGE OF

PETITIONER:

RESPONDENT:

CLAIMANT:

PLEADING ON JOINDER—EMPLOYEE BENEFIT PLAN	CASE NUMBER:

TO THE CLAIMANT: You have been joined as a party claimant in this proceeding because an interest is claimed in the employee benefit plan that is or may be subject to disposition by this court. The party who obtained the order for your joinder declares:

1. Information concerning the employee covered by the plan:
   a. Name:
   b. Employer *(name)*:
   c. ☐ Name of labor union representing employee:
   d. ☐ Employee identification number:
   e. Other *(specify)*:

2. Petitioner's

   a. ☐ Attorney *(name, address, and telephone number)*:

   b. ☐ Address and telephone number, if unrepresented by an attorney:

3. Respondent's

   a. ☐ Attorney *(name, address, and telephone number)*:

   b. Address and telephone number, if unrepresented by an attorney:

Form Adopted for Mandatory Use
Judicial Council of California
FL-370 [Rev. January 1, 2003]

PLEADING ON JOINDER—EMPLOYEE BENEFIT PLAN

Family Code, §§ 2060–2065
www.courtinfo.ca.gov

PETITIONER:	CASE NUMBER:
RESPONDENT:	

4. Petition for dissolution ☐ and response states
   a. Date of marriage:
   b. Date of separation:

5. ☐ Response states
   a. Date of marriage:
   b. Date of separation:

6. Judgment
   a. ☐ has not been entered
   b. ☐ was entered on *(date)*:
      (1) ☐ and disposes of each spouse's interest in the employee benefit plan.
      (2) ☐ and does not dispose of each spouse's interest in the employee benefit plan.

7. The following relief is sought:
   a. ☐ An order determining the nature and extent of both employee and nonemployee spouse's interest in employee's benefits under the plan.
   b. ☐ An order restraining claimant from making benefit payments to employee spouse pending the determination and disposition of nonemployee spouse's interest, if any, in employee's benefits under the plan.
   c. ☐ An order directing claimant to notify nonemployee spouse when benefits under the plan first become payable to employee.
   d. ☐ An order directing claimant to make payment to nonemployee spouse of said spouse's interest in employee's benefits under the plan when they become payable to employee.
   e. ☐ Other *(specify):*

   f. Such other orders as may be appropriate.

Dated:

▶

_____
(SIGNATURE OF ☐ ATTORNEY FOR)

☐ PETITIONER   ☐ RESPONDENT

_____
(TYPE OR PRINT NAME)

0180

ATTORNEY OR PARTY WITHOUT ATTORNEY *(Name, state bar number, and address):*	FOR COURT USE ONLY
TELEPHONE NO.: FAX NO. *(Optional):* E-MAIL ADDRESS *(Optional):* ATTORNEY FOR *(Name):*	

SUPERIOR COURT OF CALIFORNIA, COUNTY OF
STREET ADDRESS:
MAILING ADDRESS:
CITY AND ZIP CODE:
BRANCH NAME:

MARRIAGE OF
PETITIONER:

RESPONDENT:

NOTICE OF MOTION AND DECLARATION FOR JOINDER	CASE NUMBER:

NOTICE OF MOTION

1. TO ☐ Petitioner ☐ Respondent

2. A hearing on this motion for joinder will be held as follows:

    a. Date: Time: Dept.:   Rm.:

    b. The address of court: ☐ is shown above ☐ is:

    c. ☐ Petitioner ☐ Respondent ☐ Claimant will apply to this court for an order joining claimant as a party to this proceeding on the grounds set forth in the Declaration below.

3. The pleading on joinder accompanies this notice of motion.

Dated:

▶

_____   _____
(TYPE OR PRINT NAME)   (SIGNATURE)

DECLARATION FOR JOINDER

4. The name of the person to be joined is:

5. Facts showing that each person sought or seeking to be joined possesses or controls or claims to own any property subject to disposition by this court, or that such person has or claims custody, physical control, or visitation rights with respect to any minor child of the marriage, are *(specify):*

Form Adopted for Mandatory Use
Judicial Council of California
FL-371 [Rev. January 1, 2003]

NOTICE OF MOTION AND DECLARATION FOR JOINDER

Family Code, § 2021
www.courtinfo.ca.gov

PETITIONER:	CASE NUMBER:
RESPONDENT:	

6. Facts showing that it would be appropriate for this court to determine the particular issue in the proceedings are:

7. Facts showing that each person sought or seeking to be joined is either indispensable to a determination of the particular issue or necessary to the enforcement of any judgment rendered on the issue are:

I declare under penalty of perjury under the laws of the State of California that the foregoing is true and correct.

Date:

_____   ▶   _____
(TYPE OR PRINT NAME)   (SIGNATURE OF DECLARANT)

0182

ATTORNEY OR PARTY WITHOUT ATTORNEY *(Name, state bar no., and address):*	FOR COURT USE ONLY

TELEPHONE NO.:   FAX NO. *(Optional):*

E–MAIL ADDRESS *(Optional):*

ATTORNEY FOR *(Name):*

SUPERIOR COURT OF CALIFORNIA, COUNTY OF

STREET ADDRESS:

MAILING ADDRESS:

CITY AND ZIP CODE:

BRANCH NAME:

MARRIAGE OF

PETITIONER:

RESPONDENT:

CLAIMANT:

REQUEST FOR JOINDER OF EMPLOYEE BENEFIT PLAN AND ORDER	CASE NUMBER:

TO THE CLERK

1. Please join as a party claimant to this proceeding *(specify name of employee benefit plan):*

2. The pleading on joinder is submitted with this application for filing.

Dated:

▶ _____

(SIGNATURE OF [ ] ATTORNEY FOR)

[ ] PETITIONER   [ ] RESPONDENT

_____

(TYPE OR PRINT NAME)

ORDER OF JOINDER

3. IT IS ORDERED

   a. The claimant listed in item 1 is joined as a party claimant to this proceeding.

   b. The pleading on joinder be filed.

   c. Summons be issued.

   d. Claimant be served with a copy of the pleading on joinder, a copy of this request for joinder and order, the summons, and a blank *Notice of Appearance and Response of Employee Benefit Plan* (form FL-374).

Dated:

Clerk, By _____, Deputy

Page 1 of 1

Form Adopted for Mandatory Use
Judicial Council of California
FL-372 [Rev. January 1, 2003]

**REQUEST FOR JOINDER OF EMPLOYEE
BENEFIT PLAN AND ORDER**

Family Code, §§ 2010, 2021,
2060–2065, 2070–2074
www.courtinfo.ca.gov

FL-373

ATTORNEY OR PARTY WITHOUT ATTORNEY *(Name, state bar number, and address)*:	FOR COURT USE ONLY
TELEPHONE NO. *(Optional)*: FAX NO. *(Optional)*:	
E–MAIL ADDRESS *(Optional)*:	
ATTORNEY FOR *(Name)*:	

SUPERIOR COURT OF CALIFORNIA, COUNTY OF
STREET ADDRESS:
MAILING ADDRESS:
CITY AND ZIP CODE:
BRANCH NAME:

MARRIAGE OF
PETITIONER:

RESPONDENT:

CLAIMANT:

RESPONSIVE DECLARATION TO MOTION FOR JOINDER ☐ CONSENT ORDER OF JOINDER	CASE NUMBER:

1. ☐ Petitioner ☐ Respondent

    a. ☐ Consents to the requested joinder and stipulates to an order joining claimant as a party to this proceeding.

    b. ☐ Does not consent to the requested joinder of claimant as a party to this proceeding.

2. ☐ The statements contained in the declaration for joinder are incorrect or insufficient as follows *(specify)*:

I declare under penalty of perjury under the laws of the State of California that the foregoing is true and correct.

dated:

_____
(TYPE OR PRINT NAME)

_____
(SIGNATURE OF DECLARANT)

Page 1 of 2

Form Adopted for Mandatory Use
Judicial Council of California
FL-373 [Rev. January 1, 2003]

**RESPONSIVE DECLARATION TO MOTION FOR JOINDER
CONSENT ORDER OF JOINDER**

www.courtinfo.ca.gov

0184

CONSENT ORDER

3. ☐ Petitioner ☐ Respondent having consented and good cause appearing,
   IT IS ORDERED that
   a. The claimant is joined as a party to this proceeding.
   b. The clerk file the original of the submitted pleadings.
   c. ☐ *Summons (Joinder)* be issued and claimant be served with a copy of the motion for joinder with pleading
      attached and a copy of the *Summons (Joinder)*.
   d. ☐ The hearing on the motion for joinder is taken off calendar for *(date):*

Dated: _____   _____
                                  JUDICIAL OFFICER

0185

ATTORNEY OR PARTY WITHOUT ATTORNEY *(Name, state bar number and address):*

FOR COURT USE ONLY

TELEPHONE NO. *(Optional):*   FAX NO. *(Optional):*

E–MAIL ADDRESS *(Optional):*

ATTORNEY FOR *(Name):*

SUPERIOR COURT OF CALIFORNIA, COUNTY OF

STREET ADDRESS:

MAILING ADDRESS:

CITY AND ZIP CODE:

BRANCH NAME:

MARRIAGE OF

PETITIONER:

RESPONDENT:

CLAIMANT:

NOTICE OF APPEARANCE ☐ **AND RESPONSE OF EMPLOYEE BENEFIT PLAN**

CASE NUMBER:

1. An appearance in this proceeding is entered by claimant employee benefit plan *(name):*

2. Service on claimant may be made as follows

    a. ☐ Attorney for claimant *(name, address, and telephone number):*

    b. ☐ Other *(name, title, address, and telephone number):*

3. ☐ Claimant responds to the pleading on joinder and states that the allegations of the pleadings are

    a. ☐ correct

    b. ☐ incorrect as set forth in ☐ attachment 3b or ☐ as follows *(specify):*

Dated:

Claimant

_____   By _____
(TYPE OR PRINT NAME)   (SIGNATURE)

Page 1 of 1

Form Adopted for Mandatory Use
Judicial Council of California
FL-374 [Rev. January 1, 2003]

NOTICE OF APPEARANCE AND RESPONSE OF EMPLOYEE BENEFIT PLAN

Family Code, §§ 80, 2010, 2021,
2060–2065, 2070–2074
www.courtinfo.ca.gov

0186

FL-375

ATTORNEY OR PARTY WITHOUT ATTORNEY *(Name, state bar number, and address):*	FOR COURT USE ONLY

TELEPHONE NO. *(Optional):* FAX NO. *(Optional):*
E–MAIL ADDRESS *(Optional):*
ATTORNEY FOR *(Name):*

SUPERIOR COURT OF CALIFORNIA, COUNTY OF
STREET ADDRESS:
MAILING ADDRESS:
CITY AND ZIP CODE:
BRANCH NAME:

MARRIAGE OF

PETITIONER:

RESPONDENT:

CLAIMANT:

SUMMONS (JOINDER)	CASE NUMBER:

NOTICE! You have been sued. The court may decide against you without your being heard unless you respond within 30 days. Read the information below.

If you wish to seek the advice of an attorney in this matter, you should do so promptly so that your response or pleading, if any, may be filed on time.

¡AVISO! Usted ha sido demandado. El tribunal puede decidir contra Ud. sin audiencia a menos que Ud. responda dentro de 30 dias. Lea la información que sigue.

Si Usted desea solicitar el consejo de un abogado en este asunto, debería hacerlo inmediatamente, de esta manera, su respuesta o alegación, si hay alguna, puede ser registrada a tiempo.

1. ☐ TO THE ☐ PETITIONER ☐ RESPONDENT ☐ CLAIMANT
A pleading has been filed under an order joining *(name of claimant):*

as a party in this proceeding. If you fail to file an appropriate pleading within **30** days of the date this summons is served on you, your default may be entered and the court may enter a judgment containing the relief requested in the pleading, court costs, and such other relief as may be granted by the court, which could result in the garnishment of wages, taking of money or property, or other relief.

2. ☐ TO THE CLAIMANT EMPLOYEE BENEFIT PLAN
A pleading on joinder has been filed under the clerk's order joining *(name of employee benefit plan):*

as a party claimant in this proceeding. If the employee benefit plan fails to file an appropriate pleading within **30** days of the date this summons is served on it, a default may be entered and the court may enter a judgment containing the relief requested.

Dated: _____ Clerk, By _____, Deputy

(SEAL)

3. NOTICE TO THE PERSON SERVED: You are served
a. ☐ As an individual.
b. ☐ As (or on behalf of) the person sued under the fictitious name of:

c. ☐ On behalf of:

Under: ☐ CCP 416.10 (Corporation) ☐ CCP 416.60 (Minor)
☐ CCP 416.20 (Defunct Corporation) ☐ CCP 416.70 (Incompetent)
☐ CCP 416.40 (Association or Partnership) ☐ CCP 416.90 (Individual)
☐ Other: ☐ FC 2062 (Employee Benefit Plan)

d. ☐ By personal delivery on *(date):*

Page 1 of 2

Form Adopted for Mandatory Use
Judicial Council of California
FL-375 [Rev. January 1, 2003]

SUMMONS (JOINDER)

www.courtinfo.ca.gov.

PROOF OF SERVICE—SUMMONS (JOINDER)
(Use separate proof of service for each person served)

1. I served the

   a. *Summons and (1)* ☐ *Request for Joinder of Employee Benefit Plan and Order, Pleading on Joinder-Employee Benefit Plan, blank Notice of Appearance and Response of Employee Benefit Plan*

     (2) ☐ *Notice of Motion and Declaration for Joinder*   (3) ☐ Order re Joinder

     (4) ☐ *Pleading on Joinder* (specify title):

     (5) ☐ Other:

   b. On *(name of party or claimant):*

   c. By serving   (1) ☐ Party or claimant.   (2) ☐ Other *(name and title or relationship to person served):*

   d. ☐ By delivery at ☐ home   ☐ business (1) Date of:

     (2)   Time of: (3) Address:

   e. ☐ By mailing (1) Date of: (2) Place of:

2. Manner of service: *(check proper box)*

   a. ☐ **Personal service.** By personally delivering copies. (CCP 415.10)

   b. ☐ **Substituted service on corporation, unincorporated association (including partnership), or public entity.** By leaving, during usual office hours, copies in the office of the person served with the person who apparently was in charge and thereafter mailing (by first-class mail, postage prepaid) copies to the person served at the place where the copies were left. (CCP 41 5.20(a))

   c. ☐ **Substituted service on natural person, minor, incompetent, or candidate.** By leaving copies at the dwelling house, usual place of abode, or usual place of business of the person served in the presence of a competent member of the household or a person apparently in charge of the office or place of business, at least 18 years of age, who was informed of the general nature of the papers, and thereafter mailing (by first-class mail, postage prepaid) copies to the person served at the place where the copies were left. (CCP 415.20(b)) **(Attach separate declaration or affidavit stating acts relied on to establish reasonable diligence in first attempting personal service.)**

   d. ☐ **Mail and acknowledgment service.** By mailing (by first-class mail or airmail) copies to the person served, together with two copies of the form of notice and acknowledgment and a return envelope, postage prepaid, addressed to the sender. (CCP 415.30) **(Attach completed acknowledgment of receipt.)**

   e. ☐ **Certified or registered mail service.** By mailing to address outside California (by registered or certified airmail with return receipt requested) copies to the person served. (CCP 415.40) **(Attach signed return receipt or other evidence of actual delivery to the person served.)**

   f. ☐ Other *(specify code section):*

     ☐ Additional page is attached.

3. The notice to the person served (item 3 on the copy of the summons served) was completed as follows (CCP 412.30, 415.10, and 474):

   a. ☐ As an individual.

   b. ☐ As the person sued under the fictitious name of:

   c. ☐ On behalf of:

     Under: ☐ CCP 416.10 (Corporation)   ☐ CCP 416.60 (Minor)

           ☐ CCP 416.20 (Defunct Corporation)   ☐ CCP 416.70 (Incompetent)

           ☐ CCP 416.40 (Association or partnership)   ☐ CCP 416.90 (Individual)

                               ☐ FC 2062 (Employee Benefit Plan)

   d. By personal delivery on *(date):*

4. At the time of service I was at least 18 years of age and not a party to this action.

5. Fee for service: $ . . . .

6. Person serving

   a. ☐ Not a registered California process server.

   b. ☐ Registered California process server.

   c. ☐ Exempt from registration under Bus. & Prof. Code 22350(b).

   d. ☐ California sheriff, marshal, or constable.

   e. Name, address, telephone number, and, if applicable, county of registration and number:

I declare under penalty of perjury that the foregoing is true and correct and that this declaration is executed on *(date):*

     at *(place):*
     , California.

(For California sheriff, marshal, or constable use only)

I certify that the foregoing is true and correct and that this certificate is executed on *(date):*

     at *(place):*
     , California.

_____
(Signature)

_____
(Signature)

0188

ATTORNEY OR PARTY WITHOUT ATTORNEY OR GOVERNMENTAL AGENCY *(pursuant to FC §§ 17400, 17406) (Name, State Bar Number, and Address):*	TELEPHONE NO.:	*FOR COURT USE ONLY*

SUPERIOR COURT OF CALIFORNIA, COUNTY OF

STREET ADDRESS:

MAILING ADDRESS:

CITY AND ZIP CODE:

BRANCH NAME:

PETITIONER/PLAINTIFF:

RESPONDENT/DEFENDANT:

OTHER PARENT:

NOTICE OF MOTION AND MOTION FOR SIMPLIFIED MODIFICATION OF ORDER **FOR** ☐ **CHILD SUPPORT** ☐ **SPOUSAL SUPPORT** ☐ **FAMILY SUPPORT**	CASE NUMBER:

TO *(name):*

1. A hearing on this motion for the relief requested below will be held as follows:

   a. Date: Time: Dept.:   Room:

   b. Address of court: ☐ same as noted above ☐ other *(specify):*

2. I am requesting the court to change the amount currently payable by
   ☐ petitioner/plaintiff ☐ respondent/defendant ☐ other parent   to the following:
   a. ☐ child support pursuant to the California child support guideline commencing *(date):*
   b. ☐ spousal support of: $ per month beginning *(date):*
   c. ☐ family support of: $ per month beginning *(date):*
   or such other sums as may be appropriate pursuant to applicable guidelines.

3. ☐ I am requesting issuance of modified earnings assignment.

4. ☐ I am requesting the court to order the ☐ petitioner/plaintiff ☐ respondent/defendant ☐ other parent
   to provide health insurance coverage for the children as obligated by law, and to issue a Health Insurance Coverage
   Assignment (form FL-470).

5. *(Check whichever statements are true, if any)*
   a. ☐ An application for public assistance (TANF) for the children is pending in *(county name):*   County.
   b. ☐ The children are receiving public assistance from *(county name):*   County.
   c. ☐ This request is made by the governmental agency providing support enforcement services in this action.

6. This request is based on
   a. the attached completed *Financial Statement (Simplified)* (form FL-155) or *Income and Expense Declaration* (form FL-150)
      for the applicant.
   b. ☐ a significant change in the income of ☐ petitioner/plaintiff ☐ respondent/defendant ☐ other parent
   c. ☐ the attached guideline support calculation sheet.
   d. ☐ other *(specify):*

I declare under penalty of perjury under the laws of the State of California that the foregoing is true and correct.

Date:

▶

_____
(TYPE OR PRINT NAME)

_____
(SIGNATURE OF DECLARANT)

Page 1 of 2

Form Adopted for Mandatory Use
Judicial Council of California
FL-390 [Rev. January 1, 2003]

NOTICE OF MOTION AND MOTION FOR SIMPLIFIED
MODIFICATION OF ORDER FOR CHILD, SPOUSAL, OR FAMILY SUPPORT

Family Code, § 3680
www.courtinfo.ca.gov.

0189

	CASE NUMBER:
PETITIONER/PLAINTIFF:	
RESPONDENT/DEFENDANT:	
OTHER PARENT:	

PROOF OF SERVICE

The *Notice* of *Motion and Motion* must be served on the other party. If the action was brought by the local child support agency, the local child support agency is enforcing the order, or the children are receiving TANF, the *Notice of Motion and Motion* must also be served on the local child support agency of the county where the action is filed. Service of the motion on the local child support agency and other party may be made by anyone at least 18 years EXCEPT you. Service is made in one of the following ways:

(1) Personally delivering it to the office of the local child support agency and to the other party.

OR

(2) Mailing it, postage prepaid, to the office of the local child support agency, and to the last known address of the other party.

Anyone at least 18 years of age EXCEPT A PARTY in this action may personally serve or mail the motion. Be sure whoever served the motion fills out and signs this proof of service. The *Notice of Motion and Motion* cannot be filed with the court until the local child support agency and the other party (or attorney) are served and this proof of service is properly completed. If this motion is brought after judgment has been entered in the case, service must be made on the party and not the attorney for the party.

1. At the time of service I was at least 18 years of age and not a party to the legal action.

2. I served a copy of the foregoing *Notice of Motion and Motion* as follows (check either a. or b. below for each person served):

a. ☐ **Personal service.** I personally delivered a copy of the *Notice of Motion and Motion for Simplified Modification of Order for Child, Spousal, or Family Support* and all attachments as follows:

   ☐ (1) Name of party or attorney served: ☐ (2) Name of local child support agency served:

   (a) Address where delivered: (a) Address where delivered:

   (b) Date of delivery: (b) Date of delivery:
   (c) Time of delivery: (c) Time of delivery:

b. ☐ **Mail.** I deposited a copy of the *Notice* of *Motion and Motion for Simplified Modification of Order for Child, Spousal, or Family Support* (form FL-390) and all attachments in the United States mail, in a sealed envelope with postage fully prepaid, addressed as follows:

   ☐ (1) Name of party or attorney served: ☐ (2) Name of local child support agency served:

   (a) Address: (a) Address:

   (b) Date of mailing: (b) Date of mailing:
   (c) Time of mailing: (c) Time of mailing:

I declare under penalty of perjury under the laws of the State of California that the foregoing is true and correct.

Date:

▶

_____   _____
(TYPE OR PRINT NAME)   (SIGNATURE OF PERSON WHO SERVED MOTION)

FL-390 [Rev. January 1, 2003]   **NOTICE OF MOTION AND MOTION FOR SIMPLIFIED MODIFICATION OF ORDER FOR CHILD, SPOUSAL, OR FAMILY SUPPORT**   www.courtinfo.ca.gov

INFORMATION SHEET
SIMPLIFIED WAY TO CHANGE CHILD, SPOUSAL, OR FAMILY SUPPORT

New laws make it easier for a person to ask the court to raise or lower the amount paid for child, spousal, or family support.

How to Ask for a Change

1. Get copies of these forms:
   * *Notice of Motion and Motion for Simplified Modification of Order for Child, Spousal, or Family Support ("Notice of Motion")* (form FL-390).
   * *Responsive Declaration to Motion for Simplified Modification for Child, Spousal, or Family Support* (form FL-392).
   * *Findings and Order After Hearing* (form FL-340) and *Child Support Information and Order Attachment* (form FL-342).
   * *Financial Statement (Simplified)* (form FL-155) or *Income and Expense Declaration* (form FL-150).
   The court clerk's office, the office of the family law facilitator, or the local child support agency can tell you where to get these forms. You can get them at the Judicial Council website: *www.courtinfo.ca.gov*

2. Fill out and sign the form *Notice of Motion*. **Check with your local court clerk's office or the office of the family law facilitator to see if the forms must be typewritten.**

3. Fill out the form *Financial Statement (Simplified),* if you are allowed to use the form. See the instructions on the back side of the form to see if you qualify; otherwise you must fill out the *Income and Expense Declaration.* You must attach copies of your most recent W-2 form(s) and three most recent paycheck stubs, to the form *Financial Statement (Simplified)* or the form *Income and Expense Declaration.*

4. You must schedule a hearing date with your court clerk's office before filing and serving these papers. You must enter the hearing date in item 1 of the *Notice of Motion.*

5. Make at least three copies of these forms after you have completed them:
   * *Notice of Motion and Motion for Simplified Modification of Order for Child, Spousal, or Family Support* (form FL-390).
   * *Financial Statement (Simplified)* (form FL-155) or *Income and Expense Declaration* (form FL-150).

6. You must have one copy of each of the following papers served on the local child support agency **and on the other party,** if the other party is not the county:
   * Your *Notice of Motion and Motion for Simplified Modification of Order for Child, Spousal, or Family Support* (form FL-390).
   * Your *Financial Statement (Simplified)* (form FL-155) or *Income and Expense Declaration* (form FL-150).
   * A blank *Responsive Declaration to Motion for Simplified Modification of Order for Child, Spousal, or Family Support* (form FL-392).
   * A blank *Financial Statement (Simplified)* (form FL-155) or *Income and Expense Declaration* (form FL-150). *Information Sheet—How to Oppose a Request to Change Child, Spousal, or Family Support* (form FL-393).

   For instructions on how to serve these papers properly, see the information box on the Proof of Service, found on the reverse of the *Notice of Motion* (form FL-390). Whoever serves the papers should fill out and must sign the Proof of Service.

7. Take the original of each of the completed forms to the court clerk's office for filing. If you or your attorney have not filed any other papers in the case, you must do one or more of the following:
   * Pay a first appearance filing fee to the court clerk when you go to file these papers (you can find out what the amount of the fee is from the court clerk's office or the office of the family law facilitator); or
   * Pay a fee to file this motion with the court clerk, even if you or your attorney have already filed papers in this case; or
   * Apply for a fee waiver. For more information on how to request a waiver of the filing fees, get the form *Information Sheet on Waiver of Court Fees and Costs* (form FW-001-INFO).

Form Approved for Optional Use
Judicial Council of California
FL-391 [Rev. July 1, 2008]

**INFORMATION SHEET—SIMPLIFIED WAY TO CHANGE
CHILD, SPOUSAL, OR FAMILY SUPPORT**

Family Code, § 3680
www.courtinfo.ca.gov

Using an Attorney

If you use this method to modify support, you may hire an attorney to represent you in court, or you may represent yourself. If you hire an attorney, you will have to pay the cost. The court will not provide you with a free attorney.

If the county is the other party, and if one of the parties is receiving welfare benefits, or if one of the parties has asked the local child support agency to enforce support, a representative from the local child support agency will be present at the hearing.

REMEMBER: The local child support agency does not represent any individual in this lawsuit, including the child, the child's mother, or the child's father.

Agreeing to Support Before the Hearing

A court hearing may not be necessary to modify the current support order, if you are able to reach an agreement with the other party. Note that if an agreement is reached with the other party, you must prepare an order and submit it to the court for the judge's signature and file the order with the court clerk's office. If one of the parties is receiving welfare benefits or the local child support agency is enforcing the support order, the local child support agency must sign the agreement before it is filed with the court.

Hearing

Even if neither the local child support agency nor the other party has filed a response to your *Notice of Motion,* the judge may still require a hearing. Make sure you bring with you a copy of your *Notice of Motion* (form FL-390), *Financial Statement (Simplified)* (form FL-155) or *Income and Expense Declaration* (form FL-150), your most recent federal and state income tax returns and W-2 form(s), and three most recent paycheck stubs. The other party has a right to see your financial information, and you have the right to see the other party's financial information.

Court Order

Once the judge makes a decision, you may be required to prepare the form *Findings and Order After Hearing* (form FL-340) with the *Child Support Information and Order Attachment* (form FL-342). If the support order has changed, you may required to prepare a modified *Income Withholding for Support* (FL-195). You will not have to prepare these documents if the local child support agency is involved. If you have prepared these documents yourself, you must make sure that they are signed by the judge. Check with the court clerk's office or the office of the family law facilitator for the proper procedure. After the *Income Withholding for Support* (FL-195) is signed by the judge and filed, it must be served on the noncustodial parent's employer, on the other party, and on the local child support agency if the local child support agency is involved in the case.

**INFORMATION SHEET—SIMPLIFIED WAY TO CHANGE
CHILD, SPOUSAL, OR FAMILY SUPPORT**

0192

ATTORNEY OR PARTY WITHOUT ATTORNEY OR GOVERNMENTAL AGENCY *(under Family Code, §§ 17400, 17406) (Name, state bar number, and address):* TELEPHONE AND FAX NOS.:	*FOR COURT USE ONLY*

SUPERIOR COURT OF CALIFORNIA, COUNTY OF

STREET ADDRESS:

MAILING ADDRESS:

CITY AND ZIP CODE:

BRANCH NAME:

PETITIONER/PLAINTIFF:

RESPONDENT/DEFENDANT:

OTHER PARENT:

**RESPONSIVE DECLARATION TO MOTION FOR SIMPLIFIED
MODIFICATION OF ORDER FOR CHILD, SPOUSAL, OR FAMILY SUPPORT**

HEARING DATE:	TIME:	DEPT., ROOM, OR DIVISION:	CASE NUMBER:

1. ☐ I consent to the request contained in the *Notice of Motion and Motion for Simplified Modification of Order for Child, Spousal, or Family Support* (form FL-390).

2. ☐ I object to the request contained in the *Notice of Motion and Motion for Simplified Modification of Order for Child, Spousal, or Family Support* (form FL-390) for the following reasons *(check one or more):*
   a. ☐ My income is incorrectly stated.
   b. ☐ The other parent's income is incorrectly stated.
   c. ☐ I am entitled to the hardship deductions as shown in my attached *Financial Statement (Simplified)* (form FL-155) or my *Income and Expense Declaration* (form FL-150).
   d. ☐ The other parent is not entitled to hardship deductions as claimed.
   e. ☐ The amount of support is not computed correctly.
   f. ☐ OTHER *(specify):*

3. I have attached the following:
   a. A completed copy of my *Financial Statement (Simplified)* (form FL-155) or my *Income and Expense Declaration* (form FL-150).
   b. ☐ A guideline support calculation sheet.
   c. ☐ OTHER *(specify):*

NOTICE TO BOTH PARENTS
**You must bring copies of your three most recent pay stubs and your two most recent federal and
state tax returns (whether individual or joint) to the hearing.**

I declare under penalty of perjury under the laws of the State of California that the foregoing is true and correct.

Date:

▶

_____
(TYPE OR PRINT NAME)

_____
(SIGNATURE OF DECLARANT)

Page 1 of 2

PETITIONER/PLAINTIFF:	CASE NUMBER:
RESPONDENT/DEFENDANT:	
OTHER PARENT:	

PROOF OF SERVICE

This *Responsive Declaration* must be served on the other party. If the action was brought by the local child support agency, the local child support agency is enforcing the order, or the child is receiving TANF, the *Responsive Declaration* must also be served on the local child support agency of the county where the action is filed. Service of the *Responsive Declaration* on the local child support agency and other party may be made by anyone at least 18 years of age EXCEPT you.

Service is made in one of the following ways:
   (1) Personally delivering it to the office of the local child support agency and to the other party.
               OR
   (2) Mailing it, postage prepaid, to the office of the local child support agency and to the other party.
Anyone at least 18 years of age EXCEPT A PARTY to this action may personally serve or mail the *Responsive Declaration*. Be sure whoever served the declaration fills out and signs this proof of service. The *Responsive Declaration* cannot be filed with the court until the local child support agency and the other party are served and this proof of service is properly completed.

1. At the time of service I was at least 18 years of age and not a party to the legal action.

2. I served a copy of the foregoing *Responsive Declaration* as follows *(check either a. or b. below for each person served):*
  a. ☐   **Personal service.** I personally delivered a copy of the *Responsive Declaration to Motion for Simplified Modification of Order for Child, Spousal, or Family Support* as follows:

    ☐ (1) Name of party or attorney served: ☐ (2) Name of local child support agency served:

      (a) Address where delivered: (a) Address where delivered:

      (b) Date of delivery: (b) Date of delivery:
      (c) Time of delivery: (c) Time of delivery:

  b. ☐   **Mail.** I deposited a copy of the *Responsive Declaration to Motion for Simplified Modification of Order for Child, Spousal, or Family Support* in the United States mail, in a sealed envelope with postage fully prepaid, addressed as follows:

    ☐ (1) Name of party or attorney served: ☐ (2) Name of local child support agency served:

      (a) Address: (a) Address:

      (b) Date of mailing: (b) Date of mailing:
      (c) Time of mailing: (c) Time of mailing:

I declare under penalty of perjury under the laws of the State of California that the foregoing is true and correct.

Date:

▶

_____
(TYPE OR PRINT NAME)

_____
(SIGNATURE OF PERSON WHO SERVED RESPONSIVE DECLARATION)

**RESPONSIVE DECLARATION TO MOTION FOR SIMPLIFIED
MODIFICATION OF ORDER FOR CHILD, SPOUSAL, OR FAMILY SUPPORT**

INFORMATION SHEET
HOW TO OPPOSE A REQUEST TO CHANGE CHILD, SPOUSAL, OR FAMILY SUPPORT

What to Do

1. If you receive a *Notice of Motion and Motion for Simplified Modification of Order for Child, Spousal, or Family Support ("Notice of Motion")* (form FL-390) from the other party or the local child support agency, you have one of two choices:

   * Agree with the proposed changes; or

   * File a response and go to the hearing.

2. You do not need to wait to go to court before modifying the support. If you agree with the changes sought (see item 2 on the front of the *Notice of Motion),* or if you agree that the order should be changed in some way, contact the party that served you so that an agreement should be reached. If an agreement is reached with the other party, an order must be prepared and submitted to the court for the judge's signature and filed with the court clerk's office. If one of the parties is receiving welfare benefits or the local child support agency is enforcing the support order, the local child support agency must sign the agreement before it is filed with the court. If you are able to reach an agreement with the other party and the order is filed with the court clerk's office, you do not need to appear at the hearing. The hearing will simply be taken off calendar.

   NOTICE: Unless you know the hearing has been taken off calendar, you should go to the hearing as scheduled to protect your rights. You might consider calling the court the day before the hearing to see if the hearing is still on calendar.

3. If you do <u>not</u> agree with the proposed changes, you must do the following:

   * Complete the *Responsive Declaration to Motion for Simplified Modification of Order for Child, Spousal, or Family Support ("Response to Motion"* (form FL-392). If a blank *Response to Motion* was not given to you when you received the *Notice of Motion,* the court clerk's office, the office of the family law facilitator, or the local child support agency can tell you where one can be found. Or you can get one from the Judicial Council's website: *www.courtinfo.ca.gov.* **NOTICE: Check with your local court clerk's office or the office of the family law facilitator to see if the forms must be typewritten. Make at least three copies of the completed form.**

   * Fill out the form *Financial Statement (Simplified)* (form FL-155), if you are allowed to use the form. See the instructions on the back side of the form to see if you qualify; otherwise, you must fill out the form *Income and Expense Declaration* (form FL-150). You must attach copies of your most recent W-2 form(s) and three most recent paycheck stubs to the form *Financial Statement (Simplified)* (form FL-155) or the form *Income and Expense Declaration* (form FL-150). Make at least three copies of the completed form.

4. You must have one copy of each of the following papers served on the local child support agency **and on the other party,** if the other party is not the local child support agency:

   * Your *Responsive Declaration to Motion* (form FL-392).

   * Your *Financial Statement (Simplified)* (form FL-155) or *Income and Expense Declaration* (form FL-150).

   For instructions on how to serve these papers properly, see the information box on the Proof of Service, found on the reverse of the *Response to Motion* (form FL-392). Whoever serves the papers should fill out and must sign the Proof of Service. **NOTICE: Consult with the office of the family law facilitator or the local court rules to see if there are any other documents you will need to have served on the local child support agency and on the other party.**

Form Approved for Optional Use
Judicial Council of California
FL-393 [Rev. July 1, 2008]

**INFORMATION SHEET—HOW TO OPPOSE A REQUEST
TO CHANGE CHILD, SPOUSAL, OR FAMILY SUPPORT**

Page 1 of 2
Family Code, § 3680
www.courtinfo.ca.gov

5. Take the original of each of the completed forms to the court clerk's office for filing. If you or your attorney have not filed any other papers in the case, you must do one of two things:

- Pay a first appearance filing fee to the court clerk when you go to file these papers (you can find out what the amount of the fee is from the court clerk's office or the office of the family law facilitator); or

- Apply for a fee waiver. For more information on how to request a waiver of the filing fees, get the form *Information Sheet on Waiver of Court Fees and Costs* (form FW-001-INFO).

NOTICE: The existing support order remains in effect and payments must be made according to its terms until any new order is made.

Using an Attorney

If you use this method to modify support, you may hire an attorney to represent you in court, or you may represent yourself. If you hire an attorney, you will have to pay the cost. The court will not provide you with a free attorney.

If the county is the other party, and if one of the parties is receiving welfare benefits, or if one of the parties has asked the local child support agency to enforce support, a representative from the local child support agency will be present at the hearing.

REMEMBER: The local child support agency does not represent any individual in this lawsuit, including the child, the child's mother, and the child's father.

Hearing

Make sure you bring with you a copy of your *Response to Motion* (form FL-392), *Financial Statement (Simplified)* (form FL-155) or *Income and Expense Declaration* (form FL-150), your most recent federal and state income tax returns and W-2 form(s), and three most recent pay check stubs. The other party has a right to see your financial information, and you have the right to see the other party's financial information.

Court Order

Whether you win or lose, once the judge makes a decision, you may be required to prepare the form *Findings and Order After Hearing* (form FL-340) and *Child Support Information and Order Attachment* (form FL-342). If the support order has changed, you may also be required to prepare a modified *Income Withholding for Support* (form FL-195). Usually, the party bringing the motion is supposed to prepare these papers. If that party does not, you must be ready to do it. You will not have to prepare these documents if the local child support agency is involved.

If you have prepared these documents yourself, you must make sure that they are signed by the judge. Check with the court clerk's office or the office of the family law facilitator for the proper procedure. After the *Income Withholding for Support* (form FL-195) is signed by the judge and filed, it must be served on the noncustodial parent's employer, on the other party, and on the local child support agency if it is involved in the case.

0196

ATTORNEY OR PARTY WITHOUT ATTORNEY *(Name and Address):*	TELEPHONE NO.:	*FOR COURT USE ONLY*

ATTORNEY FOR *(Name):*

SUPERIOR COURT OF CALIFORNIA, COUNTY OF

STREET ADDRESS:

MAILING ADDRESS:

CITY AND ZIP CODE:

BRANCH NAME:

MARRIAGE OF

PETITIONER:

RESPONDENT:

EX PARTE APPLICATION FOR RESTORATION OF FORMER NAME AFTER ENTRY OF JUDGMENT AND ORDER	CASE NUMBER:

APPLICATION

1. A judgment of dissolution or nullity was entered on *(date):*

2. Applicant now requests that his or her former name be restored. The applicant's former name is *(specify):*

Date:

_____
(TYPE OR PRINT NAME)

▶

_____
(SIGNATURE OF APPLICANT)
(USE CURRENT NAME)

ORDER

3. IT IS ORDERED that applicant's former name is restored to *(specify):*

Date: _____

JUDICIAL OFFICER

[SEAL]

CLERK'S CERTIFICATE

I certify that the foregoing is a true and correct copy of the original on file in my office.

Date: Clerk, by _____, Deputy

Page 1 of 1

Form Adopted for Mandatory Use
Judicial Council of California
FL-395 [Rev. January 1, 2003]

EX PARTE APPLICATION FOR RESTORATION OF FORMER NAME AFTER ENTRY OF JUDGMENT AND ORDER
(Family Law)

Family Code, § 2080
www.courtinfo.ca.gov

0197

ATTORNEY OR PARTY WITHOUT ATTORNEY *(Name and Address):*	TELEPHONE NO.:	*FOR COURT USE ONLY*

ATTORNEY FOR *(Name):*

SUPERIOR COURT OF CALIFORNIA, COUNTY OF

STREET ADDRESS:

MAILING ADDRESS:

CITY AND ZIP CODE:

BRANCH NAME:

PETITIONER/PLAINTIFF:

RESPONDENT/DEFENDANT:

REQUEST FOR PRODUCTION OF AN INCOME AND EXPENSE DECLARATION AFTER JUDGMENT	CASE NUMBER:

(NOTE: This request must be served on the petitioner or respondent and not on an attorney who was or is representing that party.)

To *(name):*

1. a. As permitted by Family Code section 3664(a), declarant requires that you complete and return the attached *Income and Expense Declaration* (form FL-150) within 30 days after the date this request is served on you. Family Code section 3665(a) requires you to attach copies of your most recent state and federal income tax returns (whether individual or joint) to the completed *Income and Expense Declaration* (form FL-150).

   b. The completed *Income and Expense Declaration* (form FL-150) should be mailed to the following person at the following address *(specify):*

2. You may consult an attorney about completion of the *Income and Expense Declaration* (form FL-150) or you may proceed without an attorney. The information provided will be used to determine whether to ask for a modification of child, spousal, or family support at this time.

3. If you wish to do so, you may serve a request for a completed *Income and Expense Declaration* (form FL-150) on me. Each of us may use this procedure once a year after judgment even though no legal matter is pending.

Date:

_____
(TYPE OR PRINT NAME)

▶

_____
(SIGNATURE OF DECLARANT)

WARNING: If a court later finds that the information provided in response to this request is incomplete or inaccurate or missing the prior year's tax returns, or that you did not submit the information in good faith, the court may order you to pay all costs necessary for me to get complete and accurate information. In addition you could be found to be in contempt and receive other penalties.

Form Adopted for Mandatory Use
Judicial Council of California
FL-396 [Rev. January 1, 2003]

**REQUEST FOR PRODUCTION OF AN INCOME
AND EXPENSE DECLARATION AFTER JUDGMENT**

Family Code, §§ 3664,
3665, 3668
www.courtinfo.ca.gov

PETITIONER/PLAINTIFF:	CASE NUMBER:
RESPONDENT/DEFENDANT:	

PROOF OF SERVICE BY MAIL
REQUEST FOR PRODUCTION OF AN INCOME AND EXPENSE DECLARATION AFTER JUDGMENT

1.   I am at least 18 years old and **not a party to this cause.** I am a resident of or employed in the county where the mailing took place, and my residence or business address is *(specify):*

2. I served a copy of the following documents:
   a. a completed *Request for Production of an Income and Expense Declaration After Judgment,* and
   b. a **blank** *Income and Expense Declaration* (a four-page form) (form FL-150).

3. I served a copy of the foregoing documents by mailing them in a sealed envelope with postage fully prepaid, certified mail, return receipt requested, as follows:
   a.   ☐ I deposited the envelope with the United States Postal Service.
   b.   ☐ I placed the envelope for collection and processing for mailing following this business's ordinary practice with which I am readily familiar. On the same day correspondence is placed for collection and mailing, it is deposited in the ordinary course of business with the United States Postal Service.

4. Manner of service
   a. Date of mailing:
   b. Place mailed from:
   c. Addressed as follows:
         Name:

         Street:

      City, state, and zip code:

   I declare under penalty of perjury under the laws of the State of California that the foregoing is true and correct.

Date:

▶

(TYPE OR PRINT NAME)	(SIGNATURE OF DECLARANT)

FL-396 [Rev. January 1, 2003]

**REQUEST FOR PRODUCTION OF AN INCOME
AND EXPENSE DECLARATION AFTER JUDGMENT**

0199

ATTORNEY OR PARTY WITHOUT ATTORNEY *(Name, state bar number, and address):*	FOR COURT USE ONLY
TELEPHONE NO. *(Optional):*　　　　FAX NO. *(Optional):* E–MAIL ADDRESS *(Optional):* ATTORNEY FOR *(Name):*	

SUPERIOR COURT OF CALIFORNIA, COUNTY OF
STREET ADDRESS:
MAILING ADDRESS:
CITY AND ZIP CODE:
BRANCH NAME:

PETITIONER/PLAINTIFF:

RESPONDENT/DEFENDANT:

REQUEST FOR INCOME AND BENEFIT **INFORMATION FROM EMPLOYER**	CASE NUMBER:

To *(employer name):*

1. This notice is served on you, under California Family Code section 3664(b), in regard to your employee *(name):*

2. I previously served a request for an *Income and Expense Declaration* (form FL-150) after judgment on your employee and:
   a. ☐ There was no response within 35 days
   　　　or
   b. ☐ The response was incomplete as to wage information.

3. I request that the information sought be sent to me on or before *(date):*　　　　　　　　, which is at least 15 days from the date of this request.

4. I request that you, as the employer of the above employee, provide the following information (indicated by checked boxes below). If you wish, you may return a copy of this form with the information filled out or provide the information on a separate form.
   a. ☐ Occupation of employee:
   b. ☐ (1) Presently employed:　☐ Yes　☐ No
   　　　　(2) If employed, current employment status:　☐ Full time　☐ Part time
   　　　　(3) If not presently employed:
   　　　　　　(a) Date of separation:
   　　　　　　(b) Reasons for separation:
   c. ☐ Starting date of employment:
   d. ☐ Gross salary or wages for the previous month (including commissions, bonuses, and overtime):
   e. ☐ Total salary or wages for the previous 12 months (including commissions, bonuses, and overtime):
   f. ☐ Federal income tax withheld for the previous month:
   g. ☐ State income tax withheld for the previous month:
   h. ☐ Social Security and Medicare Tax ("FICA" and "MEDI") deducted for the previous month:
   i. ☐ Any other deductions from the paycheck for the previous month *(for each deduction state purpose and amount):*

Form Adopted for Mandatory Use
Judicial Council of California
FL-397 [Rev. January 1, 2003]
**REQUEST FOR INCOME AND BENEFIT
INFORMATION FROM EMPLOYER**
Family Code, § 3664
www.courtinfo.ca.gov

PETITIONER/PLAINTIFF:	CASE NUMBER:
RESPONDENT/DEFENDANT:	

j. ☐ Benefits provided:

(1) ☐ Vision insurance ☐ Not available ☐ Not enrolled ☐ Enrolled *(specify value to employee)*:

(2) ☐ Life insurance ☐ Not available ☐ Not enrolled ☐ Enrolled *(specify value to employee)*:

(3) ☐ Health insurance ☐ Not available ☐ Not enrolled ☐ Enrolled *(specify value to employee)*:

(4) ☐ Contributions toward ☐ Not available ☐ Not enrolled ☐ Enrolled *(specify asset value to*
retirement plan *employee)*:

(5) ☐ Use of company assets *(vehicle, housing, health club facility, etc.)*
☐ Not available ☐ Not enrolled ☐ Enrolled *(specify value to employee)*:

k. ☐ Attach a copy of the employee's three most recent pay stubs.

5. You are entitled to have me pay the reasonable costs of copying the information in this request.

6. Under Family Code section 3664(f), your compliance with this request is voluntary except upon order of the court or upon agreement of the parties, employers, and employee affected.

Date:

▶

_____
(TYPE OR PRINT NAME)

_____
(SIGNATURE OF REQUESTING PARTY)

NOTICE TO EMPLOYEE

I have served a copy of the attached *Request for Income and Benefit Information From Employer* on your employer under Family Code section 3664(b).

Under Family Code section 3664(c), you are notified that:

1. The information sought by me is limited to the income and benefits provided to you by your employer.

2. The information may be protected by right of privacy.

3. If you object to the production of this information by the employer to me, you must notify the court, in writing, of this objection prior to the date specified in paragraph 3 of the attached request.

4. If, upon your objection, I do not agree, in writing, to cancel or narrow the scope of my request, you should consult an attorney regarding your right to privacy and how to protect this right.

5. You may have other rights provided by Family Code section 3664 and otherwise.

NOTICE TO REQUESTING PARTY

Under Family Code section 3664(e), service of this request on the employer and of the copy of the request on the employee must be by certified mail, postage prepaid, return receipt requested, to the last known address of the party to be served, or by personal service.

**REQUEST FOR INCOME AND BENEFIT
INFORMATION FROM EMPLOYER**

0201

FL-410

ATTORNEY OR PARTY WITHOUT ATTORNEY *(name, State Bar number, and address):*	FOR COURT USE ONLY

TELEPHONE NO.:   FAX NO. *(optional):*
E-MAIL ADDRESS *(optional):*
ATTORNEY FOR *(name):*

SUPERIOR COURT OF CALIFORNIA, COUNTY OF
    STREET ADDRESS:
    MAILING ADDRESS:
    CITY AND ZIP CODE:
    BRANCH NAME:

PETITIONER/PLAINTIFF:

RESPONDENT/DEFENDANT:

OTHER PARTY/PARENT:

ORDER TO SHOW CAUSE AND AFFIDAVIT FOR CONTEMPT	CASE NUMBER:

NOTICE!	**¡AVISO!**
A contempt proceeding is criminal in nature. If the court finds you in contempt, the possible penalties include jail sentence, community service, and fine.	Un proceso judicial por desacato es de índole criminal. Si la corte le declara a usted en desacato, las sanciones posibles incluyen penas de prisión y de servicio a la comunidad, y multas.
You are entitled to the services of an attorney, who should be consulted promptly in order to assist you. If you cannot afford an attorney, the court may appoint an attorney to represent you.	Usted tiene derecho a los servicios de un abogado, a quien debe consultar sin demora para obtener ayuda. Si no puede pagar a un abogado, la corte podrá nombrar a un abogado para que le represente.

1. TO CITEE *(name of person you allege has violated the orders):*

2. YOU ARE ORDERED TO APPEAR IN THIS COURT AS FOLLOWS, TO GIVE ANY LEGAL REASON WHY THIS COURT SHOULD NOT FIND YOU GUILTY OF CONTEMPT, PUNISH YOU FOR WILLFULLY DISOBEYING ITS ORDERS AS SET FORTH IN THE AFFIDAVIT BELOW AND ANY ATTACHED *AFFIDAVIT OF FACTS CONSTITUTING CONTEMPT;* AND REQUIRE YOU TO PAY, FOR THE BENEFIT OF THE MOVING PARTY, THE ATTORNEY FEES AND COSTS OF THIS PROCEEDING.

  a. Date: Time: Dept.:   Rm.:

  b. Address of court: ☐ same as noted above ☐ other *(specify):*

Date: _____ ▶ _____
                                 JUDICIAL OFFICER

AFFIDAVIT SUPPORTING ORDER TO SHOW CAUSE FOR CONTEMPT

3. ☐ An *Affidavit of Facts Constituting Contempt* (form FL-411 or FL-412) is attached.

4. Citee has willfully disobeyed certain orders of this court as set forth in this affidavit and any attached affidavits.

5. a. Citee had knowledge of the order in that
    (1) ☐ citee was present in court at the time the order was made.
    (2) ☐ citee was served with a copy of the order.
    (3) ☐ citee signed a stipulation upon which the order was based.
    (4) ☐ other *(specify):*

    ☐ Continued on Attachment 5a(4).
  b. Citee was able to comply with each order when it was disobeyed.

6. Based on the instances of disobedience described in this affidavit
  a. ☐ I have not previously filed a request with the court that the citee be held in contempt.
  b. ☐ I have previously filed a request with the court that the citee be held in contempt *(specify date filed and results):*

  ☐ Continued on Attachment 6b.

Page 1 of 4

Form Adopted for Mandatory Use
Judicial Council of California
FL-410 [Rev. January 1, 2015]

ORDER TO SHOW CAUSE AND AFFIDAVIT FOR CONTEMPT

Family Code, § 292;
Code of Civil Procedure, §§ 1211.5, 2015.5
www.courts.ca.gov

PETITIONER/PLAINTIFF: RESPONDENT/DEFENDANT: OTHER PARTY/PARENT:	CASE NUMBER:

7. ☐ Citee has previously been found in contempt of a court order *(specify case, court, date):*

☐ Continued on Attachment 7.

8. ☐ Each order disobeyed and each instance of disobedience is described as follows:

a. ☐ Orders for child support, spousal support, family support, attorney fees, and court or other litigation costs (see attached *Affidavit of Facts Constituting Contempt* (form FL-411))

b. ☐ Domestic violence restraining orders and child custody and visitation orders (see attached *Affidavit of Facts Constituting Contempt* (form FL-412))

c. ☐ Injunctive or other order *(specify which order was violated, how the order was violated, and when the order was violated):*

☐ Continued on Attachment 8c.

d. ☐ Other material facts, including facts indicating that the violation of the orders was without justification or excuse *(specify):*

☐ Continued on Attachment 8d.

e. ☐ I am requesting that attorney fees and costs be awarded to me for the costs of pursuing this contempt action. (A copy of my *Income and Expense Declaration* (form FL-150) is attached.)

WARNING: IF YOU PURSUE THIS CONTEMPT ACTION, IT MAY AFFECT THE ABILITY OF THE DISTRICT ATTORNEY TO PROSECUTE THE CITEE CRIMINALLY FOR THE SAME VIOLATIONS.

I declare under penalty of perjury under the laws of the State of California that the foregoing is true and correct.

Date:

▶

_____
(TYPE OR PRINT NAME)

_____
(SIGNATURE)

INFORMATION SHEET FOR ORDER TO SHOW CAUSE
AND AFFIDAVIT FOR CONTEMPT

(Do NOT deliver this Information Sheet to the court clerk.)

Please follow these instructions to complete the *Order to Show Cause and Affidavit for Contempt* (form FL-410) if you do not have an attorney to represent you. Your attorney, if you have one, should complete this form, as well as the *Affidavit of Facts Constituting Contempt* (form FL-411 or form FL-412). You may wish to consult an attorney for assistance. Contempt actions are very difficult to prove. An attorney may be appointed for the citee.

INSTRUCTIONS FOR COMPLETING THE ORDER TO SHOW CAUSE AND AFFIDAVIT FOR CONTEMPT (TYPE OR PRINT FORM IN INK):

If the top section of the form has already been filled out, skip down to number 1 below. If the top section of the form is blank, you must provide this information.

Front page, first box, top of form, left side: Print your name, address, telephone number, and fax number, if any, in this box. If you have a restraining order and wish to keep your address confidential, you may use any address where you can receive mail. **You can be legally served court papers at this address.**

Front page, second box, left side: Print the name of the county where the court is located and insert the address and any branch name of the court building where you are seeking to obtain a contempt order. You may get this information from the court clerk. This should be the same court in which the original order was issued.

Front page, third box, left side: Print the names of the Petitioner, Respondent, and Other Party/Parent (if any) in this box. Use the same names as appear on the most recent court order disobeyed.

Front page, first box, top of form, right side: Leave this box blank for the court's use.

Front page, second box, right side: Print the court case number in this box. This number is also shown on the most recent court order disobeyed.

Item 1: Insert the name of the party who disobeyed the order ("the citee").

Item 2: The court clerk will provide the hearing date and location.

Item 3: Either check the box in item 3 and attach an *Affidavit of Facts Constituting Contempt* (form FL-411 for financial orders or form FL-412 for domestic violence, or custody and visitation orders), or leave the box in item 3 blank but check and complete item 8.

Item 5: Check the box that describes how the citee knew about the order that has been disobeyed.

Item 6: a. Check this box if you have not previously applied for a contempt order.

   b. Check this box if you have previously applied for a contempt order and briefly explain when you requested the order and results of your request. If you need more space, check the box that says "continued on Attachment 6b" and attach a separate sheet to this order to show cause.

Item 7: Check this box if the citee has previously been found in contempt by a court of law. Briefly explain when the citee was found in contempt and for what. If there is not enough space to write all the facts, check the box that says "continued on Attachment 7" and attach a separate sheet to this order to show cause.

Item 8: a. Check this box if the citee has disobeyed orders for child support, custody, visitation, spousal support, family support, attorney fees, and court or litigation costs. Refer to item 1a on *Affidavit of Facts Constituting Contempt* (form FL-411).

   b. Check this box if the citee has disobeyed domestic violence orders or child custody and visitation orders. Refer to *Affidavit of Facts Constituting Contempt* (form FL-412).

Information Sheet *(continued)*

<u>Item 8:</u> c. If you are completing this item, use facts personally known to you or known to the best of your knowledge. State the facts in detail. If there is not enough space to write all the facts, check the box that says "continued on Attachment 8c" and attach a separate sheet to this order to show cause, including facts indicating that the violation of the orders was without justification or excuse.

      d. Use this item to write other facts that are important to this order. If you are completing this item, insert facts personally known to you, or known to the best of your knowledge. State facts in detail. If there is not enough space to write all the facts, check the box that says "Continued on Attachment 8d" and attach a separate sheet to the order to show cause.

      e. If you request attorney fees and/or costs for pursuing this contempt action, check this box. Attach a copy of your *Income and Expense Declaration* (form FL-150).

Type or print and sign your name at the bottom of page 2.

If you checked the boxes in item 3 and item 8a or 8b, complete the appropriate *Affidavit of Facts Constituting Contempt* (form FL-411), following the instructions for the affidavit above.

Make at least three copies of the *Order to Show Cause and Affidavit for Contempt* (form FL-410) and any supporting *Affidavit of Facts Constituting Contempt* (form FL-411 or FL-412) and the *Income and Expense Declaration* (form FL-150) for the court clerk, the citee, and yourself. If the district attorney or local child support agency is involved in your case, you must provide a copy to the district attorney or local child support agency.

Take the completed form(s) to the court clerk's office. The clerk will provide hearing date and location in item 2, obtain the judicial officer's signature, file the originals, and return the copies to you.

Have someone who is at least 18 years of age, who is not a party, serve the order and any attached papers on the disobedient party. For example, a process server or someone you know may serve the papers. **You may not serve the papers yourself. Service must be personal; service by mail is insufficient.** The papers must be served at least 16 court days before the hearing. The person serving papers must complete a *Proof of Personal Service* (form FL-330) and give the original to you. Keep a copy for yourself and file the original *Proof of Personal Service* (form FL-330) with the court.

If you need assistance with these forms, contact an attorney or the Family Law Facilitator in your county.

0205

PETITIONER/PLAINTIFF:	CASE NUMBER:
RESPONDENT/DEFENDANT:	
OTHER PARENT:	

AFFIDAVIT OF FACTS CONSTITUTING CONTEMPT
Financial and Injunctive Orders
Attachment to *Order to Show Cause and Affidavit for Contempt* **(form FL-410)**

1. a. Orders for child support, spousal support, family support, attorney fees, and court and litigation costs *(separately itemize each default on installment payments):*

DATE DUE	TYPE OF ORDER AND DATE FILED	PAYABLE TO	AMOUNT ORDERED	AMOUNT PAID	AMOUNT DUE
☐ Continued on Attachment 1a.			TOTAL AMOUNT ORDERED	TOTAL AMOUNT PAID	TOTAL AMOUNT DUE
Summary of contempt counts alleged (including all attachments):					
Child support: Spousal support: Family support: Attorney fees: Court and other costs:					
Total			$	$	$

b. ☐ Other orders *(specify which order was violated, how the order was violated, and when the violation occurred):*

☐ Continued on Attachment 1b.

c. ☐ Other material facts *(specify):*

☐ Continued on Attachment 1c.

I declare under penalty of perjury under the laws of the State of California that the foregoing is true and correct.
Date:

▶

_____
(TYPE OR PRINT NAME)

_____
(SIGNATURE)

Page 1 of 1

Form Adopted for Mandatory Use
Judicial Council of California
FL-411 [Rev. January 1, 2003]

AFFIDAVIT OF FACTS CONSTITUTING CONTEMPT
Financial and Injunctive Orders

Family Code, § 292;
Code of Civil Procedure,
§§ 1209, 1211, 1211.5, 2015.5
www.courtinfo.ca.gov

FL-430

ATTORNEY OR PARTY WITHOUT ATTORNEY *(Name, State Bar number, and address):*	FOR COURT USE ONLY

TELEPHONE NO.: FAX NO. *(Optional):*

E-MAIL ADDRESS *(Optional):*

ATTORNEY FOR *(Name):*

SUPERIOR COURT OF CALIFORNIA, COUNTY OF

STREET ADDRESS:

MAILING ADDRESS:

CITY AND ZIP CODE:

BRANCH NAME:

PETITIONER/PLAINTIFF:

RESPONDENT/DEFENDANT:

OTHER PARTY/PARENT:

EX PARTE APPLICATION TO ☐ ISSUE, ☐ MODIFY, OR ☐ TERMINATE AN EARNINGS ASSIGNMENT ORDER	CASE NUMBER:

APPLICANT DECLARES

1. ☐ **Child support** was ordered as follows on *(date):*

   a. Child's name   b. Date of birth   c. Monthly amount d. Payable by *(party):* e. Payable to *(party):*

   f. Total amount unpaid (arrears) is at least: $ as of *(date):*

2. ☐ **Spousal or domestic partner support** ☐ **family support** was ordered as follows:

   a. Date of order:

   b. Payable by ☐ petitioner ☐ respondent ☐ other parent

   c. Payable to ☐ petitioner ☐ respondent ☐ other *(specify):*

   d. Total amount unpaid (arrears) is at least: $ as of *(date):*

3. ☐ **Interest and penalties**

   a. The amount of arrears stated in items 1f and 2d ☐ does ☐ does not include interest at the legal rate. *(If interest is not included, it is not waived.)*

   b. The amount of arrears stated in items 1f and 2d ☐ does ☐ does not include penalties at the legal rate. *(If penalties are not included, they are not waived.)*

4. ☐ *(Complete for support ordered before July 1, 1990, only)*

   Payment of ☐ child support ☐ spousal or partner support is overdue in the sum of at least one month's payment.

   Written notice of my intent to seek an earnings assignment was

   a. ☐ given at least 15 days before the date of filing this application

   (1) ☐ by first class mail.

   (2) ☐ by personal service.

   (3) ☐ contained in the support order described in item 1 or 2.

   (4) ☐ other *(specify):*

   b. ☐ waived *(explain):*

5. ☐ An earnings assignment order has not been issued for support ordered after July 1, 1990.

Page 1 of 3

Form Adopted for Mandatory Use
Judicial Council of California
FL-430 [Rev. January 1, 2014]

EX PARTE APPLICATION TO ISSUE, MODIFY, OR TERMINATE AN EARNINGS ASSIGNMENT ORDER

Family Code, §§ 3901, 5230, 5240, 5252
www.courts.ca.gov

PETITIONER/PLAINTIFF:	CASE NUMBER:
RESPONDENT/DEFENDANT:	
OTHER PARTY/PARENT:	

ISSUANCE OF EARNINGS ASSIGNMENT ORDER

6. **I request** an earnings assignment order issue for the following monthly deductions:
   a. ☐ $ _____ per month current **child support.**
   b. ☐ $ _____ per month current **spousal or domestic partner support.**
   c. ☐ $ _____ per month current **family support.**
   d. ☐ $ _____ per month **child support arrears.**
   e. ☐ $ _____ per month **spousal or domestic partner support arrears.**
   f. ☐ $ _____ per month **family support arrears.**
   g. **Total deductions per month:** $

MODIFICATION OF CHILD SUPPORT EARNINGS ASSIGNMENT ORDER

7. ☐ The existing earnings assignment order for child support should be modified as follows *(specify):*

   The modified earnings assignment order is requested because *(check all that apply):*

   a. ☐ One or more of the following children listed in the child support order are emancipated (support is no longer required by law) as of the following dates (name each emancipated child and date of emancipation):

   b. ☐ The support arrears in this case are paid in full, including interest.

   c. ☐ The earnings assignment order must be conformed to the most recent support order as follows *(specify):*

   d. ☐ The local child support agency is no longer enforcing the current support obligation in this case but is required to collect and enforce any arrears owing.

   e. ☐ Other *(specify):*

TERMINATION OF CHILD SUPPORT EARNINGS ASSIGNMENT ORDER

8. ☐ The earnings assignment order for child support should be terminated because *(check all that apply):*
   a. Past due support has been paid in full, including any interest due.
   b. ☐ There is no current support order.
   c. ☐ The child reached age 18 and completed the 12th grade on *(date):*
   d. ☐ The child reached 18 and is no longer a full-time high school student as of *(date):*
   e. ☐ The child reached age 19.
   f. ☐ The child died on *(date):*
   g. ☐ The child married on *(date):*
   h. ☐ The child went on active duty with the armed forces of the United States on *(date):*
   i. ☐ The child received a declaration of emancipation under Family Code section 7122 *(name each child and give details):*

**EX PARTE APPLICATION TO ISSUE, MODIFY, OR
TERMINATE AN EARNINGS ASSIGNMENT ORDER**

FL-430

PETITIONER/PLAINTIFF: RESPONDENT/DEFENDANT: OTHER PARTY/PARENT:	CASE NUMBER:

8. *(continued)*

j. ☐ The previous stay of the earnings assignment was improperly terminated *(specify):*

k. ☐ The State Disbursement Unit has been unable to deliver payment for a period of six months due to the failure of the support recipient to notify the State Disbursement Unit of a change in his or her address.

l. ☐ Other *(specify):*

MODIFICATION OF SPOUSAL, DOMESTIC PARTNER, OR FAMILY SUPPORT EARNINGS ASSIGNMENT ORDER

9. ☐ The existing earnings assignment order for spousal, domestic partner, or family support should be changed as follows *(specify):*

The modified earnings assignment order is requested because *(check all that apply):*

a. ☐ The support arrears in this case are paid in full, including interest.

b. ☐ The earnings assignment order must be conformed to the most recent support order as follows *(specify):*

c. ☐ Other *(specify):*

TERMINATION OF SPOUSAL, DOMESTIC PARTNER, OR FAMILY SUPPORT EARNINGS ASSIGNMENT ORDER

10. ☐ The earnings assignment order for spousal, domestic partner, or family support should be terminated because *(specify):*

a. Past due support has been paid in full, including any interest due.

b. ☐ There is no current support order.

c. ☐ The supported spouse or domestic partner remarried or registered a domestic partnership on *(date):*

d. ☐ The supported spouse or partner died on *(date):*

e. ☐ By terms of the current order, spousal, partner, or family support terminated on *(date):*

f. ☐ A previous stay of wage assignment was improperly terminated *(specify):*

g. ☐ The ☐ employer ☐ State Disbursement Unit has been unable to deliver payment for a period of six months due to the failure of the support recipient to notify that employer or the State Disbursement Unit of a change in his or her address.

h. ☐ Other *(specify):*

I declare under penalty of perjury under the laws of the State of California that the foregoing is true and correct.

Date:

_____
(TYPE OR PRINT NAME)

▸ _____
SIGNATURE

FL-430 [Rev. January 1, 2014]

**EX PARTE APPLICATION TO ISSUE, MODIFY, OR
TERMINATE AN EARNINGS ASSIGNMENT ORDER**

Page 3 of 3

FL-435

ATTORNEY OR PARTY WITHOUT ATTORNEY *(Name, State Bar number, and address)*:	FOR COURT USE ONLY

TELEPHONE NO.:   FAX NO. *(Optional)*:

E-MAIL ADDRESS *(Optional)*:

ATTORNEY FOR *(Name)*:

SUPERIOR COURT OF CALIFORNIA, COUNTY OF

STREET ADDRESS:

MAILING ADDRESS:

CITY AND ZIP CODE:

BRANCH NAME:

PETITIONER/PLAINTIFF:

RESPONDENT/DEFENDANT:

OTHER PARENT:

EARNINGS ASSIGNMENT ORDER FOR SPOUSAL OR PARTNER SUPPORT ☐ **Modification**	CASE NUMBER:

TO THE PAYOR: This is a court order. You must withhold a portion of the earnings of *(specify obligor's name and birthdate)*:

and pay as directed below. *(An explanation of this order is printed on page 2 of this form.)*

THE COURT ORDERS

1. You must pay part of the earnings of the employee or other person who has been ordered to pay support, as follows:
   a. ☐ $ _____ per month current **spousal or partner support**
   b. ☐ $ _____ per month **spousal or partner support arrearages**
   c. **Total deductions per month:** $ _____

2. ☐ The payments ordered under item 1a must be paid to *(name, address)*:

3. ☐ The payments ordered under item 1b must be paid to *(name, address)*:

4. The payments ordered under item 1 must continue until further written notice from the payee or the court.

5. ☐ This order modifies an existing order. **The amount you must withhold may have changed.** The existing order continues in effect until this modification is effective.

6. This order affects all earnings that are payable beginning as soon as possible but not later than 10 days after you receive it.

7. You must give the obligor a copy of this order and the blank *Request for Hearing Regarding Earnings Assignment* (form FL-450) within 10 days.

8. ☐ Other *(specify)*:

9. For the purposes of this order, spousal or partner support arrearages are set at: $ _____ as of *(date)*:

Date: _____

_____
JUDICIAL OFFICER

Page 1 of 2

**EARNINGS ASSIGNMENT ORDER FOR SPOUSAL
OR PARTNER SUPPORT
(Family Law)**

Family Code, §§ 299(d), 5208;
Code of Civil Procedure, § 706.031;
15 U.S.C. §§ 1672–1673
www.courtinfo.ca.gov

INSTRUCTIONS FOR EARNINGS ASSIGNMENT ORDER

1. **DEFINITION OF IMPORTANT WORDS IN THE EARNINGS ASSIGNMENT ORDER**

   a. **Earnings:**

      (1) Wages, salary, bonuses, vacation pay, retirement pay, and commissions paid by an employer;

      (2) Payments for services of independent contractors;

      (3) Dividends, interest, rents, royalties, and residuals;

      (4) Patent rights and mineral or other natural resource rights;

      (5) Any payments due as a result of written or oral contracts for services or sales, regardless of title;

      (6) Payments due for workers' compensation temporary benefits, or payments from a disability or health insurance policy or program; and

      (7) Any other payments or credits due, regardless of source.

   b. **Earnings assignment order:** a court order issued in every court case in which one person is ordered to pay for the support of another person. This order has priority over any other orders such as garnishments or earnings withholding orders.

      Earnings should not be withheld for any other order until the amounts necessary to satisfy this order have been withheld in full. However, an *Order/Notice to Withhold Income for Child Support* for child support or family support has priority over this order for spousal or partner support.

   c. **Obligor:** any person ordered by a court to pay support. The obligor is named before item 1 in the order.

   d. **Obligee:** the person or governmental agency to whom the support is to be paid.

   e. **Payor:** the person or entity, including an employer, that pays earnings to an obligor.

2. **INFORMATION FOR ALL PAYORS.** Withhold money from the earnings payable to the obligor as soon as possible but no later than 10 days after you receive the *Earnings Assignment Order for Spousal or Partner Support.* Send the withheld money to the payee(s) named in items 2 and 3 of the order within 10 days of the pay date. You may deduct $1 from the obligor's earnings for each payment you make.

   When sending the withheld earnings to the payee, state the date on which the earnings were withheld. You may combine amounts withheld for two or more obligors in a single payment to each payee, and identify what portion of that payment is for each obligor.

   You will be liable for any amount you fail to withhold and can be cited for contempt of court.

3. **SPECIAL INSTRUCTIONS FOR PAYORS WHO ARE EMPLOYERS**

   a. State and federal laws limit the amount you can withhold and pay as directed by this order. This limitation applies only to earnings defined above in item 1a(1) and are usually half the obligor's disposable earnings.

      Disposable earnings are different from gross pay or take-home pay. Disposable earnings are earnings left after subtracting the money that state or federal law requires an employer to withhold. Generally these required deductions are (1) federal income tax, (2) social security, (3) state income tax, (4) state disability insurance, and (5) payments to public employees' retirement systems.

      After the obligor's disposable earnings are known, withhold the amount required by the order, **but never withhold more than 50 percent of the disposable earnings unless the court order specifies a higher percentage.** Federal law prohibits withholding more than 65 percent of disposable earnings of an employee in any case.

      If the obligor has more than one assignment for support, add together the amounts of support due for all the assignments. If 50 percent of the obligor's net disposable earnings will not pay in full all of the assignments for support, prorate it first among all of the current support assignments in the same proportion that each assignment bears to the total current support owed. Apply any remainder to the assignments for arrearage support in the same proportion that each assignment bears to the total arrearage owed. If you have any questions, please contact the office or person who sent this form to you. This office or person's name appears in the upper left-hand corner of the order.

   b. If the employee's pay period differs from the period specified in the order, prorate the amount ordered withheld so that part of it is withheld from each of the obligor's paychecks.

   c. If the obligor stops working for you, notify the office that sent you this form of that, no later than the date of the next payment, by first-class mail. Give the obligor's last known address and, if known, the name and address of any new employer.

   d. California law prohibits you from firing, refusing to hire, or taking any disciplinary action against any employee ordered to pay support through an earnings assignment. Such action can lead to a $500 civil penalty per employee.

4. **INFORMATION FOR ALL OBLIGORS.** You should have received a *Request for Hearing Regarding Earnings Assignment* (form FL-450) with this *Earnings Assignment Order for Spousal or Partner Support.* If not, you may get one from either the court clerk or the family law facilitator. If you want the court to stop or modify your earnings assignment, you must file (by hand delivery or mail) an original copy of the form with the court clerk within 10 days of the date you received this order. Keep a copy of the form for your records.

   If you think your support order is wrong, you can ask for a modification of the order or, in some cases, you can have the order set aside and have a new order issued. You can talk to an attorney or get information from the family law facilitator about this.

5. **SPECIAL INFORMATION FOR THE OBLIGOR WHO IS AN EMPLOYEE.** State law requires you to notify the payees named in items 2 and 3 of the order if you change your employment. You must provide the name and address of your new employer.

**EARNINGS ASSIGNMENT ORDER FOR SPOUSAL
OR PARTNER SUPPORT**
(Family Law)

ATTORNEY OR PARTY WITHOUT ATTORNEY *(Name, State Bar number, and address):*	FOR COURT USE ONLY

TELEPHONE NO.:   FAX NO. *(Optional):*

E-MAIL ADDRESS *(Optional):*

ATTORNEY FOR *(Name):*

SUPERIOR COURT OF CALIFORNIA, COUNTY OF

STREET ADDRESS:

MAILING ADDRESS:

CITY AND ZIP CODE:

BRANCH NAME:

PETITIONER/PLAINTIFF:

RESPONDENT/DEFENDANT:

OTHER PARENT:

REQUEST FOR HEARING REGARDING EARNINGS ASSIGNMENT	CASE NUMBER:

NOTICE: Complete and file this form with the court clerk to request a hearing *only* if you object to the *Income Withholding for Support* (form FL-195/OMB0970-0154) or *Earnings Assignment Order for Spousal or Partner Support* (form FL-435). This form may not be used to modify your current child support amount. (See page 2 of form FL-192, *Information Sheet on Changing a Child Support Order*.) Page 3 of this form is instructional only and does not need to be delivered to the court.

1. A hearing on this application will be held as follows *(see instructions for getting a hearing date on page 3)*:

   a.   Date: Time: ☐ Dept.:   ☐ Div.:   ☐ Room:

   b. The address of the court is: ☐ same as noted above ☐ other *(specify):*

2. ☐ I request that service of the *Earnings Assignment Order for Spousal or Partner Support* (form FL-435) or *Income Withholding for Support* (form FL-195/OMB0970-0154) be quashed (set aside) because

   a. ☐ I am not the obligor named in the earnings assignment.

   b. ☐ There is good cause to recall the earnings assignment because **all** of the following conditions exist:

      (1) Recalling the earnings assignment would be in the best interest of the children for whom I am ordered to pay support *(state reasons):*

      (2) I have paid court-ordered support fully and on time for the last 12 months without either an earnings assignment or another mandatory collection process.

      (3) I do not owe any arrearage (back support).

      (4) Service of the earnings assignment would cause extraordinary hardship for me, as follows *(state reasons; you must prove these reasons at any hearing on this application by clear and convincing evidence):*

   c. ☐ The other parent and I have a written agreement that allows the support order to be paid by an alternative method. A copy of the agreement is attached. **(NOTE: If the support obligation is paid to the local child support agency, this agreement must be signed by a representative of that agency.)**

Page 1 of 3

Form Adopted for Mandatory Use Judicial Council of California FL-450 [Rev. July 1, 2008]	**REQUEST FOR HEARING REGARDING EARNINGS ASSIGNMENT** **(Family Law—Governmental—UIFSA)**	Family Code, § 5246 *www.courtinfo.ca.gov*

FL-450

PETITIONER/PLAINTIFF:	CASE NUMBER:
RESPONDENT/DEFENDANT:	
OTHER PARENT:	

3. ☐ I request that the earnings assignment be modified because

    a. ☐ the total amount of arrearages claimed as owing is incorrect. *(Check one or more of the following reasons.)*

        (1) ☐ I did not receive credit for all of the payments I have made. *(Check (a), (b), or both.)*

            (a) ☐ I have attached my statement of the payment history, which includes a monthly breakdown of amounts ordered and amounts paid.

            (b) ☐ I made the following payments that were not credited *(for each payment, specify the date, the amount, and the name of the person or agency paid):*

        (2) ☐ Child support was terminated *(specify name of child, child's date of birth, date of termination, and reason support was terminated):*

        (3) ☐ Other *(specify):*

    b. ☐ the monthly payment specified in the earnings assignment is more than half of my total net income each month from all sources.

    c. ☐ the monthly arrearage payment stated in the earnings assignment creates an undue hardship because *(describe the hardship and state the amount you are able to pay on your arrearage):*

    (NOTE: If you want to change the amount of money being deducted for arrearage because it creates a hardship, please attach a completed *Financial Statement (Simplified)* (form FL-155) or *Income and Expense Declaration* (form FL-150).)

I declare under penalty of perjury under the laws of the State of California that the foregoing is true and correct.

Date:

▶

_____
(TYPE OR PRINT NAME OF PERSON REQUESTING HEARING)

_____
(SIGNATURE OF PERSON REQUESTING HEARING)

CLERK'S CERTIFICATE OF MAILING

I certify that I am not a party to this action and that a true copy of the *Request for Hearing Regarding Earnings Assignment* (form FL-450) was mailed, with postage fully prepaid, in a sealed envelope addressed as shown below, and that the request was mailed at *(place):*   on *(date):*

Date:

Clerk, by _____, Deputy

REQUEST FOR HEARING REGARDING EARNINGS ASSIGNMENT
(Family Law—Governmental—UIFSA)

INFORMATION SHEET AND INSTRUCTIONS
FOR REQUEST FOR HEARING REGARDING EARNINGS ASSIGNMENT
(Do *not* deliver this information sheet to the court clerk.)

Please follow these instructions to complete the *Request for Hearing Regarding Earnings Assignment* (form FL-450) if you do not have an attorney representing you. Your attorney, if you have one, should complete this form. You must file the completed *Request for Hearing* form and its attachments with the court clerk **within 10 days** after the date your employer gave you a copy of *Earnings Assignment Order for Spousal or Partner Support* (form FL-435) or an *Income Withholding for Support* (form FL-195/OMB0970-0154). The address of the court clerk is the same as the one shown for the superior court on the earnings assignment order. You may have to pay a filing fee. If you cannot afford to pay the filing fee, the court may waive it, but you will have to fill out some forms first. For more information about the filing fee and waiver of the filing fee, contact the court clerk or the family law facilitator in your county.

(TYPE OR PRINT IN INK)

Front page, first box, top of form, left side: Print your name, address, and telephone number in this box if they are not already there.

Item 1. a–b. You must contact the court clerk's office and ask that a hearing date be set for this motion. The court clerk will give you the information you need to complete this section.

Item 2. Check this box if you want the court to stop the local child support agency or the other parent from collecting any support from your earnings. If you check this box, you must check the box for either a, b, or c beneath it.

  a. Check this box if you are not the person required to pay support in the earnings assignment.

  b. Check this box if you believe that there is "good cause" to recall the earnings assignment. **Note:** The court must find that **all** of the conditions listed in item 2b exist in order for good cause to apply.

  c. Check this box if you and the other parent have a written agreement that allows you to pay the support another way. **You must attach a copy of the agreement,** which must be signed by both the other parent and a representative of the local child support agency if payments are made to a county office.

Item 3. Check this box if you want to change the earnings assignment. If you check this box, you must check the box for either a, b, or c beneath it.

  a. Check this box if the total arrearages listed in item 9 on the earnings assignment order are wrong. If you check this box, you must check one or more of (1), (2), and (3). You must attach the original of your statement of arrearages. Keep one copy for yourself.

   (1) Check this box if you believe the amount of arrearages listed on the earnings assignment order does not give you credit for all the payments you have made. If you check this box, you must check one or both of the boxes beneath it.

    (a) Check this box if you are attaching your own statement of arrearages. This statement must include a monthly listing of what you were ordered to pay and what you actually paid.

    (b) Check this box if you wish to list any payments that you believe were not included in the arrearages amount. For each payment you must list the date you paid it, the amount paid, and the person or agency (such as the local child support agency) to whom you made the payment. Bring to the hearing proof of any payment that is in dispute.

   (2) Check this box if the child support for any of the children in the case has been terminated (ended). If you check this box, you must list the following information for each child:
   - The name and birthdate of each child.
   - The date the child support order was terminated.
   - The reason child support was terminated.

   (3) Check this box if there is another reason you believe the amount of arrearages is incorrect. You must explain the reasons in detail.

  b. Check this box if the total monthly payment shown in item 1 of the earnings assignment order is more than half of your monthly net income.

  c. Check this box if the total monthly payment shown in item 1 of the earnings assignment order causes you a serious hardship. You must write the reasons for the hardship in this space.

You must date this *Request for Hearing* form, print your name, and sign the form under penalty of perjury. You must also complete the certificate of mailing at the bottom of page 2 of the form by printing the name and address of the other parties in brackets and providing a stamped envelope addressed to each of the parties. When you sign this *Request for Hearing* form, you are stating that the information you have provided is true and correct. After you file the request, the court clerk will notify you by mail of the date, time, and location of the hearing.

You must file your request within 10 days of receiving the *Earnings Assignment Order for Spousal or Partner Support* or the *Income Withholding for Support* from your employer. You may file your request in person at the clerk's office or mail it to the clerk. In either event, it must be received by the clerk within the 10-day period.

If you need additional assistance with this form, contact an attorney or the family law facilitator in your county. Your family law facilitator can help you, for free, with any questions you have about the above information. For more information on finding a lawyer or family law facilitator, see the California Courts Online Self-Help Center at *www.courtinfo.ca.gov/selfhelp/*.

NOTICE: Use form FL-450 to request a hearing only if you object to the *Income Withholding for Support* (form FL-195/OMB0970-0154) or *Earnings Assignment Order for Spousal or Partner Support* (form FL-435). This form will *not* modify your current support amount. (See page 2 of form FL-192, *Information Sheet on Changing a Child Support Order*.)

REQUEST FOR HEARING REGARDING EARNINGS ASSIGNMENT
(Family Law—Governmental—UIFSA)

FL-455

ATTORNEY OR PARTY WITHOUT ATTORNEY *(Name and address):*	FOR COURT USE ONLY

TELEPHONE NO.:

ATTORNEY FOR *(Name):*

SUPERIOR COURT OF CALIFORNIA, COUNTY OF

STREET ADDRESS:

MAILING ADDRESS:

CITY AND ZIP CODE:

BRANCH NAME:

PETITIONER/PLAINTIFF:

RESPONDENT/DEFENDANT:

OTHER PARENT:

☐ **STAY** ☐ **TERMINATION OF STAY**
OF SERVICE OF EARNINGS ASSIGNMENT ORDER

CASE NUMBER:

APPLICATION FOR STAY

(NOTICE: If this application is made separately from a hearing on support, you must get a hearing date from the clerk and give notice. See below.)

I request that the court stay the service of the earnings assignment order in this case because *(check one or more applicable reasons):*

1. ☐ I have paid fully and on time the previously ordered support for the last 12 months, and I do not owe any back support (arrearages).

2. ☐ I have not been subject to a support order for the last 12 months, but I have posted ☐ cash ☐ a cash bond with the clerk of the court in the amount of $ _____ , which is equal to three months' support, and I do not owe any back support (arrearages).

3. ☐ Service of the earnings assignment would cause extraordinary hardship on me as follows *(state reasons):*
   (Note: You must prove these reasons at any hearing on this application by clear and convincing evidence.)

4. ☐ I have a written agreement with the party receiving support that provides a stay of service of the earnings assignment order. A copy of the agreement is attached. *(Note: This agreement must be signed by the local child support agency if support is payable to a county officer designated for that purpose.)*

5. ☐ My employer or the local child support agency has been unable to deliver the support payments to the recipient for at least six months because the recipient has not notified my employer or the local child support agency of a change of address. *(Attach a statement made under oath by employer or local child support agency.)*

I declare under penalty of perjury under the laws of the State of California that the foregoing is true and correct.

Date:

▶

_____
(TYPE OR PRINT NAME)

_____
(SIGNATURE OF APPLICANT)

NOTICE OF HEARING

A hearing on this application will be held as follows:

a. Date:	Time:	Dept.:	Room:

b. The address of the court ☐ is shown above ☐ is:

Page 1 of 2

Form Adopted for Mandatory Use Judicial Council of California FL-455 [Rev. January 1, 2003]	**STAY OF SERVICE OF EARNINGS ASSIGNMENT ORDER**	Family Code, §§ 5260, 5261 www.courtinfo.ca.gov

PETITIONER/PLAINTIFF:	CASE NUMBER:
RESPONDENT/DEFENDANT:	
OTHER PARENT:	

APPLICATION FOR TERMINATION OF STAY

I request that the court terminate the stay of service of the earnings assignment previously issued in this case
on (date):   because (check one or more applicable reasons):

1. ☐ The person required to make payments has missed at least one payment of support, which continues unpaid. (Note: A false statement about missed payments is punishable as contempt.)

2. ☐ I am ☐ the person required to make the payments ☐ the local child support agency, and I wish the stay terminated.

3. ☐ The reasons for granting the stay no longer exist. (A hearing is required. See page 1 for notice of hearing.)

(State facts showing that the previous reasons for granting the stay no longer exist.)

I declare under penalty of perjury under the laws of the State of California that the foregoing is true and correct.
Date:

▶

_____   _____
(TYPE OR PRINT NAME)   (SIGNATURE OF APPLICANT)

PROOF OF SERVICE BY MAIL

1. I am at least 18 years of age and **not a party to this cause.** I am a resident of or employed in the county where the mailing took place, and my residence or business address is (specify):

2. I served a copy of this Stay of Service of Earnings Assignment Order by enclosing it in a sealed envelope with first-class postage fully prepaid and depositing it in the United States Postal Service as follows:

   a. Date of deposit:
   b. Place of deposit (city, state):
   c. Addressed as follows:

I declare under penalty of perjury under the laws of the State of California that the foregoing is true and correct.

Date:

▶

_____   _____
(TYPE OR PRINT NAME)   (SIGNATURE OF DECLARANT)

ORDER

GOOD CAUSE APPEARING:

1. ☐ Service of the earnings assignment order issued in this action is stayed.
2. ☐ The stay of service granted above will terminate without further order on (date):
3. ☐ The previous stay of service of the earnings assignment order made on (date):   is terminated, and the earnings assignment order previously issued in this case may be served.

Date: _____   _____
                                              (JUDICIAL OFFICER)

FL-570

SUPERIOR COURT OF CALIFORNIA, COUNTY OF STREET ADDRESS: MAILING ADDRESS: CITY AND ZIP CODE: BRANCH NAME:	*FOR COURT USE ONLY*
PETITIONER/PLAINTIFF: RESPONDENT/DEFENDANT:	
NOTICE OF REGISTRATION OF OUT-OF-STATE SUPPORT ORDER ☐ **Support Order**　　☐ **Income Withholding Order**	CASE NUMBER:

1. To *(name)*:

2. You are notified that an ☐ Out-of-State Support Order ☐ Out-of-State Order for Income Withholding   has been registered with this court. A copy of the order and the Letter of Transmittal Requesting Registration are attached.

3. The amount of arrears is specified in section 1 on the attached Letter of Transmittal Requesting Registration.

   The amount of the alleged arrears is:　　　　　　　　as of　　　　　　　　.

   ☐ The arrears have a U.S. dollar equivalence of　　　　　　as of　　　　　　　　.

4. The registered order is enforceable in the same manner as a support order made by a California court as of the date that the Letter of Transmittal Requesting Registration is filed.

5. If you want to contest the validity or enforcement of the registered order, you must request a hearing within 20 days after notice. You can request a hearing by completing and filing a *Request for Hearing Regarding Registration of Support Order* (form FL-575).

6. If you fail to contest the validity or enforcement of the attached order within 20 days after notice, the order will be confirmed by the court and you will be unable to contest any portion of the order including the amount of arrears as specified in item 1 of the Letter of Transmittal Requesting Registration.

CLERK'S CERTIFICATE OF MAILING

7. I certify that I am not a party to this cause and that a copy of the Letter of Transmittal Requesting Registration with a copy of the out-of-state order were sent to the person named in item 1 by first-class mail. The copies were enclosed in an envelope with postage fully prepaid. The envelope was addressed to the person named in item 1 only at the address in the Personal Information Form, sealed, and deposited with the U.S. Postal Service

   at *(place)*:

   on *(date)*:

8. A copy was sent to the local child support agency on *(date)*:

Date:　　　　　　　　　　Clerk, by _____, Deputy

Page 1 of 1

Form Approved for Optional Use
Judicial Council of California
FL-570 [Rev. July 1, 2017] **NOTICE OF REGISTRATION OF OUT-OF-STATE SUPPORT ORDER** Family Code, §§ 5700.603, 5700.605
www.courts.ca.gov

0217

ATTORNEY OR PARTY WITHOUT ATTORNEY (Name, State Bar number, and address):	FOR COURT USE ONLY

TELEPHONE NO.:   FAX NO. (Optional):

E-MAIL ADDRESS (Optional):

ATTORNEY FOR (Name):

SUPERIOR COURT OF CALIFORNIA, COUNTY OF

STREET ADDRESS:

MAILING ADDRESS:

CITY AND ZIP CODE:

BRANCH NAME:

PETITIONER:

RESPONDENT:

REGISTRATION OF OUT-OF-STATE CUSTODY ORDER	CASE NUMBER:

1. The minor children covered by the out-of-state custody order are (name each):

Child's name	Date of birth	Age	Sex

2. a. Petitioner has been awarded ☐ custody ☐ visitation of those minor children.

   b. Petitioner is the ☐ mother ☐ father ☐ other (specify):   of those minor children.

   c. Petitioner's address is:*

3. a. Respondent has been awarded ☐ custody ☐ visitation of those minor children.

   b. Respondent is the ☐ mother ☐ father ☐ other (specify):   of those minor children.

   c. Respondent's address is:*

4. ☐ a. Another person (specify name):   has been awarded

      ☐ custody ☐ visitation of those minor children.

   b. That person is the ☐ mother ☐ father ☐ other (specify):   of those minor children.

   c. That person's address is:*

    * If there are issues of domestic violence or child abuse, you may give a mailing address instead.

5. A completed *Declaration Under Uniform Child Custody Jurisdiction and Enforcement Act (UCCJEA)* (form FL-105) is attached to this registration.

6. I request that the attached out-of-state custody order be registered in this court.

   a. The court, county, and state where order was made are (specify):

   b. The date when the most recent order for child custody/visitation was made in that case (specify):

   c. Two copies, including one certified copy of that out-of-state order, are attached to this registration and made a part of it.

   d. To the best of my knowledge and belief, this order has not been modified.

Date:

I declare under penalty of perjury under the laws of the State of California that the foregoing is true and correct.

▶

_____   _____
(TYPE OR PRINT NAME)   (SIGNATURE)

Form Approved for Optional Use
Judicial Council of California
FL-580 [Rev. January 1, 2006]

REGISTRATION OF OUT-OF-STATE CUSTODY ORDER

Family Code, §§ 3429, 3445
www.courtinfo.ca.gov

PETITIONER:	CASE NUMBER:
RESPONDENT:	

NOTICE OF REGISTRATION OF OUT-OF-STATE CUSTODY ORDER

1. To:
    a. Petitioner at address on 2(c) on page 1

    b. Respondent at address on 3(c) on page 1

    c. ☐ Other person who has been awarded custody or visitation in this custody order at address on 4(c) on page 1

2. The attached out-of-state custody order can be enforced as of the date of registration in the same manner as an order issued by a California court.

3. If you want to contest the validity of this registered out-of-state custody order, you must request a hearing date that is within 20 days of the date that this notice was mailed to you (see clerk's date of mailing below). A request for a hearing must be in writing and filed in this case.

4. If you do not request this hearing, the out-of-state order will be confirmed in California and you will not be able to challenge its validity in the future.

5. At the hearing, the court will confirm the out-of-state order unless you can prove one of the following:
    a. The issuing court did not have jurisdiction under chapter 2 of the California Family Code (commencing with section 3421).
    b. The child custody determination sought to be registered has been vacated, stayed, or modified by a court having jurisdiction to do so under chapter 2 of the California Family Code (commencing with section 3421).
    c. You were entitled to notice of the original order, but did not receive that notice in accordance with the standards of California Family Code section 3408 in the proceedings before the court that issued the order for which registration is sought.

CLERK'S CERTIFICATE OF MAILING

I certify that I am not a party to this case and that a copy of this *Registration of Out-of-State Custody Order* and all attachments was sent to each person named in item 1 above by first-class mail. The copies were enclosed in envelopes with postage fully prepaid. The envelopes were addressed to the persons named in item 1 at the addresses listed above, sealed, and deposited with the United States Postal Service.

At *(place):* _____

On *(date):* _____

Date: _____   Clerk by: _____, Deputy

FL-585

ATTORNEY OR PARTY WITHOUT ATTORNEY *(Name, state bar number, and address)*:	FOR COURT USE ONLY
TELEPHONE NO.: FAX NO.:	
ATTORNEY FOR *(Name)*:	

SUPERIOR COURT OF CALIFORNIA, COUNTY OF
STREET ADDRESS:
MAILING ADDRESS:
CITY AND ZIP CODE:
BRANCH NAME:

PETITIONER:

RESPONDENT:

REQUEST FOR HEARING REGARDING REGISTRATION OF OUT-OF-STATE CUSTODY DECREE	CASE NUMBER:

NOTICE OF HEARING

1. A hearing on this application will be held as follows:

a. Date:	Time:	Dept:	Div.:	Room:

   b. The address of the court is ☐ same as noted above ☐ other *(specify):*

2. I request that service of the registration of custody be vacated (canceled) because:

   a. ☐ The court or tribunal that issued the order did not have personal jurisdiction over me.

   b. ☐ The custody order has been vacated, stayed, or modified by a later order made by a court having jurisdiction to do so. *(Please attach a copy of the later order.)*

   c. ☐ I was entitled to notice of the original order, but did not receive that notice in the proceedings before the court that issued the order.

   d. ☐ Other *(specify):*

I declare under penalty of perjury under the laws of the State of California that the foregoing is true and correct.

Date:

▶

_____
(TYPE OR PRINT NAME)

_____
(SIGNATURE OF DECLARANT)

Page 1 of 2

Form Approved for Optional Use
Judicial Council of California
FL-585 [New January 1, 2003]

**REQUEST FOR HEARING REGARDING
REGISTRATION OF OUT-OF-STATE CUSTODY DECREE**

Family Code, § 3445
www.courtinfo.ca.gov

PETITIONER:	CASE NUMBER:
RESPONDENT:	

CLERK'S CERTIFICATE OF MAILING

I certify that I am not a party to this cause and that a true copy of the *Request for Hearing Regarding Registration of Out-of-State Custody Decree* was mailed first class, postage fully prepaid, in a sealed envelope addressed as shown below, and that the notice was mailed

at *(place):*   , California,

on *(date):*

Date: _____   Clerk, by _____ , Deputy

REQUEST FOR HEARING REGARDING
REGISTRATION OF OUT-OF-STATE CUSTODY DECREE

FL-590A

PETITIONER/PLAINTIFF:	CASE NUMBER:
RESPONDENT/DEFENDANT:	
OTHER PARENT:	

UIFSA CHILD SUPPORT ORDER JURISDICTIONAL ATTACHMENT

TO ☐ *Order After Hearing* (form FL-687)

☐ *Stipulation and Order* (form FL-625)

☐ **Other** *(specify):*

THE COURT FINDS THE FOLLOWING:

1. ☐ All parties have left *(issuing state or foreign country):* ☐ Petitioner ☐ Respondent
☐ Other Parent is the party requesting modification and resides in *(state or foreign country):*
☐ Petitioner ☐ Respondent ☐ Other Parent is the nonrequesting party and resides in California. This court assumes continuing, exclusive jurisdiction under Family Code section 5700.611 and modifies the order.

2. ☐ is the issuing state of the support order. ☐ Petitioner ☐ Respondent
☐ Other Parent resides in the issuing state. ☐ Petitioner ☐ Respondent ☐ Other Parent resides in California. Under Family Code section 5700.611(a)(2), the court finds that the parties consented in the issuing state for California to assume continuing, exclusive jurisdiction over support. This court assumes jurisdiction and modifies the order accordingly.

3. ☐ California is the issuing state of the support order. ☐ Petitioner ☐ Respondent ☐ Other Parent is the party requesting modification and resides in *(state or foreign country):* ☐ Petitioner
☐ Respondent ☐ Other Parent resides outside the United States, in *(country):*
Under Family Code section 5700.611(f), California retains jurisdiction to modify the order.

4. ☐ All parties have left *(issuing state):* and reside in California. This court assumes jurisdiction under Family Code section 5700.613 to modify support and domesticates the support issues.

5. ☐ Under Family Code section 5700.615, this court finds that the foreign country that issued the foreign support order *(country):* , cannot or will not modify its order. This court assumes jurisdiction and modifies the order accordingly.

6. ☐ The parties have agreed that neither of them currently reside in California, which is the state that issued the support order.
☐ Petitioner ☐ Respondent ☐ Other Parent resides in *(state or foreign country):*
☐ Petitioner ☐ Respondent ☐ Other Parent resides in *(state or foreign country):*
Under Family Code section 5700.205(a)(2), the parties consent for California to retain continuing, exclusive jurisdiction to modify the support order.

7. ☐ The parties have agreed that California is the state that issued the support order. ☐ Petitioner ☐ Respondent
☐ Other Parent resides in California. ☐ Petitioner ☐ Respondent ☐ Other Parent resides in *(state):* . The parties consent under Family Code section 5700.205(b)(1) for *(state):* to assume continuing, exclusive jurisdiction and modify the order.

8. ☐ Other:

THIS IS A COURT ORDER.

Page 1 of 1

Form Adopted for Mandatory Use
Judicial Council of California
FL-590A [Rev. July 1, 2017]

UIFSA CHILD SUPPORT ORDER JURISDICTIONAL ATTACHMENT

Family Code, §§ 5700.102,
5700.205, 5700.611,
5700.613, 5700.615
www.courts.ca.gov

FL-592

SUPERIOR COURT OF CALIFORNIA, COUNTY OF	FOR COURT USE ONLY
STREET ADDRESS: MAILING ADDRESS: CITY AND ZIP CODE: BRANCH NAME:	
PETITIONER/PLAINTIFF: RESPONDENT/DEFENDANT:	
NOTICE OF REGISTRATION OF AN INTERNATIONAL HAGUE CONVENTION SUPPORT ORDER	CASE NUMBER:

1. To *(name)*:

2. You are notified that an International Hague Convention Support Order has been registered with this court. A copy of the following is attached:

   ☐ Complete text of the order

   ☐ Abstract of the order

   ☐ Record stating the support order is enforceable in the issuing country

   ☐ Record attesting proper notice and opportunity to be heard, if respondent did not appear and was not represented

   ☐ Record showing the amount of arrears, if any

   ☐ Record showing a requirement for automatic adjustment of support, if any

   ☐ Record showing the extent to which the applicant received free legal assistance, if necessary

3. The amount of arrears is specified in item 1 on the attached Transmittal Form under Article 12(2).

   The amount of the alleged arrears is: as of   .

   ☐ The arrears have a U.S. dollar equivalence of   as of   .

4. The registered order is enforceable in the same manner as a support order made by a California court as of the date the Transmittal Form under article 12(2) is filed.

5. If you want to contest the validity or enforcement of the registered order, you must request a hearing within 30 days if you reside in the United States, or within 60 days if residing outside the United States, of the date that the notice was mailed to you *(see below for clerk's date of mailing)*. You can request a hearing by completing and filing a *Request for Hearing Regarding Registration of an International Hague Convention Support Order* (form FL-594).

6. If you fail to contest the validity or enforcement of the attached order within 30 days, or 60 days if residing outside the United States, of the date this notice was mailed, the order will be confirmed by the court and you will be unable to contest any portion of the order including the amount of arrears as specified in item 1 of the Transmittal Form under article 12(2).

CLERK'S CERTIFICATE OF MAILING

7. I certify that I am not a party to this cause and that a copy of the Transmittal Form with a copy of the International Hague Convention Support Order were sent to the person named in item 1 by first-class mail. The copies were enclosed in an envelope with postage fully prepaid. The envelope was addressed to the person named in item 1 only at the address in the Transmittal Form, sealed, and deposited with the U.S. Postal Service

   at *(place)*:

   on *(date)*:

8. Copy sent to local child support agency on *(date)*:

Date: Clerk, by   , Deputy

Page 1 of 1

Form Adopted for Mandatory Use
Judicial Council of California
FL-592 [Rev. July 1, 2017]

NOTICE OF REGISTRATION OF AN INTERNATIONAL HAGUE CONVENTION SUPPORT ORDER

Family Code, §§ 5700.706,
5700.707
www.courts.ca.gov

PARTY WITHOUT ATTORNEY OR ATTORNEY *(name, state bar number, and address)*:	FOR COURT USE ONLY
NAME: STATE BAR NO.:	
FIRM NAME:	
STREET ADDRESS:	
CITY: STATE: ZIP CODE:	
TELEPHONE NO.: FAX NO.:	
E-MAIL ADDRESS:	
ATTORNEY FOR *(name)*:	

SUPERIOR COURT OF CALIFORNIA, COUNTY OF
STREET ADDRESS:
MAILING ADDRESS:
CITY AND ZIP CODE:
BRANCH NAME:

PETITIONER/PLAINTIFF:

RESPONDENT/DEFENDANT:

OTHER PARENT:

REQUEST FOR HEARING REGARDING REGISTRATION OF AN INTERNATIONAL HAGUE CONVENTION SUPPORT ORDER	CASE NUMBER:

NOTICE OF HEARING

1. A hearing on this application will be held as follows *(see instructions on how to get a hearing date and for more information about what an International Hague Convention Support Order is and how to fill out this form)*:

   a. Date: Time: Dept: Div: Room:

   b. The address of the court is ☐ same as noted above   ☐ Other *(specify)*:

2. I request that the court refuse recognition and enforcement of the International Hague Convention Support Order because:

   a. ☐ recognition and enforcement of the order is manifestly incompatible with public policy, including the failure of the issuing court or tribunal to observe minimum standards of due process, which include notice and an opportunity to be heard.

   b. ☐ the court or tribunal that issued the order did not have personal jurisdiction as listed in Family Code section 5700.201.

   c. ☐ the order is not enforceable in the country that issued it.

   d. ☐ the order was obtained by fraud in connection with a matter of procedure.

   e. ☐ a record registering this order as required by Family Code section 5700.706 is not authentic or lacks integrity.

   f. ☐ a case between the same parties and having the same purpose is pending before a court in California, and that case was the first to be filed.

   g. ☐ the order is incompatible with a more recent support order involving the same parties and having the same purpose. The more recent support order is entitled to recognition and enforcement under Family Code sections 5700.101–5700.905.

   h. ☐ the alleged arrears have been paid in whole or in part.

   i. ☐ I did not attend the hearing, nor did I have a lawyer in the country that issued the order. The law of the issuing country provides for prior notice of proceedings, but I did not have proper notice of the proceedings or an opportunity to be heard.

   j. ☐ I did not attend the hearing, nor did I have a lawyer in the country that issued the order. The law of that county **does not** provide for prior notice of the proceedings, and I did not have proper notice of the order or an opportunity to be heard in a challenge or appeal on fact or law before a tribunal.

   k. ☐ the order was made in violation of Family Code section 5700.711.

I declare under penalty of perjury under the laws of the State of California that the foregoing is true and correct.

Date:

_____
(TYPE OR PRINT NAME)

▶

_____
(SIGNATURE OF DECLARANT)

Page 1 of 4

Form Adopted for Mandatory Use
Judicial Council of California
FL-594 [New January 1, 2017]

**REQUEST FOR HEARING REGARDING REGISTRATION OF
AN INTERNATIONAL HAGUE CONVENTION SUPPORT ORDER**

Family Code, §§ 5700.707, 5700.708
www.courts.ca.gov

FL-594

PETITIONER/PLAINTIFF:	CASE NUMBER:
RESPONDENT/DEFENDANT:	
OTHER PARENT:	

CLERK'S CERTIFICATE OF MAILING

I certify that I am not a party to this cause and that a true copy of the *Request for Hearing Regarding Registration of an International Hague Convention Support Order* was mailed first class, postage fully prepaid, in a sealed envelope addressed as shown below, and that the notice was mailed

at *(place)*:   , California

on *(date)*:

Date: Clerk, by _____ , Deputy

**REQUEST FOR HEARING REGARDING REGISTRATION OF
AN INTERNATIONAL HAGUE CONVENTION SUPPORT ORDER**

INFORMATION SHEET FOR REQUEST FOR HEARING REGARDING REGISTRATION OF AN INTERNATIONAL HAGUE CONVENTION SUPPORT ORDER
(Do NOT deliver this information sheet to the court clerk.)

Please follow these instructions to complete the *Request for Hearing Regarding Registration of an International Hague Convention Support Order* (form FL-594) if you do not have an attorney representing you. Your attorney, if you have one, should complete this form.

This form should be used if you received a notice or statement of registration telling you that a support order made in another country is being registered in a California court but you do not want that support order registered. To request a hearing regarding an out-of-state or foreign order, which is not an International Hague Convention Support Order, use form FL-575.

An International Hague Convention Support Order is one that was made under the Convention on the International Recovery of Child Support and Other Forms of Family Maintenance, concluded at The Hague on November 23, 2007. The Convention is now part of Family Code sections 5700.101–5700.905.

You must file your completed request for hearing with the court clerk. You must also give the court clerk addressed envelopes with postage paid to mail copies of your request for hearing to the other parties. The address of the court clerk is the same as the one shown for the superior court on the notice or statement of registration you received. You may have to pay a filing fee to request a hearing. If you cannot afford to pay the filing fee, you must file a *Request to Waive Court Fees* (form FW-001). You can get this form from the court clerk, family law facilitator, or California Courts website at *www.courts.ca.gov*.

INSTRUCTIONS FOR COMPLETING THE REQUEST FOR HEARING REGARDING REGISTRATION FORM (YOU CAN COMPLETE THE FORM ON A COMPUTER, BY TYPING, OR BY PRINTING IN INK):

Page 1, first box, top of form, left side: Print your name, address, and phone number in this box.

Page 1, second box, left side: Print the court's address in this box. Use the same address for the court that is on the notice or statement of registration form you received.

Page 1, third box, left side: Print the names of the Petitioner/Plaintiff, Respondent/Defendant, and Other Parent in this box. Use the same names as listed on the notice or statement of registration form you received.

Page 1, first box, top of form, right side: Leave this box blank for the court's use.

Page 1, second box, right side: Print your case number in this box. This number is also shown on the notice or statement of registration you received.

1. Before you file your request for hearing with the court clerk, ask the court clerk to set a hearing date for you. The court clerk will give you the information you need to complete this section.

2. In this section you are telling the court why you do not want the support order to be recognized or enforced in California. Check the box by your reason(s). Check the corresponding box, a–k, if

   a. recognition and enforcement of the order conflicts with public policy. This includes the failure of the court or tribunal issuing the order to provide you with an opportunity to be heard through notice and due process.

   b. the court or tribunal that issued the support order did not have jurisdiction over you to issue the order.

   c. the order cannot be enforced in the country that issued it.

   d. your support order was obtained by fraud.

   e. the required document(s) accompanying this order is not authentic or lacks integrity.

   f. if there is a case between the same parties and having the same purpose awaiting a decision before a court in California, and that case was filed first.

   g. the order is conflicting with a more recent support order between the same parties and having the same purpose.

   h. you have paid all of the alleged arrears or some of the alleged arrears.

   i. the country issuing the order requires prior notice of a hearing, but you did not receive notice of the hearing and you did not attend the hearing, and you did not have an attorney representing you in the hearing.

   j. the country issuing the order **does not** require prior notice of proceedings, you did not receive notice of the hearing and you did not have the opportunity to be heard in the proceeding.

   k. the order was made in violation of Family Code section 5700.711 because it was changed when you were a resident of the country where the support order was issued, and you did not agree to the case being heard in California either expressly or by defending yourself without objecting to the case being heard in California as soon as possible. If the country where your order was issued will not or cannot change the support order or make a new one, the case may be heard in California.

REQUEST FOR HEARING REGARDING REGISTRATION OF AN INTERNATIONAL HAGUE CONVENTION SUPPORT ORDER

INFORMATION SHEET FOR REQUEST FOR HEARING REGARDING
REGISTRATION OF AN INTERNATIONAL HAGUE CONVENTION SUPPORT ORDER
(continued)

You must date the form, print your name, and sign the form under penalty of perjury. When you sign the form, you are stating that the information you have provided is true and correct.

Top of page 2, box on left side: Print the names of Petitioner/Plaintiff, Respondent/Defendant, and Other Parent in this box. Use the same names as on the front page.

Top of page 2, box on right side: Print your case number in this box. Use the same number as on the front page.

The court clerk will sign and date the request for hearing form before mailing it to the Petitioner/Plaintiff, Respondent/Defendant, and Other Parent.

You must print the name and address of the Petitioner/Plaintiff, Respondent/Defendant, and Other Parent in the brackets. The names are the same as those at the top of the page. You also must provide the court clerk with stamped envelopes addressed to each of the other parties.

If you need assistance with this form, contact an attorney or the family law facilitator in your county. The family law facilitator can help you with this form for free.

**REQUEST FOR HEARING REGARDING REGISTRATION OF
AN INTERNATIONAL HAGUE CONVENTION SUPPORT ORDER**

0227

ATTORNEY:	STATE BAR NO.:		FOR COURT USE ONLY
NAME:			
FIRM NAME:			
STREET ADDRESS:			
CITY:	STATE:	ZIP CODE:	
TELEPHONE NO.:	FAX NO.:		
E-MAIL ADDRESS:			
ATTORNEY FOR (name):			

SUPERIOR COURT OF CALIFORNIA, COUNTY OF

STREET ADDRESS:

MAILING ADDRESS:

CITY AND ZIP CODE:

BRANCH NAME:

PETITIONER:

RESPONDENT:

OTHER PARENT/CLAIMANT:

NOTICE OF LIMITED SCOPE REPRESENTATION ☐ AMENDED	CASE NUMBER:

1. Attorney (name):

   and party (name):

   have an agreement that attorney will provide limited scope representation to the party.

2. The attorney will represent the party as follows:

   ☐ At the hearing on (date): ☐ and for any continuance of that hearing

   ☐ Until resolution of the issues checked on this form by trial or settlement

   ☐ Other (specify duration of representation):

   ☐ Submitting to the court an order after hearing or judgment is not within the scope of the attorney's representation.

3. Attorney will serve as "attorney of record" for the party **only** for the following issues in the case:

   a. ☐ Child custody and visitation (parenting time): (1) ☐ Establish (2) ☐ Enforce (3) ☐ Modify (specify):

   b. ☐ Child support: (1) ☐ Establish (2) ☐ Enforce (3) ☐ Modify (describe in detail):

   c. ☐ Spousal or domestic partner support: (1) ☐ Establish (2) ☐ Enforce (3) ☐ Modify (describe in detail):

   d. ☐ Restraining order: (1) ☐ Establish (2) ☐ Enforce (3) ☐ Modify (describe in detail):

   e. ☐ Division of property (describe in detail):

Form Adopted for Mandatory Use
Judicial Council of California
FL-950 [Rev. September 1, 2017]

NOTICE OF LIMITED SCOPE REPRESENTATION

Cal. Rules of Court, rule 5.425
www.courts.ca.gov

PETITIONER: RESPONDENT: OTHER PARENT/CLAIMANT:	CASE NUMBER:

3. f. ☐ Pension issues *(describe in detail):*

g. ☐ Contempt *(describe in detail):*

h. ☐ Other *(describe in detail):*

i. ☐ See attachment 3i.

4. **By signing this form, the party agrees to sign** *Substitution of Attorney—Civil* **(form MC-050) when the representation is completed.**

5. The attorney named above is "attorney of record" and available for service of documents only for those issues specifically checked on pages 1 and 2. For all other matters, the party must be served directly. The party's name, address, and phone number are listed below for that purpose.

Name:

Address *(for the purpose of service):*

Phone: Fax Number:

This notice accurately sets forth all current matters on which the attorney has agreed to serve as "attorney of record" for the party in this case. The information provided in this document is not intended to set forth all of the terms and conditions of the agreement between the party and the attorney for limited scope representation.

Date: _____

_____
(TYPE OR PRINT NAME)

▶ _____
(SIGNATURE OF PARTY)

Date: _____

_____
(TYPE OR PRINT NAME)

▶ _____
(SIGNATURE OF ATTORNEY)

0229

PETITIONER: RESPONDENT: OTHER PARENT/CLAIMANT:	CASE NUMBER:

PROOF OF SERVICE: ☐ **PERSONAL SERVICE** ☐ **MAIL** ☐ **OVERNIGHT DELIVERY** ☐ **ELECTRONIC SERVICE**

1. At the time of service, I was at least 18 years of age and **not a party to this legal action** (not applicable to electronic service).

2. I served a copy of *Notice of Limited Scope Representation* (form FL-950) as follows:

    a. ☐ **Personal service.** The document listed above was given to

       (1) Name of person served:
           Address where served:
           Date served:
           Time served:

       (2) Name of person served:
           Address where served:
           Date served:
           Time served:

    b. ☐ **Mail.** I placed a copy of the form listed above in the U.S. mail, in a sealed envelope with postage fully prepaid. The envelope was addressed and mailed as indicated below. I live or work in the county where the form was mailed.

       (1) Name of person served:
           Address where served:
           Date of mailing:
           Place of mailing *(city and state):*

       (2) Name of person served:
           Address where served:
           Date of mailing:
           Place of mailing *(city and state):*

    c. ☐ **Overnight delivery.** I placed a copy of the form listed above in a sealed envelope, with Express Mail postage fully prepaid, and deposited it in a post office mailbox, subpost office, substation, mail chute, or other like facility maintained by the U.S. Postal Service for receipt of Express Mail. The envelope was addressed and mailed as indicated below. I live or work in the county where the form was deposited for overnight delivery.

       (1) Name of person served:
           Address where served:
           Date of mailing:
           Place of mailing *(city and state):*

       (2) Name of person served:
           Address where served:
           Date of mailing:
           Place of mailing *(city and state):*

    d. ☐ **Electronic service.** I electronically served the document listed above as described in the attached proof of electronic service *Proof of Electronic Service* ((form POS-050)) may be used for this purpose).

3. Server's information
    a. Name:
    b. Home or work address:
    c. Telephone number:

I declare under penalty of perjury under the laws of the State of California that the information above is true and correct.

Date:

_____
(TYPE OR PRINT NAME)

▶

_____
(SIGNATURE OF PERSON SERVING NOTICE)

| Print this form | Save this form | | Clear this form |

0230

PARTY WITHOUT ATTORNEY OR ATTORNEY:	STATE BAR NO:	
NAME:		
FIRM NAME:		
STREET ADDRESS:		
CITY:	STATE: ZIP CODE:	
TELEPHONE NO.:	FAX NO. :	
E-MAIL ADDRESS:		
ATTORNEY FOR (Name):		

SUPERIOR COURT OF CALIFORNIA, COUNTY OF
STREET ADDRESS:
MAILING ADDRESS:
CITY AND ZIP CODE:
BRANCH NAME:

MARRIAGE OR PARTNERSHIP OF
PETITIONER 1:
PETITIONER 2:

JOINT PETITION FOR SUMMARY DISSOLUTION ☐ MARRIAGE ☐ DOMESTIC PARTNERSHIP	CASE NUMBER:

We petition for a summary dissolution of marriage, registered domestic partnership, or both and declare that all the following conditions exist on the date this petition is filed with the court:

1. We have read and understand the *Summary Dissolution Information* booklet (form FL-810).

2. a. ☐ We were married on *(date):*

   b. ☐ We registered as domestic partners on *(date):*

3. ☐ We separated on *(date):*

4. Less than five years have passed between the date of our marriage and/or registration of our domestic partnership and the date of our separation.

5. a. ☐ One of us has lived in California for at least six months and in the county of filing for at least the three months preceding the date of filing. Or we are only asking to end a domestic partnership registered in California.

   b. ☐ We are the same sex and were married in California but are not residents of California. Neither of us lives in a place that will allow us to divorce. We are filing this case in the county in which we married.

6. There are no minor children who were born of our relationship before or during our marriage or domestic partnership or adopted by us during our marriage or domestic partnership. Neither one of us, to our knowledge, is pregnant.

7. Neither of us has an interest in any real property anywhere. **(You may have a lease for a residence in which one of you lives. It must terminate within a year from the date of filing this petition. The lease must not include an option to purchase.)**

8. Except for obligations with respect to cars, on obligations incurred by either or both of us during our marriage or domestic partnership, we owe no more than $6,000.

9. The total fair market value of community property assets, not including what we owe on those assets and not including cars, is less than $43,000.

10. Neither of us has separate property assets, not including what we owe on those assets and not including cars, in excess of $43,000.

11. We each have filled out and given the other an *Income and Expense Declaration* (form FL-150).

12. We have complied with the preliminary disclosure requirements as follows:

    a. We each have disclosed information about the value and division of our property by filling out and giving each other copies of the documents listed in (1) or (2) below (specify):

       (1) ☐ The worksheets on pages 7, 9, and 11 of the *Summary Dissolution Information* booklet (form FL-810).

       (2) ☐ A *Declaration of Disclosure* (form FL-140), a *Schedule of Assets and Debts* (form FL-142), or *Property Declaration (form FL-160),* and all attachments to these forms.

    b. We have told each other in writing about any investment, business, or other income-producing opportunities that came up after we were separated based on investments made or work done during the marriage or domestic partnership and before our separation.

    c. We have exchanged all tax returns each of us has filed within the two years before disclosing the information described in 12a.

Page 1 of 2

Form Adopted for Mandatory Use
Judicial Council of California
FL-800 [Rev. July 1, 2017]

JOINT PETITION FOR SUMMARY DISSOLUTION
(Family Law——Summary Dissolution)

Family Code, § 299, 2109, 2320, 2400-2406
www.courts.ca.gov

PETITIONER 1:	CASE NUMBER:
PETITIONER 2:	

13. *(Check whichever statement is true.)*

    a. ☐ We have no community assets or liabilities.

    b. ☐ We have signed an agreement listing and dividing all our community assets and liabilities and have signed all the papers necessary to carry out our agreement. A copy of our agreement is attached to the *Judgment of Dissolution and Notice of Entry of Judgment* (form FL-825).

14. Irreconcilable differences have caused the irremediable breakdown of our marriage and/or domestic partnership, and each of us wishes to have the court dissolve our marriage and/or domestic partnership without our appearing before a judge.

15.   a. ☐ Petitioner 1 desires to have his or her former name restored. That name is *(specify):*

    b. ☐ Petitioner 2 desires to have his or her former name restored. That name is *(specify):*

16. We each give up our rights to appeal and to move for a new trial after the effective date of our *Judgment of Dissolution.*

17. **Each of us forever gives up any right to spousal or partner support from the other.**

18. We each agree to keep the court and each other informed of any change of mailing address or phone number occurring within six months from the filing of this joint petition using the *Notice of Change of Address or Other Contact Information* (form MC-040).

19. We are submitting the original and three copies of the proposed *Judgment of Dissolution and Notice of Entry of Judgment* (form FL-825) and two stamped envelopes together with this petition. One envelope is addressed to Petitioner 1 and the other to Petitioner 2.

20. We agree that this matter may be determined by a commissioner sitting as a temporary judge.

21. **Mailing address of Petitioner 1**

    Name:

    Address:

    City:

    State:

    Zip Code:

22. **Mailing address of Petitioner 2**

    Name:

    Address:

    City:

    State:

    Zip Code:

23. Number of pages attached: _____

I declare under penalty of perjury under the laws of the State of California that the foregoing and all attached documents are true and correct.

Date:

▶ _____
       (SIGNATURE OF PETITIONER 1)

I declare under penalty of perjury under the laws of the State of California that the foregoing and all attached documents are true and correct.

Date:

▶ _____
       (SIGNATURE OF PETITIONER 2)

NOTICES

Your marriage and/or domestic partnership will end six months from the date of filing this joint petition. Both petitioners will receive a stamped copy from the court of the *Judgment of Dissolution and Notice of Entry of Judgment* (from FL-825) stating the effective date of your dissolution. Until the effective date specified on form FL-825 for the dissolution of your marriage and/or domestic partnership, either one of you can stop this joint petition by filing a *Notice of Revocation of Petition for Summary Dissolution* (form FL-830). If you stop this joint petition, you will STILL be married or in a domestic partnership.

Dissolution may automatically cancel the rights of a spouse or domestic partner under the other spouse's or domestic partner's will, trust, retirement plan, power of attorney, pay-on-death bank account, transfer-on-death vehicle registration, survivorship rights to any property owned in joint tenancy, and any other similar instrument. It does not automatically cancel the rights of a spouse or domestic partner as beneficiary of the other spouse's or domestic partner's life insurance policy. You should review these matters, as well as any credit card accounts, other credit accounts, insurance policies, and credit reports to determine whether they should be changed or whether you should take any other actions. However, some changes may require the agreement of your spouse or domestic partner or a court order. (See Fam. Code, §§ 231–235.)

JOINT PETITION FOR SUMMARY DISSOLUTION
(Family Law—Summary Dissolution)

For your protection and privacy, please press the Clear This Form button after you have printed the form.

| Print this form | Save this form | | Clear this form |

0232

PARTY WITHOUT ATTORNEY OR ATTORNEY *(Name, State Bar number, and address)*:	FOR COURT USE ONLY
TELEPHONE NO.: FAX NO. *(Optional)*: E-MAIL ADDRESS *(Optional)*: ATTORNEY FOR *(Name)*:	

SUPERIOR COURT OF CALIFORNIA, COUNTY OF

> STREET ADDRESS:
>
> MAILING ADDRESS:
>
> CITY AND ZIP CODE:
>
> BRANCH NAME:

MARRIAGE OF

> HUSBAND:
>
> WIFE:

REQUEST FOR JUDGMENT, JUDGMENT OF DISSOLUTION OF MARRIAGE, AND NOTICE OF ENTRY OF JUDGMENT	CASE NUMBER:

1. The *Joint Petition for Summary Dissolution* (form FL-800) was filed on *(date)*:
   (Use this form ONLY if the Joint Petition for Summary Dissolution *(form FL-800) was filed before January 1, 2011. If it was filed after January 1, 2011, use* Judgment of Dissolution and Notice of Entry of Judgment *(form FL-825) instead.)*

2. No notice of revocation has been filed, and the parties have not become reconciled.

3. I request that judgment of dissolution of marriage be
   a. ☐ entered to be effective now.
   b. ☐ entered to be effective (nunc pro tunc) as of *(date)*:
      for the following reason:

I declare under penalty of perjury under the laws of the State of California that the foregoing is true and correct.
Date:

_____
(TYPE OR PRINT NAME)

▶ _____
(SIGNATURE OF HUSBAND OR WIFE)

4. Husband ☐   Wife ☐   who did **not** request that his or her own former name be restored when he or she signed the joint petition, now requests that it be restored. The applicant's former name is:

Date:

_____
(TYPE OR PRINT NAME)

▶ _____
(SIGNATURE OF PARTY WISHING TO HAVE HIS OR HER NAME RESTORED)

(For Court Use Only)
JUDGMENT OF DISSOLUTION

THE COURT ORDERS

5. A judgment of dissolution of marriage will be entered, and the parties are restored to the status of unmarried persons.
   a. ☐ The judgment of dissolution of marriage will be entered nunc pro tunc as of *(date)*:
   b. ☐ Wife's former name is restored *(specify)*:
   c. ☐ Husband's former name is restored *(specify)*:
   Husband and wife must comply with any agreement attached to the petition.

Date:

_____
JUDICIAL OFFICER

Page 1 of 2

Form Adopted for Mandatory Use
Judicial Council of California
FL-820 [Rev. January 1, 2012]

**REQUEST FOR JUDGMENT, JUDGMENT OF DISSOLUTION
OF MARRIAGE, AND NOTICE OF ENTRY OF JUDGMENT**
(Family Law—Summary Dissolution)

Family Code, § 2403
www.courts.ca.gov

0233

HUSBAND:	CASE NUMBER:
WIFE:	

NOTICE: Dissolution may automatically cancel the rights of a spouse under the other spouse's will, trust, retirement benefit plan, power of attorney, pay-on-death bank account, transfer-on-death vehicle registration, survivorship rights to any property owned in joint tenancy, and any other similar instrument. It does not automatically cancel the rights of a spouse as beneficiary of the other spouse's life insurance policy. You should review these matters, as well as any credit cards, other credit accounts, insurance policies, retirement benefit plans, and credit reports, to determine whether they should be changed or whether you should take any other actions.

NOTICE OF ENTRY OF JUDGMENT

6. You are notified that a judgment of dissolution of marriage was entered on *(date)*:

Date: _____   Clerk, by _____, Deputy

CLERK'S CERTIFICATE OF MAILING

I certify that I am not a party to this cause and that a true copy of the *Notice of Entry of Judgment* was mailed first class, postage fully prepaid, in a sealed envelope addressed as shown below, and that the notice was mailed

at *(place)*:   California,

on *(date)*:

Date: _____   Clerk, by _____, Deputy

HUSBAND'S ADDRESS	WIFE'S ADDRESS

FL-820 [Rev. January 1, 2012]

**REQUEST FOR JUDGMENT, JUDGMENT OF
DISSOLUTION, AND NOTICE OF ENTRY OF JUDGMENT
(Family Law—Summary Dissolution)**

0234

PARTY WITHOUT ATTORNEY OR ATTORNEY *(Name, State Bar number, and address):*	FOR COURT USE ONLY
TELEPHONE NO.: FAX NO. *(Optional):* E-MAIL ADDRESS *(Optional):* ATTORNEY FOR *(Name):*	

SUPERIOR COURT OF CALIFORNIA, COUNTY OF

STREET ADDRESS:

MAILING ADDRESS:

CITY AND ZIP CODE:

BRANCH NAME:

MARRIAGE OR DOMESTIC PARTNERSHIP OF

PETITIONER 1:

PETITIONER 2:

JUDGMENT OF DISSOLUTION AND NOTICE OF ENTRY OF JUDGMENT ☐ **MARRIAGE** ☐ **DOMESTIC PARTNERSHIP**	CASE NUMBER:

Use this form ONLY if the *Joint Petition for Summary Dissolution* (form FL-800) was filed after January 1, 2011. If the *Joint Petition for Summary Dissolution* was filed before January 1, 2011, use *Request for Judgment, Judgment of Dissolution, and Notice of Entry of Judgment* (form FL-820) instead.

1. **THE COURT ORDERS**

   a. A judgment of dissolution of marriage and/or domestic partnership will be entered, and the parties are restored to the status of single persons, effective *(date):* [   ]

   b. ☐ The former name of Petitioner 1 is restored *(specify):*

   c. ☐ The former name of Petitioner 2 is restored *(specify):*

   Both petitioners must comply with any agreement attached to this judgment.

Date: _____

_____
JUDICIAL OFFICER

NOTICE: Dissolution may automatically cancel the rights of a spouse or domestic partner under the other spouse or domestic partner's will, trust, retirement benefit plan, power of attorney, pay-on-death bank account, transfer-on-death vehicle registration, survivorship rights to any property owned in joint tenancy, and any other similar instrument. It does not automatically cancel the rights of a spouse or domestic partner as beneficiary of the other spouse's or domestic partner's life insurance policy. You should review these matters, as well as any credit cards, other credit accounts, insurance policies, retirement benefit plans, and credit reports to determine whether they should be changed or whether you should take any other actions.

NOTICE OF ENTRY OF JUDGMENT

2. You are notified that a judgment of dissolution of

   a. ☐ marriage

   b ☐ domestic partnership

   was entered on *(date):*

Date: _____   Clerk, by _____ , Deputy

The date the judgment of dissolution is entered is NOT the date your divorce or termination of your domestic partnership is final. For the effective date of the dissolution of your marriage and/or domestic partnership, see the date in item 1a.

Page 1 of 2

Form Adopted for Mandatory Use Judicial Council of California FL-825 [New January 1, 2012]	**JUDGMENT OF DISSOLUTION AND** **NOTICE OF ENTRY OF JUDGMENT** **(Family Law—Summary Dissolution)**	Family Code, § 2403 *www.courts.ca.gov.*

0235

PETITIONER 1:	CASE NUMBER:
PETITIONER 2:	

CLERK'S CERTIFICATE OF MAILING

I certify that I am not a party to this cause and that a true copy of the *Judgment of Dissolution* and *Notice of Entry of Judgment* was mailed first class, postage fully prepaid, in a sealed envelope addressed as shown below, and that the notice was mailed

at *(place):*   California,

on *(date):*

Date: Clerk, by _____ , Deputy

ADDRESS OF PETITIONER 1	ADDRESS OF PETITIONER 2

0236

ATTORNEY OR PARTY WITHOUT ATTORNEY:	STATE BAR NO:	FOR COURT USE ONLY
NAME:		
FIRM NAME:		
STREET ADDRESS:		
CITY: STATE: ZIP CODE:		
TELEPHONE NO.: FAX NO. :		
E-MAIL ADDRESS:		
ATTORNEY FOR (Name):		

SUPERIOR COURT OF CALIFORNIA, COUNTY OF
  STREET ADDRESS:
  MAILING ADDRESS:
  CITY AND ZIP CODE:
  BRANCH NAME:

MARRIAGE OR DOMESTIC PARTNERSHIP OF
Petitioner 1
Petitioner 2

NOTICE OF REVOCATION OF JOINT PETITION FOR SUMMARY DISSOLUTION	CASE NUMBER:

Notice is given that the undersigned terminates the summary dissolution proceedings and revokes the *Joint Petition for Summary Dissolution* (form FL-800) filed on *(date):*

I declare under penalty of perjury under the laws of the State of California that the foregoing is true and correct.

Date:

_____
(TYPE OR PRINT NAME)

_____
(SIGNATURE OF DECLARANT)

Complete this notice. Submit the original and two copies to the court clerk's office. If the effective date of the judgment has not yet occurred, the clerk will notify you that this notice of revocation has been filed by completing the certificate below.

Name and address of Petitioner 1   Name and address of Petitioner 2

CLERK'S CERTIFICATE OF MAILING (For court use only)

I certify that I am not a party to this cause and that a copy of the foregoing was mailed first class, postage fully prepaid, in a sealed envelope as shown above, and that the mailing of the foregoing and execution of this certificate occurred at

(place):   California, on

Date: Clerk, by _____, Deputy

NOTICE

If the clerk's certificate of mailing above has been dated and signed by the clerk, this summary dissolution case is ended. You are still married and/or domestic partners. If you still want to get divorced, you will have to file a regular divorce case using the *Petition—Marriage/Domestic Partnership* (form FL-100).

Page 1 of 1

Form Adopted for Mandatory Use
Judicial Council of California
FL-830 [Rev. July 1, 2015]

**NOTICE OF REVOCATION OF PETITION
FOR SUMMARY DISSOLUTION**
(Family Law—Summary Dissolution)

Family Code, § 2402
www.courts.ca.gov

For your protection and privacy, please press the Clear This Form button after you have printed the form.   Print this form   Save this form   Clear this form

0237

FL-910

Request of Minor to Marry or Establish a Domestic Partnership

Clerk stamps date here when form is filed.

(1) Minor Requesting Court Order

Date of birth: _____

Name: _____

Street address: _____

City: _____ State: _____ Zip: _____

Telephone number: _____

(2) Minor's Proposed Spouse or Domestic Partner

Date of birth: _____

Name: _____

Street address: _____

City: _____ State: _____ Zip: _____

Telephone number: _____

Fill in court name and street address:

Superior Court of California, County of

Clerk fills in case number when form is filed.

Case Number:

(3) Your Lawyer's Information *(if you have a lawyer):*

Name: _____

Telephone number: _____ E-mail: _____

Address: _____

State Bar number: _____

(4) Request

The people listed in (1) and (2) above request that the court grant permission for them to
☐ Marry   ☐ Establish a domestic partnership.

(5) Written Permission

You must attach permission to marry or establish a domestic partnership in writing from the parent or guardian of each person under 18. Describe the permissions attached to this form. *(Check all that apply):*

a. ☐ Permission from (1)'s *(check one):* ☐ mother ☐ father ☐ guardian
   ☐ Other *(explain):* _____

b. ☐ Permission from (2)'s *(check one):* ☐ mother ☐ father ☐ guardian
   ☐ Other *(explain):* _____

(6) Premarital Counseling

If requesting permission to marry, the judge may require you to go to premarital counseling to learn about the social, economic, and personal responsibilities of marriage.

(7) I declare under penalty of perjury under the laws of the State of California that the foregoing is true and correct.

Date: _____   ▶ _____
                                  Person (1) *signs here*

Date: _____   ▶ _____
                                  Person (2) *signs here*

Judicial Council of California, *www.courts.ca.gov*
Revised January 1, 2012, Optional Form
Family Code §§ 297, 297.1, 302–304

Request of Minor to Marry or Establish a Domestic Partnership
(Family Law)

FL-910, Page 1 of 1

0238

ATTORNEY OR PARTY WITHOUT ATTORNEY *(Name, State Bar number, and address)* or GOVERNMENTAL AGENCY:	FOR COURT USE ONLY

TELEPHONE NO. *(Optional):*   FAX NO. *(Optional):*

E-MAIL ADDRESS *(Optional):*

ATTORNEY FOR *(Name):*

SUPERIOR COURT OF CALIFORNIA, COUNTY OF

STREET ADDRESS:

MAILING ADDRESS:

CITY AND ZIP CODE:

BRANCH NAME:

CHILD'S NAME:

PETITIONER:

RESPONDENT:

OTHER PARENT:

APPLICATION AND ORDER FOR APPOINTMENT OF GUARDIAN AD LITEM OF MINOR—FAMILY LAW ☐ **EX PARTE**	CASE NUMBERS:

NOTE: This form is for use in family law proceedings with the exception of dissolution proceedings. For appointment of a guardian ad litem in civil proceedings, use form CIV-010. For appointment of a guardian ad litem in probate proceedings, use form DE-350/GC-100.

1. I *(name):*   am the
   a. ☐ attorney for
      (1) ☐ minor.
      (2) ☐ parent of the minor.
      (3) ☐ other interested person *(specify name and relationship):*
   b. ☐ parent of the minor.
   c. ☐ other interested person.
   d. ☐ minor *(answer all that apply to you):*
      (1) My date of birth is *(specify):*
      (2) I live with my ☐ mother ☐ father ☐ legal guardian ☐ other *(specify name and relationship):*

      (3) My mother's name is *(specify):*   , and her address is:

      (4) My father's name is *(specify):*   , and his address is:

      (5) ☐ I have a legal guardian. My legal guardian's name is *(specify):*   , and his
          or her address is:
          The guardianship was established in: County, case no. *(if known):*

2. I ask the court to appoint the following personas guardian ad litem for the minor *(state name, address, and telephone no.):*

3. The relationship of the person listed in item 2 to the minor is
   a. ☐ parent
   b. ☐ other *(specify):*

4. Appointment of a guardian ad litem is necessary because *(specify):*

☐ Continued on Attachment 4 *(describe in detail, attach additional pages if necessary).*

Page 1 of 2

Form Approved for Optional Use
Judicial Council of California
FL-935 [Rev. January 1, 2008]

APPLICATION AND ORDER FOR APPOINTMENT OF GUARDIAN AD LITEM OF MINOR—FAMILY LAW

Code of Civil Procedure, § 373;
Family Code, § 7635

CHILD'S NAME:	CASE NUMBERS:
PETITIONER:	
RESPONDENT:	
OTHER PARENT:	

5. The proposed guardian ad litem is fully competent to understand and protect the rights of the minor and has no interests conflicting with those of the minor.

Date:

_____   ▶   _____
(TYPE OR PRINT NAME)   (SIGNATURE OF APPLICANT)

CONSENT TO ACT AS GUARDIAN AD LITEM

I consent to the appointment as guardian ad litem and agree to assume the responsibilities.

Date:

_____   ▶   _____
(TYPE OR PRINT NAME)   (SIGNATURE OF PROPOSED GUARDIAN)

CONSENT TO GUARDIAN BY MINOR 14 YEARS OF AGE OR OLDER

I, *(name):*   , am *(specify age):*   years of age and hereby nominate
(name):   to be my guardian ad litem to represent my interests for the
reasons set forth in items 4 and 5 of this application.

Date:

_____   ▶   _____
(TYPE OR PRINT NAME)   (SIGNATURE OF PETITIONER)

ORDER   ☐ EX PARTE

THE COURT FINDS
It is reasonable and necessary to appoint a guardian ad litem for the person named in the application, as requested above.

THE COURT ORDERS that *(name):*   is hereby appointed guardian ad
litem of *(name):*   for the purposes set
forth in item 4 of the application.

Application for Appointment of Guardian ad Litem filed *(date):*
  a. ☐ is denied.
  b. ☐ is granted.
  c. ☐ is set for hearing on *(date):*   at *(time):*

Date:

                                                    _____
                                                              JUDICIAL OFFICER
                                                    ☐ SIGNATURE FOLLOWS LAST ATTACHMENT

FL-955

ATTORNEY:	STATE BAR NO.:	FOR COURT USE ONLY
NAME:		
FIRM NAME:		
STREET ADDRESS:		
CITY: STATE: ZIP CODE:		
TELEPHONE NO.: FAX NO.:		
E-MAIL ADDRESS:		
ATTORNEY FOR (name):		

SUPERIOR COURT OF CALIFORNIA, COUNTY OF
  STREET ADDRESS:
  MAILING ADDRESS:
  CITY AND ZIP CODE:
  BRANCH NAME:

PETITIONER:
RESPONDENT:
OTHER PARENT/CLAIMANT:

NOTICE OF COMPLETION OF LIMITED SCOPE REPRESENTATION	CASE NUMBER:
☐ Proposed ☐ Final	

1. In accordance with the terms of an agreement between *(name):*   ☐ petitioner
☐ respondent ☐ other party/claimant   and myself, I agreed to provide limited scope representation.

2. I was retained as attorney of record for the services described in the attached ☐ *Notice of Limited Scope Representation*
(form FL-950) ☐ Other *(specify):*   *(Do not include your fee agreement.)*

3. I completed all services within the scope of my representation on *(date):*

4. The last known information for the ☐ petitioner ☐ respondent ☐ other party/claimant *(for the purpose of service)* is
  Mailing address:
  Telephone number:
  E-mail address:

NOTICE TO PARTY/CLIENT:

Your attorney has served this *Notice of Completion of Limited Scope Representation* stating that he or she has completed the tasks that you agreed the attorney would perform. For more information, read *Information for Client About Notice of Completion of Limited Scope Representation* (form FL-955-INFO).

IF THIS FORM IS MARKED " ☒ PROPOSED"	**IF THIS FORM IS MARKED " ☒ FINAL"**
You have the right to object if you believe that the attorney has not finished everything that he or she agreed to do. To object, you must do the following:	You did not object to the proposed *Notice of Completion,* which was served on *(date):* _____ by *(specify type of service):* _____
(1) Complete the enclosed *Objection to Notice of Completion of Limited Scope Representation* (form FL-956).	(1) The attorney no longer represents you in your limited scope action.
(2) Have the *Objection* served on your limited scope attorney and the other parties in the case by a person who is at least 18 years of age and not a party in the case.	(2) YOU NOW REPRESENT YOURSELF IN ALL ASPECTS OF THIS CASE.
(3) File the *Objection* and proof of service with the court.	(3) All legal documents will be directed to you at your last known address, shown above in item 4.
(4) Have the *Objection* filed and served by the following date: _____	If that address is incorrect, you need to let the court and the other parties in the case know your correct mailing address as soon as possible. You may use *Notice of Change of Address or Other Contact Information (form MC-040)* for this purpose.

I declare under penalty of perjury under the laws of the State of California that the information above is true and correct.

Date:

_____
(TYPE OR PRINT NAME)

▶

_____
(SIGNATURE OF ATTORNEY)

Page 1 of ___

Form Adopted for Mandatory Use
Judicial Council of California
FL-955 [Rev. September 1, 2017]

NOTICE OF COMPLETION OF LIMITED SCOPE REPRESENTATION

Cal. Rules of Court, rule 5.425
www.courts.ca.gov

FL-955

PETITIONER:	CASE NUMBER:
RESPONDENT:	
OTHER PARENT/CLAIMANT:	

PROOF OF SERVICE: ☐ **PROPOSED** ☐ **FINAL** **NOTICE OF COMPLETION OF LIMITED SCOPE REPRESENTATION**

1. At the time of service, I was at least 18 years of age and **not a party to this legal action.**

2. I served a copy of *(specify)*:
   ☐ Proposed *Notice of Completion of Limited Scope Representation* (form FL-955), a blank *Objection to Proposed Notice of Completion of Limited Scope Representation* (form FL-956), and *Information for Client About Notice of Completion of Limited Scope Representation* (form FL-955-INFO).
   ☐ Final *Notice of Completion of Limited Scope Representation* (form FL-955).

3. I served the above forms as follows:
   a. ☐ **Personal service.** The documents listed above were given to
      (1) Name of person served:
          Address where served:
          Date served:
          Time served:
      (2) Name of person served:
          Address where served:
          Date served:
          Time served:

   b. ☐ **Mail.** I placed a copy of the forms listed above in the U.S. mail in a sealed envelope with postage fully prepaid. The envelope was addressed and mailed as indicated below. I live or work in the county where the forms were mailed.
      (1) Name of person served:
          Address where served:
          Date of mailing:
          Place of mailing *(city and state)*:
      (2) Name of person served:
          Address where served:
          Date of mailing:
          Place of mailing *(city and state)*:

   c. ☐ **Overnight delivery.** I placed a copy of the forms listed above in a sealed envelope, with Express Mail postage fully prepaid, and deposited it in a post office mailbox, subpost office, substation, mail chute, or other like facility maintained by the U.S. Postal Service for receipt of Express Mail. The envelope was addressed and mailed as indicated below. I live or work in the county where the forms were deposited for overnight delivery.
      (1) Name of person served:
          Address where served:
          Date of mailing:
          Place of mailing *(city and state)*:
      (2) Name of person served:
          Address where served:
          Date of mailing:
          Place of mailing *(city and state)*:

   d. ☐ **Electronic service.** I electronically served the document listed above as described in the attached proof of electronic service (*Proof of Electronic Service* (form POS-050) may be used for this purpose).

4. Server's information
   a. Name:
   b. Home or work address:
   c. Telephone number:

I declare under penalty of perjury under the laws of the State of California that the information above is true and correct.

Date:

▶

_____
(TYPE OR PRINT NAME)

_____
(SIGNATURE OF PERSON SERVING NOTICE)

FL-955 [Rev. September 1, 2017] **NOTICE OF COMPLETION OF LIMITED SCOPE REPRESENTATION** Page ___ of ___

For your protection and privacy, please press the Clear This Form button after you have printed the form. | Print this form | | Save this form | | Clear this form |

FL-955-INFO | Information for Client About Notice of Completion of Limited Scope Representation

(1) Why did I get this Proposed *Notice of Completion of Limited Scope Representation* (form FL-955)?

When you and the limited scope attorney signed the *Notice of Limited Scope Representation* (form FL-950), you agreed to sign the *Substitution of Attorney—Civil* (form MC-050) when the attorney completed the tasks listed on form FL-950.

You have not yet signed that *Substitution of Attorney* form. By serving you a Proposed *Notice of Completion* (form FL-955), your attorney is telling you that he or she has completed the tasks agreed to and is taking action to be removed from your case.

(2) Why is it marked "Proposed"?

The attorney wants to give you a chance to respond if you agree or disagree that he or she completed the work for you.

(3) What do I do if I agree?

You can contact the attorney and say that you agree. But you don't have to take any action.

(4) What if I don't take any action?

After the 10th day, the attorney will serve you and the other party a *Notice of Completion* form marked "Final." It will then be filed with the court along with the proofs of service of the "Proposed" and "Final" *Notices of Completion*. When the "Final" *Notice* is served on you, the attorney no longer represents you. Unless you have a new attorney, you now represent yourself.

(5) What if I don't agree and think that the attorney is not finished with the work we agreed to?

Contact the attorney right away and see if you can work it out. But, if you can't, YOU MUST ACT RIGHT AWAY to file papers and ask for a court hearing.

(6) How fast do I have to act?

You have only **10 days** from the date that form FL-955 was personally served on you to file papers with the court. If the form was served another way, the time to act is increased slightly.

Look at the *Objection to Proposed Notice of Completion of Limited Scope Representation* (form FL-956). The attorney is required to fill in the date by which you have to file the form. To understand how that date was calculated, read **(7)**.

(7) What do I have to do by the 10th day if I disagree?

☑ Fill out form FL-956, *Objection to Proposed Notice of Completion of Limited Scope Representation.*
You should have been served with a blank form FL-956 along with the *Notice of Completion of Limited Scope Representation* that was marked "Proposed." Form FL-956 is also available online at *courts.ca.gov/documents/fl956.pdf.*

☑ Next, make two copies of the completed *Objection* (form FL-956).

☑ File the original *Objection* with the court clerk by the following deadlines:

10 calendar days	from the date that form FL-955 was personally served on you
10 calendar days, PLUS 2 court days	from the date that form FL-955 was served on you by e-mail, facsimile, express mail, or other overnight delivery
10 calendar days, PLUS 5 calendar days	from the date that form FL-955 was served on you by mail within the state of California

Note: The court clerk may reject your *Objection* if it is not served and filed by the correct deadline.

☑ The court clerk will set the hearing no later than 25 court days from the date you file the *Objection* and give you filed copies of the *Objection* so that they can be served as described in item **(11)**.

(8) Is there a filing fee for the *Objection*?

Yes, a fee is due when you file the *Objection* (form FL-956) because the court will have to set a hearing on the *Objection*. If you cannot afford to pay and do not yet have a fee waiver order for your case, you can ask the court to waive the fee by completing and filing form FW-001, *Request to Waive Court Fees* and form FW-003, *Order on Court Fee Waiver.*

Form Approved for Optional Use
Judicial Council of California
www.courts.ca.gov
New September 1, 2017

Information for Client About Notice of Completion of Limited Scope Representation

FL-955-INFO, Page 1 of 2 →

FL-955-INFO Information for Client About Notice of Completion of
Limited Scope Representation

9 What else needs to be done?

Copies of the filed *Objection* have to be "served" on your attorney and the other party in the case, or the other party's attorney. Someone else who is at least 18 years old must do it (for example, a friend, relative, sheriff, or professional process server). The server must complete a proof of service, which must be filed with the court.

10 How can the *Objection* be served?

A copy of the filed *Objection* can be served by:

- *Personal service*. The server hand delivers the papers. The server may leave the papers near the person if he or she will not take them.

- *Mail service*. The server places a copy of all documents in a sealed envelope and mails them to the address of each person being served. The server must be at least 18 years old and live or work in the county where the mailing took place.

- *Electronic* service. If you and your attorney have agreed in writing that you can send each other documents by e-mail or other electronic transmission, you can serve each other that way.

- *Service by express mail or overnight delivery*. An authorized courier or driver authorized by the express service can deliver the papers to a person's business or residence.

11 When does the *Objection* need to be served?

Everyone in the case needs to be served with the *Objection*, as described below, unless otherwise ordered by the court:

16 court days before the hearing	if personal service is used
16 court days PLUS 2 court days before the hearing	if service is by fax, electronic service, or overnight delivery
16 court days PLUS 5 calendar days before the hearing	if service is by mail within California. *For service outside of California, see item* (15)

12 What will my limited scope attorney do if I file the *Objection*?

The attorney may file form FL-957, *Response to Objection to Proposed Notice of Completion of Limited Scope Representation*, with the court at least nine court days before the hearing, and serve a copy on you and all the parties (or their attorneys) in the case. The hearing will go forward even if the attorney does not file and serve a *Response*.

13 How should I prepare for my hearing?

- ☑ Take at least two copies of your documents and filed forms to the hearing.

- ☑ Write down the tasks that the attorney agreed to do but has not completed and bring that list to court.

- ☑ Bring any paperwork that helps prove that the work is incomplete.

  Important! Your agreement with your attorney is private and should not go into the court file. Letters between you and your lawyer are also private. If you want to bring these documents to court to show why you don't think the tasks are completed, make two copies. Keep the original and give one copy to the judge and the other to the attorney at the hearing. These documents will help the judge make the decision, but they should not be filed with form FL-956, *Objection*.

14 What will happen at the hearing?

The judge will decide if your attorney has finished the work agreed to or not. You will get an *Order on Completion of Limited Scope Representation* (form FL-958) signed by the judge. The attorney will usually prepare the order, unless the court decides otherwise.

15 Do you have questions or need help?

Talk to a lawyer or contact the Family Law Facilitator or Self-Help Center for information and assistance about any subject included in this form. Go to www.courts.ca.gov/selfhelp-courtresources. htm.

For your protection and privacy, please press the Clear This Form button after you have printed the form.   [Print this form]   [Save this form]   [Clear this form]

0244

ATTORNEY OR PARTY WITHOUT ATTORNEY:	STATE BAR NO.:	FOR COURT USE ONLY

ATTORNEY OR PARTY WITHOUT ATTORNEY: STATE BAR NO.:

NAME:

FIRM NAME:

STREET ADDRESS:

CITY: STATE: ZIP CODE:

TELEPHONE NO.:   FAX NO.:

E-MAIL ADDRESS:

ATTORNEY FOR *(name)*:

FOR COURT USE ONLY

SUPERIOR COURT OF CALIFORNIA, COUNTY OF

STREET ADDRESS:

MAILING ADDRESS:

CITY AND ZIP CODE:

BRANCH NAME:

PETITIONER:

RESPONDENT:

OTHER PARENT/CLAIMANT:

ORDER ON COMPLETION OF LIMITED SCOPE REPRESENTATION

CASE NUMBER:

1. The proceeding on the party's *(name):*   objection to the attorney's *(name):*
   proposed *Notice of Completion of Limited Scope Representation* (form FL-955) was heard

   a. on *(date):*   at *(time):*   in Dept.:   Room:

        by Judge *(name):*   ☐ Temporary Judge

   b. The following persons were present at the hearing:
   - ☐ Petitioner   ☐ Attorney *(name):*
   - ☐ Respondent   ☐ Attorney *(name):*
   - ☐ Other Parent/Claimant   ☐ Attorney *(name):*

2. **THE COURT FINDS**

   a. ☐ The attorney demonstrated that he or she has completed the services that the party and attorney agreed that the attorney would perform in the *Notice of Limited Scope Representation* (form FL-950).

   b. ☐ The party demonstrated that the attorney has not completed the services that the party and the attorney agreed would be performed in the *Notice of Limited Scope Representation* (form FL-950).

   c. ☐ Other *(specify):*

3. **THE COURT ORDERS**

   a. ☐ The request of the attorney to be relieved of limited scope representation is denied.

   b. ☐ The attorney is relieved as the limited scope attorney of record for the party/client.
   - (1) ☐ effective immediately.
   - (2) ☐ effective upon the filing of the proof of service of this signed order on the client.
   - (3) ☐ effective on *(specify date):*

   c. ☐ The court further orders *(specify):*

   d. ☐ All legal documents and notices must be served directly on the party using the following address or contact information:
   Mailing address:
   Telephone number: E-mail address:

   e. Unless otherwise directed by the court, the attorney must serve copies of this order on the parties and their attorneys of record and and file the proof of service with the court.

Date: _____

_____
JUDGE OF THE SUPERIOR COURT

> **NOTICE TO PARTY/CLIENT:** If the court relieved the limited scope attorney as your attorney of record, **you now represent yourself in the case.** You may wish to seek other legal counsel to represent you. You must keep the court and the other parties in your case informed of your current mailing address and contact information. You may use *Notice of Change of Address or Other Contact Information* (form MC-040) for this purpose.

Page 1 of 1

Form Adopted for Mandatory Use
Judicial Council of California
FL-958 [Rev. January 1, 2018]

ORDER ON COMPLETION OF LIMITED SCOPE REPRESENTATION

Cal. Rules of Court, rule 5.425
www.courts.ca.gov

For your protection and privacy, please press the Clear   [Print this form]   [Save this form]   [Clear this form]

0245

ATTORNEY OR PARTY WITHOUT ATTORNEY *(Name, state bar number, and address):*

TELEPHONE NO.:   FAX NO.:

ATTORNEY FOR *(Name):*

FOR COURT USE ONLY

SUPERIOR COURT OF CALIFORNIA, COUNTY OF

STREET ADDRESS:

MAILING ADDRESS:

CITY AND ZIP CODE:

BRANCH NAME:

PETITIONER/PLAINTIFF:

RESPONDENT/DEFENDANT:

NOTICE OF WITHDRAWAL OF ATTORNEY OF RECORD

CASE NUMBER:

1. In accordance with the provisions of section 285.1 of the Code of Civil Procedure, I withdraw as Attorney of Record for:
   ☐ Petitioner   ☐ Respondent

2. The final judgment of dissolution, legal separation, nullity, parentage, or postjudgment order was entered on *(specify date):*
   and no motions or other proceedings are pending at this time.

3. The last known address for the   ☐ Petitioner   ☐ Respondent   is:

4. The last known telephone number for the   ☐ Petitioner   ☐ Respondent   is:

5. I mailed a copy of this *Notice of Withdrawal* to   ☐ Petitioner   ☐ Respondent   at the address set forth in item 3.

I declare under penalty of perjury under the laws of the State of California that the foregoing is true and correct.

Date:

_____
(TYPE OR PRINT NAME)

▶

_____
(SIGNATURE)

WARNING
This form may not be used after a status-only judgment.

Form Adopted for Mandatory Use
Judicial Council of California
FL-960 [Rev. January 1, 2003]

NOTICE OF WITHDRAWAL OF ATTORNEY OF RECORD

Code of Civil Procedure, § 285.1
www.courtinfo.ca.gov

PETITIONER/PLAINTIFF:	CASE NUMBER:
RESPONDENT/DEFENDANT:	

PROOF OF SERVICE BY ☐ PERSONAL SERVICE ☐ MAIL

1. At the time of service I was at least 18 years of age and **not a party to this legal action.**

2. I served a copy of the *Notice of Withdrawal of Attorney of Record* as follows *(check either a. or b. below):*

   a. ☐ **Personal service.** I personally delivered the *Notice of Withdrawal of Attorney of Record* as follows:
   (1) Name of person served:
   (2) Address where served:

   (3) Date served:
   (4) Time served:

   b. ☐ **Mail.** I deposited the *Notice of Withdrawal of Attorney of Record* in the United States mail, in a sealed envelope with postage fully prepaid. The envelope was addressed and mailed as follows:
   (1) Name of person served:
   (2) Address:

   (3) Date of mailing:
   (4) Place of mailing *(city and state):*
   (5) I am a resident of or employed in the county where the *Notice* was mailed.

   c. My residence or business address is *(specify):*

   d. My phone number is *(specify):*

I declare under penalty of perjury under the laws of the State of California that the foregoing is true and correct.

Date:

▶

_____
(TYPE OR PRINT NAME)

_____
(SIGNATURE OF PERSON SERVING NOTICE)

0247

ATTORNEY OR PARTY WITHOUT ATTORNEY *(Name, State Bar number, and address)*:	FOR COURT USE ONLY

TELEPHONE NO.: FAX NO. *(Optional)*:
E-MAIL ADDRESS *(Optional)*:
ATTORNEY FOR *(Name)*:

SUPERIOR COURT OF CALIFORNIA, COUNTY OF

STREET ADDRESS:
MAILING ADDRESS:
CITY AND ZIP CODE:
BRANCH NAME:

PETITIONER:

RESPONDENT:

OTHER PARTY/PARENT:

APPLICATION FOR ORDER FOR ☐ PUBLICATION OR ☐ POSTING	CASE NUMBER:

1. ☐ **Publication Request:** The petitioner requests that the court issue an order directing service of the summons listed in item 3 based on Code of Civil Procedure section 413.30, and that the summons be published in the following newspaper of general circulation *(name of proposed newspaper of general circulation where respondent is most likely to receive actual notice)*:

2. ☐ **Posting Request:** The petitioner requests that the court issue an order directing service of the summons listed in item 3 by posting at the location listed below. The petitioner has submitted a *Request to Waive Court Fees* (form FW-001). This request is based on Code of Civil Procedure section 413.30.

   Posting location *(name, city, and state of proposed location to post where respondent is most likely to receive actual notice)*:

3. **The legal documents to be served are:**
   a. ☐ *Summons (Family Law)* (form FL-110)
   b. ☐ *Summons (Uniform Parentage—Petition for Custody and Support)* (form FL-210)
   c. ☐ Other *(specify)*:

Form Approved for Optional Use
Judicial Council of California
FL-980 [New January 1, 2013]

**APPLICATION FOR ORDER
FOR PUBLICATION OR POSTING
(Family Law)**

Code of Civil Procedure §§ 413.30, 415.50
www.courts.ca.gov

FL-980

	CASE NUMBER:
PETITIONER:	
RESPONDENT:	
OTHER PARTY/PARENT:	

4 The respondent cannot with reasonable diligence be served in any manner specified in Code of Civil Procedure sections 415.10 through 415.40 based on the declaration below.

5. **Declaration:**

   Describe how you tried to find the respondent. This search may include checking with respondent's last known address; respondent's friends and family, respondent's current and past employers and any unions, Internet research, and the tax assessor records in the county of respondent's last known address or any county in which you think the respondent may live. List all steps, the date you took each step, and the results. (You may want to check with your local court's self-help center or the California courts on-line self-help center for additional ideas about how to locate someone).

   a. I last saw or had contact with the respondent on *(date):*
       at *(location):*

   b. The last address I have for respondent is:

   c. The last work or business address I have for respondent is:

   d. I have taken the following steps to try to find the respondent:

   ☐ Continued on the attached declaration. Number of pages attached: _____
   ☐ Search results attached.

I declare under penalty of perjury under the laws of the State of California that the foregoing is true and correct.

Date:

_____
(TYPE OR PRINT NAME)

▶ _____
(SIGNATURE OF PETITIONER)

**APPLICATION FOR ORDER
FOR PUBLICATION OR POSTING**
(Family Law)

0249

ATTORNEY OR PARTY WITHOUT ATTORNEY *(Name, State Bar number, and address)*:	FOR COURT USE ONLY
TELEPHONE NO.: FAX NO. *(Optional)*: E-MAIL ADDRESS *(Optional)*: ATTORNEY FOR *(Name)*:	

SUPERIOR COURT OF CALIFORNIA, COUNTY OF
STREET ADDRESS:
MAILING ADDRESS:
CITY AND ZIP CODE:
BRANCH NAME:

PETITIONER:

RESPONDENT:

OTHER PARTY/PARENT:

ORDER FOR ☐ **PUBLICATION OR** ☐ **POSTING**	CASE NUMBER:

1. ☐ **Publication Granted:** The court finds that the respondent cannot be served in any other manner specified in the California Code of Civil Procedure. The court orders that the documents listed in item 6 be served by publication at least once per week for four successive weeks in the following newspaper *(specify)*:

2. ☐ **Posting Granted:** The court finds that the respondent cannot be served in any other manner specified in the California Code of Civil Procedure and that the petitioner cannot afford to serve by publication. The court orders that the documents listed in item 6 be served by posting for 28 continuous days at the following location *(address)*:

   And that the documents in item 6, along with this order, be mailed to respondent's last known address *(specify)*:

3. ☐ **Publishing Denied:** The court denies the request to publish.
   a. ☐ Other methods of service are possible.
   b. ☐ Insufficient attempts have been made to locate the respondent *(specify)*:

4. ☐ **Posting Denied:** The court denies the request to post.
   a. ☐ Other methods of service are possible.
   b. ☐ Petitioner is able to pay fees required for publication.
   c. ☐ Insufficient attempts have been made to locate the respondent *(specify)*:

5. ☐ **Hearing Required:** The court orders that a hearing be set to determine the petitioner's financial circumstances. If at this hearing the court decides that the petitioner, based on financial circumstances, does not qualify for posting, then the court may order that the documents listed in item 6 be served by publication.

   Hearing date: Time: Dept:

6. Documents to be served by publication or posting:
   a. ☐ *Summons (Family Law)* (form FL-110)
   b. ☐ *Summons (Uniform Parentage—Petition for Custody and Support)* (form FL-210)
   c. ☐ Other *(specify)*:

7. If, during the 28 days of publication or posting, you locate the respondent's address, you must have someone 18 years of age or older mail the documents listed in item 6 to the respondent along with this order. The server must complete and file with the court a *Proof of Service by Mail* (form FL-335).

Date: _____ _____
JUDICIAL OFFICER

Page 1 of 2

Form Approved for Optional Use
Judicial Council of California
FL-982 [New January 1, 2013]

ORDER FOR PUBLICATION OR POSTING
(Family Law)

Code of Civil Procedure, § 415.50
www.courts.ca.gov

PETITIONER:	CASE NUMBER:
RESPONDENT:	
OTHER PARTY/PARENT:	

INSTRUCTIONS

Publication:

1. **Publication:** Take this order to the approved newspaper for publication and pay the fee to publish the documents listed in item 6 of this order for at least once a week for four successive weeks.

2. **Proof of Service by Publication:** After the newspaper publication is complete, the newspaper will send you a declaration or affidavit of publication and a copy of the publication notice that appeared in the newspaper. You must file this declaration or affidavit of publication with the court clerk if it has not been filed by the newspaper. Be sure to make a copy for yourself.

3. **Service by Publication Completed:** Service by publication is complete at the end of the 28th day of publication in the newspaper. If no response has been filed by the respondent, the petitioner may file *a Request to Enter Default* (form FL-165) starting on the 59th day after the first day of publication.

4. **Mailing:** If during the time of publication, you locate the respondent's address, you must have someone 18 years of age or older mail the this order and all documents listed in item 6 of this order to the respondent. Be sure the person who mails these documents completes and files a proof of service of this mailing. The server may use *Proof of Service by Mail* (form FL-335).

Posting:

1. **Posting Location:** You must have someone, 18 years of age or older and not a party to the case, post a copy of this *Order for Publication or Posting* (form FL-982) and all documents listed in item 6 of this order at the court-ordered posting location leaving it posted for 28 days in a row.

2. **Mailing to last known address:** You must have someone, 18 years or older and not a party to the case, mail this *Order for Publication or Posting* (form FL-982) and all documents listed in item 6 of this order to the respondent's last known address. The person who mails these documents completes a proof of service of this mailing. The server may use *Proof of Service by Mail* (form FL-335).

3. **Proof of Service by Posting:** The person (server) who posts and/or mails these documents must complete and file a declaration under penalty of perjury of such proof of posting. The server may use *Proof of Service of Posting* (form FL-985).

4. **Service by Posting Completed:** Service by posting is complete at the end of the 28th day of posting. If no response has been filed by the respondent, the petitioner may file *a Request to Enter Default* (form FL-165) on the 59th day after the first day of posting.

5. **Mailing:** If during the time of posting, you locate the respondent's address, you must have someone 18 years of age or older mail the this order and all documents listed in item 6 of this order to the respondent. Be sure the person who mails these documents completes and files a proof of service of this mailing. The server may use *Proof of Service by Mail* (form FL-335).

ORDER FOR PUBLICATION OR POSTING
(Family Law)

0251

FL-985

ATTORNEY OR PARTY WITHOUT ATTORNEY *(Name, State Bar number, and address)*:	FOR COURT USE ONLY

TELEPHONE NO.:   FAX NO. *(Optional)*:

E-MAIL ADDRESS *(Optional)*:

ATTORNEY FOR *(Name)*:

SUPERIOR COURT OF CALIFORNIA, COUNTY OF

STREET ADDRESS:

MAILING ADDRESS:

CITY AND ZIP CODE:

BRANCH NAME:

PETITIONER:

RESPONDENT:

OTHER PARTY/PARENT:

PROOF OF SERVICE BY POSTING	CASE NUMBER:

1. At the time of service I was at least 18 years of age and not a party to this action. I served the respondent by posting copies of:

   a. ☐ *Summons (Family Law)* (form FL-110)

   b. ☐ *Summons (Uniform Parentage—Petition for Custody and Support)* (form FL-210)

   c. ☐ Other *(specify)*:

2. Location where documents were posted:

3. Date when documents were first posted:

   Date when documents were removed *(document must be posted at least 28 days)*:

4. My Name:

   My Address:

   My Telephone No.:

   I am *(specify)*:

   a. ☐ exempt from registration under Business and Professions Code section 22350(b).

   b. ☐ not a registered California process server.

   c. ☐ a registered California process server: ☐ an employee or ☐ an independent contractor

       (1) Registration No.:

       (2) County:

5. ☐ I declare under penalty of perjury under the laws of the State of California that the foregoing is true and correct.

   —or—

6. ☐ I am a California sheriff, marshal, or constable, and I certify that the foregoing is true and correct.

Date:

▶

_____   _____

(NAME OF PERSON WHO SERVED PAPERS)   (SIGNATURE OF PERSON WHO SERVED PAPERS)

Page 1 of 1

Form Approved for Optional Use
Judicial Council of California
FL-985 [New January 1, 2013]

PROOF OF SERVICE BY POSTING
(Family Law)

Code of Civil Procedure, §§ 413.30
and 415.50
www.courts.ca.gov

CLETS-001

California Law Enforcement Telecommunications System (CLETS) Information Form

☐ This form is submitted with the initial filing *(date)*: _____

☐ This is an amended form *(date)*: _____

Important: **This form MUST NOT become part of the public court file. It is confidential and private.**

Fill out as much of this form as you can and give it to the court clerk. If the court issues a restraining order, this form will provide law enforcement with information that will help them enforce it. If any of this information changes, fill out a new (amended) form.

Case Number *(if you know it):* _____

---

(1) **Person to Be Protected** *(Name):* _____

Sex: ☐ M ☐ F Height: _____ Weight: _____ Race: _____
Hair Color: _____ Eye Color: _____ Age: _____ Date of Birth: _____
Mailing Address *(listed on restraining order):* _____
City: _____ State: _____ Zip: _____ Telephone *(optional):* _____
Vehicle *(Type, Model, Year):* _____ *(License Number and State):* _____

(2) **Person to Be Restrained** *(Name):* _____

Sex: ☐ M ☐ F Height: _____ Weight: _____ Race: _____
Hair Color: _____ Eye Color: _____ Age: _____ Date of Birth: _____
Residence Address: _____
City: _____ State: _____ Zip: _____ Telephone: _____
Business Address: _____
City: _____ State: _____ Zip: _____ Telephone: _____
Employer: _____
Occupation/Title: _____ Work Hours: _____
Driver's License Number and State: _____ Social Security Number: _____
Vehicle *(Type, Model, Year):* _____ *(License Number and State):* _____
Describe any marks, scars, or tattoos: _____
Other names used by the restrained person: _____

(3) **Guns or Firearms** Describe any guns or firearms that you believe the person in **(2)** owns or has access to *(Number, types, and locations):*

_____
_____

(4) **Other People to Be Protected**

Name	Date of Birth	Sex	Race	Relation to Person in **(1)**
_____	_____	_____	_____	_____
_____	_____	_____	_____	_____

☐ Additional persons to be protected are listed on Attachment 4.

This is not a Court Order—Do not place in court file.

Judicial Council of California, *www.courts.ca.gov*
New January 1, 2012, Mandatory Form
Cal. Rules of Court, rule 1.51

Confidential CLETS Information

CLETS-001, Page 1 of 1

0253

DV-100	**Request for Domestic Violence Restraining Order**

You must also complete Form CLETS-001, Confidential CLETS Information, and give it to the clerk when you file this Request.

(1) Name of Person Asking for Protection:

_____ Age: _____

Your lawyer in this case *(if you have one):*

Name: _____ State Bar No.: _____

Firm Name: _____

Address *(If you have a lawyer for this case, give your lawyer's information. If you do not have a lawyer and want to keep your home address private, give a different mailing address instead. You do not have to give your telephone, fax, or e-mail.):*

Address: _____

City: _____ State: _____ Zip: _____

Telephone: _____ Fax: _____

E-Mail Address: _____

Clerk stamps date here when form is filed.

Fill in court name and street address:

Superior Court of California, County of

Court fills in case number when form is filed.

Case Number:

(2) Name of Person You Want Protection From:

_____

Description of person you want protection from:

Sex: ☐ M ☐ F   Height: _____   Weight: _____   Hair Color: _____   Eye Color: _____

Race: _____   Age: _____   Date of Birth: _____

Address *(if known):* _____

City: _____   State: _____   Zip: _____

(3) Do you want an order to protect family or household members?   ☐ Yes ☐ No

If yes, list them:

Full name	Sex	Age	Lives with you?	Relationship to you
_____	_____	_____	☐ Yes ☐ No	_____
_____	_____	_____	☐ Yes ☐ No	_____
_____	_____	_____	☐ Yes ☐ No	_____

☐ *Check here if you need more space. Attach a sheet of paper and write "DV-100, Protected People" for a title.*

(4) What is your relationship to the person in ②? *(Check all that apply):*

a. ☐ We are now married or registered domestic partners.

b. ☐ We used to be married or registered domestic partners.

c. ☐ We live together.

d. ☐ We used to live together.

e. ☐ We are related by blood, marriage, or adoption *(specify relationship):* _____

f. ☐ We are dating or used to date, or we are or used to be engaged to be married.

g. ☐ We are the parents together of a child or children under 18:

    Child's Name: _____ Date of Birth: _____

    Child's Name: _____ Date of Birth: _____

    Child's Name: _____ Date of Birth: _____

    ☐ *Check here if you need more space. Attach a sheet of paper and write "DV-100, Additional Children" for a title.*

h. ☐ We have signed a Voluntary Declaration of Paternity for our child or children. *(Attach a copy if you have one).*

If you do not have one of these relationships, the court may not be able to consider your request. Read Form DV-500-INFO for help.

This is not a Court Order.

Judicial Council of California, *www.courts.ca.gov*
Revised July 1, 2016, Mandatory Form
Family Code, § 6200 et seq.

Request for Domestic Violence Restraining Order
(Domestic Violence Prevention)

DV-100, Page 1 of 6

→

0254

(5) Other Restraining Orders and Court Cases

a. Are there any restraining/protective orders currently in place OR that have expired in the last six months (emergency protective orders, criminal, juvenile, family)?

☐ No ☐ Yes *(date of order):* and *(expiration date):* *(Attach a copy if you have one).*

b. Have you or any other person named in ③ been involved in another court case with the person in ②?

☐ No ☐ Yes *If yes, check each kind of case and indicate where and when each was filed:*

Kind of Case	County or Tribe Where Filed	Year Filed	Case Number *(if known)*
☐ Divorce, Nullity, Legal Separation			
☐ Civil Harassment			
☐ Domestic Violence			
☐ Criminal			
☐ Juvenile, Dependency, Guardianship			
☐ Child Support			
☐ Parentage, Paternity			
☐ Other *(specify):* _____			

☐ *Check here if you need more space. Attach a sheet of paper and write "DV-100, Other Court Cases" for a title.*

Check the orders you want. ☑

(6) ☐ Personal Conduct Orders

I ask the court to order the person in ② not to do the following things to me or anyone listed in ③:

a. ☐ Harass, attack, strike, threaten, assault (sexually or otherwise), hit, follow, stalk, molest, destroy personal property, disturb the peace, keep under surveillance, impersonate (on the Internet, electronically or otherwise), or block movements

b. ☐ Contact, either directly or indirectly, in any way, including but not limited to, by telephone, mail or e-mail or other electronic means

The person in ② will be ordered not to take any action to get the addresses or locations of any protected person unless the court finds good cause not to make the order.

(7) ☐ Stay-Away Order

a. I ask the court to order the person in ② to stay at least _____ yards away from *(check all that apply):*

☐ Me ☐ My school
☐ My home ☐ Each person listed in ③
☐ My job or workplace ☐ The child(ren)'s school or child care
☐ My vehicle ☐ Other *(specify):* _____

b. If the person listed in ② is ordered to stay away from all the places listed above, will he or she still be able to get to his or her home, school, job, workplace, or vehicle? ☐ Yes ☐ No *(If no, explain):*

_____

(8) ☐ Move-Out Order

(If the person in ② lives with you and you want that person to stay away from your home, you must ask for this move-out order.)

I ask the court to order the person in ② to move out from and not return to *(address):*

_____

I have the right to live at the above address because (explain):

_____

This is not a Court Order.

0255

Case Number: _____

⑨ Guns or Other Firearms or Ammunition

I believe the person in ② owns or possesses guns, firearms, or ammunition. ☐ Yes ☐ No ☐ I don't know
If the judge approves the order, the person in ② will be ordered not to own, possess, purchase, or receive a firearm or ammunition. The person will be ordered to sell to, or store with, a licensed gun dealer, or turn in to law enforcement, any guns or firearms that he or she owns or possesses.

⑩ ☐ Record Unlawful Communications

I ask for the right to record communications made to me by the person in ② that violate the judge's orders.

⑪ ☐ Care of Animals

I ask for the sole possession, care, and control of the animals listed below. I ask the court to order the person in ② to stay at least _____ yards away from and not take, sell, transfer, encumber, conceal, molest, attack, strike, threaten, harm, or otherwise dispose of the following animals:

_____
_____

I ask for the animals to be with me because:

_____
_____

⑫ ☐ Child Custody and Visitation

a. ☐ I do not have a child custody or visitation order and I want one.
b. ☐ I have a child custody or visitation order and I want it changed.
If you ask for orders, you must fill out and attach Form DV-105, Request for Child Custody and Visitation Orders.
You and the other parent may tell the court that you want to be legal parents of the children (use Form DV-180, Agreement and Judgment of Parentage).

⑬ ☐ Child Support *(Check all that apply):*

a. ☐ I do not have a child support order and I want one.
b. ☐ I have a child support order and I want it changed.
c. ☐ I now receive or have applied for TANF, Welfare, CalWORKS, or Medi-Cal.
If you ask for child support orders, you must fill out and attach form FL-150, Income and Expense Declaration or *Form FL-155,* Financial Statement (Simplified).

⑭ ☐ Property Control

I ask the court to give *only* me temporary use, possession, and control of the property listed here:

_____
_____

⑮ ☐ Debt Payment

I ask the court to order the person in ② to make these payments while the order is in effect:
☐ *Check here if you need more space. Attach a sheet of paper and write "DV-100, Debt Payment" for a title.*
Pay to: _____ For: _____ Amount: $ _____ Due date: _____

⑯ ☐ Property Restraint

I am married to or have a registered domestic partnership with the person in ②. I ask the judge to order that the person in ② not borrow against, sell, hide, or get rid of or destroy any possessions or property, except in the usual course of business or for necessities of life. I also ask the judge to order the person in ② to notify me of any new or big expenses and to explain them to the court.

⑰ ☐ Spousal Support

I am married to or have a registered domestic partnership with the person in ② and no spousal support order exists. I ask the court to order the person in ② to pay spousal support. *(You must complete, file, and serve Form FL-150,* Income and Expense Declaration, *before your hearing).*

This is not a Court Order.

Revised July 1, 2016

Request for Domestic Violence Restraining Order
(Domestic Violence Prevention)

DV-100, Page 3 of 6 →

Case Number: _____

18 ☐ **Rights to Mobile Device and Wireless Phone Account**

   a. ☐ **Property control of mobile device and wireless phone account**
     I ask the court to give **only** me temporary use, possession, and control of the following mobile devices:
     _____ and the wireless phone account for the
     following wireless phone numbers because the account currently belongs to the person in ② :
     (including area code): _____ ☐ my number ☐ number of child in my care
     (including area code): _____ ☐ my number ☐ number of child in my care
     (including area code): _____ ☐ my number ☐ number of child in my care
     ☐ *Check here if you need more space. Attach a sheet of paper and write "DV-100, Rights to Mobile Device*
      and Wireless Phone Account" for a title.

   b. ☐ **Debt Payment**
     I ask the court to order the person in ② to make the payments for the wireless phone accounts listed in 18a
     because: _____
     Name of the wireless service provider is: _____ Amount: $ _____ Due Date: _____
     If you are requesting this order, you must complete, file, and serve Form FL-150, Income and Expense
     Declaration, before your hearing.

   c. ☐ **Transfer of Wireless Phone Account**
     I ask the court to order the wireless service provider to transfer the billing responsibility and rights to the
     wireless phone numbers listed in 18a to me because the account currently belongs to the person in ② .
     If the judge makes this order, you will be financially responsible for these accounts, including monthly service
     fees and costs of any mobile devices connected to these phone numbers. You may be responsible for other fees.
     You must contact the wireless service provider to find out what fees you will be responsible for and whether you
     are eligible for an account.

19 ☐ **Insurance**

   I ask the court to order the person in ② NOT to cash, borrow against, cancel, transfer, dispose of, or change the
   beneficiaries of any insurance or coverage held for the benefit of me or the person in ②, or our child(ren), for
   whom support may be ordered, or both.

20 ☐ **Lawyer's Fees and Costs**

   I ask that the person in ② pay some or all of my lawyer's fees and costs.
   You must complete, file, and serve form FL-150, Income and Expense Declaration, before your hearing.

21 ☐ **Payments for Costs and Services**

   I ask the court to order the person in ② to pay the following:
   You can ask for lost earnings or your costs for services caused directly by the person in ② (damaged property,
   medical care, counseling, temporary housing, etc.). You must bring proof of these expenses to your hearing.
   Pay to: _____ For: _____ Amount: $ _____
   Pay to: _____ For: _____ Amount: $ _____

22 ☐ **Batterer Intervention Program**

   I ask the court to order the person listed in ② to go to a 52-week batterer intervention program and show proof
   of completion to the court.

23 ☐ **Other Orders**

   What other orders are you asking for? _____
   _____
   _____
   _____

   ☐ *Check here if you need more space. Attach a sheet of paper and write "DV-100, Other Orders" for a title.*

This is not a Court Order.

Case Number:

24 ☐ **Time for Service (Notice)**

The papers must be personally served on the person in ② at least five days before the hearing, unless the court orders a shorter time for service. If you want there to be fewer than five days between service and the hearing, explain why below. For help, read Form DV-200-INFO, "What Is Proof of Personal Service"?

_____

_____

25 **No Fee to Serve (Notify) Restrained Person**

If you want the sheriff or marshal to serve (notify) the restrained person about the orders for free, ask the court clerk what you need to do.

26 **Court Hearing**

The court will schedule a hearing on your request. If the judge does not make the orders effective right away ("temporary restraining orders"), the judge may still make the orders after the hearing. If the judge does not make the orders effective right away, you can ask the court to cancel the hearing. Read form DV-112, *Waiver of Hearing on Denied Request for Temporary Restraining Order,* for more information.

27 **Describe Abuse**

Describe how the person in ② abused you. Abuse means to intentionally or recklessly cause or attempt to cause bodily injury to you; or to place you or another person in reasonable fear of imminent serious bodily injury; or to harass, attack, strike, threaten, assault (sexually or otherwise), hit, follow, stalk, molest, keep you under surveillance, impersonate (on the Internet, electronically or otherwise), batter, telephone, or contact you; or to disturb your peace; or to destroy your personal property. (For a complete definition, see Fam. Code, §§ 6203, 6320.)

a. Date of most recent abuse: _____

   1. Who was there? _____

   2. Describe how the person in ② abused you or your child(ren):

   _____

   _____

   _____

   _____

   _____

   ☐ *Check here if you need more space. Attach a sheet of paper and write "DV-100, Recent Abuse" for a title.*

   3. Did the person in ② use or threaten to use a gun or any other weapon? ☐ No ☐ Yes *(If yes, describe):*

   _____

   _____

   4. Describe any injuries: _____

   _____

   _____

   5. Did the police come? ☐ No ☐ Yes

   If yes, did they give you or the person in ② an Emergency Protective Order? ☐ Yes ☐ No ☐ I don't know

   Attach a copy if you have one.

   The order protects ☐ you or ☐ the person in ②

This is not a Court Order.

Case Number:

(27) Describe Abuse (continued)

Has the person in (2) abused you (or your child(ren)) other times?

    b. Date of abuse: _____

       1. Who was there? _____

       2. Describe how the person in (2) abused you or your child(ren):

           _____
           _____
           _____
           _____
           _____

          ☐ *Check here if you need more space. Attach a sheet of paper and write "DV-100, Recent Abuse" for a title.*

       3. Did the person in (2) use or threaten to use a gun or any other weapon? ☐ No ☐ Yes *(If yes, describe):*

           _____

       4. Describe any injuries: _____
           _____

       5. Did the police come? ☐ No ☐ Yes

          If yes, did they give you or the person in (2) an Emergency Protective Order?

          ☐ Yes ☐ No ☐ I don't know *Attach a copy if you have one.*

          The order protects ☐ you or ☐ the person in (2)

          If the person in (2) abused you other times, check here ☐ and use Form DV-101, Description of Abuse or describe any previous abuse on an attached sheet of paper and write "DV-100, Previous Abuse" for a title.

(28) Other Persons to Be Protected

The persons listed in item (3) need an order for protection because *(describe):* _____
_____
_____
_____
_____
_____
_____

(29) Number of pages attached to this form, if any: _____

I declare under penalty of perjury under the laws of the State of California that the information above is true and correct.

Date: _____

_____
Type or print your name

▶ _____
Sign your name

Date: _____

_____
Lawyer's name, if you have one

▶ _____
Lawyer's signature

This is not a Court Order.

0259

Case Number:

This form is attached to DV-100, *Request for Domestic Violence Restraining Order* .

(1) **Name of person asking for protection:** _____

(2) **Name of person you want protection from:** _____

(3) **Describe abuse to you or your children.**

    a. Date of abuse: _____

    b. Who was there? _____
_____

    Describe how the person in (2) abused you or your children:

_____
_____
_____
_____
_____
_____
_____
_____
_____
_____
_____
_____
_____
_____
_____
_____
_____

    d. Describe any use or threatened use of guns or other weapons:

_____
_____
_____
_____

    e. Describe any injuries: _____
_____
_____
_____
_____

    f. Did the police or other law enforcement come? ☐ No ☐ Yes
      If yes, did they give you or the person in (2) an Emergency Protective Order? ☐ Yes ☐ No ☐ I don't know
      The Emergency Protective Order protects ☐ You ☐ The person in (2)
      Attach a copy of the Emergency Protective Order if you have one.

Judicial Council of California, *www.courts.ca.gov*
Rev. January 1, 2017, Optional Form
Family Code, § 6200 et seq.

Description of Abuse
(Domestic Violence Prevention)

DV-101, Page 1 of 2
→

0260

Case Number: _____

④ **Describe abuse to you or your children.**

Has the person in ② abused you (or your children) other times?

a. Date of abuse: _____

b. Who was there? _____

c. Describe how the person in ② abused you or your children:

_____
_____
_____
_____
_____
_____
_____
_____
_____
_____
_____
_____
_____
_____
_____
_____

d. Describe any use or threatened use of guns or other weapons:

_____
_____
_____
_____

e. Describe any injuries: _____

_____
_____
_____
_____

f. Did the police or other law enforcement come? ☐ No ☐ Yes
If yes, did they give you or the person in ② an Emergency Protective Order? ☐ Yes ☐ No ☐ I don't know
The Emergency Protective Order protects ☐ You ☐ The person in ②
Attach a copy of the Emergency Protective Order if you have one.

⑤ **Describe abuse to you or your children.**

_____
_____
_____
_____

☐ *Check here if you need more space. Attach a sheet of paper and write "DV-101—Description of Abuse" for a title.*

0261

<table>
<tr><td>**DV-105**</td><td>**Request for Child Custody and Visitation Orders**</td><td>**Case Number:**</td></tr>
</table>

This form is attached to DV-100, *Request for Domestic Violence Restraining Order.*

Check the orders you want ☑.

(1) Your name: _____ ☐ Mom ☐ Dad ☐ Other*

(2) Other parent's name: _____ ☐ Mom ☐ Dad ☐ Other*

If Other, specify relationship to child: _____

(3) ☐ **Child Custody**

I ask the court for custody as follows:

Legal Custody to: *(Person who makes decisions about health, education, and welfare)*

Physical Custody to: *(Person you want the child to live with)*

Child's Name	Date of Birth	Mom	Dad	Other	Mom	Dad	Other
a. _____	_____	☐	☐	☐	☐	☐	☐
b. _____	_____	☐	☐	☐	☐	☐	☐
c. _____	_____	☐	☐	☐	☐	☐	☐
d. _____	_____	☐	☐	☐	☐	☐	☐

☐ *Check here if you need more space. Attach a sheet of paper and write "DV-105, Child Custody" for a title.*

(4) ☐ **Change Current Court Order**

I want to change a current child custody or visitation court order.

Case Number *(if you have it):* _____ County: _____

Explain your current order and why you want a change. _____
_____

☐ *Check here if you need more space. Attach a sheet of paper and write "DV-105, Change Current Court Order" for a title.*

(5) **Child's Address**

Where has the child in **(3)**(a) lived for the last 5 years? Give each city and state the child has lived unless it is unknown to the other parent and you want to keep it confidential because of domestic violence or child abuse. Start with where the child lives now and work backwards in time. *(If the current address is confidential, check the box below and just provide the current state).*

Child **(3)**(a) addresses *(city and state):*

Child **(3)**(a) lived with: Mom Dad Other

Dates lived there:

☐ Confidential

	Mom	Dad	Other			
_____	☐	☐	☐	From _____	to present	
_____	☐	☐	☐	From _____	to _____	
_____	☐	☐	☐	From _____	to _____	
_____	☐	☐	☐	From _____	to _____	

☐ *Check here if you need more space. Attach a sheet of paper and write "DV-105, Child's Address" for a title.*

This is not a Court Order.

Judicial Council of California, www.courts.ca.gov
Rev. January 1, 2012, Mandatory Form
Family Code, § 3063

Request for Child Custody and Visitation Orders
(Domestic Violence Prevention)

DV-105, Page 1 of 3 ➔

Case Number: _____

(6) Other Children's Addresses

☐ Check here if the other child's (or children's) address information is the same as listed in ⑤ .

☐ *If it is different, check here. Attach a sheet of paper and write "DV-105, Other Children's Addresses" for a title. List other children's address information, including dates, and name of person child lived with.*

(7) Other Custody Case

Were you involved in, or do you know of, any other custody case for any child listed in this form?

☐ No ☐ Yes *If yes, fill out below and attach a copy of any custody or visitation orders if you have them:*

a. Name of each child in other custody case: _____

_____

b. Type of case: ☐ Parentage (Paternity) ☐ Divorce ☐ Child Support ☐ Guardianship
☐ Juvenile/Dependency ☐ Domestic Violence
☐ Other *(specify):* _____

c. I was a ☐ Party ☐ Witness ☐ Other *(specify):* _____

d. Court *(name):* _____

Address: _____ County: _____ State: _____

e. Date of court order: _____

f. Case number *(if you have it):* _____

(8) Other People With or Claiming to Have Custody or Visitation Rights

Do you know of anyone who is not involved in this case who has or claims to have custody or visitation

rights with any child listed on this form? ☐ No ☐ Yes *If yes, fill out below:*

Name and address of that person:

_____

☐ Has custody ☐ Claims custody rights ☐ Claims visitation rights

For these children *(name of each child):*

_____

_____

☐ *Check here if you need more space. Attach a sheet of paper and write "DV-105, Other People With or Claiming Custody or Visitation" for a title.*

(9) ☐ Visitation

I ask the court to order that the person in ② have the following temporary visitation rights:
(Check all that apply)

a. ☐ No visitation until the hearing

b. ☐ No visitation after the hearing

c. ☐ The following visitation ☐ until the hearing ☐ after the hearing

(1) ☐ **Weekends** *(starting):* _____ *(The 1st weekend of the month is the 1st weekend with a Saturday.)*

☐ 1st ☐ 2nd ☐ 3rd ☐ 4th ☐ 5th weekend of month

from _____ at _____ ☐ a.m. ☐ p.m. to _____ at _____ ☐ a.m. ☐ p.m.
(day of week) *(time)* *(day of week)* *(time)*

(2) ☐ **Weekdays** *(starting):* _____

from _____ at _____ ☐ a.m. ☐ p.m. to _____ at _____ ☐ a.m. ☐ p.m.
(day of week) *(time)* *(day of week)* *(time)*

This is not a Court Order.

Case Number: _____

(10) ☐ **Other Visitation**

Attach a sheet of paper with other visitation days and times, like summer vacation, holidays, and birthdays. List dates and times. Write "DV-105, Visitation" for a title.

(11) ☐ **Responsibility for Transportation**

The parent will take or pick up the child or make arrangements for someone else to do so.

I ask the court to order that:

a. ☐ Mom ☐ Dad ☐ Other *(name):* _____ **take children to** the visits.

b. ☐ Mom ☐ Dad ☐ Other *(name):* _____ **pick up children from** the visits.

c. ☐ Drop-off / pick-up of children will be at *(address):* _____

d. ☐ Check here if other arrangement. Attach a sheet of paper and write *"DV-105, Responsibility for Transportation"* for a title.

(12) ☐ **Supervised Visitation**

a. I ask that the visitation in **(9)** be supervised by

☐ A professional supervisor ☐ A non-professional supervisor ☐ Other _____

Name and telephone number, if known: _____

b. I ask that the visitation in **(10)** be supervised by

☐ A professional supervisor ☐ A non-professional supervisor ☐ Other _____

Name and telephone number, if known: _____

c. I ask that any costs for supervision be paid by:

Mom _____ % Dad _____ % Other *(name)* _____ _____ %

(13) ☐ **Travel With Children**

I ask the court to order that:

☐ Mom ☐ Dad ☐ Other *(name):* _____ **must** have written permission from the other parent, or a court order, to take the children outside of:

a. ☐ The State of California ☐ County of: _____

b. ☐ Other place(s) *(list):* _____

(14) ☐ **Child Abduction Risk**

☐ I believe that there is a risk the other parent will take our child out of California and hide the child from me.

If you check this box you must fill out and attach Form DV-108, Request for Order: No Travel with Children.

Important Instructions

- **You must tell the court if you find out any other information about a custody case in any court for the children listed on this form.**
- **If the court makes a temporary custody order, the parent receiving custody must not take the child out of California without a noticed hearing. (See Family Code §3063.)**

This is not a Court Order.

0264

**Request for Order:
No Travel with Children**

Case Number:

This form is attached to DV-105, *Request for Child Custody and Visitation Orders.*

(1) Your name: _____   ☐ Mom   ☐ Dad   ☐ Other*

(2) Other parent's name: _____   ☐ Mom   ☐ Dad   ☐ Other*

If "Other," specify relationship with children: _____

(3) Do you think the other parent may take the children without your permission to:

a. ☐ Another county in California?   ☐ Yes   ☐ No   *If "yes," what county?* _____

b. ☐ Another state?   ☐ Yes   ☐ No   *If "yes," what state?* _____

c. ☐ A foreign country?   ☐ Yes   ☐ No   *If "yes," what country ?* _____

If "Yes," is the other parent a citizen of that country?   ☐ Yes   ☐ No

If "Yes," does the other parent have family or emotional ties to that country?   ☐ Yes   ☐ No

Explain:

_____

_____

(4) Why do you think the other parent may take the children without your permission?
The other parent: *(Check all that apply)*

a. ☐ Has violated — or threatened to violate — a custody or visitation order in the past.

b. ☐ Does not have strong ties to California.

c. ☐ Has done things recently that make it easy for him or her to take the children away without permission.
He or she has: *(Check all that apply)*

☐ Quit his or her job   ☐ Sold his or her home
☐ Closed a bank account   ☐ Ended a lease
☐ Sold or gotten rid of assets   ☐ Hidden or destroyed documents
☐ Applied for a passport, birth certificate, or school or medical records

d. ☐ Has a history of: *(Check all that apply)*
☐ Domestic violence
☐ Child abuse
☐ Not cooperating with me in parenting
☐ Child abduction

e. ☐ Has a criminal record

f. Please explain your answers to a–e:

_____

_____

_____

_____

_____

This is not a Court Order.

Judicial Council of California, *www.courts.ca.gov*
Revised January 1, 2012, Mandatory Form
Family Code, § 3048

Request for Order: No Travel with Children
(Domestic Violence Prevention)

DV-108, Page 1 of 2 →

What orders do you want? Check the boxes that apply to your case. ☑

(5) ☐ **Post a Bond**

I ask the court to order the other parent to post a bond for $ _____ . If the other parent takes the children without my permission, I can use this money to bring the children back.

(6) ☐ **Do Not Move Without My Permission or Court Order**

I ask the court to order the other parent *not* to move with the children without my written permission or a court order.

(7) ☐ **No Travel Without My Permission**

I ask the court to order the other parent *not* to travel with the children outside: *(Check all that apply)*

☐ This county ☐ California ☐ The United States ☐ Other *(specify):* _____

(8) ☐ **Notify Other State of Travel Restrictions**

I ask the court to order the other parent to register this order in the state of _____ before the children can travel to that state for visits.

(9) ☐ **Turn In and Do Not Apply for Passports or Other Vital Documents**

I ask the court to order the other parent to turn in and *not* apply for passports or other documents (such as visas or birth certificates) that can be used for travel.

(10) ☐ **Provide Itinerary and Other Travel Documents**

If the other parent is allowed to travel with the children, I ask the court to order the other parent to give me before leaving:

☐ The children's travel itinerary

☐ Copies of round-trip airline tickets

☐ Addresses and telephone numbers where the children can be reached

☐ An open airline ticket for me in case the children are not returned

☐ Other *(specify):*

(11) ☐ **Notify Foreign Embassy or Consulate of Passport Restrictions**

I ask the court to order the other parent to notify the embassy or consulate of _____ of this order and to provide the court with proof of that notification within _____ calendar days.

(12) ☐ **Foreign Custody and Visitation Order**

I ask the court to order the other parent to get a custody and visitation order equal to the most recent U.S. order before the child can travel to that country for visits. I understand that foreign orders may be changed or enforced depending on the laws of the country.

(13) I declare under penalty of perjury under the laws of the State of California that the information on this form is true and correct.

Date: _____

_____   ▶ _____
Type or print your name   *Sign your name*

This is not a Court Order.

0266

DV-109   Notice of Court Hearing

Clerk stamps date here when form is filed.

(1) Name of Person Asking for Order:

_____

Your lawyer in this case *(if you have one):*
Name: _____ State Bar No.: _____
Firm Name: _____

Address *(If you have a lawyer for this case, give your lawyer's information. If you do not have a lawyer and want to keep your home address private, give a different mailing address instead. You do not have to give your telephone, fax, or e-mail.)*
Address: _____
City: _____ State: _____ Zip: _____
Telephone: _____ Fax: _____
E-Mail Address: _____

Fill in court name and street address:

Superior Court of California, County of

(2) Name of Person to Be Restrained:

_____

The court will fill out the rest of this form.

Court fills in case number when form is filed.

Case Number:

(3) Notice of Hearing

A court hearing is scheduled on the request for restraining orders against the person in (2):

Name and address of court if different from above:

Hearing Date → Date: _____ Time: _____

Dept.: _____ Room: _____

_____
_____
_____

(4) Temporary Restraining Orders (Any orders granted are attached on form DV-110.)

a. Temporary Restraining Orders for personal conduct and stay-away orders as requested in form DV-100, *Request for Domestic Violence Restraining Order,* are *(check only one box below):*
   (1) ☐ All **GRANTED** until the court hearing.
   (2) ☐ All **DENIED** until the court hearing. *(Specify reasons for denial in b, below.)*
   (3) ☐ Partly **GRANTED** and partly **DENIED** until the court hearing. *(Specify reasons for denial in b, below.)*

b. Reasons for denial of some or all of those personal conduct and stay-away orders as requested in form DV-100, *Request for Domestic Violence Restraining Order,* are:
   (1) ☐ The facts as stated in form DV-100 do not show reasonable proof of a past act or acts of abuse. (Family Code, §§ 6320 and 6320.5.)

   (2) ☐ The facts do not describe in sufficient detail the most recent incidents of abuse, such as what happened, the dates, who did what to whom, or any injuries or history of abuse.

   (3) ☐ Further explanation of reason for denial, or reason not listed above:

   _____
   _____

Judicial Council of California, *www.courts.ca.gov*
Revised January 1, 2019, Mandatory Form
Family Code § 242
Approved by DOJ

Notice of Court Hearing
(Domestic Violence Prevention)

DV-109, Page 1 of 3

Case Number:

⑤ Confidential Information Regarding Minor

a. ☐ A *Request to Keep Minor's Information Confidential* (form DV-160) was made and **GRANTED** *(see form DV-165, Order on Request to Keep Minor's Information Confidential, served with this form.)*

b. **If the request was granted, the information described on the order (form DV-165, item ⑧) must be kept CONFIDENTIAL. The disclosure or misuse of the information is punishable as contempt of court, with a fine of up to $1,000 or possible sanctions.**

⑥ Service of Documents by the Person in ①

At least ☐ **five** ☐ _____ **days before the hearing,** someone age 18 or older—**not you or anyone to be protected**—must personally give (serve) a court file-stamped copy of this form (DV-109, *Notice of Court Hearing)* to the person in ② along with a copy of all the forms indicated below:

a. DV-100, *Request for Domestic Violence Restraining Order* (file-stamped)

b. ☐ DV-110, *Temporary Restraining Order* (file-stamped) **IF GRANTED**

c. DV-120, *Response to Request for Domestic Violence Restraining Order* (blank form)

d. DV-120-INFO, *How Can I Respond to a Request for Domestic Violence Restraining Order?*

e. DV-250, *Proof of Service by Mail* (blank form)

f. ☐ DV-170, *Notice of Order Protecting Information of a Minor,* and DV-165, *Order on Request to Keep Minor's Information Confidential* (file-stamped), **IF GRANTED**

g. ☐ Other *(specify):* _____

Date: _____   _____
                                              Judicial Officer

Right to Cancel Hearing: Information for the Person in ①

- If item ④(a)(2) or ④(a)(3) is checked, the judge has denied some or all of the temporary orders you requested until the court hearing. The judge may make the orders you want after the court hearing. You can keep the hearing date, or you can cancel your request for orders so there is no court hearing.

- If you want to cancel the hearing, use form DV-112, *Waiver of Hearing on Denied Request for Temporary Restraining Order.* Fill it out and file it with the court as soon as possible. You may file a new request for orders, on the same or different facts, at a later time.

- If you cancel the hearing, do not serve the documents listed in item ⑥ on the other person.

- If you want to keep the hearing date, you must have all of the documents listed in item ⑥ served on the other person within the time listed in item ⑥.

- At the hearing, the judge will consider whether denial of any requested orders will jeopardize your safety and the safety of children for whom you are requesting custody or visitation.

- You must come to the hearing if you want the judge to make restraining orders or continue any orders already made. If you cancel the hearing or do not come to the hearing, any restraining orders made on form DV-110 will end on the date of the hearing.

Case Number:

To the Person in ❶ :

- The court cannot make the restraining orders after the court hearing unless the person in ② has been personally given (served) a copy of your request and any temporary orders. To show that the person in ② has been served, the person who served the forms must fill out a proof of service form. form DV-200, *Proof of Personal Service,* may be used.

- For information about service, read form DV-200-INFO, *What Is "Proof of Personal Service"?*

- If you are unable to serve the person in ② in time, you may ask for more time to serve the documents. Read form DV-115-INFO, *How to Ask for a New Hearing Date.*

To the Person in ❷ :

- If you want to respond in writing, mail a copy of your completed form DV-120, *Response to Request for Domestic Violence Restraining Order,* to the person in ① and file it with the court. You cannot mail form DV-120 yourself. Someone age 18 or older — **not you** — must do it.

- To show that the person in ① has been served by mail, the person who mailed the form must fill out a proof of service form. Form DV-250, *Proof of Service by Mail,* may be used. File the completed form with the court before the hearing and bring a copy with you to the hearing.

- For information about responding to a restraining order and filing your answer, read form DV-120-INFO, *How Can I Respond to a Request for Domestic Violence Restraining Order?.*

- Whether or not you respond in writing, go to the hearing if you want the judge to hear from you before making an order. You may tell the judge why you agree or disagree with the orders requested. You may bring witnesses and other evidence.

- **At the hearing, the judge may make restraining orders against you that could last up to five years.**

- **The judge may also make other orders about your children, child support, spousal support, money, and property and may order you to turn in or sell any firearms that you own or possess.**

 ### Request for Accommodations

Assistive listening systems, computer-assisted real-time captioning, or sign language interpreter services are available if you ask at least five days before the hearing. Contact the clerk's office or go to *www.courts.ca.gov/forms* for *Request for Accommodations by Persons with Disabilities and Response* (form MC-410). (Civ. Code, § 54.8.)

(Clerk will fill out this part.)

—Clerk's Certificate—

*Clerk's Certificate
[seal]*

I certify that this *Notice of Court Hearing* is a true and correct copy of the original on file in the court.

Date: _____ Clerk, by _____, Deputy

0269

DV-110 | Temporary Restraining Order

Person in ① must complete items ①, ②, and ③ only.

① Name of Protected Person:

_____

Your lawyer in this case *(if you have one)*:

Name: _____ State Bar No.: _____

Firm Name: _____

Address *(If you have a lawyer for this case, give your lawyer's information. If you do not have a lawyer and want to keep your home address private, give a different mailing address instead. You do not have to give your telephone, fax, or e-mail.):*

Address: _____

City: _____ State: _____ Zip: _____

Telephone: _____ Fax: _____

E-mail Address: _____

Clerk stamps date here when form is filed.

Fill in court name and street address:

Superior Court of California, County of

Court fills in case number when form is filed.

Case Number:

② Name of Restrained Person:

_____

Description of restrained person:

Sex: ☐ M ☐ F   Height: _____ Weight: _____ Hair Color: _____ Eye Color: _____
Race: _____ Age: _____ Date of Birth: _____
Address *(if known):* _____
City: _____ State: _____ Zip: _____
Relationship to protected person: _____

③ ☐ Additional Protected Persons

In addition to the person named in ①, the following persons are protected by temporary orders as indicated in items ⑥ and ⑦ *(family or household members):*

Full name	Relationship to person in ①	Sex	Age
_____	_____	____	____
_____	_____	____	____
_____	_____	____	____

☐ *Check here if there are additional protected persons. List them on an attached sheet of paper and write, "DV-110, Additional Protected Persons" as a title.*

The court will complete the rest of this form.

④ Court Hearing

This order expires at the end of the hearing stated below:

Hearing Date: _____ Time: _____ ☐ a.m. ☐ p.m.

This is a Court Order.

Judicial Council of California, *www.courts.ca.gov*
Revised July 1, 2016, Mandatory Form
Family Code, § 6200 et seq.
Approved by DOJ

**Temporary Restraining Order
(CLETS—TRO)
(Domestic Violence Prevention)**

DV-110, Page 1 of 6

Case Number: _____

⑤ ☐ **Criminal Protective Order**

a. ☐ A criminal protective order on form CR-160, *Criminal Protective Order—Domestic Violence,* is in effect.
   Case Number: _____ County: _____ Expiration Date: _____

b. ☐ No information has been provided to the judge about a criminal protective order.

To the person in ❷

The court has granted the temporary orders checked below. If you do not obey these orders, you can be arrested and charged with a crime. You may be sent to jail for up to one year, pay a fine of up to $1,000, or both.

⑥ **Personal Conduct Orders** ☐ Not requested ☐ Denied until the hearing ☐ Granted as follows:

a. You must **not** do the following things to the person in ① and ☐ persons in ③ :

   ☐ Harass, attack, strike, threaten, assault *(sexually or otherwise),* hit, follow, stalk, molest, destroy personal property, disturb the peace, keep under surveillance, impersonate *(on the Internet, electronically or otherwise),* or block movements

   ☐ Contact, either directly or indirectly, in any way, including but not limited to, by telephone, mail, e-mail or other electronic means

   ☐ Take any action, directly or through others, to obtain the addresses or locations of the persons in① *and*③. *(If this item is not checked, the court has found good cause not to make this order.)*

b. Peaceful written contact through a lawyer or process server or another person for service of Form DV-120 *(Response to Request for Domestic Violence Restraining Order)* or other legal papers related to a court case is allowed and does not violate this order.

c. ☐ Exceptions: Brief and peaceful contact with the person in ①, and peaceful contact with children in ③, as required for court-ordered visitation of children, is allowed unless a criminal protective order says otherwise.

⑦ **Stay-Away Order** ☐ Not requested ☐ Denied until the hearing ☐ Granted as follows:

a. You **must** stay at least *(specify):* _____ yards away from *(check all that apply):*

   ☐ The person in①   ☐ School of person in ①
   ☐ Home of person in ①   ☐ The persons in ③
   ☐ The job or workplace of person in①   ☐ The child(ren)'s school or child care
   ☐ Vehicle of person in①   ☐ Other *(specify):* _____

b. ☐ Exceptions: Brief and peaceful contact with the person in ①, and peaceful contact with children in ③, as required for court-ordered visitation of children, is allowed unless a criminal protective order says otherwise.

⑧ **Move-Out Order** ☐ Not requested ☐ Denied until the hearing ☐ Granted as follows:

You must take only personal clothing and belongings needed until the hearing and move out immediately from *(address):* _____

This is a Court Order.

Revised July 1, 2016   **Temporary Restraining Order**   DV-110, Page 2 of 6
(CLETS—TRO)
(Domestic Violence Prevention)   →

Case Number: _____

⑨ No Guns or Other Firearms or Ammunition

a. You cannot own, possess, have, buy or try to buy, receive or try to receive, or in any other way get guns, other firearms, or ammunition.

b. You must:

- Sell to, or store with, a licensed gun dealer, or turn in to a law enforcement agency, any guns or other firearms within your immediate possession or control. Do so within 24 hours of being served with this order.
- Within 48 hours of receiving this order, file with the court a receipt that proves guns have been turned in, stored, or sold. (You may use Form DV-800, *Proof of Firearms Turned In, Sold, or Stored,* for the receipt.) Bring a court filed copy to the hearing.

c. ☐ The court has received information that you own or possess a firearm.

⑩ Record Unlawful Communications

☐ **Not requested** ☐ **Denied until the hearing** ☐ **Granted as follows:**

The person in ① can record communications made by you that violate the judge's orders.

⑪ Care of Animals ☐ **Not requested** ☐ **Denied until the hearing** ☐ **Granted as follows:**

The person in ① is given the sole possession, care, and control of the animals listed below. The person in ② must stay at least _____ yards away from and not take, sell, transfer, encumber, conceal, molest, attack, strike, threaten, harm, or otherwise dispose of the following animals:

_____

_____

⑫ Child Custody and Visitation ☐ **Not requested** ☐ **Denied until the hearing** ☐ **Granted as follows:**

Child custody and visitation are ordered on the attached form DV-140, *Child Custody and Visitation Order* or *(specify other form):* _____ . The parent with temporary custody of the child must not remove the child from California unless the court allows it after a noticed hearing (Fam. Code, § 3063).

⑬ Child Support

Not ordered now but may be ordered after a noticed hearing.

⑭ Property Control ☐ **Not requested** ☐ **Denied until the hearing** ☐ **Granted as follows:**

Until the hearing, *only* the person in ① can use, control, and possess the following property:

_____

⑮ Debt Payment ☐ **Not requested** ☐ **Denied until the hearing** ☐ **Granted as follows:**

The person in ② must make these payments until this order ends:

Pay to: _____ For: _____ Amount: $ _____ Due date: _____

Pay to: _____ For: _____ Amount: $ _____ Due date: _____

⑯ Property Restraint ☐ **Not requested** ☐ **Denied until the hearing** ☐ **Granted as follows:**

If the people in ① and ② are married to each other or are registered domestic partners, ☐ the person in ① ☐ the person in ② must not transfer, borrow against, sell, hide, or get rid of or destroy any property, including animals, except in the usual course of business or for necessities of life. In addition, each person must notify the other of any new or big expenses and explain them to the court. *(The person in ② cannot contact the person in ① if the court has made a "no contact" order.)*

Peaceful written contact through a lawyer or a process server or other person for service of legal papers related to a court case is allowed and does not violate this order.

This is a Court Order.

Case Number: _____

(17) Spousal Support

Not ordered now but may be ordered after a noticed hearing.

(18) Rights to Mobile Device and Wireless Phone Account

    a. Property control of mobile device and wireless phone account

      ☐ Not requested   ☐ Denied until the hearing   ☐ Granted as follows:

      Until the hearing, only the person in ① can use, control, and possess the following property:

      Mobile device *(describe)* _____ and account *(phone number):* _____

      Mobile device *(describe)* _____ and account *(phone number):* _____

      Mobile device *(describe)* _____ and account *(phone number):* _____

      ☐ *Check here if you need more space. Attach a sheet of paper and write "DV-110 Rights to Mobile Device and Wireless Phone Account" as a title.*

    b. Debt Payment   ☐ Not requested   ☐ Denied until the hearing   ☐ Granted as follows:

      The person in ② must make these payments until this order ends:

      Pay to *(wireless service provider):* _____ Amount: $_____ Due date: _____

    c. Transfer of Wireless Phone Account

      Not ordered now but may be ordered after a noticed hearing.

(19) Insurance

    ☐ The person in ①   ☐ the person in ② is ordered NOT to cash, borrow against, cancel, transfer, dispose of, or change the beneficiaries of any insurance or coverage held for the benefit of the parties, or their child(ren), if any, for whom support may be ordered, or both.

(20) Lawyer's Fees and Costs

Not ordered now but may be ordered after a noticed hearing.

(21) Payments for Costs and Services

Not ordered now but may be ordered after a noticed hearing.

(22) Batterer Intervention Program

Not ordered now but may be ordered after a noticed hearing.

(23) Other Orders   ☐ **Not requested**   ☐ **Denied until the hearing**   ☐ **Granted as follows:**

_____

_____

_____

_____

_____

_____

_____

    ☐ *Check here if there are additional orders. List them on an attached sheet of paper and write "DV-110, Other Orders" as a title.*

(24) No Fee to Serve (Notify) Restrained Person

If the sheriff serves this order, he or she will do so for free.

Date: _____   _____

                                              Judge (or Judicial Officer)

This is a Court Order.

Case Number:

Warnings and Notices to the Restrained Person in ❷

If You Do Not Obey This Order, You Can Be Arrested And Charged With a Crime.

- If you do not obey this order, you can go to jail or prison and/or pay a fine.
- It is a felony to take or hide a child in violation of this order.
- If you travel to another state or to tribal lands or make the protected person do so, with the intention of disobeying this order, you can be charged with a federal crime.

You Cannot Have Guns, Firearms, And/Or Ammunition.

You cannot own, have, possess, buy or try to buy, receive or try to receive, or otherwise get guns, other firearms, and/or ammunition while the order is in effect. If you do, you can go to jail and pay a $1,000 fine. You must sell to or store with a licensed gun dealer or turn in to a law enforcement agency any guns or other firearms that you have or control. The judge will ask you for proof that you did so. If you do not obey this order, you can be charged with a crime. Federal law says you cannot have guns or ammunition while the order is in effect.

Service of Order by Mail

If the judge makes a restraining order at the hearing, which has the same orders as in this form, you will get a copy of that order by mail at your last known address, which is written in ❷. If this address is incorrect, or to find out if the orders were made permanent, contact the court.

Child Custody, Visitation, and Support

- **Child custody and visitation:** If you do not go to the hearing, the judge can make custody and visitation orders for your children without hearing from you.
- **Child support:** The judge can order child support based on the income of both parents. The judge can also have that support taken directly from a parent's paycheck. Child support can be a lot of money, and usually you have to pay until the child is age 18. File and serve a *Financial Statement (Simplified)* (form FL-155) or an *Income and Expense Declaration* (form FL-150) if you want the judge to have information about your finances. Otherwise, the court may make support orders without hearing from you.
- **Spousal support:** File and serve an *Income and Expense Declaration* (form FL-150) so the judge will have information about your finances. Otherwise, the court may make support orders without hearing from you.

Instructions for Law Enforcement

This order is effective when made. It is enforceable by any law enforcement agency that has received the order, is shown a copy of the order, or has verified its existence on the California Law Enforcement Telecommunications System (CLETS). If the law enforcement agency has not received proof of service on the restrained person, and the restrained person was not present at the court hearing, the agency shall advise the restrained person of the terms of the order and then shall enforce it. Violations of this order are subject to criminal penalties.

Arrest Required if Order Is Violated

If an officer has probable cause to believe that the restrained person had notice of the order and has disobeyed the order, the officer must arrest the restrained person. (Pen. Code, §§ 836(c)(1), 13701(b).) A violation of the order may be a violation of Penal Code section 166 or 273.6.

This is a Court Order.

If the Protected Person Contacts the Restrained Person

Even if the protected person invites or consents to contact with the restrained person, the orders remain in effect and must be enforced. The protected person cannot be arrested for inviting or consenting to contact with the restrained person. The orders can be changed only by another court order. (Pen. Code, §13710(b).)

Conflicting Orders–Priorities for Enforcement

If more than one restraining order has been issued protecting the protected person from the restrained person, the orders must be enforced according to the following priorities (see Pen. Code, § 136.2, and Fam. Code, §§ 6383(h), 6405(b)):

1. *EPO:* If one of the orders is an *Emergency Protective Order* (form EPO-001), and it is more restrictive than other restraining or protective orders, it has precedence in enforcement over all other orders.

2. *No-Contact Order:* If there is no EPO, a no-contact order that is included in a restraining or protective order has precedence in enforcement over any other restraining or protective order.

3. *Criminal Order:* If none of the orders includes a no-contact order, a domestic violence protective order issued in a criminal case takes precedence in enforcement over any conflicting civil court order. Any nonconflicting terms of the civil restraining order remain in effect and enforceable.

4. *Family, Juvenile, or Civil Order:* If more than one family, juvenile, or other civil restraining or protective order has been issued, the one that was issued last must be enforced.

Child Custody and Visitation

- The custody and visitation orders are on form DV-140, items ③ and ④ They are sometimes also written on additional pages or referenced in DV-140 or other orders that are not part of the restraining order.

- **Forms DV-100 and DV-105 are not orders. Do not enforce them.**

Certificate of Compliance With VAWA

This temporary protective order meets all "full faith and credit" requirements of the Violence Against Women Act, 18 U.S.C. § 2265 (1994) (VAWA), upon notice of the restrained person. This court has jurisdiction over the parties and the subject matter; the restrained person has been or will be afforded notice and a timely opportunity to be heard as provided by the laws of this jurisdiction. **This order is valid and entitled to enforcement in each jurisdiction throughout the 50 states of the United States, the District of Columbia, all tribal lands, and all U.S. territories, commonwealths, and possessions and shall be enforced as if it were an order of that jurisdiction.**

(Clerk will fill out this part.)

—Clerk's Certificate—

Clerk's Certificate
[seal]

I certify that this *Temporary Restraining Order* is a true and correct copy of the original on file in the court.

Date: _____ Clerk, by _____ , Deputy

This is a Court Order.

Temporary Restraining Order
(CLETS—TRO)
(Domestic Violence Prevention)

0275

DV-112 — Waiver of Hearing on Denied Request for Temporary Restraining Order

*Use this form **only** to waive (cancel) the hearing date in item ③ on Form DV-109, Notice of Court Hearing.*

① Name of Person Asking for Protection:

_____

② Name of Person to Be Restrained:

_____

Fill in court name and street address:

Superior Court of California, County of

Fill in case number:

Case Number:

To the Person in ❶

- Some or all of the temporary restraining orders you requested were denied for the reasons listed on Form DV-109, *Notice of Court Hearing.*
- The court has set a hearing and might make the orders you want after the hearing.
- Use this form **only** if you want to cancel the hearing date listed on Form DV-109, item ③. If you want to cancel the hearing, sign this form below and file it with the court clerk. Do not serve Form DV-109 and other papers on the person in ②.
- If you already served Form DV-109 and other papers on the person in ②, you must notify that person that you have canceled the hearing. If the person in ② files a response before you file this form, the court may still hear the case.
- If the hearing is canceled, any temporary orders made on Form DV-110, *Temporary Restraining Order* will end on the hearing date. You may file a new request for temporary restraining orders on the same or different facts at a later date.

I have read this form and I understand that I have a right to a court hearing. By signing below, I am asking the court to cancel the hearing listed on Form DV-109, *Notice of Court Hearing.* I understand that any orders already made by the court on Form DV-110, *Temporary Restraining Order* will end on the hearing date.

I declare under penalty of perjury under the laws of the State of California that the information above is true and correct.

Date: _____

_____   ▶ _____
Type or print your name   *Sign your name*

This is not a Court Order.

Judicial Council of California, *www.courts.ca.gov*
Revised January 1, 2012, Optional Form
Family Code, § 6320.5

**Waiver of Hearing on Denied Request
for Temporary Restraining Order**
(Domestic Violence Prevention)

DV-112, Page 1 of 1

DV-115   **Request to Continue Hearing**

Use this form to ask the court to change the hearing date listed on form DV-109, *Notice of Court Hearing.* (Read DV-115-INFO, *How to Ask for a New Hearing Date,* for more information).

Clerk stamps date here when form is filed.

Fill in court name and street address:

Superior Court of California, County of

Fill in case number:

Case Number:

① Party Seeking Continuance

a. Full Name: _____

I am the: ☐ Party seeking protection.
            ☐ Restrained Party.

Your Lawyer *(if you have one for this case):*
Name: _____ State Bar No.: _____
Firm Name: _____

b. Your Address *(If you have a lawyer, give your lawyer's information. If you do not have a lawyer and want to keep your home address private, you may give a different mailing address instead. You do not have to give telephone, fax, or e-mail.)*
Address: _____
City: _____ State: _____ Zip: _____
Telephone: _____ Fax: _____
E-Mail Address: _____

② Other Party

Full Name: _____

③ Request to Continue Hearing

a. I ask the court to continue the hearing currently scheduled for *(date):* _____

b. I request that the hearing be continued because *(check any that apply):*

   (1) ☐ I could not get the papers served before the hearing date.

   (2) ☐ I am the restrained party, and this is my first request to continue the hearing.

   (3) ☐ I need more time to hire a lawyer or prepare for the hearing or trial.

   (4) ☐ Other good cause as stated ☐ below ☐ on Attachment 3b(4).

_____
_____
_____
_____
_____
_____
_____
_____

This is not a Court Order.

Judicial Council of California, *www.courts.ca.gov*
Revised July 1, 2016, Mandatory Form
Family Code, § 245, Approved by DOJ

**Request to Continue Hearing
(Temporary Restraining Order)
(Domestic Violence Prevention)**

DV-115, Page 1 of 2

Case Number:

④ Extension of Temporary Restraining Order

a. ☐ A *Temporary Restraining Order* (Form DV-110) was issued on *(date):* _____ .
   Please attach a copy of the order if you have one.

b. **Notice: If the hearing date is continued, the *Temporary Restraining Order* (Form DV-110) will remain in effect until the end of the new hearing, unless otherwise ordered by the court.**

I declare under penalty of perjury under the laws of the State of California that the information above is true and correct.

Date:_____

_____
Type or print name of
☐ Lawyer   ☐ Party Without Lawyer

▶ _____
Sign your name

DV-120

Response to Request for Domestic Violence Restraining Order

Clerk stamps date here when form is filed.

(1) Name of Person Asking for Protection:
(See Form DV-100, item (1)):

_____

(2) Your Name:

_____

Your lawyer in this case *(if you have one):*
Name: _____ State Bar No.: _____
Firm Name: _____
Address *(If you have a lawyer for this case, give your lawyer's information. If you do not have a lawyer and want to keep your home address private, give a different mailing address instead. You do not have to give your telephone, fax, or e-mail.):*
Address: _____
City: _____ State: _____ Zip: _____
Telephone: _____ Fax: _____
E-Mail Address: _____

Fill in court name and street address:

Superior Court of California, County of

Fill in case number:

Case Number:

(3) Use this form to respond to the *Request for Domestic Violence Restraining Order* (Form DV-100).

- Fill out this form and take it to the court clerk.
- Have the person in (1) served by mail with a copy of this form and any attached pages. (See Form DV-250, *Proof of Service by Mail.*)
- For more information, read Form DV-120-INFO, *How Can I Respond to a Request for Domestic Violence Restraining Order?*
- This form is for a response to a restraining order request. For more information about how to request your own restraining order, read Form DV-505-INFO and Form DV-120-INFO (see the section called *"What if I need a restraining order against the other person?"*)

> **The judge will consider your Response at the hearing.**
> Write your hearing date, time, and place from Form DV-109, *Notice of Court Hearing,* item (3), here:
>
> **Hearing Date →** Date: _____ Time: _____
> Dept.: _____ Room: _____
>
> **You must obey the orders in Form DV-110, *Temporary Restraining Order,* until the hearing.** At the hearing, the court may make restraining orders against you that could last up to five years and could be renewed.

(4) ☐ Relationship to Person Asking for Protection
　a. ☐ I agree to the relationship listed in item (4) on Form DV-100.
　b. ☐ I do not agree that the other party and I have or had the relationship listed in item (4) on Form DV-100 because: _____

(5) ☐ Other Protected People
　a. ☐ I agree to the order requested.
　b. ☐ I do not agree to the order requested, ☐ but I would agree to: _____

_____

(Specify your reasons in item 25, page 5, of this form.)

This is not a Court Order.

Judicial Council of California, *www.courts.ca.gov*
Revised July 1, 2016, Mandatory Form
Family Code, § 6200 et seq.

**Response to Request for Domestic Violence
Restraining Order**
(Domestic Violence Prevention)

Case Number: _____

(6) ☐ **Personal Conduct Orders**
   a. ☐ I agree to the orders requested.
   b. ☐ I do not agree to the order requested,   ☐ but I would agree to: _____
   _____
   (Specify your reasons in item 25, page 5, of this form.)

(7) ☐ **Stay-Away Order**
   a. ☐ I agree to the order requested.
   b. ☐ I do not agree to the order requested,   ☐ but I would agree to: _____
   _____
   (Specify your reasons in item 25, page 5, of this form.)

(8) ☐ **Move-Out Order**
   a. ☐ I agree to the order requested.
   b. ☐ I do not agree to the order requested,   ☐ but I would agree to: _____
   _____
   (Specify your reasons in item 25, page 5, of this form.)

(9) **Guns or Other Firearms or Ammunition**
   If you were served with Form DV-110, Temporary Restraining Order, *you must turn in any guns or firearms in your immediate possession or control. You must file a receipt with the court from a law enforcement agency or a licensed gun dealer within 48 hours after you received Form DV-110.*
   a. ☐ I do not own or have any guns or firearms.
   b. ☐ I ask for an exemption from the firearms prohibition under Family Code section 6389(h) because
       (specify): _____
   c. ☐ I have turned in my guns and firearms to law enforcement or sold them to, or stored them with, a
       licensed gun dealer. A copy of the receipt showing that I turned in, sold, or stored my firearms
       (check all that apply):
       ☐ is attached   ☐ has already been filed with the court.

(10) ☐ **Record Unlawful Communications**
   a. ☐ I agree to the order requested.
   b. ☐ I do not agree to the order requested,   ☐ but I would agree to: _____
   _____
   (Specify your reasons in item 25, page 5, of this form.)

(11) ☐ **Care of Animals**
   a. ☐ I agree to the order requested.
   b. ☐ I do not agree to the order requested,   ☐ but I would agree to: _____
   _____
   (Specify your reasons in item 25, page 5, of this form.)

This is not a Court Order.

**Response to Request for Domestic Violence
Restraining Order**
(Domestic Violence Prevention)

Case Number: _____

(12) ☐ **Child Custody and Visitation**
   a. ☐ I agree to the order requested.
   b. ☐ I do not agree to the order requested. *(Specify your reasons in item 25, page 5, of this form.)*
   c. ☐ I am not the parent of the child listed in Form DV-105, *Request for Child Custody and Visitation Orders.*
   d. ☐ I ask for the following custody order *(specify):* _____
   _____

   e. ☐ I do ☐ I do not   agree to the orders requested to limit the child's travel as listed in Form DV-108, *Request for Order: No Travel with Children.*

   You and the other parent may tell the court that you want to be legal parents of the children (use Form DV-180, Agreement and Judgment of Parentage).

(13) ☐ **Child Support** *(Check all that apply):*
   a. ☐ I agree to the order requested.
   b. ☐ I do not agree to the order requested. *(Specify your reasons in item 25, page 5, of this form.)*
   c. ☐ I agree to pay guideline child support.

   Whether or not you agree to pay support, you must fill out, serve, and file Form FL-150, Income and Expense Declaration, or Form FL-155, Financial Statement (Simplified).

(14) ☐ **Property Control**
   a. ☐ I agree to the order requested.
   b. ☐ I do not agree to the order requested,   ☐ but I would agree to: _____
   _____
   (Specify your reasons in item 25, page 5, of this form.)

(15) ☐ **Debt Payment**
   a. ☐ I agree to the order requested.
   b. ☐ I do not agree to the order requested,   ☐ but I would agree to: _____
   _____
   (Specify your reasons in item 25, page 5, of this form.)

(16) ☐ **Property Restraint**
   a. ☐ I agree to the order requested.
   b. ☐ I do not agree to the order requested,   ☐ but I would agree to: _____
   _____
   (Specify your reasons in item 25, page 5, of this form.)

(17) ☐ **Spousal Support**
   a. ☐ I agree to the order requested.
   b. ☐ I do not agree to the order requested,   ☐ but I would agree to: _____
   _____
   (Specify your reasons in item 25, page 5, of this form.)

   Whether or not you agree, you must fill out, serve, and file Form FL-150, Income and Expense Declaration.

This is not a Court Order.

**Response to Request for Domestic Violence
Restraining Order**
(Domestic Violence Prevention)

Case Number:

(18) ☐ **Rights to Mobile Device and Wireless Phone Account**
    a. ☐ I agree to the order requested.
    b. ☐ I do not agree to the order requested,   ☐ but I would agree to: _____
    _____
    (Specify your reasons in item 25, page 5, of this form.)

(19) ☐ **Insurance**
    a. ☐ I agree to the order requested.
    b. ☐ I do not agree to the order requested,   ☐ but I would agree to: _____
    _____
    (Specify your reasons in item 25, page 5, of this form.)

(20) ☐ **Lawyer's Fees and Costs**
    a. ☐ I agree to the order requested.
    b. ☐ I do not agree to the order requested,   ☐ but I would agree to: _____
    _____
    (Specify your reasons in item 25, page 5, of this form.)
    c. ☐ I request the court to order payment of my lawyer's fees and costs.
    Whether or not you agree, you must fill out, serve, and file Form FL-150, Income and Expense Declaration.

(21) ☐ **Payments for Costs and Services**
    a. ☐ I agree to the order requested.
    b. ☐ I do not agree to the order requested,   ☐ but I would agree to: _____
    _____
    (Specify your reasons in item 25, page 5, of this form.)

(22) ☐ **Batterer Intervention Program**
    a. ☐ I agree to the order requested.
    b. ☐ I do not agree to the order requested,   ☐ but I would agree to: _____
    _____
    (Specify your reasons in item 25, page 5, of this form.)

(23) ☐ **Other Orders** *(see item 22 on Form DV-100)*
    a. ☐ I agree to the order requested.
    b. ☐ I do not agree to the order requested,   ☐ but I would agree to: _____
    _____
    (Specify your reasons in item 25, page 5, of this form.)

(24) ☐ **Out-of-Pocket Expenses**
    I ask the court to order payment of my out-of-pocket expenses because the temporary restraining order was issued without enough supporting facts. The expenses are:
    Item: _____   Amount: $ _____   Item: _____   Amount: $ _____
    You must fill out, serve, and file Form FL-150, Income and Expense Declaration.

This is not a Court Order.

Case Number:

25 ☐ Reasons I Do Not Agree to the Orders Requested

Explain your answers to each of the orders requested *(give specific facts and reasons):*

☐ *Check here if there is not enough space below for your answer. Put your complete answer on an attached sheet of paper and write, "DV-120, Reasons I Do Not Agree" as a title.*

_____
_____
_____
_____
_____
_____
_____
_____
_____
_____
_____
_____
_____
_____
_____
_____
_____
_____
_____
_____
_____
_____
_____

26 Number of pages attached to this form, if any: _____

I declare under penalty of perjury under the laws of the State of California that the information above is true and correct.

Date: _____

_____
Type or print your name

▶ _____
Sign your name

Date: _____

_____
Lawyer's name, if you have one

▶ _____
Lawyer's signature

This is not a Court Order.

DV-120-INFO How Can I Respond to a Request for Domestic Violence Restraining Order?

What is a Domestic Violence Restraining Order?

It is a court order that can help protect people who have been abused or threatened with abuse.

Abuse can be physical or emotional. It can be spoken or written.

What does the order do?

The court can order you to:

- Not contact or harm the protected person, including children or others listed as protected people
- Stay away from all protected people
- Not have any guns or ammunition
- Move out of the place that you share with the protected person
- Follow custody and visitation orders
- Pay child support
- Pay spousal support
- Obey property orders
- Follow other types of orders (listed on *Form DV-100*)

Who can ask for a domestic violence restraining order?

The person requesting the order must have a relationship with you:

- Someone you date or used to date
- Married, registered domestic partners, separated, engaged, or divorced
- Someone you live or lived with (more than just a roommate)
- A parent, grandparent, sibling, child, or grandchild related by blood, marriage, or adoption

I've been served with a request for domestic violence restraining order. What do I do now?

Read the papers very carefully. You must follow all the orders the judge made. The *Notice of Court Hearing* tells you when to appear in court. You should go to the hearing, if you do not agree to the orders requested. If you do not go to the hearing, the judge can make orders against you without hearing from you.

What if I don't obey the order?

The police can arrest you. You can go to jail and pay a fine. You must still follow the orders even if you are not a U.S. citizen. If you are worried about your immigration status, talk to an immigration lawyer.

How long does the order last?

If there is a *Temporary Restraining Order* in effect, it will last until the hearing date. At the hearing, the judge will decide whether to extend the order or cancel the order. The judge can extend the order for up to five years. Custody, visitation, child support, and spousal support orders can last longer than five years and they do not end when the restraining order ends.

What if I don't agree with what the order says?

You still must obey the orders until the hearing. If you do NOT agree with the orders the person is asking for, fill out Form DV-120, *Response to Request for Domestic Violence Restraining Order*. After you fill out the form, file it with the court clerk and "serve" the form on the person asking for the restraining order. "Serve" means to have someone 18 years or older—**not you**—mail a copy to the other party. The person who serves your form must fill out Form DV-250, *Proof of Service by Mail*. After Form DV-250 is completed, make sure it is filed with the court clerk. You will also have a chance at the hearing to tell your side of the story. For more information on how to prepare for the hearing, read Form DV-520-INFO, *Get Ready for the Restraining Order Court Hearing*.

Is there a cost to file my Response (Form DV-120)?

No.

What if I also have criminal charges against me?

See a lawyer. Anything you say or write, including in this case, can be used against you in your criminal case.

DV-120-INFO How Can I Respond to a Request for Domestic Violence Restraining Order?

What if I have a gun or ammunition?

If a restraining order is issued, you cannot own, possess, or have a gun, other firearm, or ammunition while the order is in effect. If you have a gun or other firearm in your immediate possession or control, you must sell it to, or store it with, a licensed gun dealer, or turn it in to a law enforcement agency. You must also prove to the court that you turned in or sold your gun. Read Form DV-800-INFO, *How Do I Turn In, Sell, or Store My Firearms?,* for more information.

Do I need a lawyer?

You are not entitled to a free court-appointed lawyer for this case but having a lawyer represent you or getting legal advice from a lawyer is a good idea, especially if you have children. If you cannot afford a lawyer, you can represent yourself. There is free or low-cost help available in every county. For help, ask the court clerk how to find free or low-cost legal services and self-help centers in your area. You can also get free help with child support at your local family law facilitator's office.

What if I do not speak English?

When you file Form DV-120, ask the court clerk if a court interpreter is available for your hearing. If an interpreter is not available, bring someone to interpret for you. Do NOT ask a child, a witness, or anyone to be protected by the order to interpret for you.

What if I am deaf or hard of hearing?

 Assistive listening systems, computer-assisted real-time captioning, or sign language interpreter services are available if you ask at least five days before the proceeding. Contact the clerks' office or go to *www.courts.ca.gov/forms* for *Request for Accommodations by Persons With Disabilities and Response* (Form MC-410). (Civ. Code, § 54.8.)

Can I use the restraining order to get divorced or terminate a domestic partnership?

No. These forms will not end your marriage or registered domestic partnership. You must file other forms to end your marriage or registered domestic partnership.

What if I have children with the other person?

The judge can make temporary orders for child custody and visitation. If the judge makes a temporary order for child custody, the parent with custody may not remove the child from California before notice to the other parent and a court hearing. Read the order for any other restrictions. There may be some exceptions. Ask a lawyer for more information.

What if I want to leave the county or state?

You must still comply with the restraining order, including custody and visitation orders. The restraining order is valid anywhere in the United States.

Will I see the person who asked for the order at the court hearing?

Yes. Assume that the person who is asking for the order will attend the hearing. Do not talk to him or her unless the judge or that person's attorney says that you can. Any temporary restraining order made by the court is in effect until the end of the hearing.

What if I need a restraining order against the other person?

Do not use this form to request a domestic violence restraining order. For information on how to file your own restraining order, read Form DV-505-INFO. You can also ask the court clerk about free or low-cost legal help.

What if I am a victim of domestic violence?

For a referral to a local domestic violence or legal assistance program, call the National Domestic Violence Hotline:

1-800-799-7233
TDD: 1-800-787-3224

It's free and private.
They can help you in more than 100 languages.

For help in your area, contact:

[Local information may be inserted]

0285

DV-130 Restraining Order After Hearing (Order of Protection)

☐ **Original Order** ☐ _____ **Amended Order**

(1) Name of Protected Person:

_____

Your lawyer in this case _(if you have one)_:
Name: _____ State Bar No.: _____
Firm Name: _____
Address _(If you have a lawyer for this case, give your lawyer's information. If you do not have a lawyer and want to keep your home address private, give a different mailing address instead. You do not have to give your telephone, fax, or e-mail.):_
Address: _____
City: _____ State: _____ Zip: _____
Telephone: _____ Fax: _____
E-Mail Address: _____

Fill in court name and street address:

Superior Court of California, County of

Clerk fills in case number when form is filed.

Case Number:

(2) Name of Restrained Person:

_____

Description of restrained person:

Sex: ☐ M ☐ F   Height: _____ Weight: _____ Hair Color: _____ Eye Color: _____
Race: _____ Age: _____ Date of Birth: _____
Mailing Address _(if known)_: _____
City: _____ State: _____ Zip: _____
Relationship to protected person: _____

(3) ☐ Additional Protected Persons

In addition to the person named in (1), the following persons are protected by orders as indicated in items (6) and (7) _(family or household members)_:

Full name	Relationship to person in (1)	Sex	Age
_____	_____	___	___
_____	_____	___	___

☐ _Check here if there are additional protected persons. List them on an attached sheet of paper and write, "DV-130, Additional Protected Persons," as a title._

(4) Expiration Date

The orders, except as noted below, end on

(date): _____ at _(time):_ _____ ☐ a.m. ☐ p.m. or ☐ midnight

- _If no date is written, the restraining order ends three years after the date of the hearing in item (5)(a)._
- _If no time is written, the restraining order ends at midnight on the expiration date._
- _Note: Custody, visitation, child support, and spousal support orders remain in effect after the restraining order ends. Custody, visitation, and child support orders usually end when the child is 18._
- **_The court orders are on pages 2, 3, 4, and 5 and attachment pages (if any)._**

This order complies with VAWA and shall be enforced throughout the United States. See page 5.

This is a Court Order.

Judicial Council of California, _www.courts.ca.gov_
Revised July 1, 2016, Mandatory Form
Family Code, § 6200 et seq. Approved by DOJ

Restraining Order After Hearing (CLETS—OAH)
(Order of Protection)
(Domestic Violence Prevention)

DV-130, Page 1 of 7
→

Case Number: _____

⑤ Hearings

a. The hearing was on *(date):* _____ with *(name of judicial officer):* _____

b. These people were at the hearing *(check all that apply):*
- ☐ The person in ①
- ☐ The lawyer for the person in ①*(name):* _____
- ☐ The person in ②
- ☐ The lawyer for the person in ②*(name):* _____

c. The people in ① and ② must **return to Dept.** _____ **of the court** on (date): _____
at *(time):* _____ ☐ a.m. ☐ p.m. to review *(specify issues):* _____

To the person in ❷ :

The court has granted the orders checked below. Item ⑨ is also an order. If you do not obey these orders, you can be arrested and charged with a crime. You may be sent to jail for up to one year, pay a fine of up to $1,000, or both.

⑥ ☐ Personal Conduct Orders

a. The person in ② must **not** do the following things to the protected people in ① and ③ :

- ☐ Harass, attack, strike, threaten, assault *(sexually or otherwise)*, hit, follow, stalk, molest, destroy personal property, disturb the peace, keep under surveillance, impersonate *(on the Internet, electronically or otherwise)*, or block movements.
- ☐ Contact, either directly or indirectly, by any means, including, but not limited to, by telephone, mail, e-mail, or other electronic means.
- ☐ Take any action, directly or through others, to obtain the addresses or locations of any protected persons. *(If this item is not checked, the court has found good cause not to make this order.)*

b. Peaceful written contact through a lawyer or process server or another person for service of legal papers related to a court case is allowed and does not violate this order.

c. ☐ Exceptions: Brief and peaceful contact with the person in ①, and peaceful contact with children in ③, as required for court-ordered visitation of children, is allowed unless a criminal protective order says otherwise.

⑦ ☐ Stay-Away Order

a. The person in ② **must** stay at least *(specify):* _____ yards away from *(check all that apply):*
- ☐ The person in ①
- ☐ School of person in ①
- ☐ Home of person in ①
- ☐ The persons in ③
- ☐ The job or workplace of person in ①
- ☐ The child(ren)'s school or child care
- ☐ Vehicle of person in ①
- ☐ Other *(specify):* _____

b. ☐ Exceptions: Brief and peaceful contact with the person in ①, and peaceful contact with children in ③, as required for court-ordered visitation of children, is allowed unless a criminal protective order says otherwise.

⑧ ☐ Move-Out Order

The person in ② must move out immediately from *(address):* _____

⑨ No Guns or Other Firearms or Ammunition

a. The person in ② cannot own, possess, have, buy or try to buy, receive or try to receive, or in any other way get guns, other firearms, or ammunition.

This is a Court Order.

Restraining Order After Hearing (CLETS—OAH)
(Order of Protection)
(Domestic Violence Prevention)

0287

Case Number:

(9) b. The person in **(2)** must:
- Sell to, or store with, a licensed gun dealer, or turn in to a law enforcement agency, any guns or other firearms within his or her immediate possession or control. Do so within 24 hours of being served with this order.
- Within 48 hours of receiving this order, file with the court a receipt that proves guns have been turned in, sold, or stored. *(Form DV-800, Proof of Firearms Turned In, Sold, or Stored*, may be used for the receipt.) Bring a court filed copy to the hearing.

c. ☐ The court has received information that the person in **(2)** owns or possesses a firearm.

d. ☐ The court has made the necessary findings and applies the firearm relinquishment exemption under Family Code section 6389(h). Under California law, the person in **(2)** is not required to relinquish this firearm *(specify make, model, and serial number of firearm):* _____
The firearm must be in his or her physical possession only during scheduled work hours and during travel to and from his or her place of employment. Even if exempt under California law, the person in **(2)** may be subject to federal prosecution for possessing or controlling a firearm.

(10) ☐ **Record Unlawful Communications**
The person in **(1)** has the right to record communications made by the person in **(2)** that violate the judge's orders.

(11) ☐ **Care of Animals**
The person in **(1)** is given the sole possession, care, and control of the animals listed below. The person in **(2)** must stay at least _____ yards away from and not take, sell, transfer, encumber, conceal, molest, attack, strike, threaten, harm, or otherwise dispose of the following animals: _____

(12) ☐ **Child Custody and Visitation**
Child custody and visitation are ordered on the attached Form DV-140, *Child Custody and Visitation Order* or *(specify other form):* _____

(13) ☐ **Child Support**
Child support is ordered on the attached Form FL-342, *Child Support Information and Order Attachment* or *(specify other form):* _____

(14) ☐ **Property Control**
Only the person in **(1)** can use, control, and possess the following property: _____

(15) ☐ **Debt Payment**
The person in **(2)** must make these payments until this order ends:

Pay to: _____ For: _____ Amount: $ _____ Due date: _____
Pay to: _____ For: _____ Amount: $ _____ Due date: _____
Pay to: _____ For: _____ Amount: $ _____ Due date: _____

☐ *Check here if more payments are ordered. List them on an attached sheet of paper and write "DV-130, Debt Payments" as a title.*

(16) ☐ **Property Restraint**
The ☐ person in **(1)** ☐ person in **(2)** must not transfer, borrow against, sell, hide, or get rid of or destroy any property, including animals, except in the usual course of business or for necessities of life. In addition, the person must notify the other of any new or big expenses and explain them to the court. *(The person in **(2)** cannot contact the person in **(1)** if the court has made a "No-Contact" order.)*
Peaceful written contact through a lawyer or a process server or other person for service of legal papers related to a court case is allowed and does not violate this order.

This is a Court Order.

Case Number: _____

(17) ☐ **Spousal Support**

Spousal support is ordered on the attached Form FL-343, *Spousal, Partner, or Family Support Order Attachment* or *(specify other form):* _____

(18) ☐ **Rights to Mobile Device and Wireless Phone Account**

a. ☐ **Property Control of Mobile Device and Wireless Phone Account**

Only the person in **(1)** can use, control, and possess the following property:

Mobile device *(describe)* _____ and account *(phone number):* _____

Mobile device *(describe)* _____ and account *(phone number):* _____

☐ *Check here if you need more space. Attach a sheet of paper and write "DV-130 Rights to Mobile Device and Wireless Phone Account" as a title.*

b. ☐ **Debt Payment**

The person in **(2)** must make these payments until this order ends:

Pay to *(wireless service provider):* _____ Amount: $_____ Due date: _____

c. ☐ **Transfer of Wireless Phone Account**

The court has made an order transferring one or more wireless service accounts from the person in **(2)** to the person in **(1)**. These orders are contained in a separate order (Form DV-900).

(19) ☐ **Insurance**

☐ The person in **(1)** ☐ the person in **(2)** is ordered NOT to cash, borrow against, cancel, transfer, dispose of, or change the beneficiaries of any insurance or coverage held for the benefit of the parties, or their child(ren), if any, for whom support may be ordered, or both.

(20) ☐ **Lawyer's Fees and Costs**

The person in **(2)** must pay the following lawyer's fees and costs:

Pay to: _____ For: _____ Amount: $_____ Due date: _____

Pay to: _____ For: _____ Amount: $_____ Due date: _____

(21) ☐ **Payments for Costs and Services**

The person in **(2)** must pay the following:

Pay to: _____ For: _____ Amount: $_____ Due date: _____

Pay to: _____ For: _____ Amount: $_____ Due date: _____

Pay to: _____ For: _____ Amount: $_____ Due date: _____

☐ *Check here if more payments are ordered. List them on an attached sheet of paper and write "DV-130, Payments for Costs and Services" as a title.*

(22) ☐ **Batterer Intervention Program**

The person in **(2)** must go to and pay for a 52-week batterer intervention program and show written proof of completion to the court. This program must be approved by the probation department under Penal Code § 1203.097. The person in **(2)** must enroll by *(date):* _____ or if no date is listed, must enroll within 30 days after the order is made. The person in **(2)** must complete, file and serve Form 805, Proof of Enrollment for Batterer Intervention Program.

(23) ☐ **Other Orders**

Other orders *(specify):* _____

_____

_____

(24) **No Fee to Serve (Notify) Restrained Person**

If the sheriff or marshal serves this order, he or she will do it for free.

This is a Court Order.

0289

Case Number: _____

(25) Service

a. ☐ The people in ① and ② were at the hearing or agreed in writing to this order. No other proof of service is needed.

b. ☐ The person in ① was at the hearing on the request for original orders. The person in ② was not present.

   (1) ☐ Proof of service of Form DV-109 and Form DV-110 (if issued) was presented to the court. The judge's orders in this form are the same as in Form DV-110 except for the end date. The person in ② must be served. This order can be served by mail.

   (2) ☐ Proof of service of Form DV-109 and Form DV-110 (if issued) was presented to the court. The judge's orders in this form are different from the orders in Form DV-110, or Form DV-110 was not issued. The person in ② must be personally "served" (given) a copy of this order.

c. ☐ Proof of service of Form FL-300 to modify the orders in Form DV-130 was presented to the court.

   (1) ☐ The people in ① and ② were at the hearing or agreed in writing to this order. No other proof of service is needed.

   (2) ☐ The person in ☐ ① ☐ ② was not at the hearing and must be personally "served" (given) a copy of this amended order.

(26) ☐ Criminal Protective Order

a. ☐ Form CR-160, *Criminal Protective Order—Domestic Violence*, is in effect.
   Case Number: _____ County: _____ Expiration Date: _____

b. ☐ Other Criminal Protective Order in effect *(specify):* _____
   Case Number: _____ County: _____ Expiration Date: _____

   (List other orders on an attached sheet of paper. Write "DV-130, Other Criminal Protective Orders" as a title.)

c. ☐ No information has been provided to the judge about a criminal protective order.

(27) ☐ Attached pages are orders.

- Number of pages attached to this seven-page form: _____
- All of the attached pages are part of this order.
- Attachments include *(check all that apply):*
  ☐ DV-140 ☐ DV-145 ☐ DV-150 ☐ FL-342 ☐ FL-343 ☐ DV-900
  ☐ Other *(specify):* _____

Date: _____   _____
                                     Judge (or Judicial Officer)

Certificate of Compliance With VAWA

This restraining (protective) order meets all "full faith and credit" requirements of the Violence Against Women Act, 18 U.S.C. § 2265 (1994) (VAWA) upon notice of the restrained person. This court has jurisdiction over the parties and the subject matter; the restrained person has been or will be afforded notice and a timely opportunity to be heard as provided by the laws of this jurisdiction. **This order is valid and entitled to enforcement in each jurisdiction throughout the 50 states of the United States, the District of Columbia, all tribal lands, and all U.S. territories, commonwealths, and possessions and shall be enforced as if it were an order of that jurisdiction.**

This is a Court Order.

Case Number:

Warnings and Notices to the Restrained Person in ❷

If you do not obey this order, you can be arrested and charged with a crime.

- If you do not obey this order, you can go to jail or prison and/or pay a fine.
- It is a felony to take or hide a child in violation of this order.
- If you travel to another state or to tribal lands or make the protected person do so, with the intention of disobeying this order, you can be charged with a federal crime.

You cannot have guns, firearms, and/or ammunition.

You cannot own, have, possess, buy or try to buy, receive or try to receive, or otherwise get guns, other firearms, and/or ammunition while the order is in effect. If you do, you can go to jail and pay a $1,000 fine. Unless the court grants an exemption, you must sell to, or store with, a licensed gun dealer, or turn in to a law enforcement agency, any guns or other firearms that you have or control. The judge will ask you for proof that you did so. If you do not obey this order, you can be charged with a crime. Federal law says you cannot have guns or ammunition while the order is in effect. Even if exempt under California law, you may be subject to federal prosecution for possessing or controlling a firearm.

Instructions for Law Enforcement

Start Date and End Date of Orders

The orders *start* on the earlier of the following dates:
- The hearing date in item ⑤ (a) on page 2, or
- The date next to the judge's signature on this page.

The orders *end* on the expiration date in item ④ on page 1. If no date is listed, they end three years from the hearing date.

Arrest Required if Order Is Violated

If an officer has probable cause to believe that the restrained person had notice of the order and has disobeyed the order, the officer must arrest the restrained person. (Pen. Code, §§ 836(c)(1), 13701(b).) A violation of the order may be a violation of Penal Code section 166 or 273.6.

Notice/Proof of Service

Law enforcement must first determine if the restrained person had notice of the orders. If notice cannot be verified, the restrained person must be advised of the terms of the orders. If the restrained person then fails to obey the orders, the officer must enforce them. (Fam. Code, § 6383.)

Consider the restrained person "served" (notified) if:
- The officer sees a copy of the *Proof of Service* or confirms that the *Proof of Service* is on file; *or*
- The restrained person was at the restraining order hearing or was informed of the order by an officer. (Fam. Code, § 6383; Pen. Code, § 836(c)(2).) An officer can obtain information about the contents of the order in the Domestic Violence Restraining Order System (DVROS). (Fam. Code, § 6381(b)-(c).)

If the Protected Person Contacts the Restrained Person

Even if the protected person invites or consents to contact with the restrained person, the orders remain in effect and must be enforced. The protected person cannot be arrested for inviting or consenting to contact with the restrained person. The orders can be changed only by another court order. (Pen. Code, § 13710(b).)

This is a Court Order.

Case Number:

Child Custody and Visitation

The custody and visitation orders are on Form DV-140, items ③ and ④. They are sometimes also written on additional pages or referenced in DV-140 or other orders that are not part of the restraining order.

Enforcing the Restraining Order in California

Any law enforcement officer in California who receives, sees, or verifies the orders on a paper copy, in the California Law Enforcement Telecommunications System (CLETS), or in an NCIC Protection Order File must enforce the orders.

Conflicting Orders—Priorities for Enforcement

If more than one restraining order has been issued protecting the protected person from the restrained person, the orders must be enforced in the following priority (see Pen. Code, § 136.2 and Fam. Code, §§ 6383(h)(2), 6405(b)):

1. *EPO:* If one of the orders is an *Emergency Protective Order* (Form EPO-001) and it is more restrictive than other restraining or protective orders, it has precedence in enforcement over all other orders.
2. *No-Contact Order:* If there is no EPO, a no-contact order that is included in a restraining or protective order has precedence in enforcement over any other restraining or protective order.
3. *Criminal Order:* If none of the orders includes a no-contact order, a domestic violence protective order issued in a criminal case takes precedence in enforcement over any conflicting civil court order. Any nonconflicting terms of the civil restraining order remain in effect and enforceable.
4. *Family, Juvenile, or Civil Order:* If more than one family, juvenile, or other civil restraining or protective order has been issued, the one that was issued last must be enforced.

(Clerk will fill out this part.)

—Clerk's Certificate—

Clerk's Certificate
[seal]

I certify that this *Restraining Order After Hearing (Order of Protection)* is a true and correct copy of the original on file in the court.

Date: _____ Clerk, by _____ , Deputy

This is a Court Order.

0292

<table>
<tr><td>**DV-140**</td><td>**Child Custody and Visitation Order**</td><td>Case Number:</td></tr>
</table>

This form is attached to *(check one):* ☐ DV-110 ☐ DV-130

(1) Name of Protected Person: _____ ☐ Mom ☐ Dad ☐ Other*

(2) Other Parent's Name: _____ ☐ Mom ☐ Dad ☐ Other*

　　* If Other, *specify relationship to child:* _____

The Court Orders:

(3) ☐ **Child Custody** is ordered as follows:

Legal Custody to: *(Person who makes decisions about health, education. Check at least one.)*

Physical Custody to: *(Person the child lives with. Check at least one.)*

Child's Name	Date of Birth	Mom	Dad	Other*	Mom	Dad	Other*
a. _____	_____	☐	☐	☐	☐	☐	☐
b. _____	_____	☐	☐	☐	☐	☐	☐
c. _____	_____	☐	☐	☐	☐	☐	☐

☐ *If more children, check here. Attach a sheet of paper and write "DV-140, Child Custody" for a title.*

* If Other, *specify relationship to child and name of person:* _____

(4) ☐ **Child Visitation** is ordered as follows:

　　a. ☐ No visitation to ☐ Mom ☐ Dad ☐ Other *(name):* _____

　　b. ☐ See the attached _____ - page document, dated: _____

　　c. ☐ The parties must go to mediation at: _____

　　d. ☐ Until the next court order, visitation for ☐ Mom ☐ Dad ☐ Other *(name):* _____ will be:

　　　　(1) ☐ **Weekends** *(starting):* _____ *(The 1st weekend of the month is the 1st weekend with a Saturday.)*

　　　　☐ 1st ☐ 2nd ☐ 3rd ☐ 4th ☐ 5th weekend of month

　　　　from _____ at _____ ☐ a.m. ☐ p.m. to _____ at _____ ☐ a.m. ☐ p.m.
　　　　　　(day of week) 　　*(time)* 　　　　　　　　　*(day of week)* 　　*(time)*

　　　　(2) ☐ **Weekdays** *(starting):* _____

　　　　from _____ at _____ ☐ a.m. ☐ p.m. to _____ at _____ ☐ a.m. ☐ p.m.
　　　　　　(day of week) 　　*(time)* 　　　　　　　　　*(day of week)* 　　*(time)*

　　　　(3) ☐ **Other Visitation**

　　　　Check here and attach a sheet of paper if there are other visitation days and times, like holidays, birthdays, sports events. List dates and times. Write "DV- 140, Other Visitation" for a title.

(5) ☐ **Supervised Visitation or Exchange**

　　Visits and/or exchanges of children are supervised as specified on Form DV-150, *Supervised Visitation and Exchange Order.*

This is a Court Order.

Judicial Council of California, *www.courts.ca.gov*
Rev. January 1, 2012, Mandatory Form
Family Code, §§ 3020, 3022, 3040–3043, 3100, 6340,7604

Child Custody and Visitation Order
(Domestic Violence Prevention)

DV-140, Page 1 of 2
→

Case Number: _____

(6) ☐ Responsibility for Transportation for Visitation

"Responsibility for transportation" means the parent will take or pick up the child or make arrangements for someone else to do so.

a. ☐ Mom ☐ Dad ☐ Other *(name):* _____ **take children to** the visits.

b. ☐ Mom ☐ Dad ☐ Other *(name):* _____ **pick up children from** the visits.

c. ☐ Drop-off / pick-up of children will be at *(address):*

_____

(7) ☐ Travel with Children

☐ Mom ☐ Dad ☐ Other *(name):* _____ *must* have written permission from the other parent, or a court order, to take the children outside of:

a. ☐ The State of California

b. ☐ The United States of America

c. ☐ Other place(s) *(list):* _____

(8) ☐ Child Abduction

There is a risk that one of the parents will take the children out of California without the other parent's permission. ☐ The orders in Form DV-145, *Order: No Travel with Children,* are attached and must be obeyed. *(Fill out and attach Form DV-145 to this form.)*

(9) ☐ Other Orders

Check here and attach any other orders to this form. Write "DV-140, Other Orders" as a title.

(10) Jurisdiction

This court has jurisdiction to make child custody orders in this case under the Uniform Child Custody Jurisdiction and Enforcement Act (part 3 of the California Family Code starting with § 3400).

(11) Notice and Opportunity to Be Heard

The responding party was given reasonable notice and an opportunity to be heard as provided by the laws of the State of California.

(12) Country of Habitual Residence

The country of habitual residence of the child or children in this case is ☐ The United States of America or ☐ Other *(specify):* _____ .

(13) Penalties for Violating This Order

If you violate this order, you may be subject to civil or criminal penalties, or both.

(14) Duration of Child Custody, Visitation, and Support Orders

If this form is attached to Form DV-130 *(Restraining Order After Hearing),* the custody and visitation orders in this form remain in effect after the restraining orders on Form DV-130 end.

This is a Court Order.

Child Custody and Visitation Order
(Domestic Violence Prevention)

DV-200 **Proof of Personal Service**

(1) Name of Party Asking for Protection:

_____

(2) Name of Party to Be Restrained:

_____

(3) Notice to Server

The server must:

- Be 18 years of age or older.
- Not be listed in items **(1)** or **(3)** of form DV-100, _Request for Domestic Violence Restraining Order._
- Give a copy of all documents checked in **(4)** to the restrained party in **(2)** (you cannot send them by mail). Then complete and sign this form, and give or mail it to the party in **(1)**.

Fill in court name and street address:

Superior Court of California, County of

(4) I gave the party in **(2)** a copy of all the documents checked:

a. ☐ DV-109 with DV-100 and a blank DV-120 _(Notice of Court Hearing; Request for Domestic Violence Restraining Order; blank Response to Request for Domestic Violence Restraining Order)_

Court clerk fills in case number when form is filed.

Case Number:

b. ☐ DV-110 _(Temporary Restraining Order)_
c. ☐ DV-105 and DV-140 _(Request for Child Custody and Visitation Orders, Child Custody and Visitation Order)_
d. ☐ FL-150 with a blank FL-150 _(Income and Expense Declaration)_
e. ☐ FL-155 with a blank FL-155 _(Financial Statement (Simplified))_
f. ☐ DV-115 _(Request to Continue Hearing)_
g. ☐ DV-116 _(Order on Request to Continue Hearing)_
h. ☐ DV-130 _(Restraining Order After Hearing)_
i. ☐ Other _(specify):_

(5) I personally gave copies of the documents checked above to the party in **(2)** on:

a. Date: _____ b. Time: _____ ☐ a.m. ☐ p.m.

c. At this address: _____

City: _____ State: _____ Zip: _____

(6) Server's Information

Name: _____

Address: _____

City: _____ State: _____ Zip: _____

Telephone: _____

(If you are a registered process server):

County of registration: _____ Registration number: _____

(7) I declare under penalty of perjury under the laws of the State of California that the information above is true and correct.

Date: _____

_____   _____
Type or print server's name   _Server to sign here_

Judicial Council of California, www.courts.ca.gov
Revised July 1, 2016, Optional Form
Family Code, §§ 243, 245, and 6345

Proof of Personal Service (CLETS)
(Domestic Violence Prevention)

DV-250   Proof of Service by Mail

Clerk stamps date here when form is filed.

(1) Name of Person Asking for Protection:

_____

(2) Name of Person to Be Restrained:

_____

(3) Notice to Server

The server must:

- Be 18 years of age or over.
- Not be listed in items (1) or (2) or (3) of form DV-100, *Request for Domestic Violence Restraining Order.*
- Mail a copy of all documents checked in (4) to the person in (5).

Fill in court name and street address:

Superior Court of California, County of

Fill in case number:

Case Number:

(4) I (the server) am 18 years of age or over and live in or am employed in the county where the mailing took place. I mailed a copy of all documents checked below to the person in (5):

a. ☐ DV-112, *Waiver of Hearing on Denied Request for Temporary Restraining Order*
b. ☐ DV-120, *Response to Request for Domestic Violence Restraining Order*
c. ☐ FL-150, *Income and Expense Declaration*
d. ☐ FL-155, *Simplified Financial Statement*
e. ☐ DV-130, *Restraining Order After Hearing (Order of Protection)*
f. ☐ Other *(specify):* _____

Note: You cannot serve DV-100, DV-105, DV-109, or DV-110 by mail.

(5) I placed copies of the documents checked above in a sealed envelope and mailed them as described below:

a. Name of person served: _____
b. To this address: _____

   City: _____ State: _____ Zip: _____

c. Mailed on *(date):* _____
d. Mailed from: City: _____ State: _____

(6) Server's Information

Name: _____

Address: _____

City: _____ State: _____ Zip: _____

Telephone: _____

(If you are a registered process server):

County of registration: _____ Registration number: _____

(7) I declare under penalty of perjury under the laws of the State of California that the information above is true and correct.

Date: _____

_____   ▶ _____
Type or print server's name   *Server to sign here*

Judicial Council of California, *www.courts.ca.gov*
Rev. January 1, 2012, Optional Form
Family Code, §§ 6324, 6340-6344

Proof of Service by Mail (CLETS)
(Domestic Violence Prevention)

DV-250, Page 1 of 1

0296

DV-400 | Findings and Order to Terminate Restraining Order After Hearing

Complete only items 1 and 2. The remaining items are for court use.

(1) Name of Protected Party: _____

(2) Name of Restrained Party: _____

(3) Court Findings (Fam. Code, § 6345 (a) & (d))

a. ☐ The **Protected Party** filed the request to terminate the restraining orders in *Restraining Order After Hearing* (form DV-130). A proof of service (by mail or personal service) of the request on the Restrained Party is filed with the court.

b. ☐ The **Restrained Party** filed the request to terminate restraining orders. The filed proof of service shows that the Protected Party received notice of the Request by:

   1. ☐ Personal service.

   2. ☐ Service on the Secretary of State (the Protected Person is registered in the Safe at Home Program).

   3. ☐ An alternative, court-ordered method of service that gives actual notice of the request and the hearing.

c. ☐ The **Restrained Party** filed the request to terminate the restraining orders in form DV-130. The Protected Party was physically present in court on the hearing date, waived his or her right to notice, and does not challenge the sufficiency of the notice.

d. ☐ The **Protected Party** was physically present at the hearing and verified his or her identity.

e. ☐ The **Protected Party and the Restrained Party** submitted a written stipulation (agreement) to terminate the restraining orders in *Restraining Order After Hearing* (form DV-130).

f. ☐ Other *(specify):*

_____

Clerk stamps date here when form is filed.

Fill in court name and street address:

Superior Court of California, County of

Court fills in case number when form is filed.

Case Number:

---

(4) Court Orders

The protective orders in *Restraining Order After Hearing* (form DV-130) that were issued or modified on *(date):* _____ are terminated. This order is effective when made.

a. ☐ Child custody, visitation (parenting time), and child support orders in *Restraining Order After Hearing* (form DV-130)

   1. ☐ Remain in effect.

   2. ☐ Have been modified on *(date):* _____

   3. ☐ Are also terminated.

b. ☐ Spousal or domestic partner support orders in *Restraining Order After Hearing* (form DV-130)

   1. ☐ Remain in effect.

   2. ☐ Have been modified on *(date):* _____

   3. ☐ Are also terminated.

c. Unless modified or terminated by court order, any existing orders for child custody, child visitation (parenting time), child support, and spousal or partner support made in a Domestic Violence Prevention Act case after a noticed hearing survive the termination of the protective order, and remain in effect. Family Code sections 6340(a), 6345(b).

d. This order does not modify or terminate any existing criminal, juvenile, or probate court orders.

This is a Court Order.

Judicial Council of California, *www.courts.ca.gov*
New July 1, 2016, Mandatory Form
Family Code, § 6345, Approved by DOJ

**Findings and Order to Terminate
Restraining Order After Hearing (CLETS–CANCEL)**
(Domestic Violence Prevention)

DV-400, Page 1 of 2

Case Number:

---

(5) ☐ **Hearings**

a. The hearing was on *(date):* _____ with *(name of judicial officer):* _____

b. These people were at the hearing *(check all that apply):*

☐ The Protected Party   ☐ Protected Party's lawyer *(name):* _____

☐ The Restrained Party   ☐ Restrained Party's lawyer *(name):* _____

☐ Other *(name):* _____ ☐ Lawyer *(name):* _____

☐ Other *(name):* _____ ☐ Lawyer *(name):* _____

(6) CLETS Entry

The court or its designee will transmit this form within one business day to law enforcement personnel for entry into the California Restraining and Protective Orders System via CLETS.

(7) Service of this Order

a. ☐ The **Protected Party** and the **Restrained Party** were at the hearing or agreed in writing to this order. No other proof of service is needed.

b. ☐ The **Protected Party** (party who asked for the order) was at the hearing. The **Restrained Party** was not. Someone 18 or over—not anyone else protected or restrained by the restraining order—must personally "serve" the Restrained Party with a filed copy of this order.

c. ☐ The **Restrained Party** (party who asked for the order) was at the hearing. The **Protected Party** was not. Someone 18 or over—not anyone else protected or restrained by the restraining order—must personally "serve" the Protected Party with a filed copy of this order.

d. ☐ Other *(specify):*

_____
_____
_____
_____
_____
_____
_____
_____

Date: _____

_____
Judge (or Judicial Officer)

(Clerk will fill out this part.)
—Clerk's Certificate—

Clerk's Certificate
[seal]

I certify that this *Findings and Order to Terminate Restraining Order After Hearing* is a true and correct copy of the original on file in the court.

Date: _____ Clerk, by _____, Deputy

This is a Court Order.

**Findings and Order to Terminate
Restraining Order After Hearing (CLETS–CANCEL)**
(Domestic Violence Prevention)

DV-710 Notice of Hearing to Renew Restraining Order

(1) Name of Protected Person:

_____

Your lawyer in this case *(if you have one):*

Name: _____ State Bar No.: _____

Firm Name: _____

Address *(If you have a lawyer for this case, give your lawyer's information. If you do not have a lawyer and want to keep your home address private, give a different mailing address instead. You do not have to give your telephone, fax, or e-mail.):*

Address: _____

City: _____ State: _____ Zip: _____

Telephone: _____ Fax: _____

E-mail Address: _____

Fill in court name and street address:

Superior Court of California, County of

Clerk fills in case number when form is filed.

Case Number:

(2) Name of Restrained Person:

_____

Description of restrained person:

Sex: ☐ M ☐ F Height: _____ Weight: _____ Hair Color: _____ Eye Color: _____

Race: _____ Age: _____ Date of Birth: _____

Mailing Address *(if known):* _____

City: _____ State: _____ Zip: _____

Relationship to protected person: _____

The court will fill in the rest of this form.

(3) Court Hearing

The judge has set a court hearing date.

The *Restraining Order After Hearing (Order of Protection)* **stays in effect until the expiration date on that order or the end of the hearing below, whichever is later.**

| Hearing Date & Time | → Date: _____ Time: _____ Dept.: _____ Room: _____ | Name and address of court if different from above: _____ |

To the person in (2):

At the hearing, the judge can renew the current restraining order for another five years or permanently. Before the hearing, you can file a response on Form DV-720. You *must* continue to obey the current restraining orders until the expiration date on the current orders or the hearing date, whichever is later. At the hearing, you can tell the judge why you agree or disagree with the request to renew the orders. If the restraining orders are renewed, you *must* obey the orders even if you do not attend the hearing.

This is a Court Order.

Judicial Council of California, *www.courts.ca.gov*
Revised July 1, 2014, Mandatory Form
Family Code, § 6345 et seq.

**Notice of Hearing to Renew Restraining Order
(CLETS) (Domestic Violence Prevention)**

DV-710, Page 1 of 2

→

Case Number:

---

(4) Service and Response

To the Person in ❶

Someone 18 or over—**not you or anyone else protected by the restraining order**—must personally "serve" a copy of the following forms on the person in ❷ at least _____ days before the hearing.

- DV-700, *Request to Renew Restraining Order* (file stamped);
- DV-710, *Notice of Hearing to Renew Restraining Order* (this form);
- DV-720, *Response to Request to Renew Restraining Order* (blank copy);
- DV-130, the current *Restraining Order After Hearing (Order of Protection)* that you want to renew.

After the person in ❷ has been served, file Form DV-200, *Proof of Personal Service,* with the court clerk. For help with service, read Form DV-200-INFO, *What Is "Proof of Personal Service"?* **Bring a copy of Form DV-200, *Proof of Personal Service,* to the court hearing.**

To the Person in ❷

If you want to respond in writing to the request to renew the restraining order, fill out Form DV-720, *Response to Request to Renew Restraining Order.* File the original with the court, and have someone 18 or over—**not you**—mail a copy of it to the person in ❶ before the hearing. Also file Form DV-250, *Proof of Service by Mail,* with the court before the hearing. **Bring a copy of Form DV-250, *Proof of Service by Mail,* to the court hearing.**

Date: _____   _____
                                                                              Judicial Officer

Request for Accommodations

Assistive listening systems, computer-assisted real-time captioning, or sign language interpreter services are available if you ask at least five days before the hearing. Contact the clerk's office or go to *www.courts.ca.gov/forms* for *Request for Accommodations by Persons with Disabilities and Response* (Form MC-410). (Civ. Code, § 54.8.)

(Clerk will fill out this part.)

—Clerk's Certificate—

Clerk's Certificate
[seal]

I certify that this *Temporary Restraining Order* is a true and correct copy of the original on file in the court.

Date: _____ Clerk, by _____ , Deputy

DV-720	Response to Request to Renew Restraining Order

Use this form to respond to the *Request to Renew Restraining Order* (Form DV-700)
- Fill out this form and then take it to the court clerk.
- Have someone—**age 18 or older**—not you or anyone in ③ on Form DV-130 serve the person in ① by mail with a copy of this form and any attached pages. *(Use Form DV-250, Proof of Service by Mail.)*

Clerk stamps date here when form is filed.

Fill in court name and street address:
Superior Court of California, County of

Fill in case number:
Case Number:

① **Protected Person** *(See Form DV-700, item ①):*
_____

② **Restrained Person:**
_____

Your lawyer in this case *(if you have one):*
Name: _____ State Bar No.: _____
Firm Name: _____

Address *(If you have a lawyer for this case, give your lawyer's information. If you do not have a lawyer and want to keep your home address private, give a different mailing address instead. You do not have to give your telephone, fax, or e-mail.):*

Address: _____
City: _____ State: _____ Zip: _____
Telephone: _____ Fax: _____
E-Mail Address: _____

③ **Response**

   a. ☐ I agree to renew the order.

   b. ☐ I do not agree to renew the order.

④ ☐ I ask the court not to renew the order because *(specify):*

_____
_____
_____
_____
_____
_____

The court will consider your Response at the hearing. Write your hearing date, time, and place from Form DV-710, item ③ here:

Hearing Date → Date: _____
   Time: _____
Dept.: _____ Room: _____

You must continue to obey the current restraining order on Form DV-130 *(Restraining Order After Hearing)* until the hearing. If you do not come to the hearing, the court may renew the order against you 5 years or permanently.

☐ *Check here if you need more space. Attach a sheet of paper and write "DV-720, Reason to Not Renew" for a title.*

I declare under penalty of perjury under the laws of the State of California that the information above is true and correct.

Date: _____   _____   ▶ _____
                    Type or print your name   *Sign your name*

Date: _____   _____   ▶ _____
                    Your lawyer's name, if you have one   *Lawyer's signature*

Judicial Council of California, *www.courts.ca.gov*
New January 1, 2012, Mandatory Form
Family Code § 6345

Response to Request to Renew Restraining Order
(Domestic Violence Prevention)

DV-720, Page 1 of 1

DV-800/JV-252 Proof of Firearms Turned In, Sold, or Stored

Clerk stamps date here when form is filed.

(1) Protected Person

Name: _____

(2) Restrained Person

a. Your Name: _____

Your Lawyer *(if you have one for this case):*

Name: _____ State Bar No.: _____

Firm Name: _____

b. Your Address *(If you have a lawyer, give your lawyer's information. If you do not have a lawyer and want to keep your home address private, you may give a different mailing address instead. You do not have to give telephone, fax, or e-mail.):*

Address: _____

City: _____ State: _____ Zip: _____

Telephone: _____ Fax: _____

E-Mail Address: _____

Fill in court name and street address:

Superior Court of California, County of

Court fills in case number when form is filed.

Case Number:

(3) To the Restrained Person:

If the court has ordered you to turn in, sell, or store your firearms, you may use this form to prove to the court that you have obeyed its orders. When you deliver your unloaded weapons, ask the law enforcement officer or the licensed gun dealer to complete item **(4)** or **(5)** and item **(6)**. After the form is signed, file it with the court clerk. Keep a copy for yourself. For help, read form DV-800-INFO/JV-252-INFO, *How Do I Turn In, Sell, or Store My Firearms?*

(4) | **To Law Enforcement**

Fill out items **(4)** and **(6)** of this form. Keep a copy and give the original to the person who turned in the firearms.

The firearms listed in **(6)** were turned in on:

Date: _____ at: _____ ☐ a.m. ☐ p.m.

To: _____
Name and title of law enforcement agent

_____
Name of law enforcement agency

_____

_____
Address

I declare under penalty of perjury under the laws of the State of California that the information above is true and correct.

▶ _____
Signature of law enforcement agent

(5) | **To Licensed Gun Dealer**

Fill out items **(5)** and **(6)** of this form. Keep a copy and give the original to the person who sold you the firearms or stored them with you.

The firearms listed in **(6)** were
☐ sold to me ☐ transferred to me for storage on:

Date: _____ at: _____ ☐ a.m. ☐ p.m.

To: _____
Name of licensed gun dealer

_____
License number *Telephone*

_____

_____
Address

I declare under penalty of perjury under the laws of the State of California that the information above is true and correct.

▶ _____
Signature of licensed gun dealer

Judicial Council of California, *www.courts.ca.gov*
Revised January 1, 2019, Optional Form
Family Code, § 6389 et seq., Cal. Rules of Court, rules 5.630 and 5.495

Proof of Firearms Turned In, Sold, or Stored
(Domestic Violence Prevention)

DV-800/JV-252, Page 1 of 2

→

6 **Firearms**

	Make	Model	Serial Number
a.			
b.			
c.			
d.			
e.			

☐ *Check here if you turned in, sold, or stored more firearms. Attach a sheet of paper and write "DV-800/ JV-252, Item 6—Firearms Turned In, Sold, or Stored" for a title. Include make, model, and serial number of each firearm. You may use form MC-025,* Attachment.

7 Do you have, own, possess, or control any other firearms besides the firearms listed in **6**? ☐ Yes ☐ No

If you answered yes, have you turned in, sold, or stored those other firearms? ☐ Yes ☐ No
If yes, check one of the boxes below:

a. ☐ I filed a *Proof of Firearms Turned In, Sold, or Stored* for those firearms with the court on *(date):*

b. ☐ I am filing the proof for those firearms along with this proof.

c. ☐ I have not yet filed the proof for the other firearms *(explain why not):*

☐ *Check here if there is not enough space below for your answer. Put your complete answer on the attached sheet of paper or form MC-025 and write "Attachment 7c" for a title.*

_____

_____

_____

_____

_____

I declare under penalty of perjury under the laws of the State of California that the information above is true and correct.

Date: _____

_____
Type or print your name

▶
_____
Sign your name

55326860R00171